Federal Indian Policy
in the Kennedy and Johnson
Administrations
1961–1969

FEDERAL INDIAN POLICY

IN THE KENNEDY AND JOHNSON ADMINISTRATIONS

1961–1969

THOMAS CLARKIN

UNIVERSITY OF NEW MEXICO PRESS
ALBUQUERQUE

Library of Congress Cataloging-in-Publication Data:
Clarkin, Thomas, 1961–
Federal Indian policy in the Kennedy and Johnson
Administrations, 1961–1969 / Thomas Clarkin. — 1st ed.
    p. cm.
Includes bibliographical references and index.
    ISBN 0-8263-2262-X (cloth : alk. paper)
1. Indians of North America—Government relations.
2. Indians of North America—Politics and government.
3. Kennedy, John F. (John Fitzgerald), 1917–1963. 4. Johnson,
Lyndon B. (Lyndon Baines), 1908–1973. 5. United States—
Politics and government—1961–1963. 6. United States—Politics
and government—1963–1969. I. Title.
    E93 .C65 2001
    323.1'197073'09046—dc21
                                        00-012079

CONTENTS

ACKNOWLEDGMENTS

This study was completed with the expert assistance of several archivists, including Linda Seelke at the Johnson Library; Dennis Bilger, Sam Rushay, Liz Safly, and Randy Sowell at the Truman Library; June Payne at the Kennedy Library; Dan Linke, and John Weeren at Princeton's Seely G. Mudd Library; and Todd Kosmerick at the Carl Albert Congressional Research and Studies Center. I received generous financial support from the History Department and Graduate School at the University of Texas; a Visiting Scholars grant from the Carl Albert Center; a Moody Grant from the Lyndon Baines Johnson Foundation; a Research Grant from the Harry S. Truman Library Institute; and a Research Fellowship from the Friends of the Princeton Library.

Byron Hulsey, Jon Lee, Shelley Sallee, Mark Young, and Nancy Beck Young, all friends and fellow scholars, formed a communal support group as we researched, wrote, and revised our dissertations. Chris Riggs, the very model of a "gentleman and a scholar," kindly shared a draft of his dissertation and his 1999 interview with Vine Deloria, Jr. Thomas Cowger reviewed the manuscript and made many helpful suggestions. He also rescued me from potential embarrassment in pointing out some passages that carried meanings that I did not intend. David Holtby of the University of New Mexico Press expressed interest in and support for this project from the outset—everyone should be blessed with such an editor.

Two people deserve special thanks. Lewis L. Gould of the University of Texas has remained a valuable mentor long after his responsibilities as my dissertation supervisor were fulfilled. My skills as a historian stand to his credit; my weaknesses I of course claim as my own. Kimberly Zborowski Clarkin—friend, proofreader, sympathetic ear, and, as this project progressed, spouse and mother to our children— knows that although my name graces the cover of this book, it was really a family project all along.

INTRODUCTION

The 1960s were the first decade in what has become known as the era of Indian self-determination. Scholarly assessments of the federal Indian policy that the Democratic administrations of John Kennedy and Lyndon Johnson conducted during the 1960s have been mixed. Some historians have referred to a "turnabout in the 1960s" that brought a "new orientation to United States Indian policy," and have claimed that "after 1960, major changes took place in federal policy and in Indian thought and behavior." They have deemed the last years of the decade to have been "an exceptional period in the history of federal-Indian affairs." Other scholars have been more critical, dismissing the period through 1965 as "barren years," condemning Kennedy as a "hollow icon" for his poor leadership in Indian affairs, and asserting that "though [Johnson's] Administration set the foundation for contemporary American Indian self-determination, clearly his heart or mind, or that of the Administration was not in it."[1]

These varied historical assessments are based on little archival research. The Kennedy and Johnson Indian policies have in fact received little scholarly attention. The neglect of federal Indian affairs in Kennedy's New Frontier and Johnson's Great Society stems in part from the difficulties in reconciling the development of self-determination as a goal of federal policy with the minimal gains realized during the decade. At first glance it may seem as if the 1960s were devoid of the conflicts and achievements in Indian affairs that marked the decades that preceded and followed it. House Concurrent Resolution 108 and Public Law 280, both passed during the 1950s, marked the zenith of termination, the policy of ending federal obligations to Indian communities. The Indian Self-Determination and Education Assistance Act of 1975 marked the acceptance of self-determination as the goal of federal Indian policy. Most of the legislation passed during the 1960s that affected Indians, however, was not targeted specifically at Indians, and the effect of one major act of the era, the Indian Civil Rights Act, remains a matter of debate (or confusion). Although the 1961 American Indian Chicago Conference and the fishing rights protests of the 1960s have received some scholarly attention, the 1964 American Indian Capital Conference on Poverty and the 1966 emergency meeting in Santa Fe, while not forgotten, are not nearly as well known as the dynamic protests of the 1970s such as the occupation of the BIA building and Wounded Knee II.[2]

The 1960s were a decade of transition, of moving toward Indian self-determination. To demand significant achievements in the early years of any policy era would be unrealistic. However, explaining the disparity between goals and gains in Indian affairs during the 1960s as the understandable result of the transitional nature of the decade does not lend much to understanding the early years of the self-determination era. A more complete explanation is necessary.

The Democrats who came to power in 1961 sought to devise programs that would end the dependency of Indian communities and allow Indians opportunities available to other Americans. As liberals open to the ideal of cultural pluralism, these Democrats were not hostile to the survival of Native American cultures and heritages. As such, the policies of the Kennedy and Johnson administrations have much in common with those of the New Deal era, which attempted to increase economic opportunities for Indians and evidenced respect for Indian cultures.

The Kennedy and Johnson years also resemble those of the New Deal in that paternalism, the belief that the bureaucrat knows what is best for the Indian, marred the conduct of Indian policy. The paternalism prevalent in both the executive branch and the Congress limited the ability of Native Americans to determine their own fates and to maintain their communities in accord with traditional values. It also curbed their influence on the policy process. For most of the twentieth century, Native American efforts to influence federal policy proved weak and ineffective. Apart from the obstacles that paternalism created, most Indians lacked the organizational skills and the political sophistication necessary to pressure the federal government into responding to their demands. However, by mid-century some Native Americans had become familiar enough with the workings of the federal government to organize politically across tribal lines in an effort to lobby for their goals. During the 1950s, the termination policy contributed to a sense of crisis in Indian country, leading groups such as the National Congress of American Indians gradually to assume a greater (though still limited) role in the policy process. This trend continued into the 1960s, and Native American efforts to gain control over the creation of policy and the operation of government programs constituted an important feature of policy formulation and implementation during that decade.[3]

The Department of the Interior formulated the administrations' policy initiatives and ran the majority of programs involving Native Americans. However, Interior Secretary Stewart Udall and his commissioners of Indian affairs did not operate with a free hand. Members of Congress, specifically those serving on the Senate and House Interior Committees, held sway over the conduct of Indian policy. The ability of a few key congressmen on these committees, especially a small group of senators from western states, to restrict the nature of federal initiatives proved detrimental to the interests of Native Americans during the 1960s. Through their dedication to the flawed policy of terminating federal services to the tribes, the western senators slowed progress toward Indian self-sufficiency and self-determination.

It was no accident that those federal initiatives that most effectively promoted Indian self-determination, the war on poverty programs, were outside the purview of the western senators. Their authority over Indian affairs and the growing opposition within Congress to their position on policy matters were central elements in the conduct of federal Indian policy during the 1960s.

The persistence of termination is the key to understanding the 1960s as a transitional era. The decade not only marked the move toward self-determination, but the move away from termination. While historians have noted that termination had its supporters well into the 1960s, they have misunderstood or understated its power, both in its ability to distort the formulation of policies aimed at promoting self-determination and to create fear and suspicion among Native Americans toward federal programs that benefited them. Self-determination policy developed under the shadow of termination, a shadow that diminished in length and intensity over the course of the 1960s but nonetheless limited the objectives of policymakers and the gains that American Indians realized during this period.

In addition to making contributions to American Indian history, the study of the Kennedy and Johnson Indian policies also offers new insights into the workings of those administrations and into the controversial liberal programs of the contentious 1960s. Liberalism has not fared well in the estimations of many Americans in the decades following the New Frontier and the Great Society. By the end of the twentieth century, the belief that these programs had not only failed to achieve their objectives but had exacerbated racial and social tensions within the nation contributed to demands to cut the size and responsibility of the federal government. The scholarly examination of the impact of the programs and their importance to Native Americans is necessary before a final judgment on the efficacy and the legacy of liberalism can be rendered.

In order to meet the standards that historians strive to achieve in writing the histories of American Indians, it is essential that policy studies abandon older forms of interpretation that relegated Indians to the status of victims reacting to the directives of Euroamericans in positions of power. Instead, policy studies must articulate the perceptions of Native Americans as they responded to federal policies and programs, as they struggled to resist the implementation of policies inimical to their interests, and, increasingly in the twentieth century, as they worked to influence the formulation of policy and to assert the right to determine the future of their communities.

Although Indian activism plays an essential role in this study, most of the individuals who populate its pages are non-Indians. Because I focus on the process of policy formulation, I have restricted my discussion of Indian activism to those organizations, individuals, incidents, and events that captured the attention of policymakers, most of whom were white. With few exceptions American Indians did not hold positions of authority in federal Indian affairs until the late 1960s. This does not render my study any less a part of Native American history; rather, it again evidences the importance of interactions between Indians and non-Indians in the lives of Native Americans.

A Note on Terminology

The native peoples who lived in the Americas had names for their communities and for those of their neighbors. They did not have a term for native peoples as a whole. The collective term *Indian*, which Columbus coined in error, remained in general use through the 1970s. In recent years the term *Native American* has gained favor among some native peoples and in academic circles. Lacking any consensus on the issue, and recognizing the continued use of the word *Indian* as a means of self-identification that lends validity to that term, I have used *Indians* and *Native Americans* interchangeably throughout this study. When identifying individual Native Americans, I have whenever possible included that person's tribal affiliation.

Similar problems with terminology arise when discussing non-Indians. I have used the word *white* when referring to the descendants of the Europeans and the political, social, and cultural systems they established in North America. I have also used the less than euphonious but more appropriate term *Euroamerican* when referring to non-Indian individuals and attitudes discussed in this study.

ABBREVIATIONS

AAIA	Association of American Indian Affairs
AFN	Alaska Federation of Natives
AICC	American Indian Chicago Conference
ARA	Area Redevelopment Administration
BIA	Bureau of Indian Affairs
BOB	Bureau of the Budget
CAA or CAAs	Community Action Agencies
CAP or CAPs	Community Action Programs
EOA	Economic Opportunity Act
EDA	Economic Development Administration
ESEA	Elementary and Secondary Education Act
FBI	Federal Bureau of Investigation
HCR	House Concurrent Resolution
HEW	Health, Education and Welfare (Department)
ICC	Indian Claims Commission
JUA	Joint Use Area
NCAI	National Congress of American Indians
NIYC	National Indian Youth Council
OEO	Office of Economic Opportunity
ONEO	Office of Navajo Economic Opportunity
PHA	Public Housing Administration
PL	Public Law
SIRP	Selected Indian Reservation Program
VISTA	Volunteers in Service to America

CHAPTER ONE

THE TERMINATION ERA

In April 1961, a writer for the *Gallup Navajo Times* enthused that "the greatest Redskin invasion of Chicago since the Ft. Dearborn invasion" would take place that summer. The promised invasion, formally titled the American Indian Chicago Conference (AICC), commenced on 13 June 1961, with over 800 Indians in attendance, 467 of whom were registered delegates representing ninety communities from throughout the United States. After a calumet ceremony, a dance performance, and a welcome feast, conferees gathered to hear University of Arizona anthropologist Edward Dozier, Santa Clara Pueblo, deliver the keynote address. Dozier reminded his audience that "our purpose at this conference is to compile a series of suggestions and recommendations. . . . While we differ as groups and individuals, our problems have a commonality. Pooling our efforts toward policies of greater benefits for ourselves is our goal."[1]

As Dozier noted, Native Americans had crossed tribal and community boundaries to attend the AICC, the largest pan-tribal meeting held to date, because the problems they faced as a group in American society demanded intertribal cooperation and coordination in order to bring about solutions. D'Arcy McNickle, enrolled member of the confederated Salish and Kutenai tribes, later wrote that participants "had a common sense of being under attack." The sense of crisis that American Indians experienced in 1961 stemmed from the crushing poverty that plagued them and from federal policies that threatened the very existence of their communities.[2]

NATIVE AMERICA IN 1961

The 1960 census, the first to incorporate self-identification as the means of determining racial classifications, counted 546,228 Native Americans in the United States. Slightly more than half of all Indians lived in the West, a region that encompassed the Rocky Mountain and Pacific states and Alaska and Hawaii. Thirty percent of Indians lived in urban areas, a result of migration to cities in search of employment during and after World War II and, in small part, to a government policy of relocating Native Americans to cities that was first implemented in the 1950s.[3]

The census revealed that Indians were an undereducated and impoverished people. The median school years completed was 8.45 years. Of Indians aged fourteen and over, ten percent had never attended school; only twelve percent had completed four years of high school. Some 9,000 Native American children did not attend school at all in 1961. Only one percent of Indians had four or more years of post-secondary education—in 1961 a mere sixty-six Indians received degrees from four-year colleges. Employment sector statistics reflected the low levels of educational achievement. The census classified 90,560 Indians as "heads of household"; only forty-seven percent of family heads worked more than forty weeks in 1959, and roughly a quarter of all family heads did not work at all that year. The median income for all Indians who received income in 1959 was $1,348, with male median income at $1,792, and that of females at less than $1,000. The same census listed the median income for white males as $4,300 and for nonwhite males as $2,300. Thus, extreme poverty was the norm for most Native Americans. Mary Crow Dog, who grew up on the Rosebud Sioux reservation during the 1960s, recalled that "we had no shoes and went barefoot most of the time. I never had a new dress." However, she claimed that "we kids did not suffer from being poor" because "we did not know that somewhere there was a better, more comfortable life."[4]

Low income levels limited access to adequate housing. Robert Burnette, Rosebud Sioux, remembered that many Indians lived in "tarpaper shacks, rickety log houses, ragged tents, abandoned automobile bodies and hillside caves." Wretched housing and rural isolation contributed to health problems. Infant mortality rates for Indians stood at twice that of the rest of the nation. The average age at death for Native Americans was forty-two years, more than twenty years fewer than that of other Americans. Native Americans suffered from diseases such as diphtheria, meningitis, trichinosis, and trachoma at rates far above the national averages—the Indian death rate from tuberculosis in 1961 was five times that of the rest of the American population.[5]

THE FEDERAL GOVERNMENT AND INDIAN AFFAIRS

Over time, the federal government incurred numerous obligations to American Indians, primarily through the signing of treaties from 1776 to 1871 but also through other mechanisms including executive action and legislation. These obligations included the recognition of tribes and their governments as semi-sovereign bodies, assistance in the form of goods and services, and the protection of Indian lands and resources, which were held in trust by the federal government for Indians.[6]

Because federal services were limited to individuals living on or near reservations, Native Americans who lived along the east coast, in cities, or who were members of terminated tribes received no direct services.

In 1961, the federal government provided assistance to approximately 345,000 Native Americans, and held nearly 52.5 million acres of Indian land in trust.[7]

The Bureau of Indian Affairs (BIA), an agency within the Department of the Interior, provided most government services to Indians and managed Indian lands. Until 1977, the head of the BIA was the commissioner of Indian affairs, who reported to the assistant secretary of public land management. For most of its history, the position of commissioner was regarded as a political appointment and, in the words of one commissioner, was held by "lawyers, legislators, Indians, Indian fighters, Indian lovers, scholars, at least one poet and mystic, and plenty of hacks and scoundrels."[8]

As a member of the executive branch, the commissioner carried out the policies of the president. However, Indian policy was by no means the exclusive province of the executive branch. Through its control of public laws, purse strings, and appointments, the United States Congress played a major role in determining the direction of Indian policy. Congress approved all legislation and appropriations concerning Indian affairs. In addition, the U.S. Senate confirmed the nominations of many Interior Department officials, including the secretary of the interior and the commissioner of Indian affairs (one of the few bureau chiefs that required Senate confirmation).[9]

In Congress, the conduct of Indian policy was the province of the Committees on Interior and Insular Affairs and the appropriations committees in the Senate and House of Representatives. A 1973 study of congressional committees concluded that Interior Committee members in both houses had "the primary goal of helping their constituents and thereby reinsuring their re-election," and that "the making of good public policy is a distinctly secondary consideration." One committee chairman, Sen. Clinton P. Anderson (D.-N. Mex.), observed that the committee's membership was "composed almost exclusively of westerners," because "it is in the West where lie the largest tracts of public lands, the biggest Indian reservations, most of the mining of metals, the giant reclamation projects, and the extensive lumbering operations." He also noted that "businessmen involved in these matters keep a great deal of pressure on the committee and they have always had many friends among its members."[10]

Small in numbers and poor in resources, Native Americans could not match the influence that business interests had with the Interior Committee. The low level of Indian political participation led most committee members to consider Indian policy as an area that brought many troubles and few benefits. Wayne N. Aspinall (D.-Colo.), chairman of the House Interior Committee through the 1960s, recalled being "distressed a great deal" because no committee member "wanted to serve as chairman of the Indian Affairs subcommittee" in the 1970s. Thus, the fate and future of Native Americans was in the hands of congressmen who had little vested interest in promoting Indian welfare, a reality reflected in the federal Indian policy known as termination.[11]

THE TERMINATION POLICY

The goal of the termination policy was to end all federal obligations to Indians and their communities. Tribal governments would lose any sovereign rights they possessed, Indian lands would be removed from trust status, treaty rights would be extinguished, and federal assistance to Indians as such would cease. Tribes could continue to exist as private cultural, social, or business entities, but without federal recognition as communities with specific rights distinct from those of non-Indians in the United States. Thus, termination constituted yet another federal effort to assimilate American Indians into the dominant society, efforts that to date had met with abysmal failure.

The termination policy had its origins in the years immediately following World War II, when a renewed interest in Indian welfare combined with a growing concern for civil rights produced calls for an end to government involvement in Indian affairs. Increased contact with Indians during the war had led many non-Indians to reevaluate their perceptions of Native Americans, and laudable wartime service indicated that Indians were capable of managing their own affairs. Moreover, Indian patriotism contrasted poorly with the appalling conditions in which many Indians lived. Some critics blamed government management of Indian affairs for these conditions. They claimed that their legal status as wards of the government made Indians second-class citizens denied opportunities open to others in American society. President Harry Truman maintained that "the present aim (of the Indian Bureau) appears to keep the Indian an Indian and to make him satisfied with the limitations of a primitive form of existence."[12]

Fiscal conservatism, Cold War nationalism, and western development contributed to the formulation of the termination policy. Alarmed by burgeoning federal budgets, some members of Congress declared that the BIA was an unnecessary government agency whose abolition would contribute to a decrease in spending. The ideological dimensions of the growing tensions between the United States and the Soviet Union fostered a narrow nationalism that rejected cultural pluralism and regarded diversity with suspicion, prompting some critics to go so far as to charge that tribal governments were communist in nature. Finally, substantial economic growth in the American West after World War II led some westerners to advocate ending the trust status of Indian lands, which they perceived as an obstacle to the region's economic development.[13]

These larger trends in the postwar United States—liberalism, budgetary concerns, a diminished tolerance for cultures outside the "norms" of American life, and the rise of the west—coincided with the belief that a new Indian policy was necessary because New Deal reforms in Indian affairs had failed. Never comfortable with the 1934 Indian Reorganization Act (IRA), Congress listened to both Indians and non-Indians who condemned the legislation and its effect (or lack thereof) on the lives of Native Americans and their communities. Critics pointed to the lack of economic development on the reservations, factionalism within tribes, and disputes over land ownership as evidence that the IRA should be jettisoned.[14]

In 1946, Congress approved legislation that established a three-man commission charged with hearing Indian claims against the United States. The Indian Claims Commission (ICC) resolved decades-old legal controversies, offering monetary compensation to Indians who pressed successful claims. While the creation of the ICC addressed a long-overdue concern of Indians and their advocates, it was also intended to promote the assimilation of Indians into the larger American culture and society. Assimilationists maintained that cash settlements obviated the need for federal assistance. Sen. Arthur V. Watkins (R.-Utah), a leading proponent of an assimilation policy, later wrote that Congress established the ICC to "clear the way toward complete freedom of the Indians by assuring a final settlement of all obligations—real or purported—of the federal government to the Indian tribes and other groups."[15]

The postwar drive to implement an assimilation policy found its most explicit expression in House Concurrent Resolution 108 (HCR 108), which Congress passed with bipartisan support in August 1953. Concurrent resolutions do not have the force of law—they serve as a statement of purpose for the Congress that passed it. HCR 108 committed Congress to "end their (the Indians) status as wards of the government" as "rapidly as possible." It then declared that "at the earliest possible time" all Indians in California, Florida, New York, and Texas and the members of five tribes including the Klamaths of Oregon and the Menominees of Wisconsin should "be freed from Federal supervision and control and from all the disabilities and limitations specifically applicable to Indians."[16]

Although HCR 108 did not use the word, "termination" quickly became the name of the postwar Indian policy. The resolution did not establish the termination policy; it stated the direction that Indian policy had taken since the end of World War II. However, its passage marked the beginning of legislative efforts to implement termination as quickly as possible. Two weeks after approving HCR 108, Congress passed HR 1063, a bill transferring civil and criminal jurisdiction over reservations in five states from federal and tribal officials to state law enforcement agencies. The measure also permitted any state to extend its jurisdiction over Indian lands within its borders without tribal consent. While the bill was intended to solve the complex problem of overlapping jurisdictions that hampered effective law enforcement on reservations, it dealt a serious blow to tribal sovereignty and marked another step toward ending federal responsibilities to Indians. President Dwight D. Eisenhower expressed "grave doubts about the wisdom of certain provisions," but he nonetheless signed the bill, which was known as Public Law 280 (PL 280).[17]

Advocates of termination harbored no such doubts. They adopted the rhetoric of liberty to justify the policy. HCR 108 declared that Indians "should be freed from Federal supervision and control." Senator Watkins, the leading advocate of termination, called it the "Indian freedom program," and compared it to the Emancipation Proclamation. Hyperbole aside, proponents regarded termination as the end of the crippling paternalism that marred federal-Indian relations and discouraged Indian social and economic advancement. Yet the process of policy formulation indicated that policymakers retained a paternalistic perception of Native Americans. Policymakers assumed they knew best when it came to Indian affairs. Indian participation in the process was virtually nil, and Indian consultation was minimal. Although Watkins later wrote that termination did "not affect the retention of those cultural and racial qualities which people of Indian descent would wish to retain," termination advocates offered no legislation to encourage such retention or to protect Indian heritage. The provisions of PL 280 showed that policymakers had no respect or concern for tribal sovereignty. Despite protestations to the contrary, termination proffered abandonment, not liberation.[18]

In addition to the termination of specific tribes, three other policy initiatives advanced the termination policy: relocation, program transfers, and economic development. The relocation program encouraged Native Americans to leave the reservations and find employment in urban areas. While relocation offered some Indians escape from the poverty of the reservations, many found city life disorienting and dispiriting. Because relocation was intended to promote assimilation, it did nothing for Native Americans who remained on the reservations. Program transfers involved moving BIA functions to either state and local organizations or other federal departments as a means of dismantling the bureau. In 1955 BIA health services were transferred to the Public Health Service in the Department of Health, Education and Welfare, a measure that actually improved health care for many American Indians.[19]

The third policy initiative focused on the economic development of the reservations. Commissioner Glenn Emmons advocated a program that relied upon private industries locating near reservations rather than spending federal dollars to create Indian-owned enterprises. This program met with little success. Most industries had no interest in locating in the remote areas where reservations usually existed, and the few that did discovered that most Indians lacked the training necessary to perform many tasks. The recession of 1957 further hampered the program as most businesses abandoned any plans for expansion.[20]

OPPOSING TERMINATION

As the federal government implemented various aspects of the termination policy, critics from several sources attacked it as flawed. Although some highly assimilated Indians disliked trust restrictions and supported the policy, most Native Americans quickly came to regard termination as a significant threat. The paternalistic policies of the previous decades had fostered a dependency that could not be overcome by the simplistic legislation offered in Congress. Indian response to several termination bills introduced in 1954 revealed the extent of their opposition. Native Americans from many tribes journeyed to Washington D.C. to protest termination legislation at the subcommittee hearings. The protests effectively stymied some legislation, but Congress ultimately voted to terminate certain tribes, including the Menominees and the Klamaths.[21]

The National Congress of American Indians (NCAI), a pan-tribal organization founded in 1944, took the lead in opposing termination. Initially, many NCAI leaders saw termination as a means to end federal paternalism and promote Indian control over their communities. However, by February 1954 it became readily apparent that termination as defined by the U.S. Congress was not a route to self-determination. That month, as Congress held hearings that led to the passage of six bills that paved the way for terminating several tribes, the NCAI held an emergency meeting under the direction of executive director Helen Peterson. With help from her mother, Peterson had printed and collated information packets the night before the meeting began on 25 February. Her efforts paid off—the 1954 meeting galvanized the NCAI and other Indians to fight against termination and garnered national and international media coverage, drawing attention to the termination policy and Indian efforts to combat it.[22]

Termination remained at the top of the NCAI's agenda in the years that followed. During the September 1958 NCAI national convention in Missoula, Montana, NCAI president J. R. Garry deemed HCR 108 to be "the most dangerous and unwarranted piece of legislation since the enactment of the General Allotment Act." Lacy W. Maynor, a Lumbee who served as a county judge in North Carolina, pointed to the importance of Indian political participation, arguing that "Indians must become politically active if they are to protect their lands and preserve their cultural heritage." Maynor claimed that the "shortest route to all of these [Indian objectives] is the full and intelligent use of the ballot." Thus, the termination crisis promoted pan-tribal unity and a new sense of the need for concerted political action on the part of many Native Americans, an attitude that would culminate in the American Indian Chicago Conference in 1961.[23]

Non-Indian advocacy groups and supporters and some government officials also protested the termination policy. Oliver La Farge, president of the Association of American Indian Affairs (AAIA), wrote in 1957 that termination bills were created "in an atmosphere of haste, of jamming through, of bad drafting, misrepresentation, and pressure."

Former BIA Commissioner John Collier argued that the U.S. government was "defying its contractual obligations and ignoring prior experience" and was "seeking to disinherit the Indians materially and culturally." State governments, which had received jurisdiction over reservations under the provisions of PL-280, complained that they had not received the necessary funds to extend services to the Indians. Several members of Congress from states with substantial Native American populations spoke out against termination. As an Army officer during World War II, Rep. Lee Metcalf (D.-Mont.) had witnessed the suffering of the displaced and relocated victims of World War II, an experience that marked him for life and engendered in him a sense of compassion for the disadvantaged. An emerging critic of Indian policy, Metcalf condemned termination as an attempt to "dispose of the 'Indian problem' by sweeping it under the rug," and called for a new direction in Indian affairs. As a guest speaker at the 1958 NCAI meeting, Metcalf declared that he was "ready to declare war on the Bureau of Indian Affairs and to reverse the Indian policies of the Eisenhower administration."[24]

The growing opposition to termination both within and outside of Congress and the obvious failure of many termination initiatives led to a retreat from the policy. In a radio broadcast given the week of the 1958 NCAI convention, Interior Secretary Fred A. Seaton announced that no tribe would be terminated until "it understands the plan under which such a program would go forward" and it "concurs in and supports the plan proposed." Although Seaton did not repudiate termination as a goal, his statement represented an important policy change and indicated that dissatisfaction with the termination policy had reached high levels in the Eisenhower administration.[25]

After Seaton's announcement, Congress passed only one more termination act during the Eisenhower years, approving legislation in September 1959 that detailed the termination of the Catawba tribe. During the 1954–1961 period only twelve Indian groups with a total combined population of 12,821 were terminated. Tribal termination thus affected only an estimated three percent of the Indian population of the United States and removed only three percent of Indian landholdings from trust status. However, the true impact of termination was not in the number of Indians immediately affected by the legislation, but in the potential threat it leveled at all Native American communities. The fear of tribal termination colored Native American perceptions of federal initiatives throughout the 1960s and hampered the implementation of policies intended to promote Indian self-sufficiency during that decade.[26]

THE 1960 PRESIDENTIAL CAMPAIGN

Indian policy became an issue, albeit a minor one, during the 1960 presidential campaign. Both party platforms contained references to Indian affairs, but neither offered specifics or wholly rejected the termination policy. The Republican platform pointed to successes in the areas of Indian health and educational services and echoed Interior Secretary Seaton's 1958 speech in stating that the party was "opposed to precipitous termination of federal Indian trusteeship responsibility," and would not "support any termination plan for any tribe which had not approved such action." The Democratic platform, written in part after consultation with NCAI members, pledged "prompt adoption of a program to assist Indian tribes in the full development of their human and natural resources and to advance the health, education, and economic well-being of Indian citizens while preserving their cultural heritage" and declared that "free consent of the Indian tribes shall be required before the Federal Government makes any change in any Federal-Indian treaty or other contractual relationship."[27]

A briefing paper prepared for Democratic nominee John F. Kennedy recommended that "Senator Kennedy stand squarely on the Democratic platform plank on American Indians." The paper stated that a Democratic administration should reevaluate the termination program, provide more funds for land acquisition, emphasize training in skills relevant to reservation life instead of urging Indians to relocate "into often hostile urban environments," and incorporate Indians "in a broad area development program."[28]

In August 1960, Kennedy met with Frank George (Nez Perce), chairman of the American Indian Section of the Nationalities Division of the Democratic National Committee and a former director of the NCAI. Coordinated for publicity purposes, the meeting was held at Kennedy's home in Hyannis Port. George praised the Indian plank of the party platform, while Kennedy declared that "there is much to be done in the field of Indian affairs and I intend to work vigorously at the job," and promised "sympathetic and dedicated leadership to the administration of Indian affairs which will end practices that have eroded Indian rights and resources, reduced the Indians' land base and repudiated Federal responsibility."[29]

In response to an offer from the AAIA to state their positions on Indian policy, Republican presidential candidate Richard M. Nixon and Kennedy elaborated upon the party platforms. Campaigning as the successor to incumbent Dwight D. Eisenhower, Nixon hailed the "constructive accomplishments which the Eisenhower administration has hammered out through its programs to the American Indian people." Largely confined to a defense of administration policies, Nixon discussed the importance of educational and vocational programs and claimed that his aim would be to provide Indians "with the greatest possible gamut of opportunity so that they can move steadily forward and participate increasingly in the dynamic growth and upward surge of 20th century American life."[30]

Kennedy promised a "sharp break with the policies of the Republican party." Placing Indian policy in the larger context of development policies for economically depressed regions of the nation, he claimed that "Indians would benefit not only from our specific program in the field of Indian affairs, but also from our programs for help to underprivileged groups generally." Kennedy pledged his administration to "a program of development of Indian communities," and offered ten specific policy points, including the enactment of area redevelopment legislation, the expansion of credit, and continued advancement in Indian health and educational services. Kennedy's statement differed from that of Nixon in that it offered expanded federal involvement in the area of economic development; but like his Republican opponent the Democratic candidate did not repudiate the long-term goal of termination.[31]

Oliver La Farge had signed the AAIA request for the candidate's statements on Indian affairs, but AAIA attorney Richard Schifter had actually written the letter—and it was Schifter who composed Kennedy's response. Schifter later noted that "I had worked out this exchange of correspondence with [Kennedy aides] before it was initiated." This incident revealed the lack of knowledge concerning Indian affairs among Kennedy's staff. It also showed poor judgment. Allowing an advocate for Indian affairs to write the candidate's response brought benefits to Native Americans, but it would later put the White House in an awkward position when Kennedy proved unwilling to keep his pledge.[32]

John F. Kennedy was elected president on 8 November 1960. Indian affairs ranked low on his list of concerns, but the nation's Indian policy was in a shambles, lacking direction and in dire need of creative leadership and innovative programs. Termination had been disastrous for the nation's Indians, perpetuating the poverty and despair that had too long been their lot. Although efforts to terminate tribes had slowed in the late 1950s, assimilation and the end of federal involvement in Indian affairs remained the goal of many influential congressmen. In 1961 most Native Americans remained deeply suspicious of the government and its representatives.

Despite the atmosphere of distrust, there were signs that Indian policy might undergo some improvement. The narrow nationalism that had contributed to assimilation policies had given way to a new awareness concerning the treatment of minorities, thus creating the potential for a return to the cultural pluralism that had inspired reformers during the New Deal era. The American economy was robust, offering at least the potential for increases in federal expenditures in Indian affairs. Finally, the release of two nongovernment reports that offered recommendations for changing the nation's Indian policy evidenced a new spirit of reform that infused Indian affairs in 1961.

THE COMMISSION ON THE RIGHTS, LIBERTIES, AND RESPONSIBILITIES OF THE AMERICAN INDIANS

The first report, *A Program For Indian Citizens: A Summary Report, January 1961*, was the product of a private study. In March 1957, the Fund for the Republic established the Commission on the Rights, Liberties, and Responsibilities of the American Indians "to promote a better understanding of the special status of this people [Indians] as United States citizens and of what should be done by and for them to facilitate their entry into the mainstream of American life." Commission members included chairman O. Meredith Wilson, president of the University of Minnesota; W. W. Keeler, principal chief of the Cherokees and an oil company executive; Karl N. Llewellyn, professor of jurisprudence at the University of Chicago; Arthur M. Schlesinger, Sr., professor of history at Harvard University; and Charles A. Sprague, an editor and publisher from Oregon. Dr. Sophie D. Aberle replaced executive director William A. Brophy, commissioner of Indian affairs from 1945 to 1948, after his resignation in 1957. Assisted by a number of consultants, the commission conducted a four-year study and released its findings in March 1961.[33]

Although the study called for Indian participation in every step of the policy process, it did not reject assimilation as a policy goal. The report argued that encouraging Indian cultural values could serve "as a force for assimilation and for enriching American culture," and discussed "the merging of the two cultures [i.e., Indian and Euroamerican]" and "the movement of Indians into the broader society." Nor did the report repudiate termination as a means to achieve assimilation—it merely called for significant reform, which if enacted, would render termination "an act of statesmanship in the best American tradition." Federal policy must prepare Indians "in advance of termination for self-reliant living in whatever is their prevailing social and economic framework. As this is accomplished tribe by tribe, termination will follow and follow from the Indians' desire." Effective termination programs would include "Indian collaboration in the development of a plan" and "adequate time . . . for the Indians, their neighbors, State and local units, and all other who might be affected . . . to work out the necessary adjustments."[34]

The report continued with assessments and recommendations in the areas of economic development, tribal governments and law and order, education, health, and the organization of the Bureau of Indian Affairs. Economic development would require "Federal money and effort," in the form of financial assistance to tribes for development programs and for educational and vocational training. The commission acknowledged that Native Americans seeking off-reservation employment faced "the difficulty of an untrained or semi-skilled worker in a highly technical society," but argued that many reservations were "too isolated to justify the establishment of industry" and thus called for creation of new employment opportunities off the reservation. It only touched upon the cultural and social disorientation that many Indians had suffered upon entering the relocation program, noting that "guidance and financial help should be made available to them [relocated Indians] until they become adjusted to their new environment, and an effort be made to locate them in neighboring quarters."[35]

In the area of tribal government and law and order, the study recognized the value of tribal governments to Native American communities but expressed some concerns about them. Because several U.S. Supreme Court decisions had concluded that tribal governments did not have to guarantee all the civil rights that most Americans enjoyed, the commission called for federal laws requiring tribal recognition of all individual civil rights. The report included recommendations regarding the jurisdictional tangles that complicated law enforcement and suggested that PL-280 be amended to require tribal consent before state jurisdiction could be extended over reservations.[36]

Recognizing that education and health services for Indians fell far below those provided to most Americans, the commission advocated increased funding and the adoption of high standards. It concluded with a call for organizational reform within the BIA, claiming that the agency "needs only revision and redirection to accomplish the purposes which the present-day situation of the Indian demands." Finally, the report recommended the creation of an advisory board to oversee and coordinate the policy process.[37]

The overall tone of *A Program For Indian Citizens* was moderate, advocating reform rather than any radical alteration in the direction of federal policy. A gradual process of economic development and cultural convergence that would ultimately allow Indians to terminate their relations with the federal government would replace the hasty termination of the 1950s. The report's most notable recommendation was the inclusion of Indians at every stage of the policy process. It stated that "no program imposed from above can serve as a substitute for one willed by Indians themselves." The emphasis on Indian participation marked a deviation from the conduct of federal Indian policy during the past decade. However, Native Americans were no longer content to wait for policymakers to include them in policy formulation, as the battle against termination during the 1950s and the 1961 American Indian Chicago Conference revealed.[38]

THE AMERICAN INDIAN CHICAGO CONFERENCE

Dr. Sol Tax, an anthropology professor at the University of Chicago, first proposed the Chicago convention. A student of community development, Tax created the concept of "action anthropology," a method of fostering development through self-determination. In 1960, after receiving a grant to study American Indian issues from the Schwartzhaupt Foundation, Tax suggested a conference that included both Indians and non-Indian scholars. At the 1960 NCAI convention in

Denver, Tax's proposal received an enthusiastic response from Indian leaders, and preparations for a meeting to be held in Chicago in June 1961 began immediately. NCAI members drafted a preliminary statement requesting comments and suggestions from Native Americans throughout the United States. Nine regional meetings and an estimated 250 tribal and intertribal meetings convened to formulate plans for the conference.[39]

When the conference assembled in June, delegates met in committees and general assemblies to discuss and debate their concerns. Inevitably, conflicts arose. One participant recalled that "at several critical moments the conference stood ready to dissolve, but on each such occasion an acceptable base for continuing discussion was found." The AICC completed its mission and produced the *Declaration of Indian Purpose*, an American Indian statement on federal policy. The report condemned termination as "a program of destroying Indian resources, of denying Indian aspirations, and arbitrarily relieving the Federal government of responsibility for specific tribes or in specific areas of interest," and called on the U.S. government to "abandon the so-called termination policy of the last administration by revoking House Concurrent Resolution 108 of the 83rd Congress." The *Declaration* called for a new policy based on a "broad educational process as the procedure best calculated to remove the disabilities which have prevented Indians from making full use of their resources." A series of specific recommendations in the areas of economic development, education, health, housing, and law followed this general policy statement.[40]

The report blamed the failure of previous economic development programs on the absence of Indians in the planning and operation of such programs. Unlike the Fund for the Republic study, which had dismissed the possibility of industries locating on or near reservations, the AICC saw the establishment of such industries as key to Indian economic development. The report placed responsibility for creating development programs in the hands of the Indians involved, with the government providing necessary technical expertise and inducements such as tax credits to encourage businesses to locate near reservations.

Increasing the Indian land base, improving Indian access to credit, and using the force account method in contracting construction work on reservations would increase Indian employment. While the study did not reject the relocation program entirely, it called for increased services and information to the those Indians who entered the program, and a promise of transportation home to those Indians who found relocation too stressful.[41]

In the areas of health, welfare, and housing, the report noted that Indians needed substantial assistance. Lamenting the deplorable health conditions that prevailed among Indians, the *Declaration* called for increased education and expanded services. The AICC asserted that many Indians were often denied services from county and state health programs for which they qualified as participants. This observation included the reception of welfare assistance from local governments. Citing the state of Indian housing as a "serious emergency," the report recommended increased federal aid to both reservation and off-reservation Indians in the form of greater funding and access to credit.[42]

Education—described by the AICC as "a process which begins at birth and continues through a life span," and "the key to salvation of whatever ills may be, wherever Indians reside"—received significant attention. In addition to suggesting numerous reforms at the elementary and secondary levels, the AICC advocated expanded educational services including vocational and on-the-job training and special education programs for children with physical and mental handicaps.[43]

Concern for Indian landholdings framed the discussion of law and jurisdiction. The *Declaration* called for the return of excess public domain holdings acquired from Indians through either land cessions or treaties. It also requested clarification of existing landholdings in order to prevent disputes over ownership. To relieve the growing problem of fractionated land ownership, the report suggested the passage of an heirship bill, but offered no specifics as to the provisions of such legislation. The amendment of PL-280 to include Indian consent, a staple of all policy recommendations, was among the report's suggestions. Finally, the AICC expressed concern over the taxation of

Indian income derived from trust holdings and called upon the United States to recognize its treaty obligations to the various Indian groups.[44]

The *Declaration of Indian Purpose* simultaneously recommended increased federal expenditures and diminished federal leadership in Indian affairs. Under the report's guidelines, the role of the BIA was largely that of offering the technical and administrative expertise that Native Americans lacked. As educational services improved and Indians gained the sophistication to manage their own affairs, the BIA's role would be increasingly limited. However, the report carefully avoided offering any time tables for this process or promising the eventual abolition of the BIA.[45]

With its explicit rejection of termination, emphasis on Indian leadership, and demand for the recognition of treaty rights, the *Declaration of Indian Purpose* recommended a significant departure from the current conduct of Indian policy. Indians recognized their dependency upon the federal government, but they would no longer tolerate government paternalism. It was the responsibility of Stewart Udall, Kennedy's choice to head the Interior Department, to respond to the growing demand for Indian participation in the policy process.

A New Secretary of the Interior

Kennedy announced that Stewart Udall was his nominee for the position of interior secretary on 7 December 1960. Udall had been an ardent campaigner for Kennedy, credited with winning the Arizona delegation's votes for Kennedy from Lyndon Johnson at the 1960 Democratic convention. Because no western senator wanted to head the Interior Department, Kennedy nominated Udall in part to reward him for his support. However, Kennedy's decision was not merely the payment of a political debt—Udall's background and the reputation he had built as a congressman made him an excellent choice for the Interior position.[46]

Tall and athletic, sporting a severe crew cut, Stewart Lee Udall partook of the popular image of youth and vigor that Americans held of their president-elect. Born in St. Johns, Arizona, on 31 January 1920, Udall came from a family committed to the Mormon faith and possessing a tradition of public service. His father, Levi Stewart Udall, had served from 1947 to 1960 as a justice on the Supreme Court of Arizona. Following service as a B-24 gunner in World War II, Stewart Udall returned to his home state to complete his education, receiving a law degree from the University of Arizona Law School in 1948. In his 1954 bid for the congressional seat in Arizona's enormous Second District, Udall defeated his Republican opponent by an impressive margin. He won reelection to the House in 1956 and again in 1958. During his three terms as a congressman, Udall earned an enviable reputation—a 1960 newspaper editorial opined that Udall's "colleagues have come to recognize him as a stout protagonist, a man of principle and an effective leader."[47]

In the area of Indian affairs Udall offered legislation in every session of Congress. In 1956 he cosponsored legislation that increased funding for vocational training for Indians. Congress approved the bill, which became Public Law 959. Like Lee Metcalf, Udall was one of the Democratic congressman critical of Indian policy during the 1950s. During that decade Udall made statements that revealed his attitudes toward Indian affairs. In a 1956 congressional debate, Udall defended the Indian Claims Commission as "a symbol of sincerity" on the grounds that "until such time as these claims are settled once and for all, our Indian people will tend to look backward at their grievances and we will have a hard time getting them to look on ahead to the future and assume their responsibilities." Speaking at the NCAI convention held in Phoenix in December 1959, Udall did not disavow the goal of ending federal responsibility toward Native Americans, but instead condemned the Eisenhower administration for failing "to lay emphasis on the step-by-step programs that make termination possible." He called for "aggressive human and resource development programs which will make it possible for our Indian people to formulate their own plans for self-determination."[48]

These statements indicated that Udall favored a gradual termination process without any declared deadline, one that emphasized development and Indian participation in the policy process. He considered the resolution of Indian claims as a necessary precursor to the implementation of an effective policy. Udall therefore considered self-determination as a variant of the termination policy and regarded the ICC as a part of the termination process. This position, a relatively moderate one during the late 1950s, would become increasingly out of step with Native American demands during the coming years and would later lead to conflict between Udall and Indian activists.

Udall expressed his continuing concern for Indian issues as he prepared for the position as interior secretary. In response to a question regarding Indian affairs posed at the 1960 press conference, Kennedy, referring to Udall, said that "I don't think there is anyone in the United States that is more familiar with this problem." Udall claimed that "I have such a deep interest in Indian affairs that it might be said that I will be my own Indian Commissioner," and he promised to "work very closely with the Indian people themselves and with their leaders."[49]

Kennedy's nominee met with general approval. A *New York Times* editorial rated Udall a "first-class man, one who has a genuine understanding of some of the major problems facing his department and a sympathy toward its basic goals," and the *New Republic* called his appointment "splendid." Oliver La Farge maintained that Udall possessed the "common sense, energy, and the political good sense essential to successful conduct of the office of Secretary of the Interio [sic]."[50]

This favorable reception was in evidence at the Senate Interior Committee hearing on Udall's nomination on 13 January 1961. Westerners controlled the committee—not a single member represented a state east of the Mississippi. Udall had the support of chairman Clinton Anderson, whom Kennedy had consulted with prior to announcing the nomination. Nor did Udall meet with significant opposition from Republican members. Sen. Henry Dworshak (R.-Idaho) noted the "unusual bipartisan support" for Udall as members from both sides of the aisle praised the nominee.[51]

The hearing focused on the issues of public power and public lands, and only two senators raised the topic of Indian affairs. Sen. Gordon Allott (R.-Colo.), a staunch terminationist and "ring leader of the conservatives" on the Interior Committee, expressed concern over the possibility of large settlements for Indian claims. Defending the mission of the Indian Claims Commission, Udall responded that the federal government must "see to it that whatever is involved in these judgements is reinvested and spent to develop their [Indian] resources, human and natural, and not squandered." He continued, claiming that "there is not an Indian problem. There are 65 or 82—or whatever the number is of Indian reservations—problems," adding that "we must approach these as special and different problems and aid them at their level." Sen. Frank Church (D.-Idaho) questioned Udall about fractionated landholdings. Udall agreed that the landholding issue created serious difficulties, noting that Indians "have economic opportunities to really get things rolling and yet you are stymied because no one owns the land. You cannot determine ownership." He then compared aid to Indians for economic development to similar foreign aid programs, arguing that "we do not have really the same type of sound, systematic program for our own undeveloped areas." The committee approved Udall's nomination, and the Senate unanimously confirmed Udall as secretary of the interior on 21 January 1961.[52]

Phillip S. Hughes, Deputy Director of the Bureau of the Budget, remembered Udall as "a guy of vast energy" with "lots of dedication and courage." In addition to possessing considerable physical stamina—he enjoyed mountain climbing, fishing, horseback riding, and other outdoors activities—Stewart Udall also harbored a great deal of ambition. He hoped to make his mark on the Interior Department and to leave office with an enduring legacy, especially in the area of conservation. His 1963 book *The Quiet Crisis*, which was written during airplane flights, was "dedicated to the proposition that men must grasp completely the relationship between human stewardship and the fullness of the American earth."[53]

Udall built a remarkable record of accomplishment as conservationist. However, he tended to focus intensely on one concern at a time, a management style that left much to be desired. One assistant secretary recalled that "Udall didn't have ten cents worth of experience as an administrator" and that "he just played it all by ear." As a result, his involvement in Indian affairs during his years in office was erratic, creating tensions within the department and with Native American activists.[54]

CREATING AN INDIAN POLICY

Udall collected recommendations regarding Indian policy before his confirmation. In December 1960 he received a study that called for a gradualist policy similar to that which he supported. It advocated continued assimilation, arguing that "Indians must take their place alongside other Americans, must accept the same responsibilities, must have the same (but no more) privileges," and claiming that "to achieve it [assimilation] as quickly as possible with minimum trauma is the goal for which those responsible for policy in Indian administration must strive." However, pointing to the need for maintaining federal trust status for Indian lands, the analysis asserted that the "immediate termination of federal services for Indians cannot be contemplated as either practical or humane." The study concluded that "preparing Indians to become 'self-reliant' is a major task of Indian administration."[55]

To facilitate the creation of new policy objectives in Indian affairs, Udall assembled a task force to study the issue shortly after he took office. He regarded the task force as "an advisory board in undertaking an administrative reorganization and policy reorganization of the Indian Bureau." On 23 January, two days after his Senate confirmation, Udall announced that William W. Keeler, a member of the Fund for the Republic Committee, had agreed to serve as Udall's principal adviser on Indian affairs for ninety days. Keeler had been strongly critical of federal Indian policy. The *New Republic* reported that his speech at the NCAI convention in December 1960 included the charge that "the government has not been consulting the Indians, that it has tried to make them forget their heritage and 'become white,' although it has not tried to stamp out the cultural identity of any other ethnic group." Keeler chaired the Udall task force. The other task force members were James E. Officer, an anthropologist and coauthor of the December 1960 recommendations who had advised Udall on Indian affairs during his years in Congress; William Zimmerman, Jr., assistant commissioner of Indian affairs from 1933 to 1950; and Philleo Nash, an anthropologist and former lieutenant governor of Wisconsin.[56]

THE SECRETARY'S TASK FORCE ON INDIAN AFFAIRS

Udall's task force held its first meeting on the afternoon of 7 February 1961, and met with Secretary Udall two days later. James Officer reported that the initial meeting of the task force consisted of discussion concerning thirteen points, some of which Udall and BIA employees had suggested. The majority of these issues concerned reservation development and Indian education and employment; other topics included the land heirship problem, amending HCR 108, and Indian housing. Education issues dominated the agenda at a meeting on 8 February at which the participants agreed that "this problem [education] is one of the most crucial and demands the immediate attention of the Task Force."[57]

At a meeting held on 9 February, Udall expressed some doubt about using a task force, claiming that "I am not at all certain that this idea of trying to reshape our policy by a committee is a good idea," but noting that "it might be worth trying." Udall dominated the discussions, offering general statements but no substantive policy positions. He argued that "in terms of the money and manpower available, that there is too little of it being felt at the Indian Reservation level" and called for "successfully drawing in new talent [to the BIA] where new talent is needed." However, Udall told those present that "we should not anticipate any great or immediate increases in the budget available for the Indian Bureau," a warning that limited the nature of the task force's suggestions.[58]

Udall's most revealing comments concerned Indian participation in the policy process. The interior secretary stated that "test[ing] our thinking against the thinking of the wisest Indians and their friends" did "not mean that we are going to let, as someone put it, the Indian people decide what the policy should be." Udall maintained that "some of them [Indians] have special axes to grind, some of them view the problem from too narrow a point of vantage." He hoped that at the conclusion of the task force review process that "there is a feeling among the Indians themselves . . . that they have been fully consulted, that whether they agree 100 percent with our conclusions, that they had a full and fair hearing." Lacking any bureaucratic tradition or mechanism to incorporate Indians into the policy formulation process, Udall continued to employ a paternalistic viewpoint that allowed him to perceive Indians as parochial and self-interested.

In addition to doubting the motivations of individual Native Americans, Udall also had his eye on congressional reaction. He reminded the task force members that "since the programs that we are here to discuss are financed by the Congress," they should "try to lay out a program for which we can secure Congressional support in terms of legislation and appropriations." His remarks indicated that the congressional position on Indian policy, which remained committed to termination, would greatly influence the formulation process.[59]

Following this meeting, the task force set about its business. It discussed policy with members of the House Subcommittee on Indian Affairs on 27 February. The next day the task force and BIA area directors and superintendents listened to Secretary Udall call for "critical thinking in Indian affairs" and urge BIA employees to "be candid in talking with the Task Force." Task force members used the suggestions offered at various policy sessions to draft a series of recommendation memorandums that offered advice to Udall concerning ongoing Indian issues and established policy goals.[60]

The task force also sought the counsel of Native Americans, meeting with a Sioux delegation on 16 February and with representatives from the Fort Berthold community the following day. Hearings were not limited to Washington, D.C. On 10 March, Udall announced that the group would travel to seven western cities, including Oklahoma City, Albuquerque, and Spokane, to meet with various tribal representatives. The task force ultimately held fifteen days of hearings with Native American leaders and visited several Indian communities. Philleo Nash later recalled that "98 percent of the [Indian] population was represented by the elected leaders that appeared before us and offered programs." Task force members also attended the American Indian Chicago Conference in June. The hearings and reservation visits represented a genuine effort to include Native Americans in the policy formulation process.[61]

THE 1961 TASK FORCE REPORT

The task force released its policy recommendations under the title "Report to the Secretary of the Interior by the Task Force on Indian Affairs" on 10 July 1961. The opening statement declared that "the programs which the Task Force suggests in the pages which follow are programs of development—development of people and development of resources," and maintained that "in order to insure the success of our endeavor, we must solicit the collaboration of those whom we hope to benefit—the Indians themselves." These goals were in line with those of Secretary Udall, who favored economic development with some Indian participation in the policy process. The bulk of the report was devoted to two areas of concern: creating programs that promoted economic growth and improved community services, and restructuring the operations of the federal bureaucracy to better its performance.[62]

Claiming that "maximum development of the resources of Indian reservations is essential," the study recommended that the BIA and the tribes conduct resource surveys and design master plans. Capital necessary for economic growth would come from expanded credit and the settlements in Indian claims cases. To provide job training and employment opportunities, funds for vocational training would be increased, a Youth Conservation Corps would be created, and Indians would receive preferential hiring on construction work done on reservations. Finally, the BIA would promote industrial development through increased expenditures in its Branch of Industrial Development, consultation with specialists, and the establishment of industrial sites to attract businesses.[63]

The study followed its discussion of development projects with the consideration of community services such as law and order, housing, and health. This section opened with an analysis of educational programs. The task force noted that "a major problem centers around the Indians' lack of formal education," and stated that "every program of the Bureau of Indian Affairs should be oriented around the education function." Although the task force called for "the ultimate transfer of the Bureau's education responsibilities" to public school districts, it recommended the construction of new schools, additional emphasis on summer school programs, and the encouragement of parental involvement in school operations. In the area of law and order, the task force concluded that the "system of divided jurisdiction produces uncertainty concerning the civil remedies available for the enforcement of contracts and the collections of judgments," which stifled economic development; however, it was critical of the solution provided to the problem by PL-280. The report raised the issue of protecting Indian civil rights, a subject that would garner increasing attention during the coming years. The study concluded that housing and health programs were best administered by other government agencies (e.g., the Federal Housing Agency and the Public Health Service) working in concert with BIA officials.[64]

The final section of the task force's report advocated organizational changes to better implement the development programs. The creation of an interdepartmental liaison committee would coordinate the activities of the many government agencies that provided Indian services, while an advisory board (which in some ways resembled an ongoing task force) would make policy recommendations directly to the interior secretary. However, the task force was curiously reluctant to suggest any significant reorganization of the Bureau of Indian Affairs. Instead, it called for a number of minor reforms intended to increase efficiency. Thus, the report failed to create any institutional mechanisms designed to increase Native American participation in the creation and conduct of Indian policy.[65]

The programs and policies recommended in the task force report did not reject termination as the ultimate goal of federal Indian policy. Arguing that "placing greater emphasis on termination than on development impairs Indian morale and produces a hostile or apathetic response," the task force members decided "not to list termination per se as a major objective of the Federal Indian program." However, the report maintained that after implementation of resource development programs "termination can be achieved with maximum benefit for all concerned." In addition, it stated that "eligibility for special Federal services should be withdrawn from Indians with substantial incomes and superior educational experience, who are as competent as most non-Indians to look after their own affairs." Thus, Udall's vision of a gradualist approach to termination lay at the heart of the task force report.[66]

The failure to repudiate termination constituted a weakness that overshadowed many of the positive proposals set forth in the study. Task force members were well aware of Native American attitudes in this regard. During the hearing on 16 February, the Sioux delegation had called for "legislation for reversal of [the] termination policy and [a] shift in emphasis from termination to progress and development." The next day members of the Fort Berthold community had declared that "termination as a policy should be disavowed." The report noted the "vigorous denunciation of the so-called 'termination policy' during the many hearings which the task force conducted with Indian leaders." James Officer later recalled that during the hearings, members of small tribes "demonstrated particular anxiety about their vulnerability, feeling themselves too politically impotent to combat the proponents of termination." Finally, the task force had made use of "the thoughtful expressions of Indian needs and aspirations embodied in this conference's [the AICC] Declaration of Indian Purpose," a document that advocated the repeal of HCR 108.[67]

Yet rather than forsake termination, the task force only recommended a "shift in emphasis," thus allowing Native Americans to perceive termination as the hidden intent of all federal programs, including those emphasizing resource development. The report had acknowledged that "many Indians see termination written into every new bill and administrative decision and sometimes are reluctant to accept help which they need and want for fear that it will carry with it a termination requirement." Secretary Udall later stated the problem in a somewhat simpler fashion when he claimed that "Indians were seeing 'termination' lurking behind every rock and every tree." Although Udall and his advisers recognized the psychological impact and effects of termination, they did not calm Indian fears on this issue. This ensured that administration policies would be met with suspicion and anxiety, thereby undermining the goal of gaining Indian collaboration and cooperation in the policy process.[68]

Amendment of HCR 108 had been one of the original concerns of the task force and had been discussed at the 7 February meeting. On 21 February James H. Gamble, an aide for the Senate Interior Committee, asserted that Congress might accept amendments, but John R. Taylor, Indian consultant for the House Interior Committee, argued that the substance of HCR 108 had to remain intact. Four days later task force members again discussed the issue but were unable to come to an agreement. The realization that many members of Congress still supported termination prevented the task force from completely addressing the problem of termination.[69]

Secretary Udall had informed the task force that all policies would ultimately require congressional approval, and Philleo Nash later recalled that the task force "had to bear in mind that Congress provides the authority and the funds and you therefore could not fly in the face of congressional opinion." Nash concluded that "we therefore scaled it [the final report] very modestly." After reading the report, Oliver La Farge remarked upon the "wording that seems less forthright than I desired," which he recognized was "cagily intended to avoid familiar expressions that arouse unfavorable reflexes in certain members of Congress."[70]

However, the attempt to create a "modest" or moderate statement yielded a document that was, in many ways, conservative. A later assessment pointed out that "although the language was more vigorous and the platform more visible, the Task Force's emphases were very similar to those of the previous administration." Its report did not abandon termination. The economic development of reservations had been a theme sounded throughout the 1950s. Although it claimed that Indian involvement in the policy process was "an essential ingredient of a successful program," the task force offered no specifics as to how Indians could be included in the formulation and implementation of policy. References to the protection of Indian cultural values were scant; and although assimilation was never discussed, the assumption that Native Americans would inevitably adopt most Euroamerican attitudes permeated the study. As one critic later asserted, the report was "not a statement of 'bold new thinking,' but rather of compromise and uncertainty."[71]

On the other hand, the recognition that federal involvement and spending were necessary for the development of Indian resources and the improvement of Indian living standards represented a departure from the policy direction of the 1950s. Most important, the ideal of Indian participation as essential to an effective policy had been stated and could not be revoked. Despite its many faults, the task force report offered Native Americans expanded opportunities denied to them in previous federal polices.

THE IMPORTANCE OF THE INDIAN POLICY REPORTS

After eleven months in office, Interior Secretary Stewart L. Udall declared that 1961 had "already proved to be a most unusual year insofar as Indian affairs are concerned." As proof, Udall referred to the release of the three policy studies. The studies were not wholly independent of one another—William Keeler was a member of the Fund for the Republic Committee and the 1961 task force; task force members attended the AICC and referred to the *Declaration of Indian Purpose*; and task force member William Zimmerman served as an observer for Udall at early planning sessions of the AICC. However, the impact and importance of each study varied. The only widely disseminated report was that of the Fund for the Republic, which was published in an expanded hardcover edition in 1966. Publication allowed this report to reach a large audience and earn frequent citations in academic works. In the long run, the *Declaration of Indian Purpose* was the most important report because it served as a statement of Native American attitudes in an era when their concerns would become increasingly important to the policy process. In addition, the AICC received significant media coverage and captured the interest of the general public in a way that previous Indian conferences had not. NCAI resolutions passed during the 1950s had set forth similar policy statements but had not garnered much attention.[72]

In regard to federal Indian policy during the 1960s, the report of Udall's task force stood apart from the other studies because it guided the direction of federal Indian policy for several years. Declaring that "the proper role of the Federal Government is to help Indians find their way along a new trail," it attempted to map that trail for policymakers. However, Secretary Udall quickly discovered that the "New Trail," which became the catchword for Indian policy in Kennedy's New Frontier, was a path that key members of Congress were most reluctant to follow.[73]

THE NASH APPOINTMENT

Udall's remark that he might serve as his own Indian commissioner evinced his interest in Indian affairs but in reality was wholly impractical. He later commented that "no cabinet member can give full attention to his post and, at the same time, direct the daily operations of any of the bureaus within a Department." While Udall immediately recognized the need to appoint a new commissioner, the selection process was complicated by a Kennedy campaign promise to appoint a Native American to the position.[74]

The notion of appointing a Native American as commissioner had the support of senators such as Barry Goldwater (R.-Az.). However, making a campaign pledge to that effect was an error. In December 1960, Udall told a reporter that he and Kennedy wanted "someone who would be widely and generally acceptable to the Indians of all tribes in all parts of the country." That goal immediately proved difficult to achieve as several Indian leaders lobbied for the position, which in turn created tensions within the Native American community. Udall received many letters supporting J. Maurice McCabe, executive secretary of the Navajo Tribal Council. McCabe secured the endorsement of Sen. Dennis Chavez (D.-N. Mex.), and his backers formed the Committee for the Promotion of an Indian Commissioner of Indian Affairs. However, the Ute Mountain Tribe expressed anxiety over McCabe, arguing that the Navajo Tribe was already too powerful and that he would not serve the interests of other Native American communities. The Ute Mountain letter noted that the previous commissioner, Glenn Emmons, had also been from the Gallup, New Mexico area.[75]

Therein lay the problem with appointing a Native American as commissioner—any selection would inevitably alienate some tribes. To complicate matters, several Indians desiring the position had congressional sponsors, so the appointment of a Native American as commissioner entangled the opinions of important congressmen in the process. Faced with these complications, Udall delayed making a final decision by naming John Crow, a Native American from Oklahoma, as acting commissioner, a move that allowed the administration to make the somewhat disingenuous claim that it had fulfilled its campaign promise. However, with the release of the task force report, Udall could no longer delay appointing a commissioner. Following the advice of

W. W. Keeler, Udall recommended Philleo Nash, a non-Indian task force member, for the position.[76]

Born on 25 October 1909, Nash earned his bachelor's degree in anthropology from the University of Wisconsin at Madison in 1932. He continued his studies at the University of Chicago, receiving his Ph.D. in 1937. As a graduate student, Nash conducted research on the Klamath Indian Reservation, an experience that he later recalled led him to "try to get into situations where I could help to make the decisions and to make it on the basis of better understanding of cultural and personal values and attitudes and responses—rather than on the bare superficiality which was so costly and so destructive to Indian-white relations."[77]

Following a stint in academia, Nash took a position in Washington, D.C., as an analyst in the Office of War Information. He eventually served in the Truman White House, first as a special assistant and then as administrative assistant to the president. He later claimed that while working for Truman "race relations were my bag." He was involved in the preparation of the seminal 1947 report "To Secure These Rights," and in 1948 he prepared the first draft of the executive order that desegregated the armed forces. In addition to his responsibilities as a government employee, Nash served as a board member for the Association of American Indian Affairs from 1942 until 1961. Although he initially supported Dillon S. Myer, Truman's commissioner of Indian affairs from 1950 to 1953, Nash soon soured on Myer's policies. He later claimed that he "told Dillon Myer that he was an idiot" for supporting the relocation program. At one point Nash briefly considered lobbying for the commissioner's position himself.[78]

Following Eisenhower's victory in 1952, Nash returned to Wisconsin, where he was active in Democratic party politics. He also served as vice president of the Menominee Tribal Trust, a position from which he resigned in 1958 when he successfully ran for Lieutenant Governor. His platform included opposition to the termination of the Menominee tribe, whose reservation lay within the state. Ousted from office in the 1960 election, Nash again looked to Washington D.C. for employment. However, as a supporter of Hubert Humphrey's campaign for the Democratic presidential nomination in 1960, Nash had earned little political capital with the new Kennedy administration. Still interested in Indian affairs, he hoped to secure an appointment as assistant secretary of public land management, and he discussed his interests with Secretary Udall. He did not receive the position of assistant secretary, but he was invited to join the secretary's task force. His political background, his familiarity with some Native American issues, and his service on the task force all led Udall to nominate Nash.[79]

Press reaction to the nomination was favorable, with the *New York Times* opining that "President Kennedy has made an excellent choice" and the *Washington Post* calling Nash "a well qualified official" who possessed "the insights of an anthropologist who understands the tribal ways of politics as well as of Indians." However, opinion within the Interior Department was not as positive. Many long-time BIA employees perceived Nash as a reformer in the Collier mode and feared that his appointment would lead to numerous troubling changes within the bureau. More important, Udall was not entirely happy with his selection. He later noted that he chose Nash "with some reluctance" and complained that "that's one of the unfortunate things, that we brought non-Indian political types in and made them Indian Commissioner." Although Nash was qualified for the job, Udall's lack of enthusiasm for his nominee did not bode well for the future.[80]

In addition to the less-than-enthusiastic attitude of the secretary, Nash faced difficulties from Congress during his confirmation hearings. As he later recalled, "I was in for a battle and I got it." Several members of Congress had expressed opposition to policies suggested in the task force report, and during the hearings Nash would be "on the hot seat with my name on a policy document that had already irritated important members of the Committee." Udall had recognized that the report might not be favorably received in Congress and distanced himself to some degree from its conclusions. In a cover letter attached to an advance copy of the final report sent to Rep. James Haley (D.-Fla.), chairman of the House Subcommittee on Indian Affairs, Udall wrote that "this is a task force report which stands on its own feet and is not, as such, a report of this Department—but rather a series of recommendations to the Secretary."[81]

Although perhaps not admirable, Udall's caution proved warranted. When he presented the report to a group of congressmen at a breakfast in the summer of 1961, it received a chilly reception. Several senators openly criticized the report. The Nash hearings provided those senators with a public forum to air their views on the Kennedy administration's "New Trail." While the Udall confirmation was an exercise in courtesy and collegiality, the Nash hearings became an arena for tense and often unpleasant policy debates.[82]

THE NASH CONFIRMATION HEARINGS

On 9 August 1961, Senate Interior Committee chairman Clinton Anderson announced that the Nash hearings would be held the following week. Anderson's congressional career began in 1941 when he entered the House of Representatives. He remained there until 1945, when he resigned to serve as Truman's secretary of agriculture. He returned to Congress as a senator after the 1948 elections. By 1960 Anderson had become one of the Senate's most powerful members. John Carver, assistant secretary of the interior, recalled that Anderson "was critically important to the Department's program," and that "there was no possible way of working out some of our administrative problems involving Indian problems when he was opposed."[83]

In the area of Indian affairs, Anderson advocated assimilation and termination. In a 1955 letter, Anderson expressed frustration at "the folly of attempting to enact termination programs in the absence of a well thought out and planned program for the management of tribal assets following termination." Nonetheless, he remained committed to termination as a means of promoting assimilation. At the Udall breakfast, Anderson supported the recommendations of a March 1961 report from the Comptroller General that sanctioned the continued termination of Indian tribes without tribal consent.[84]

An aide later recalled that Anderson had "two sides to him. One was the great, the brilliant, the intellectual side. But he could also be mean." Anderson's antipathy to the task force report quickly became apparent during the confirmation hearings that opened on 14 August, and his "mean" side came to the fore as he grilled Philleo Nash. Although Anderson stated that the report "does reveal that you aren't turning exactly in the opposite direction from what we have been following through the last few years, namely, that we were looking toward termination," he found its recommendations wanting. He rejected measures that strengthened tribal organizations, opposing the ideal of tribal jurisdiction with the claim that "we were hoping that gradually these areas [civil and criminal jurisdiction] would be placed under the jurisdiction of State courts." He also objected to a proposed Interior bill regarding the heirship problem, contending that the bill gave "a preferential right to the tribe to buy it [heirship lands], the tribe will gradually buy it all and you will never have individual ownership of property." Anderson then allowed other senators to question Nash, but throughout the hearing he offered caustic remarks that showed his disapproval of the report's recommendations.[85]

After responding to questions from several senators who were not as adversarial as Anderson, Nash encountered Frank Church, the senator from Idaho. Church's career had a remarkable beginning—although he had never held public office, the citizens of Idaho elected him to the U.S. Senate in 1955 when he was only thirty-two years old. As a western senator he naturally sought assignment on the Interior Committee. Church had little interest in American Indian issues, so it was with reluctance that he accepted the chairmanship of the Indian Affairs Subcommittee in 1960. Initially a terminationist, he had adopted a gradualist position similar to that of Udall's by the late 1950s. However, he was not pleased with the task force report. Like Anderson, Church had attended the Udall breakfast and had been critical of the report. Nash remembered that Church "threw his hands up in the air and really went up in smoke," at the breakfast, complaining that the report failed to address any of the pressing matters concerning Indians.[86]

In the weeks following the Udall breakfast, Church had not warmed to the report's recommendations. During the Nash hearings he pointed to four deficiencies that he found in the administration's Indian policy. Like Anderson, Church found fault with the Interior heirship legislation, an area in which he had a special interest. He condemned the Interior bill as "very timid" and not "commensurate with the extent and the gravity of the problem to be solved." Church then turned to the status of the termination policy, correctly observing that "what the task force did was to duck the question of what to do about House Concurrent Resolution 108." He informed Nash that amending HCR 108 was "one of those hard problems that has to be dealt with, that I see little evidence has been dealt with up to now." As to the ongoing jurisdictional difficulties, Church maintained that he found "nothing in the task force report that would indicate a formula that would prove helpful in dealing with this question." Finally, Church raised the issue of per capita distributions of settlement awards from the Indian Claims Commission. He argued against such distributions, favoring instead the use of any monies to fund development programs. Church argued that using the settlement awards in this manner "would be of tremendous help to Indians," though "there is little indication that we have been moving in that direction."[87]

Church was not antagonistic to Nash's appointment. He concluded his questioning by noting that that "we are very fortunate in having a man of his background nominated," and that Nash "has the background and training that should equip him to do an outstanding job as Commissioner." Nor did Church oppose the basic direction of administration policy, that of economic development and education. Rather, Church was frustrated with the moderate tone of the task force report. Hoping for bold solutions, he found instead cautious and politically careful recommendations. He warned Nash that "you are going to have to be willing to sponsor and endorse and back proposals that won't just nibble away at the skin of these problems but reach into the heart of these problems." This attitude evidenced the risk that the task force took in writing a report designed not to anger Congress— inevitably, no one was entirely satisfied with its conclusions, and potential congressional allies such as Church would not give wholehearted support to administration policies.[88]

The first day of hearings ended shortly after Church completed questioning Nash, and resumed three days later on 17 August. Sen. Ernest Gruening (D.-Alaska) opened the hearings, remarking that he "share[d] Senator Church's views" that "the task force report had a lot of generalities in it." Sen. Gordon Allott took a harsh tone, telling Nash that his testimony did not offer "any hope or any belief in a resolution of the Indian problem." An ardent assimilationist committed to termination, Allott demeaned Indian culture as "a semicivilized, or at least, a very backward form of life." Nash struggled to respond to Allott's questions without offending or disagreeing with the senator, so much so that Nash later recalled that "I had to be evasive in order to obtain confirmation." Allott, who dominated the remainder of the committee hearing, posed a serious threat to the Nash confirmation. As a terminationist, he represented all the senators still committed to that policy, while as a Republican he had no vested interest in supporting the Kennedy administration's nominee.[89]

In order to discredit Nash, the senators opposed to his confirmation seized upon allegations that Sen. Joseph McCarthy (R.-Wis.) had made concerning Nash's loyalty in January 1952. McCarthy had accused Nash of making "contact with the Communist underground in Washington," and charged that Nash "had officially joined the Communist party" in the early 1940s. President Truman had been satisfied of Nash's loyalty, but with Nash's appointment the charges were resurrected. Having received an FBI report on the matter in early February 1961, the Kennedy White House knew about the McCarthy accusations; apparently no one had foreseen that the old allegations would resurface during the confirmation hearings. In late August, concerns about the Nash appointment prompted the White House to request an FBI investigation to ensure that no new and damaging revelations would arise. Several senators, including Barry Goldwater, also contacted the FBI for information on Nash. On 8 September 1961 the Interior Committee met in closed session to investigate the charges.[90]

Senators at the hearing showed little interest in Native American affairs, instead questioning Nash on the loyalty issue. Gordon Allott took the lead, hammering at Nash with what another senator referred to as "technicalities and implications." Sen. Henry Jackson, who chaired the hearing, had sponsored both the bill that created the Indian Claims Commission and HCR 108. He would succeed Clinton Anderson as Interior Committee chairman in 1963, and become the principal congressional supporter of termination during the late 1960s. As such, he earned the wrath of Native American activists, one of whom declared in 1971 that Jackson had been "more detrimental to Indian causes than any other senator in the past hundred years." Despite his stance on Indian affairs, Jackson worked in his party's interest to protect the nominee while ensuring that opponents would be satisfied with the conduct of the investigation.[91]

The closed hearing led Nash to perceive his nomination to be "the center of a 'tug of war'" within the Interior Affairs Committee, with Republicans leading an "opposition which is really political." He believed that Barry Goldwater was the opposition's "strategist," and Allott was the "hatchet man." However, Nash had the support of the Democratic senators, who held a majority on the committee. Clinton Anderson had overcome his misgivings about Nash, in part because Clark Clifford, a Nash colleague from the Truman White House and a Kennedy confidant, had reassured the New Mexico senator that Nash was loyal and reliable. Following the chairman's lead, the Democratic senators lined up in support of the nominee. The committee vote split on party lines: Nash received ayes from all the Democrats but did not garner a single Republican vote.[92]

Floor debate on the Nash nomination took place on 20 September 1961. Although the opposition did not have the votes necessary to prevent confirmation, Henry Dworshak and Francis H. Case (R.-S. Dak.) made their dissatisfaction with Nash known. Dworshak predicted that confirming Nash would lead to "another reversal in Indian Bureau policy," with "Indians encouraged to remain on the reservations, where they will receive many of the benefits denied them if they left the reservations." The debate concluded with remarks from Hubert H. Humphrey (D.-Minn.), for whom Nash had stumped in the 1960 presidential election. Humphrey declared the Nash appointment to be "a happy day for the American Indians, for the Government of the United States, and also for me, personally." He read a telegram from the NCAI, which stated that the organization "viewed with general favor the policies reported by the task force on Indian affairs" and called upon the Senate to confirm Nash, which it did with unanimous approval.[93]

Nash remembered the confirmation process as "a humbling experience," and maintained that Interior Committee members used the hearings not to ascertain his abilities but to impress him with their attitudes on Indian policy. Given the nature of the questions posed during the hearing, Nash's assessment was correct. The confirmation revealed that congressional support for the administration's Indian policy was weak. Moreover, Nash believed that his confirmation "soured my relations with the Senate Interior Committee and that seemed to be reflected in the companion Committee in the House." The new commissioner's poor start with Congress indicated that implementing administration policies would meet with opposition during his tenure.[94]

THE HOUSE INTERIOR COMMITTEE

The "companion Committee in the House" played no direct role in the confirmation of administration appointees, but in other areas of Indian policy it was as powerful and influential as the Senate committee. Wayne Aspinall, first elected to the House in 1948, became House Interior Committee chairman in 1959, a position that he held until he lost a reelection bid in 1972. Stewart Udall remembered Aspinall as a "prickly person" who "was always difficult, never easy to work with." His colleagues regarded Aspinall as a fair but domineering man—a congressional staffer recalled that he ran the committee "with an iron fist," and one committee member declared that Aspinall allowed Interior Subcommittee chairmen "no autonomy at all." Because he had few Native American constituents, and because he thought "in terms of what's good for the West—for miners, for cattlemen, for sheep raisers, and farmers," Aspinall expressed little interest in Indian policy. In a speech at the NCAI's 1962 convention, Aspinall declared that "as long as I am chairman of the committee no Indian tribe in the United States will be terminated until it is ready for termination," a rather ambiguous promise that nonetheless elicited cheers from convention delegates.[95]

Unlike Aspinall, James A. Haley, the chairman of the Indian Affairs Subcommittee, harbored a great concern for Native Americans and proved receptive to administration initiatives. Haley was an anomaly in that he was an easterner involved in Interior matters. Elected to Congress in 1952, he was a conservative Democrat of the old school, ardently opposed to the civil rights initiatives that developed in the 1950s and 1960s. His attitudes toward Native American affairs were far more complex. John Carver remembered him as "a very conservative-type Democrat, but when it came to Indian matters he was liberal in the sense of wanting to do what he could," while Aspinall recalled Haley as a "man who tried to see what was good for the Indian population as well as what was good for the nation." While Haley may have been responsible for including the Florida Seminoles among the tribes listed in HCR 108, during hearings on the Seminole termination bill held in 1955 he declared that "I just hope that the gentlemen [members of Congress] will assist me in maintaining a program that will bring the Seminole Indians of Florida some of the things that they should have been receiving many years ago," thereby acknowledging that immediate termination created as many problems as it was intended to solve.[96]

Despite his stance regarding immediate termination, Haley held the federal government responsible for what he called the "Indian problem." In a March 1961 reply to a constituent letter, Haley asserted that federal programs "have pampered and kept the Indians as wards of the government without any encouragement to them toward getting on their own." Haley could best be described as a cautious terminationist, one who recognized that the federal government had obligations to its Indian citizens while regarding many of its policies as failures that perpetuated dependency.[97]

This attitude made Haley far more receptive to the administration's programs than many of his colleagues. In a letter to Udall regarding an early draft of the task force report, Haley wrote that "if a great majority of the recommendations made by the Task Force in this report could be enacted into law and placed into operation . . . you would have contributed more to the American Indians than any other Secretary of the Interior during my lifetime," and he promised Udall that he stood "ready and willing to introduce any part of the program that the Department may recommend." Thus, Haley signaled his willingness to serve as an ally to administration officials in implementing the new policy of economic development.[98]

By late 1961 the Kennedy administration possessed both a new Indian policy as outlined in the task force report and the leadership within the Interior Department and the Bureau of Indian Affairs to implement that policy. The congressional dissatisfaction with administration policies that surfaced during the Nash hearings and the consequent tensions that developed between Nash and important members of Congress foreshadowed difficulties in coming years. However, the poverty and want that marred the lives of most Native Americans, the destructive legacy of previous federal policies, and the persistence of termination sentiment within the administration and the Congress presented the greatest difficulties for the proponents of the "New Trail."

CHAPTER TWO

THE NEW TRAIL

Committed to a program emphasizing economic and human resource development on the reservations, Interior Secretary Stewart Udall and Commissioner Philleo Nash set about implementing their new Indian policy. However, the New Trail proved difficult to travel, obstructed by congressional opposition, bureaucratic inertia, interpersonal conflicts within the administration, and the consequences of decades of failed federal policies. These problems combined with a disregard for Indian treaty rights to limit the effectiveness of the Kennedy administration in assisting the nation's Indians. However, the White House's growing commitment to fighting poverty in America brought benefits to Native Americans, and, ironically, increased the legitimacy of tribal governments. As they had during the termination era, Native Americans and pro-Indian organizations turned to congressional hearings as the most effective means to make their needs and demands known to the federal government. Although Congress presented the greatest obstacle to the Native American goal of continued federal assistance within the context of self-determination, it also provided a public forum for many Indians to express their views in hopes of influencing policy development.

THE MENOMINEE TERMINATION

Before Udall and his Indian affairs team could begin the process of improving the lives of the third of a million Americans in their charge, they had to respond to the will of key members of Congress who remained dedicated to the termination policy. James Officer recalled that "from the beginning, officials of the Kennedy administration found themselves confronting termination issues on all sides." Officer did not exaggerate. While the members of the secretary's task force were formulating a new Indian policy, Interior Department officials were responding to congressional demands to adhere to the legislative time tables for tribal termination. Only four tribes had been terminated during the Eisenhower years, but Congress had passed termination legislation for another eight tribes, with three—the Menominees, the Klamaths, and the Mixed-blood Utes of Utah—scheduled for termination of federal services in 1961. In addition, Congress had instructed the Colville Indians in Washington to submit a termination plan by July 1961. The most pressing case was that of the Menominees, scheduled for termination on 30 April 1961, a mere three months after Kennedy entered the White House.[1]

By the early 1950s the Menominee Tribe was one of the most prosperous and successful Indian groups in the United States, owning nearly a quarter million acres in trust, much of it covered with valuable timber, and operating a sawmill that employed many tribal members. In addition, the tribe had $10 million in a Treasury Department account, most of it from a 1951 claims judgment. These assets and the high degree of assimilation that many Menominees evidenced made the tribe a prime target for termination. In fact, some members of Congress regarded the Menominees as "a pilot project on which we are going to try the first experiment" in termination. As a result, the Menominees were one of the tribes specifically named in HCR 108.[2]

The law authorizing termination of the Menominees directed the interior secretary to "transfer to the tribe on December 31, 1958 . . . the title to all property, real and personal, held in trust by the United States for the tribe," and declared that "thereafter individual members of the tribe shall not be entitled to any of the services performed by the United States for Indians because of their status as Indians." Because the tribe found it impossible to create the programs necessary to implement termination by the target date, Congress granted extensions in 1958 and again in 1960. As the new termination date of 30 April 1961 approached, senators from Wisconsin cosponsored legislation to grant another extension to the tribe. One bill, S. 869, left the final termination date to the discretion of the interior secretary, while a second, S. 870, scheduled termination for 30 April 1969 and authorized low-cost loans to help the tribe implement termination plans. The Senate Subcommittee on Indian Affairs held hearings in April 1961 to discuss the proposed legislation.[3]

Those calling for an extension drew hope from the fact that a new administration had taken office. In his testimony, Sen. William Proxmire (D.-Wis.) claimed that "the hopes of many Indians accompany the [Udall] task force," which "heralds a 'New Look'" in federal Indian policy." Proxmire inserted into the record articles from the *Milwaukee Sentinel*, one of which alleged that "the Indians are watching the new Kennedy administration closely." However, subcommittee members remained steadfastly opposed to yet another extension. Chairman Frank Church opened the hearings with the reminder that "this committee, following the hearings of last August, took the position that there should be no further extensions of the termination date in connection with this tribe."[4]

The Interior Department report on the proposed legislation concluded that "the Menominee termination plan is a sound one and can be made to succeed," but "may encounter serious difficulties and hardships may result to the tribe, the State [of Wisconsin], and local units of government." As such, the department recommended that transfer of services to the tribe be accomplished by 30 April 1965, an extension of four years. During this time the interior secretary could authorize loans of up to $2.5 million "for the purpose of financing an expansion or modernization" of tribal business operations. Thus, the Interior Department's recommendations were quite similar to S. 870.

Assistant Secretary of the Interior John A. Carver presented the department's position to the committee on 18 April 1961. In his testimony Carver noted that Menominee termination constituted "one of the stickiest problems that faces this committee and the Bureau [of Indian Affairs]." He blamed the tribe for the situation, claiming that the Menominees had "never really faced up to the full implications of the severance of the umbilical cord of Federal services," and had "generally resisted the progress toward the dates fixed in the act and in the various extensions." Referring to the department's recommendations "as sort of phased extension termination," Carver argued that "if the Government is to be in the Indian business, it ought to be in the Indian business based upon some trust relationship to the property of the Indians." He later reiterated this position, asserting that if "Congress wants to leave us in the business of spending this money [loans to the tribe], getting it and spending it, then I think the safest way to do it is to leave us in the trust business. Then we have some control over it."[5]

Carver's call for an extension of federal services and a postponement of termination posed the danger that the subcommittee, which clearly opposed an extension, would also refuse to offer any assistance to the tribe. Although it rejected the proposed extension, the subcommittee ultimately approved $1.5 million in loans for economic development and the modernization of the sawmill and $438,000 to upgrade the reservation sanitation system; however, disagreements with the House Interior Committee over recommended appropriations prevented the enactment of any legislation until the following year. As of 1 May 1961, the Menominee Reservation became the poorest county in Wisconsin. The Kennedy administration had proven ineffectual in the face of the terminationists who controlled the Senate Interior Committee.[6]

THE PONCA TERMINATION

The following year Congress again enacted termination legislation, in this instance at the request of the Interior Department. On 6 April 1962, John Carver transmitted proposed legislation for the "division of the tribal assets of the Ponca Tribe of Native Americans of Nebraska" to the Congress. In his letter of transmittal, Carver maintained that "the enactment of the bill will be in the best interests of the Indians." Claiming that "the tribe has asked for the enactment of this bill," he referred to a 1958 meeting at which the tribal members approved a petition calling for termination, and an August 1961 meeting at which the tribe unanimously approved a resolution reaffirming that petition. In response to Carver's request, Senator Church introduced the proposed bill, S. 3174. In keeping with Fred Seaton's 1958 promise that future terminations would proceed only with tribal consent, S. 3174 required that tribal members be given "an opportunity to indicate their agreement with the provisions of this Act." Upon a favorable vote from a majority of tribal members, the interior secretary was instructed to publish notice in the Federal Register, after which termination would then be implemented. Tribal assets were to be divided among the enrolled tribal members and federal services were to be discontinued.[7]

While both the Interior Department and the Congress paid attention to the issue of tribal consent, a survey conducted in 1989 revealed that many Poncas did not understand the implications of requesting termination in 1958. In addition, some tribal members claimed that "the younger generation was against termination in the first place. When the older people told us our vote didn't count, we walked out of the last meeting," a charge indicating that the meetings might not have accurately reflected tribal attitudes. However, neither Congress nor the Interior Department questioned the legitimacy of the meetings. Furthermore, government officials failed to take into account the role that the distribution of tribal assets played into the decision to request termination. The promise of lump sum payments undoubtedly influenced the decision of some tribal members. Congress passed the termination legislation, which President Kennedy signed into law on 5 September 1962. The Poncas were terminated in 1966.[8]

THE KENNEDY ADMINISTRATION AND TERMINATION

Tribes terminated during the Kennedy years included the Menominees, the Catawba Tribe in South Carolina, the Klamath Tribe in Oregon, the Mixed-Blood Utes, and several California rancherías. The legislation authorizing the cessation of federal services to these tribes had been passed during the 1950s. Given the attitudes that dominated in the Senate Interior Committee, administration officials had little choice but to comply with the legislative deadlines. However, the administration's feeble call for an extension for the Menominees revealed an unwillingness to challenge the terminationists on the Senate Interior Committee, and its sponsorship of the Ponca legislation indicated continued support for termination within the Interior Department.[9]

For Native Americans seeking evidence of a policy change from the new administration, the continued termination of Indian tribes was hardly reassuring. As Assiniboine Sioux activist Hank Adams later recalled, "termination was going strong in the 1960s under Philleo Nash, James Officer, Stewart Udall and President John F. Kennedy." Although Adams ignored the role that Clinton Anderson and his colleagues played in the continuation of the hated termination policy, his remark expressed the view of many Native Americans who had held great hopes for the Kennedy White House.[10]

THE KINZUA DAM CONTROVERSY

In addition to tribal terminations, the Kennedy administration inherited another pressing conflict in Native American affairs, one that involved the construction of a dam that would flood over 9,000 acres of the Allegany Reservation, home of the Seneca Nation. To make matters worse, the Upper Allegheny River flood control project (usually known as the Kinzua Dam) would displace some 130 families and necessitate moving the grave of Gaiantwaka, the Cornplanter, an honored Seneca war chief. The history of Kinzua Dam revealed the lack of importance that Indian affairs held within the federal government, and the Kennedy administration's handling of the affair raised doubts about its campaign promises to Native Americans.[11]

The Kinzua Dam project had its origins in flood control plans for the Ohio River Valley developed in the early decades of the twentieth century. In 1928, the United States Army Corps of Engineers issued a report that recommended the construction of dams on the Allegheny River, and between 1936 and 1941 Congress approved three flood control projects that included provisions for building the Kinzua Dam. Army engineers conducted surveys along the Allegheny's banks in 1939 and 1940. However, growing anxiety over events in Europe and Interior Department concerns over treaty provisions that protected Seneca lands prevented Congress from appropriating funds for the construction projects.[12]

The treaty in question was the Treaty of Canandaigua, also known as the Pickering Treaty, which had been negotiated in 1794. Signatories included members of the Seneca Nation and Timothy Pickering, a personal representative of President George Washington. The treaty stated that "the United States acknowledge all the land within the aforementioned boundaries, to be the property of the Seneka [sic] nation; and the United States will never claim the same, nor disturb the Seneka nation . . . in the free use and enjoyment thereof." It also declared that the land "shall remain theirs, until they choose to sell the same to the people of the United States, who have the right to purchase." Interior Department officials concluded that the treaty's unequivocal language rendered impossible any dam construction project that lacked the Senecas' approval. In 1940, Assistant Secretary of the Interior Oscar Chapman noted that the "desires of the Indians in the matter must be recognized and respected."[13]

Despite the treaty guarantees, the proponents of the Kinzua Dam project did not abandon their efforts, and they met with success during the 1950s. Although attentive to budget issues, the Eisenhower administration proved amenable to large-scale public works projects, while the termination sentiment of the era diminished concerns about treaty obligations. Executive branch agencies that had been reluctant to back the Kinzua Dam project now supported it. In 1957 the Justice Department, which had opposed the project in the 1940s, filed a proceeding to condemn the Seneca lands. Interior Department officials showed no interest in the affair. As for the rights of the Senecas, the executive director of the Pittsburgh Chamber of Commerce captured the prevailing attitude when he argued that "the Seneca Indians are to be treated as Americans, not as a race apart, and compensated for their land on the same basis any American received for land taken by the government. The good of the many justifiably supercedes [sic] the minority." Expressing a similar opinion, President Eisenhower stated that the Kinzua project "would be wrong if the Indians do not desire it, unless it is essential rather than merely desirable."[14]

Dam supporters set about proving that their project was indeed essential. Officials in the Army Corps of Engineers rejected a number of alternative flood control plans, including one that Arthur E. Morgan, a prominent engineer hired as a consultant for the Seneca Nation, had proposed. Known as the Cattaraugus-Conewego plan or as Morgan Plan Number Six, this proposal saved the Seneca lands but necessitated the flooding of four non-Indian towns, which from a political perspective provided no alternative at all. The Corps submitted the alternative plans to an independent engineering firm, which concluded that, although feasible, the plans would greatly increase the cost of the flood control project and the amount of land flooded and dislocate a larger number of people. However, as Morgan later noted, three of the firm's four partners were former Corps engineers, and "that for twenty years or more the Corps had been the most important client of the firm," which raised serious questions concerning the firm's analyses.[15]

In addition to supporting the alternative plans, the Seneca Nation sought relief from the courts. In early 1957, the Seneca Nation challenged the authority of the secretary of the Army to condemn Indian lands. A federal district court in New York ruled against the Senecas, declaring that "Congress authorized the construction of the Allegheny dam and reservoir, not only with presumed, but with actual, knowledge of the history of the lands within the Allegheny Indian reservation, and particularly the so-called Pickering Treaty of 1794." In a 1958 lawsuit that claimed that "to destroy such [treaty] rights Congress must specifically so say," attorneys for the Senecas claimed that an appropriations bill did not show clear congressional intent to violate the 1794 treaty. The court rejected this argument, holding that "general legislation is sufficient to override the provisions of an Indian treaty where the intent of Congress to do so is clear." The appeal eventually reached the U.S. Supreme Court, which in 1959 refused to grant a writ of *certiorari*, thus ending the legal battle that the Senecas and their supporters had mounted. The courts had upheld the plenary power of Congress to abrogate unilaterally treaty provisions through the simple mechanism of an appropriations bill.[16]

Nor did the Congress provide any assistance to the Senecas. The proposed violation of the 1794 treaty troubled a few congressmen, including John R. Saylor (R-Pa.) and House Indian Affairs Subcommittee Chairman James Haley. The only Pennsylvania congressman who opposed the project, Saylor placed the treaty violation in a Cold War context. In a 1959 letter to Eisenhower, Saylor pointed out that the president had admonished the Soviets for violating treaty agreements while at the same time the U.S. government acted in "utter disregard for the treaties between our own Nation and some of the Indian tribes," and proved willing to "readily abandon agreements one hundred and fifty years old." Haley also fretted over the government's treaty obligations and was reportedly "not impressed with the decision of the Supreme Court not to get into the fight" over the project. Despite these protestations, most Pennsylvania congressmen enthusiastically supported the Kinzua Dam project, and in May 1960 the House of Representatives voted 398 to 18 to appropriate the funds necessary to begin construction. Groundbreaking ceremonies were held on 22 October 1960.[17]

Construction did not halt the controversy over the Kinzua Dam. In his 1960 public campaign letter to the AAIA membership, John Kennedy had claimed that he would make "no change in treaty or contractual relationships without the consent of the tribes concerned," a pledge that dam construction clearly contradicted. In a letter dated 22 February 1961, Basil Williams, president of the Seneca Nation, reminded Kennedy of his campaign pledge and asked the president to "redeem that pledge by stopping the Federal government from violating our 1794 Treaty." Williams asserted that the treaty "is more than a contract, more than a symbol; to us who have lived by its terms for more than 165 years, the 1794 Treaty is a way of life." Maintaining that the Seneca Nation would not oppose Kinzua Dam if no feasible alternative could be found, Williams asked Kennedy "to make an independent investigation into the merits and comparative costs of the Kinzua Dam and Dr. Morgan's Cattaraugus-Conewego alternative, and that in the interim you direct that work be halted on the authorized project." Williams closed with the request that Kennedy "uphold the sacred honor of the United States, and, we are confident, also save our sacred homeland."[18]

Kennedy's dilemma regarding the issue of treaty rights violations was in part his own doing. The conflict illustrated the lack of foresight the candidate had shown in allowing an attorney for the AAIA to write the well-publicized campaign letter. Native Americans had taken Kennedy's promise to heart and expected him to defend their interests. Some members of the press also urged the president to abide by his pledge. In an article appearing on 17 February 1961, Brooks Atkinson, drama critic for the *New York Times*, printed a brief history of the Kinzua Dam controversy. Atkinson contended that "the roar of progress deafens the ear of conscience." In an editorial printed five days later, the *Times* asked "can't we stop in all our understandable hurry to right the wrongs of the big world, and do justice to a handful of people in one small corner of the earth?" These articles may have prompted a reporter at a press conference held on 9 March 1961 to ask Kennedy if he "had any inclination at all to halt that project [Kinzua Dam] in favor of the so-called Morgan alternate project which would not violate the treaty." Citing the 1959 Supreme Court decision, the president replied that "I have no plans to interfere with that action."[19]

The president's statement must have disheartened the Seneca leaders who sought to gain his support, especially since they had not received a reply to Basil Williams's letter of 22 February. The letter was shunted to the Bureau of the Budget, where Deputy Director Elmer B. Staats drafted a response in mid-March. Staats claimed that the congressional debates over the appropriations for the dam and the Supreme Court decision "have decided the major points of the issue." He argued that "the executive branch has no choice except to carry out the expressed will of the Congress." In fact, the executive branch did have a "choice," legally if not politically, and could have stopped the construction of the dam had it so desired. In a procedure known as impoundment, presidents possessed the authority to refuse to spend appropriated funds. In 1946 President Truman had impounded funds appropriated for a water resource program called the Kings River Project. Kennedy impounded funds in order to halt development of the B-70 bomber in 1962. However, for political reasons the impoundment of the Kinzua Dam funds was impossible, a point that Staats neglected to raise.[20]

If the White House believed that the matter had been put to rest, a highly critical *Washington Post* editorial that appeared on 8 April 1961 not only again raised the issue but generated administration concerns about the president's public image. Pointing to Kennedy's response to the Kinzua Dam question on 9 March, the *Post* editorial noted that the president "can unwittingly leave the impression of cold unconcern." The editorial did not go so far as to suggest a reexamination of the Kinzua Dam project. Noting that the "courts have ruled against the Indians," and that it "may be true that progress on the dam on the upper Allegheny has passed the point of reconsideration," the *Post* merely hoped that Kennedy would "make clear that the case of the Seneca Indians cannot be brushed aside so simply." In reference to Cold War tensions, the editorial closed with the request that "the United States will in the future treat its own minorities with the same scrupulous respect that it repeatedly urges on Mr. Khrushchev."[21]

In a memo dated 10 April 1961, Kennedy adviser Theodore Sorenson referred to the "bad editorial in the *Washington Post* on Saturday," and asked White House aide Lee White to "look into the situation of the *dam* Indians and prepare a memo to the President on it." White requested information from the BIA. He also contacted Arthur Lazarus, an attorney who worked with the AAIA and served as legal counsel for the Seneca Nation. Lazarus had been a protégé of the late Felix Cohen, famed expert on Indian law. He sent White news clippings and correspondence concerning the Kinzua Dam, noting that although he "accede[d] to the decision of the courts," he still considered the situation "immoral."[22]

While he studied the material on the Kinzua controversy, White assured Basil Williams "that the examination of this matter by the present administration will be undertaken quickly and with a sympathetic attitude toward the position urged by the Seneca Nation." "Sympathetic attitude" proved to be a poor choice of words because the White letter "was most cordially received by the Seneca Council," which found it "heartening" because it was "convinced that only action by the President now can save its homeland." The Seneca Nation was to be sorely disappointed with the president's final decision, which was revealed in a letter to Williams in August.[23]

Kennedy's decision was based on Lee White's assessment of the Kinzua situation, which White outlined in a memo sent to the president on 8 August. White concluded that "it would be inappropriate to halt construction and have the outside study" or to "continue construction and authorize Federal expenditures for the review." Instead, he counseled the president to "take a strong position in urging Executive departments and agencies to facilitate the adjustment of the Senecas to the construction of the reservoir." In that vein, he included a brief list of recommendations and closed with the suggestion that "a letter from you to the head of the Senecas will be warmly received and under the circumstances is the best alternative available." The Kennedy letter to Basil Williams was drafted the following day.[24]

In the letter, Kennedy claimed that "I fully appreciate the reasons underlying the opposition of the Seneca Nation of Indians to the construction of Kinzua Dam." The president made no direct reference to the treaty issue, noting only "the very deep sentiments over the loss of a portion of the lands which have been owned by the Seneca Nation for centuries." Nonetheless, Kennedy continued, "it is not possible to halt the construction of Kinzua Dam currently under way." As evidence, he pointed to "the long and exhaustive congressional review," the "resolution by our judicial process of the legal right of our Federal Government to acquire the property necessary to the construction," the Army Corps' rejection of the Morgan alternative, and the "need for flood protection downstream." Following Lee White's recommendations, Kennedy held out the possibility of federal assistance to the Senecas, including the possible exchange of public lands in return for the flooded areas, an assessment of special damages, the inclusion of the Seneca Nation in recreational developments along the lake that the dam would create, and special assistance to relocated families.[25]

As one dam opponent noted, to have sided with the Seneca Nation would have been an act of "courageous statesmanship." Such courage could not be expected of a new president. Kennedy owed a political debt to Pennsylvania Governor David Lawrence, a dam proponent who had helped Kennedy win his state in 1960. More important, the president did not want to alienate key members of Congress. In regard to the Kinzua Dam situation, Kennedy was in an unpleasant but not difficult position. Choosing between breaking a campaign promise to a marginal constituency or angering Congress was never a problem for administration officials. Philleo Nash later recalled that Kennedy lacked the will to "turn back the clock on Kinzua." Stewart Udall remembered that the project "bothered a lot of people in the administration, including me," but that it "had congressional support; it had the pork barrel behind it; it had all this momentum built up."[26]

The response within the Kennedy White House to the Kinzua Dam conflict reveals that concern for the president's public image, and not for the Indians or the treaty obligations of the United States, prompted Kennedy's aides and advisers to investigate the Kinzua Dam controversy. The president's response, while predictable, would lead many Native Americans to agree with one activist who later wrote that "I never felt that he [Kennedy] kept his promises to Indian people."[27]

COMMISSIONER NASH

The administration had resolved the Kinzua Dam controversy when Philleo Nash was sworn in as commissioner of Indian affairs on 26 September 1961. Nash appointed John O. Crow, a longtime BIA employee who had served as acting commissioner during the preceding months, as his deputy commissioner. Nash regarded Crow as "a very devoted and conscientious civil servant," and selected him in part to calm bureau fears that Nash would implement radical change. Fellow task force member James Officer (whom Udall later remembered as "my man in the old BIA") received the position of associate commissioner. Nash perceived these appointments as "the old and the new in a blend which was intended to combine the good things of both for the advancement of the [administration] program."[28]

Nash did not act with a free hand when he made his personnel appointments. Clinton Anderson made it clear that certain individuals were not to be associated with the bureau. When former BIA employees D'Arcy McNickle and William Zimmerman sought positions in the BIA, Nash demurred. He made no offer to McNickle, and told Zimmerman he was too old, promising him only "occasional assignments as consultant." McNickle later learned that Anderson had told Nash not to employ Zimmerman or McNickle, both of whom were associated with the progressive administration of Commissioner John Collier.[29]

Claiming that he "operated on the premise that a large organization ought to have a place for a wide variety of talents," Nash made no effort to remove old-line bureau employees. He later argued that achieving the goals of Indian policy "did not require a massive re-organization, or extensive shifting of people and their assignments." However, Nash's decision to keep many old-line employees "did not sit well with some of his closest friends." Reformers had hoped that Nash would dismiss agency employees who harbored termination sentiments or who did not meet their standards of conduct. Oliver La Farge complained to Stewart Udall that "in the Indian Bureau staff in Washington and in the field there is a dangerous proportion of those who lack that feeling for people, that dedication to a cause, that has made other cause-oriented government agencies a success."[30]

Although the retention of old-line employees calmed anxieties within the BIA and improved Nash's relations with the workers, Udall believed that it engendered a continuity with the policies of previous administrations and stifled innovation within the agency. He later complained that "Nash became, in effect, the willing prisoner of the bureaucracy," which was "quite satisfied to feel that they'd just done a little better job than the year before." Nash's personnel policy contributed to Udall's unease with his choice of commissioner, creating a sense of dissatisfaction that would gradually degenerate into hostility between the two men.[31]

BUREAU REORGANIZATION

At Nash's swearing-in ceremony, Secretary Udall told the audience of BIA employees that Nash would "put into effect as rapidly as possible, those Task Force recommendations which can be handled by administrative action." Nash first turned his attention to BIA organization. Upon the suggestion of W. W. Keeler, the task force had recommended the formation of an operating committee "composed of those whose duties are closely associated with the executive officer" in order to "greatly speed up the flow of paperwork and improve communication." Nash created such a committee, which included the deputy and associate commissioners and the congressional liaison. The operating committee met with the commissioner on a daily basis, discussing policy issues and problems. Nash later admitted that the committee "was not popular with some of my associates" who "found the endless discussions . . . to be a waste of time," but he regarded them as invaluable. Despite the complaints, he continued to meet with the operating committee during the early years of his administration.[32]

Nash implemented few additional changes in bureau organization. The changes he authorized centered on economic development, indicating the high priority given by the administration to that concern. Following the task force recommendations, Nash reorganized the Division of Economic Development in order to foster closer cooperation between the Division and those departments involved with agricultural assistance, road construction, and similar activities. The industrial development program and revolving credit fund came under the authority of the assistant commissioner who headed the Division. In addition, Nash appointed E. Reeseman "Si" Fryer to head the newly created position of economic adviser to the commissioner, which stood separate from the Division of Economic Development.[33]

Encouraging Indian Participation in the Policy Process

Nash later maintained that "the first thing we had to do around here was to restore the confidence of the Indian people in the Department and in the Bureau." To that end, he visited reservations and Indian communities throughout the country, meeting with tribal leaders to discuss problems and ideas. At a 1963 congressional hearing, Nash claimed that he had "traveled quite literally from the Everglades to Point Barrow in an effort to honor our commitment to counsel with the Indian people." He later recalled that "in the course of a couple of years

I did establish a working relationship [with the Indians] and one that I'm very happy with and very proud of." Nash's sympathetic attitude and relaxed personal style—at one NCAI convention he stayed up all night drumming and singing—earned him the respect and appreciation of many Native Americans. One Indian leader said that "I always got along with him [Nash] very well because he was more of a human being than a commissioner."[34]

However, Nash's rapport with Native Americans could not serve as an effective sounding board for Indian concerns. Although Nash encouraged tribal officials and BIA employees to work together, he never established any bureaucratic mechanisms or procedures to increase Indian participation in the policy process. As long as Indian access to policy creation remained informal, it also remained tenuous, contingent upon the good will of the commissioner.

THE NASH APPROACH TO PROGRAM DEVELOPMENT: LEGISLATION

Recognizing the terminationist attitudes that prevailed in Congress and cognizant of his own weak relations with key members such as Clinton Anderson, Nash employed a two-pronged approach toward developing programs for Native Americans. First, he "concentrate[d] on obtaining support for several important, but relatively noncontroversial, legislative amendments which could increase Indian employment and stimulate economic resource development." This was necessary because, as AAIA attorney Richard Schifter noted, Anderson's "extremely strong personality and his equally strong views on Indian affairs" made "it extremely difficult to get good substantive legislation through Congress." Thus, the Interior Department's legislative record relating to Indian policy during the Kennedy years was unimpressive. Department proposals for 1962 included the Ponca termination act and amendments to legislation relating to the sales of Indian timber and mining leases on tribal lands. The following year, proposed legislation included an increase in the revolving loan fund and amendments to a law concerning trading with Indians. An assessment of successes in Indian affairs printed in November 1963 made no specific reference to legislative achievements. During the Kennedy years, only one legislative measure was potentially controversial—an alternative to Frank Church's heirship bill. In this instance the department was responding to a congressional initiative, and the ensuing battle, which continued for over two years, indicated that Nash's avoidance of controversial measures was wise.[35]

HEIRSHIP LEGISLATION

Fractionated landholdings constituted a serious problem in Indian affairs, ironically a problem that the government itself had created during the allotment era. As heirs received increasingly smaller portions of the original allotments, bizarre mathematical calculations became necessary to determine degrees of ownership and profits from economic activities. The Comptroller General reported that one Indian "was determined to have the right to 4 trillion, 199 billion, 168 million, 842 thousand, 4 hundred/54 trillionths" of a 116-acre estate. Proceeds from the leasing of fractionated landholdings provided little income for heirs. The 1961 rental of the Frank Roy estate yielded forty dollars, which was distributed among eighty-five owners, many of whom received as little as five cents. Although they often appeared in reports and hearings, extreme cases such as these were in fact rare. However, approximately three million acres of the total fifty-three million acres of Indian land was in lots owned by six or more heirs, and the problem was growing worse as time went on. A Library of Congress analyst ably summed up the heirship problem in a 1969 report, noting that such holdings "denied the owners any opportunity for maximum utilization of the land or of its money value," and had "a direct effect on actual and potential tribal land consolidation programs and on the Federal Government in terms of ever-increasing administrative overhead."[36]

Because multiple ownership discouraged the leasing and development of Indian lands and complicated the management of the trust properties, officials in both the Congress and the Interior department regarded heirship as a pressing issue. The 1961 task force had considered it to be a "serious deterrent to more adequate utilization of resources in some areas," and Senator Church maintained that his subcommittee viewed it as "one of the major obstacles to Indian economic and social progress." In a handwritten note in the Stewart Udall papers, heirship ranked first in a list of legislative issues. However, despite the general agreement within the government that heirship legislation was needed, the problem proved irresolvable. The failure to settle this problem led to Church's resignation from the Indian Affairs Subcommittee and further damaged Nash's already poor relations with the members of Senate Interior Committee.[37]

Church opened the first hearings on S. 1392, the proposed heirship legislation, on 9 August 1961. S. 1392 permitted the interior secretary to sell or partition an heirship tract held in trust upon the request of a single heir, unless such a sale "would not be in the best interests of the Indian owners." In an effort to promote continued Indian ownership of properties, other heirs were to be given an opportunity to purchase the land. In addition, the secretary was authorized to offer low-interest loans to tribes who wished to buy any tracts up for sale.[38]

Although the bill explicitly mentioned tribal termination only once, stating that plans devised under the act could not "prevent or delay a termination of Federal trust responsibilities," S. 1392 reflected a terminationist attitude. The 1961 Comptroller General's report that had so pleased Clinton Anderson maintained that "multiple ownership of Indian lands held in trust is an obstacle" to termination, and had argued that success in carrying out HCR 108 "depends largely on the termination of Federal trusteeship over Indian property, including lands." In order to "hasten and facilitate the orderly termination of Federal supervision over Indian affairs," the Comptroller General recommended legislation that would "authorize the partition or sale of inherited Indian lands pursuant to the prescribed legal action taken by any one of the competent owners concerned," almost exactly the mechanism detailed in the Church bill. Section 10 of S. 1392 went even further, stating that in the event of a title transfer, "the title shall pass by operation of law in a nontrust and unrestricted status" unless the interior secretary found the owner to be incompetent. Moreover, "trusts or restrictions of an individual Indian that do not extend for a stated number of years" would cease as of 1 January 1964. These provisions ensured that federal trust responsibilities over almost all Indian land would end, a goal of the termination policy.[39]

In response to the subcommittee's request for a report on S. 1392, John Carver argued that the Section 10 provisions were "drastic," and would "involve a major change in Federal Indian policy." The Interior Department offered a substitute proposal in which tribes could purchase all heirship lands deemed idle or unproductive on a deferred payment plan. The interior secretary was authorized to sell productive lands upon the request of owners holding a majority interest. Addressing the problem of obtaining permission for use or development from multiple owners, the bill also permitted the secretary to "execute the lease, timber sale, or right-of-way without the consent of the Indian owners." In what he later remembered as a "very hot hearing on the subject," John Carver stated that "the substitute draft is not intended to provide a quick or a complete solution to the [heirship] problem," but he hoped that "it will permit us to take a tremendous first step."[40]

The hearings revealed that Indians did not support the Church bill. They recognized that heirship legislation, while perhaps necessary, constituted a risk to the trust status of Indian lands that might function as yet another arm of the termination policy. Helen Peterson, executive director of the NCAI, stated that "the bill meets the opposition of the NCAI through providing for termination of individual trusts," the provision found in Section 10. Paul Jones, chairman of the Navajo Tribal Council, argued that S. 1392 "would obliterate the fractionalization, but in so doing . . . makes it so difficult for the Indian to protect his interest in the land in trust status as to render it worthless." Non-Indian organizations also refused to support S. 1392. The general secretary of the Indian Rights Association argued that the bill "seems to be aimed at the termination of all Federal responsibility."[41]

Indian support for the Interior alternative was cautious, in part because many tribes had just received copies of the bill. After detailing tribal opposition to the Church bill, Robert Burnette, president of the Rosebud Sioux Tribe, claimed that "we are in agreement in principle, that is," with the Interior department alternative, and Richard Schifter, testifying as attorney for the Oglala Sioux and the Nez Perce, asked the subcommittee to "support the principle of the administration substitute."[42]

Senator Church took the various suggestions offered during the hearings and revised the bill, which he introduced in early 1962 as S. 2899. Section 11 of the new legislation provided for the continuation of the trust status of land transferred to one devisee or heir; but if more than one person received a portion, the property was no longer held in trust. This provision was intended to "prevent the problem of multiple ownership" by encouraging Indians who wanted land to remain in trust to designate only one heir. The remainder of the bill was similar to Church's 1961 proposal.[43]

Rather than submit an alternative bill, Interior Department officials chose to offer eighteen amendments to S. 2899. They again proposed that land be sold or partitioned only upon request of those holding a majority ownership. They also called for the removal of Section 11. During his testimony, Philleo Nash argued that the BIA did not consider the heirship problem "as serious as the loss of Indian land that we fear through the application of Section 11." He deemed the heirship issue to be "fundamentally a real estate management problem." He dismissed the issue of rising administrative overhead, claiming that most expenditures for trust management "would have to be spent even if there were no fractional heirship problem." The commissioner saw continued Indian ownership of the land as the long-term issue of importance, and he proposed that the federal government "go the way of economic development, which improves the capabilities of the individual and the tribes to resolve the problem by purchase."[44]

Nash's remarks reflected the attitudes of Native Americans far more than S. 2899 did. Eagle Seelatsee, Yakima, argued that "any law being proposed in Congress[,] it should fit in with the thinking of the Indian himself." During the seven months that had passed since the 1961 hearings, many Native Americans had changed their thinking, or at least become more sophisticated in their objections, in regard to heirship legislation. Land alienation, not heirship, was seen as the most important issue. Robert Burnette, now serving as executive director of the NCAI, charged that Section 11 made the bill "a non-Indian cattleman's bill." Instead of heirship legislation, Burnette demanded "imagination and aggressive management" in the area of Indian land development. Although Senator Church believed his bill recognized "the desirability of retaining the land base as an economic resource for our Indian citizens," Native Americans disagreed. Their determined opposition prompted Church to again revise the bill, which he introduced in the next session of Congress.[45]

Church's final attempt at heirship legislation represented a true attempt at compromise. His new bill, S. 1049, contained no provisions that ended the trust status on Indian land. Instead of allowing only one owner to request sale or partition, S. 1049 required owners holding a majority to make such a request if there were a total of ten owners or less. In the event that eleven or more persons shared title, the bill required an ownership of twenty-five percent to request sale. The Interior Department approved of the legislation and offered only one minor amendment.[46]

Church's sincere effort at compromise led some American Indians to support the bill, but the NCAI and many tribes still opposed heirship legislation. In the two-year battle over the various bills, many Indians had redefined the issue, and they now perceived heirship legislation as undesirable and unnecessary. Robert Burnette argued that "tribes should be allowed to work out their own land programs," and Edison Real Bird, vice chairman of the Crow Tribe, claimed that "each Indian tribe and its leaders should inaugurate its own programs to attend to its heirship lands." Despite these arguments, the approval of the Interior Department and the decline in Indian opposition allowed Church to push the measure through the upper house, which passed S. 1049 on 11 October 1963.[47]

The bill was then referred to the House Interior Committee, from which it was never reported out. Robert Burnette credited James Haley, chairman of the House Subcommittee on Indian Affairs, with blocking hearings on the bill. Burnette claimed that Haley responded positively to Indian requests for additional time to draft an alternate proposal. Heirship legislation was dead.[48]

Although Philleo Nash later cited heirship as one of "many, many phony issues in the field of Indian affairs," and charged that "bureaucrats and the experts and to some extent the Indian people themselves . . . have built up a great bogey which really doesn't even exist," James Officer recalled that Nash "worked hard for its [heirship legislation] enactment," and was "disappointed with the failure of the bill to pass." Senator Church, who according to John Carver had always "hated the job" of subcommittee chairman, saw the collapse of heirship legislation as the last straw and he eventually resigned from the position. Nash remembered that "Frank Church learned his lesson and it made him very bitter, very bitter towards the Indians and not too friendly towards me." Although Indians benefited from the collapse of Church's heirship initiative, Nash's standing with the senators on the Interior Committee fell even further.[49]

Officer credited the defeat of the heirship bills to conflicts between the House and Senate Interior Committees and to the efforts of the Indians, thus making Church's failure a triumph for Native Americans. Within a decade of HCR 108 and the passage of the first termination acts, their determined opposition stalled and eventually contributed to the abandonment of legislation that had the support of influential senators on the Interior Committee. Officer later maintained the battle over the heirship bills "made clear to Congress and the Executive Department that the fight against termination had enabled the Indians to assemble a strong lobbying force," which meant that future legislation lacking Indian support "would be doomed to failure." Stewart Udall's failure to heed this lesson would bring him great trouble in 1966 and 1967.[50]

THE NASH APPROACH TO PROGRAM DEVELOPMENT: PROGRAM SHARING

In a 1962 letter to Oliver La Farge, attorney Richard Schifter argued that the "Anderson-Allott combination on the Senate Interior Committee is so strongly opposed to the Indian development concept that it will try to block Administration efforts" in that area. Nash's second approach to program development, the inclusion of Indians in other federal aid programs, allowed the BIA to bypass potential opposition from Interior Committee members. Through the efforts of Nash, other administration officials, and sympathetic members of Congress, Native Americans received assistance from the Public Housing Administration, and, perhaps most important, the Commerce Department, which operated the Area Redevelopment Administration and the Public Works Acceleration Program.[51]

HOUSING

Program sharing met with laudable success in the improvement of Indian housing. Marie McGuire, who headed the Public Housing Administration (PHA), showed great enthusiasm in cooperating with the BIA. John Carver recalled that she "really got interested in Indian housing," and in 1964 Stewart Udall called her "somewhat a heroine of the Indian Bureau people and of Interior people." After the chief counsel of the PHA determined that the United States Housing Act of 1937, which enabled "any state, county, municipality or other governmental entity" to qualify for public housing assistance, applied to tribal governments, McGuire met with BIA officials to coordinate such a project for the Oglala Sioux Housing Authority, which received over one million dollars to build eighty-eight units. In designing this project, McGuire and the PHA showed a great deal of sensitivity to Native American cultural attitudes toward housing, rejecting duplexes on the reservation because they violated Indian standards concerning privacy. On 19 September 1961 President Kennedy publicly announced the Oglala Sioux building program, calling it "a practical fulfillment" of his campaign promises regarding Indians. That same year a similar project was launched on the Standing Rock Sioux Reservation, and McGuire later recalled that within two years the PHA had programs for six thousand houses on sixty-six reservations.[52]

In late 1961 the White Mountain Apache Tribe began a self-help housing program that allowed tribal members to borrow money from tribal funds to build their own homes. Tribal members provided the labor, receiving assistance from a carpenter that the tribe hired. Because many Indians did not have sufficient income to meet the rent requirements for government housing, the PHA and the BIA looked to the White Mountain Apache program as a model to increase Indian housing starts. In a program created in 1963, the PHA advanced funds for materials and supervision while the Indians invested "sweat equity" in their houses, providing labor in return for lower monthly payments. Under the terms of the project, Native Americans received low-cost homes and training in construction work. The San Carlos Apache Reservation began construction of ten "mutual-help" houses in November 1963, and other tribes quickly designed their own mutual-help housing projects. The program proved that Native American communities could develop innovative solutions to problems such as substandard housing. Nash and McGuire deserve credit for recognizing the value of the White Mountain Apache program and making the federal government a partner in similar projects.[53]

The housing program did have failures, some the result of the bureaucratic confusion created when several agencies attempted to coordinate activities. The houses in a 400-unit project on the Rosebud Sioux reservation were poorly constructed and had leaky roofs. Fitted with appliances before drainage facilities were installed, the houses sustained water damage. The dilapidated structures were ultimately sold to the reservation for a dollar apiece. Despite this miserable showing, many housing projects were successful and improved the lives of those Indians fortunate enough to benefit from the programs.[54]

THE AREA REDEVELOPMENT ACT OF 1961

Of all the cooperative efforts that Nash undertook, his work with the Area Redevelopment Administration (ARA) received the most attention. The ARA had its origins in legislation that Sen. Paul Douglas (D.-Ill.) introduced in 1955. Douglas's proposal provided low-cost loans to encourage development in economically depressed regions of the United States. Originally intended to offer aid to urban areas, the bill was amended to include rural regions in order to secure the support of members of Congress who represented predominantly rural areas. During hearings held in 1956, Lee Metcalf and Sen. Michael "Mike" Mansfield (D-Mont.) argued that minor changes to the bill would "make certain that Indian reservations can qualify for its benefits." Douglas agreed, and Section 6 of the amended bill listed Indian tribes among the public and private organizations permitted to propose loans or grants for public facilities.[55]

Congress passed the Douglas bill twice, in 1958 and again in 1960, but President Eisenhower vetoed the bill each time. Kennedy's victory in 1960 prompted Douglas to offer his bill at the opening of the 87th Congress in 1961. The new president's attitudes raised Douglas's hopes that his legislation would receive Kennedy's signature. While chairman of the Senate Subcommittee on Labor in 1956, Sen. Kennedy had worked for the bill's passage. During the presidential campaign, Kennedy had seized upon the issue of assisting depressed areas, in part because of the shocking conditions he witnessed in West Virginia during the primaries.[56]

Douglas began hearings on his bill, designated S. 1 and referred to as the Area Redevelopment Act, on 18 January 1961, two days before Kennedy took office. At the urging of Metcalf and Mansfield, S. 1 specifically mentioned Indian reservations in the provisions relating to rural areas. Metcalf inserted in the record a statement that he had written with Mansfield asserting that Montana reservation "land and resources are generally unproductive and the Indian families with strong tribal ties have had to depend on welfare and direct Federal assistance." The senators were "convinced that these people can improve their lot," and maintained that the act could "provide the incentive and the help." Although no Indians testified at the hearings, Metcalf included a statement from Walter Wetzel, president of the Montana Intertribal Policy Board. A supporter of S. 1, Wetzel noted that "Indians in all sections of the country were dissatisfied because the legislation was vetoed during the past administration," and claimed that Indians "want to participate in a program that will be of great benefit to our area."[57]

The Senate passed S. 1, which then moved to the House. William Batt, who would later serve as director of the Area Redevelopment Administration, recalled that during the House debates, the bill's supporters would meet "with all the labor lobbyists and the other lobbyists . . . , the Indians and other lobbies that we had interested in this legislation." These efforts were successful. The House approved the legislation, thus giving the new administration its first legislative victory. President Kennedy signed the bill into law on 1 May 1961.[58]

The new law created a "specific kit of tools to help communities rebuild their economic bases," including low-cost loans to attract industry, loans and grants to communities for infrastructure improvement, technical assistance for the creation of long-term development programs, and job training with subsistence pay for trainees. The act authorized the interior secretary to "conduct such special studies" as were necessary to allow the Commerce Secretary to determine that an area qualified for assistance. Interior Department officials immediately established criteria for the designation of Reservation Redevelopment Areas, and within four months of the passage of the act the Interior Department had designated forty-eight such areas, with another three added by mid-1962.[59]

William Batt later recalled that the Area Redevelopment Administration "worked hand in glove with Bureau of Indian Affairs employees," because "they had a mission to help put industry on the Indian reservations," and "saw us as a way to do a better job of what Congress had given them to do." The BIA assisted the tribes in formulating Overall Economic Development Programs (OEDP), the proposals required to receive funding from the ARA. Of the twenty-seven OEDPs initially submitted, twenty received provisional approval by the end of FY 1962. In addition, ARA grants that year funded nineteen feasibility studies, including programs for tourist and recreational development, management of timber and mineral resources, and the marketing of Alaskan arts and crafts. By the end of FY 1963, fifty-eight reservation projects had received approval; by FY 1964, the ARA had authorized eighty-four projects, including eight financial assistance projects, thirty technical assistance projects, and forty-six job training projects on Indian reservations at a total cost of $4.8 million. This sum far outstripped the BIA's expenditures for industrial development, which totaled less than one million dollars for the years from 1961 through 1963.[60]

ADDITIONAL FEDERAL PROGRAMS

Nash cooperated with the Department of Labor so that the Manpower Development Training Act, which funded job training programs, applied to Native Americans. Indian communities also qualified for federal assistance under the Public Works Acceleration Act, which aimed to create temporary jobs in depressed areas through increased expenditures for construction of public facilities such as hospitals, roads, sewers, and recreational sites. The original act, which President Kennedy signed into law in September 1962, did not specifically mention Indian reservations, an oversight corrected in October 1962 when Congress passed Lee Metcalf's amendment making Indian tribes eligible. Within one year, over two hundred public works projects totaling an estimated twenty-three million dollars had been approved for eighty-nine Indian reservations. Nash considered the public works acceleration projects to be among the most beneficial programs that Indians had access to during his tenure as commissioner.[61]

The Paradox of Program Sharing

Although the programs operated by the PHA and ARA undoubtedly contributed to improvements in the Indian standard of living and created new employment opportunities for some individuals, Native American participation in them was predicated upon poverty levels, not historic federal obligations to Native Americans. Thus, sharing the benefits of federal programs with Native American raised the specter of termination in two ways. First, program sharing hinted at the eventual abolition of the BIA, long a goal of the terminationists. Second, it redefined Native Americans as poor people, ignoring the cultural and social values that many Indians wished to protect. While Nash and Udall must be credited for obtaining the federal dollars necessary to advance their programs, they never questioned the long-term consequences that program sharing might have for Indian communities.

Paradoxically, the decision to allow Indian reservations and their tribal governments to qualify for these federal programs constituted a significant (and unintended) recognition of tribal sovereignty. Programs intended to assist Native Americans with economic development in order to ensure eventual assimilation empowered the very institutions that served to preserve and protect Indian identity. The poverty programs of Lyndon Johnson's Great Society would further this trend and promote growing Indian demands for tribal sovereignty and the recognition of treaty rights.[62]

Industrial and Business Development

Administration officials in both the Eisenhower and Kennedy administrations saw the promotion of industrial development as a key to the overall improvement of Indian life. Wages from industrial employment would spark the reservation economies and raise the standard of living. During the 1950s, Commissioner Glenn Emmons maintained that the promise of cheap labor would attract private enterprise; however, reservation isolation, poor (or nearly nonexistent) infrastructure, and an undereducated labor force combined to make locating on reservations an unattractive proposition for most businesses. Emmons could claim few successes by the time he left office in 1961. Udall and Nash hoped that government assistance in the form of infrastructure improvements, vocational training, and low-cost loans would spur private sector interest in the reservations. However, efforts to attract industry to the reservation still met with limited success.[63]

The BIA's Industrial Development Program worked with tribes to create development plans and negotiate with businesses and manufacturers interested in locating on or near a reservation. The program scored a success when the Wright-McGill Company, which manufactured fishhooks and fishing tackle, opened an assembly plant on the Pine Ridge Reservation in March 1961. Pleased with the performance at this plant, Wright-McGill opened two more production centers later that year. The tribe contributed tribal buildings to the enterprise, and the BIA provided nearly $160,000 in on-the-job training funds for the period from 1961 to 1963. By 1965 the plants employed 160 Native Americans who earned between $104 and $150 each per week.[64]

Although a success, the Wright-McGill story revealed some of the limitations of the industrial development program. Capital necessary to begin operations had been small and outlays for infrastructure improvement were correspondingly minimal, which made opening operations at Pine Ridge relatively simple. The work, repetitive in nature and requiring little skill, offered no hope for advancement. Native Americans were attractive as laborers because they came at low cost. In order to remain profitable, wages had to remain low. While the Wright-McGill operation contributed to the local economy, it did not revitalize the Pine Ridge reservation, and could not serve as an example for the full-scale industrial concerns necessary for the true economic development of the reservations. Wright-McGill finally ceased production in 1968 because of foreign competition.[65]

Administration officials also discovered that repetitive motion industries had an unanticipated negative impact on some American Indian communities. Although he did not specifically refer to the industry at Pine Ridge, John Carver later remembered "a big, heavy social cost" because repetitive work attracted "a very, very high percentage of women workers" that "broke the family unit up" by injuring the pride of the unemployed male in the family. Industrial development inevitably conflicted with Native American social and cultural values, a consequence the administration largely ignored.[66]

Poor coordination and planning also limited the effectiveness of the development program. With proceeds from an ARA loan, the Colorado River Tribe built a plant for the Parker Textile company, which planned to produce gray cloth. The plant opened in September 1964, and closed within nine months. Of the firm's forty employees, only one was Indian. Research on the plant's failure revealed that the BIA had provided no oversight of the plant facilities, which were outfitted with used machinery of questionable value, or of plant management, which proved to be inept. No marketing research or feasibility studies had been conducted. The bureau failed to provide the on-the-job training necessary to increase the number of Indian employees. The Parker Textile plant should never have been opened, and with its closing the ARA loan went into default and the tribe and other local interests lost over a quarter million dollars.[67]

The development program could claim some successes. In 1962, forty Pima and Papago employees cut diamonds at Harry Winston Minerals of Arizona. The Laguna Pueblo worked with Burnell and Company, a manufacturer of electronic components, to open a plant on tribal land in 1962. The tribe provided a low-cost loan for plant construction, and the BIA provided funds for training. By 1965 the firm employed 130 Indians; the following year ninety-four percent of the workers were Native American.[68]

The bureau assisted in the establishment of fifty-five businesses between 1961 and 1965, of which only eleven failed. However, the business success rate did not reveal two weaknesses of the BIA development program. First, many of the new businesses relied upon non-Indian labor. Of the 1,839 jobs created by the program through 1963, only 908 employees, or slightly less than fifty percent, were Native Americans. Two years later Indians still held less than half the jobs created. In addition, the development program did not provide adequate support for tribal ownership of businesses, and so very few tribal enterprises were established during this period. In part this could be attributed to a lack of managerial expertise among Indians; however, as long as outside interests owned the factories, economic development on the reservations would be tied to the advantages offered by low-wage employment. Such circumstances did not promote Indian self-sufficiency and self-determination; they merely perpetuated the dependent status of Indians and their communities.[69]

EDUCATION

Innovation and creativity were not the hallmarks of BIA educational services during the Kennedy years. Given the emphasis on education found in all three of the 1961 policy reports, the absence of significant reform in that area constituted a major failure. Commissioner Nash appeared satisfied with the status quo, a curious fact given his own background in academia. He retained Hildegard Thompson as director of the Branch of Education. A holdover from the termination era who had held the position since 1952, Thompson perceived education as part of the assimilation process. She ignored subjects such as Native American culture, desired by a growing number of Indians. Udall later recalled that "we inherited this nice old lady" who believed that "if you did a little better this year than last year with Indian education, why, that was good enough." Bureau organization contributed to Thompson's weakness as education director. Prior to 1952, the education director set educational policy through direct orders to the field offices. In that year, Commissioner Dillon Myer reorganized the bureau into eleven area offices, over which the education director had no line authority. Thus, effective administration of educational services would have required the reorganization of the BIA, a task Nash did not undertake.[70]

John Carver recalled that in the field of education "you . . . say that you're going to have a first-class school system . . . and go to the Congress and get the money and do what you [can], and that's what we did." Congressional appropriations committees proved cooperative, and education funding increased significantly. The education budget for 1961 was $63.7 million; for 1962, $71 million; and for 1963, $81.3 million, a thirty-one percent increase in just two years. The budget increases were necessary because the school-age population was growing. In FY 1961 slightly more than a third of enrolled Indian students, nearly 42,000 children, attended one of the 270 schools operated by the BIA; the remainder went to public or private schools. Three years later overall enrollment had increased by approximately seventeen percent, and BIA schools served over 46,000 students.[71]

The fast-growing population of Native American school-age children and the enormous backlog of those not enrolled in school—some 9,000 in 1961, over half that number because no seats were available—meant that existing facilities were insufficient to meet demand. The bureau's budget request for 1964 noted that the BIA "has been confronted with some very serious problems with respect to the construction of school facilities," pointing to student backlog, classroom overcrowding, and replacement of obsolete facilities as the sources of difficulty. School construction had quickened during the 1950s and remained a priority under Nash. Eighteen construction projects were completed in FY 1962; however, because a large percentage of the new buildings were intended to replace aged and dilapidated facilities, these projects added less than seven hundred seats to the BIA school system. During fiscal years 1963 and 1964 space for 10,000 students was constructed, but the net gain of seats remained small. Despite the intensive construction the bureau could barely keep pace, much less guarantee improvement, and in 1965 an estimated 8,600 Indian children were still not in school.[72]

The priority on construction was not matched by a revision of the curriculum. Some new programs were instituted, such as a remedial summer school program implemented in 1960 that proved popular. Enrollment in this program rose from 2,220 students in the first year to 20,444 in 1963. Enrollment figures for adult education and college preparation courses also rose during this period. However, BIA educators could not break from the assimilation model, and many Native Americans regarded their educational experiences as irrelevant. Dropout rates remained high. Critics charged that as long as BIA education limited Indian participation in the creation of programs and focused on the values of the dominant culture at the expense of traditional values, its programs were certain to fail. Although Hildegard Thompson was a dedicated and well-meaning employee, her retention as director ensured that the overall philosophy of the education branch did not change. Stewart Udall later regretted that he had not removed her immediately, replacing her with "an outstanding educator, who was an expert with disadvantaged children."[73]

ASSESSING THE NEW TRAIL: INDIAN POLICY IN THE KENNEDY YEARS

During the Kennedy years the nation's Indian policy moved in a new direction, one based on the needs of Indians as yet another minority mired in poverty. The PHA, ARA, and other federal projects benefited Native Americans, offering better housing, job training, infrastructure improvement, and wages, all of which Indians wanted and needed. The inclusion of Indians in such programs represented a reversal from the tight-fisted policies of the 1950s and stands to the credit of the Democrats who dominated the government. However, the Kennedy administration ignored issues central to the survival of American Indian communities, including treaty rights, self-determination, tribal sovereignty, and cultural integrity. The Kinzua Dam controversy revealed that, despite the misgivings of some officials, the U.S. government continued to place little value on the nation's treaty obligations or protecting Indian communities.

Under Philleo Nash's direction, the Bureau of Indian Affairs used noncontroversial legislation and took advantage of a variety of federal programs to achieve the goal of "maximum development of the resources of Indian reservations" outlined in the 1961 task force report. However, BIA achievements in fostering economic growth and improving educational services were limited. Given the magnitude of the problems that Indians faced in the early 1960s, hopes for dramatic improvements in these areas were unrealistic, but the bureau itself often made achieving the task force goals more difficult. Industrial development and job creation were by their very nature difficult tasks, but poor management and lack of oversight reduced the effectiveness of the industrial development program. In the area of human resources, Nash's policy of retaining old-line personnel contributed to the lack of substantive change. During the Kennedy years the education division expanded rather than reformed its operations to meet the needs of Indian students.[74]

The Udall task force had also suggested "helping Indians achieve an adjustment which will be contributory, rather than passive." However, the goal of Indian self-sufficiency was hardly closer in 1963 than it had been in 1961. Because the BIA's industrial development program often relied upon non-Indian ownership, management, and employees, it did not contribute to the goal of maximizing Indian self-sufficiency. Nash's reliance on personal skills rather than departmental reorganization to incorporate Indians into the policy process allowed for only limited Indian involvement. While laudable, Nash's attempts to build positive relations with Native American leaders did not constitute the creation of bureaucratic mechanisms for the inclusion of Indians in the policy process, and so did little to change the bureau's operations or perceptions concerning Indian participation.[75]

Nash was not the only administration official responsible for the problems in the conduct of Indian policy. Stewart Udall was most responsible for the creation of that policy. His attitudes were well represented in the 1961 task force report, and his administration adhered to the long-term and open-ended termination policy outlined in the study, emphasizing economic and human resource development as the keys to the gradual withdrawal of federal services. However, Udall did not play a major role in Indian affairs during the Kennedy years, instead allowing Assistant Secretary John Carver and Philleo Nash to implement policies and programs.

Nash later claimed that the administration's Indian policy was a "Kennedy-Udall-Nash" arrangement, but there is little evidence to support Nash's contention that Kennedy took an interest in Indian affairs. The few documents regarding Indian policy found in the John F. Kennedy Presidential Library reveal a profound though not surprising lack of interest in Indian affairs. As Nash noted in 1977, "JFK wanted to be a pro-Indian president—I've never known a President who didn't want to be pro-Indian. Indian affairs is one of the moral touchstones and this is how you separate Presidents who care from Presidents that don't." Thus, Nash considered Indian affairs at the presidential level as an issue of image not substance. He admitted that Kinzua Dam, which posed public image problems for the White House, was "the area that most directly involved President Kennedy." Activist and writer Vine Deloria, Jr.'s complaint that "Jack Kennedy broke the Pickering Treaty and had accomplished little besides the usual Interior Task Force study of Indians before his death," is thus largely correct.[76]

In a 1998 interview, Udall remembered Kennedy as "sympathetic. He wanted to . . . be helpful and do positive things for the Indians, but he was so consumed with the goddamned Cold War." Kennedy's lack of knowledge of Indian affairs is illustrated by an incident that took place in August 1962. A delegation of thirty-two Indians presented a copy of

the *Declaration of Indian Purpose* to the president in a White House
ceremony held on the South Lawn. Nash recalled that Kennedy "read
through a couple of pages of briefing material in about thirty seconds
and went out and greeted the crowd and talked as though he'd just been
reading a book on the subject." In fact, the president's only comments
relating to the content of the *Declaration* concerned the statement of
Indian loyalty that opened the document. For Kennedy, the South Lawn
meeting was just another one of many ceremonies that fill a president's
day.[77]

Nash might have concluded that Indian affairs was a "Congress-
Udall-Nash" arrangement. Congress, not the administration, defined
Indian policy. In February 1961, W. W. Keeler wrote that the "willingness of our new President and our new Secretary to take a new look from
stem to stern on this whole program has won me over completely." Keeler
believed that the administration's "positive leadership on this point has
certainly changed the climate with the Congress," and he hoped "for a
new resolution to come out of Congress that will first make it clear that
108 was not meant to be 'sudden death.'" In his optimism Keeler mis-
judged the will of members of Congress, especially senators such as
Clinton P. Anderson, who remained firmly committed to the continued
termination of Indian tribes. The outlook of Anderson, Gordon Allott,
and other members of the Interior Committee severely limited the leadership that the administration provided. Because of congressional
attitudes, the administration refused to hire administrators such as
D'Arcy McNickle and William Zimmerman; acquiesced in the termination of the Menominee and Ponca tribes; limited its legislative initiatives;
and relied upon program sharing in order to assist Indians.[78]

However, Congress did not present an insurmountable obstacle to
the Indians' desire for control over their affairs. Indian involvement in
PHA and ARA programs promoted the ideal of tribal sovereignty, and
the defeat of the heirship bill indicated that Indians could influence the
policy process. In the coming years Lyndon Johnson's War on Poverty
would create an environment more conducive to self-determination and
contribute to an increase in Indian activism.

The Senate Interior Committee, seen here in 1960, was dominated by terminationists. Left to Right: Ernest Gruening, Frank Church, Alan Bible, Frank Moss (standing), Henry Jackson, Oren Long (standing), Clinton Anderson, James Murray, Barry Goldwater, Gordon Allott. (*Senate Historical Office*)

Senator Anderson conferring with Gordon Allott, Republican from Colorado, whom one Senate staff member called "ringleader of the conservatives" on the committee. (*Senate Historical Office*)

Opposite: Clinton Anderson, Democratic senator from New Mexico, whose control of the Senate Interior Committee made him a key figure in Indian affairs. (*Senate Historical Office*)

Frank Church, Democratic senator from Idaho, meeting with the Nez
Perce Tribal Executive Committee in 1962. Left to right: Frank W. Penney,
Harrison Lott, Allen P. Slickpoo, Sr., Frank Church, and Angus Wilson.
(photo Ind OO1, Church Papers, Boise State University Library)

Opposite: Henry Jackson, right, was the Democratic senator from
Washington committed to the termination policy. He is shown here
conferring with Frank Church. Date of photo unknown.
(Senate Historical Office)

Philleo Nash, commissioner of Indian affairs from 1961 to 1966, prided himself on his personal contact with American Indians. He visited this unidentified Indian family in Oregon in 1963. (*photo 72-3362, courtesy Harry S. Truman Presidential Library*)

John Carver, Asst. Secy. of Interior, with Oliver La Farge of the AAIA, April 1961. (*Princeton University Library*)

President John Kennedy greets Commissioner Marie McGuire of the
Public Housing Authority and Johnson Holy Rock, Oglala Sioux, 19
September 1961. (*photo AR 6790-C, courtesy John F. Kennedy Library*)

Ernest Gruening addresses a group of Alaska Natives invited to the
White House on 2 August 1962 after they graduated from
electronics school. To Gruening's left are President Kennedy and
Secretary Udall. Philleo Nash stands in the audience at far left.
(*photo KN-C 22996, John F. Kennedy Library*)

President Kennedy with delegates
from the American Indian Chicago
Conference, 15 August 1962.
*(photo AR 7415-D, courtesy John F.
Kennedy Library)*

President Kennedy greets Edison Real Bird, Crow, and other NCAI
delegates at a White House meeting, 5 March 1963.
(KN-C 27019, *courtesy John F. Kennedy Library*)

Robert Burnette, Brulé Sioux, executive director of the National
Congress of American Indians, 1961–1964.
(*National Anthropological Archives*)

President Lyndon Johnson awards Annie Wauneka
the Medal of Freedom, 6 December 1963.
(Cecil Stoughton, photo CACH-26-63,
LBJ Library Collections)

President Johnson speaking to NCAI delegates at the White House, 20 January 1964. *(Yoichi R. Okamoto, photo W 424-21A, LBJ Library Collections)*

Seferino Martinez and Paul Bernal of the Taos Pueblo at a 1966
meeting with Interior Secretary Stewart L. Udall. (*Princeton
University Library*)

Opposite: NCAI delegates listen to President Johnson's presentation,
20 January 1964. Left to right: Frank Ducheneaux, Cheyenne River
Sioux; unidentified man, Barney Old Coyote, Crow.
(*Yoichi R. Okamoto, photo W424-23A, LBJ Library Collections*)

100

LaDonna Harris, Comanche, championed war on poverty programs.
She is seen here at the Indian school in Concho, Oklahoma, in 1966.
(photo 958, Harris Collection, Carl Albert Center Congressional Archives,
University of Oklahoma)

Opposite: Lady Bird Johnson visited several Indian communities
during her years as First Lady. She is seen here at a reservation in
Montana, 14 August 1964. *(photo 33027-15A, LBJ Library Special*
Collections)

Following: Cleota Bennett and President Johnson and Mrs. Johnson
look on as Stewart Udall swears Robert L. Bennett in as commissioner
of Indian affairs, 27 April 1966.
(Robert Knudsen, photo C 1775-1, LBJ Library Collections)

A Head Start class in 1967 in Salina, Oklahoma, with Indian and non-Indian students. *(photo 102, Monroney Papers, Carl Albert Center Congressional Archives, University of Oklahoma)*

CHAPTER THREE

NATIVE AMERICANS AND THE GREAT SOCIETY

In his first State of the Union Message, delivered a little over six weeks after he took office, President Lyndon Johnson announced that "this administration declares unconditional war on poverty in America." Pointing out that "many Americans live on the outskirts of hope—some because of their poverty, and some because of their color," Johnson called upon Americans to attack poverty "wherever it exists—in city slums and small towns, in sharecropper shacks or in migrant worker camps, on Indian reservations." Lyndon Johnson's vision of a Great Society that "rests on abundance and liberty for all" and "demands an end to poverty and racial injustice" represented the culmination of the liberal Democratic tradition of the twentieth century, and his commitment to ending poverty in America had a significant effect on the lives and the communities of the nation's Indians.[1]

In creating his Great Society Johnson received assistance from a Congress in which liberals held increasing power. Important liberal congressmen of the era included Sen. Hubert Humphrey (D.-Minn.), who was jestingly referred to as a "bomb-thrower" for his liberal stances; George McGovern (D.-S. Dak.), who joined the Senate in 1962 and would receive his party's presidential nomination in 1972; and Walter Mondale (D.-Minn.), a young Minnesotan appointed to take Humphrey's seat in late 1964 when Humphrey resigned to accept the vice presidency. Devoted to liberal causes such as civil rights, these men and many of their peers served as advocates for Native Americans during the Johnson years.

Liberal dominance of the federal government increased after the 1964 elections. Johnson captured 61.1% of the popular vote and received 486 electoral votes, carrying forty-four states and the District of Columbia. Democrats running for Congress matched his success. In the House, the Democrats picked up thirty-eight seats, bringing their total to 295; and in the Senate they gained two seats, resulting in a total of sixty-eight. The new Congress proved willing to work closely with the president. During its first session, the "Great 89th" passed 84 of Johnson's 87 legislative proposals; during the second session, it approved 97 of 113. Although none of this legislative avalanche directly addressed Native American concerns, Indian communities reaped benefits from bills aimed at assisting the impoverished, stimulating economic development, and improving the nation's education system.[2]

POLICY AND PERSONNEL CONTINUITY BETWEEN ADMINISTRATIONS

On the evening before Thanksgiving, 1963, just five days after Kennedy's death, Lyndon Johnson addressed a joint session of Congress. The new president declared that "in this moment of new resolve, I would say to my fellow Americans, let us continue." In telling Congress that "John Kennedy's death commands what his life conveyed—that America must move forward," Johnson allied his presidency with that of his predecessor and signaled his intention to be an activist in the

White House. Ever the shrewd politician, Johnson knew that presenting his administration as the heir to the hopes and dreams of the martyred Kennedy would earn him both sympathy and support. This stance was far from cynical—Johnson's first year in office constituted a continuation of the New Frontier both in policy and personnel. The new president devoted himself to the passage of the Civil Rights Act, to a tax cut intended as an economic stimulant, and to a war on poverty, measures all crafted in the Kennedy White House. In addition, Johnson retained Kennedy's top advisers, including Interior Secretary Stewart Udall.[3]

In the days immediately following Kennedy's assassination, Udall feared that he would be removed from the Cabinet. Satisfied with the direction that his department had taken and hopeful for the future, Udall was loath to lose his position; as he later recalled, "those were terrible days for me." Washington was rife with rumors that Johnson, who had a "long memory," would not tolerate the presence of Udall, the prototypical Kennedy man who had maneuvered the Arizona delegation away from him at the 1960 Democratic National Convention.[4]

Johnson, however, had concerns other than revenge in mind. As he told one friend, "you should know by now that I'm a better politician than to fire any of Kennedy's cabinet at this time." Hoping to silence critics who might claim that any Interior appointee would have to satisfy his powerful friends in the oil industry, the president told Udall that "I want you to make all the oil decisions, you to run the oil program; I want oil out of the White House," a decision that Udall later praised as a "shrewd political move." Johnson retained Udall to deflect criticism from the White House, which, in Philleo Nash's mind, was "a service to the president and a service to the country and he [Udall] performed admirably." In time Johnson came to appreciate Udall's abilities, especially his commitment to conservation issues, and Udall remained in the cabinet throughout Johnson's presidency.[5]

The president's decision to keep Udall as head of Interior meant continuity in Indian affairs. The 1961 task force report remained the guide for federal Indian policy, and Philleo Nash retained his position as commissioner. Although the phrase had fallen out of favor, the Johnson team followed the "New Trail" just as surely as it had under John F. Kennedy. Thus, the most important development in Indian affairs during the early years of the Johnson administration did not originate in the Interior Department; rather, Lyndon Johnson, a career politician with no background in Indian policy, brought the greatest changes to the lives of Native Americans through his commitment to battling poverty in America.

LYNDON JOHNSON AND NATIVE AMERICAN AFFAIRS

The new president hailed from Texas, a state that did not have a significant American Indian population. As a result, Lyndon Johnson had no important personal contact with Indians and did not develop a concern for Native American issues. Records from Johnson's congressional career housed in the Johnson Presidential Library reveal that during his twelve years in the House and twelve years in the Senate he had no direct involvement with Indian policy. During the 1960 presidential campaign Johnson visited the Blackfeet reservation, where he was decked out in a headdress, made an honorary chief, and given the name Leading Star. As vice president, he met with the AICC delegates who had presented a copy of the *Declaration of Indian Purpose* to President Kennedy earlier in the day; but after fifteen minutes with the delegation Johnson was on the telephone engaged in other business. Lacking any background in Indian affairs and far more concerned with the civil rights struggles of African Americans, the Texan had almost no interest in issues involving Native Americans.[6]

Johnson's understanding of Indian affairs did not increase after he entered the Oval Office. In a meeting with a delegation from the National Congress of American Indians held in the East Room on 20 January 1964, Johnson directed most of his remarks to the members of Congress in the audience, wooing their support on a variety of issues from protecting the nation's gold supply to cutting the Department of Defense budget. His few comments regarding Indians consisted of statistics gleaned from a briefing sheet provided by Udall. Robert Burnette later remembered of the meeting that he "did not feel the Kennedy warmth" from Johnson, and he concluded that "the President's interest was motivated by political considerations rather than by a concern for Indian problems."[7]

Despite his apparent lack of interest, Johnson pledged to put Indians in the "forefront" of the battle against poverty, a promise that America's Indians would not forget—and Native Americans and their advocacy groups kept a close watch on the president. When Johnson neglected to mention Indians in his 1965 State of the Union message, the Indian Rights Association lamented the omission, informing the president that "your inclusion of Indian reservations" in the 1964 message "was a source of encouragement and inspiration to the Indian people" and asking for continued attention to Indian affairs from the White House in the coming year.[8]

The War on Poverty

In his 1971 memoir, Johnson asserted that "my entire life, from boyhood on, had helped me recognize the work that needed to be done in America." As a teacher of impoverished Hispanic students in south Texas during the late 1920s and as Texas state director of the National Youth Association during the Great Depression, Johnson witnessed firsthand the consequences of poverty and the burdens suffered by America's poor, especially its minority groups. From the outset of the Johnson administration, the "work that needed to be done" included a war on poverty. On 23 November 1963, his first full day in the Oval Office, Johnson met with Walter Heller, chairman of the Council of Economic Advisers. Heller informed the new president that with Kennedy's approval he had been working on a project to alleviate poverty. Intrigued and excited, Johnson told Heller to "go ahead. Give it the highest priority. Push ahead full tilt."[9]

After several weeks of discussion, Johnson decided to create an independent agency to head his war on poverty. Robert Sargent Shriver, Peace Corps director and brother-in-law of the recently slain president, became director of the program. Shriver immediately created a task force that worked furiously to draft a legislative proposal for the president. The resulting legislation was daring, innovative, hastily assembled, and loaded with unproven methods for battling poverty. The Economic Opportunity Act of 1964 (EOA) created a Job Corps to "increase the employability of youths," offered work-training and work-study programs, authorized grants and loans to low-income rural families and to long-term unemployed persons, proffered small business loans, and organized the Volunteers in Service to America (VISTA), a domestic Peace Corps. It also established the Office of Economic Opportunity (OEO) to oversee the poverty programs.[10]

Title II of the bill "provided stimulation and incentive for urban and rural communities to mobilize their resources, public and private, to combat poverty through community action programs." These programs, known as CAPs, were intended to encourage "maximum feasible participation" on the part of the impoverished in creating and implementing antipoverty programs in their neighborhoods. Community residents would organize community action agencies (CAAs), craft proposals, apply for grants, and administer the local programs without interference from local, state, or federal officials. No one was certain exactly how the CAPs would function, as the notion was largely theoretical and untested.[11]

During the 1960s, CAPs became the most controversial provision of the EOA, receiving negative publicity and providing ammunition for opponents of the poverty programs. Ironically, CAPs more closely met the needs of American Indians than any other federal program of the 1960s. Native Americans desired and demanded self-determination, and the poverty bill provided them with a mechanism to work toward that goal. CAPs allowed Indians access to federal funds while permitting them to determine the allocation of those funds.

The benefits that accrued to American Indians from the Economic Opportunity Act were accidental and unintentional. Documents housed in the Johnson Library and published accounts of the early years of the war on poverty indicate that Indian welfare and well-being did not constitute a major area of concern during the planning stages of the war on poverty. The neglect of Native Americans in part reflected their marginal status in American life; it is doubtful that the theorists creating OEO knew much about Indians. Without Interior Department input, Indians were not likely to receive much attention, and neither Udall nor his staff played a significant role in the planning of the war on poverty. In late 1963 Walter Heller solicited policy proposals from top administration officials, including the heads of four Cabinet departments; but he neglected to inform Secretary Udall, whose suggestions were submitted at a later date. (Heller rejected all recommendations by the four Cabinet members as unimaginative, unrealistic, or budget busting.) No one represented the Interior Department at the 4 February 1964 planning session attended by both the secretary of labor, and the undersecretary of health, education and welfare (HEW). The Task Force on Poverty, which included officials from Agriculture, Commerce, HEW, Justice and Labor, lacked a voice dedicated to Indian affairs. Although Indians constituted the most impoverished group in America, they did not loom large in the Kennedy-Johnson efforts to organize a concerted attack on poverty in America.[12]

American Indians were also rarely mentioned because the administration hoped to craft a poverty program that was distinct from race. Civil rights was a contentious issue, and policymakers feared entangling the war on poverty in the battle over civil rights legislation being waged in Congress at the time. While this typically meant avoiding specific references to African Americans, the tendency to eschew racial distinctions may well have stifled specific discussion about Native Americans, Hispanics, and other minority groups.[13]

House hearings for H. 10440, a "bill to mobilize the human and financial resources of the nation to combat poverty in the United States," opened on 17 March 1964. In testimony given on 8 April, Udall corrected his department's lack of involvement with the poverty bill. Appearing both as a high-ranking administration official and as an advocate of Indian affairs, Udall deemed it a "pleasure to testify on this very vital national legislation." In his opening remarks Udall reminded the committee of President Johnson's promise to place Indians "in the very forefront of this program," and declared that Interior Department officials "certainly look[ed] forward to a very intensive participation, if this legislation is enacted." His prepared statement outlined the facts concerning Indian poverty and detailed the ways in which the specific titles of the bill would assist Native Americans. After citing the benefits to Indian youth offered by the Job Corps, Udall maintained that the CAP provision "offers an unprecedented opportunity for Indians to carry out local community improvement." He also claimed that the act would advance industrial development on reservations through "economic incentives" and the creation of long-term reservation plans.[14]

Representative Peter H. B. Frelinghuysen (R.-N.J.), a determined opponent of H. 10440, questioned Udall about Indian participation in the antipoverty programs. Noting that the "Department of the Interior is not even mentioned" in the text of the bill, Frelinghuysen added that there was "no assurance that there is going to be anything available for Indians, if some other competing Federal effort and program receives higher consideration." Frelinghuysen raised an important point. Native Americans were mentioned but once in the legislation, in a section permitting the assignment of VISTA volunteers to reservations. Thus, the legislation contained no guarantees that Indians would benefit from other aspects of the poverty program. Udall replied that President Johnson "has said in very flat language that he wants Indians in the forefront of the program. If you think that the Director [of OEO] will ignore the President, you may assume so. I do not."[15]

Richard Schifter, the AAIA attorney, was the only witness other than Udall to address the concerns of American Indians. Schifter built upon Udall's testimony, attempting to convince the committee that Indians would benefit greatly from the programs under discussion. He drew parallels between H. 10440 and the New Deal programs, especially the Civilian Conservation Corps, which had brought relief to the reservations during the Great Depression. Schifter also recommended two technical changes to the proposed legislation, including the explicit recognition of Indian tribes as qualifying agencies.[16]

During the House hearings most members of Congress appeared willing to extend federal assistance to the reservations, although some questioned the creation of a new federal agency to perform the task. Frelinghuysen, a moderate Republican opposed to the legislation because of the expanded powers it gave to the "poverty czar," declared that "it might well be that a case could be made that we should spend $1 billion a year on Indians," and Charles E. Goodell (R-N.Y.) stated that "the question we have is not whether Indians should participate—obviously, I think they should participate and this program holds some potential for them." Despite these expressions of congressional good will, Native Americans wanted to be certain that they would be recognized as an impoverished people under the term of the Economic Opportunity Act. To that end, the American Indian Capital Conference on Poverty convened in Washington, D.C., in May 1964.[17]

THE AMERICAN INDIAN CAPITAL CONFERENCE ON POVERTY

Organized under the auspices of the Council on Indian Affairs, an umbrella group for Indian organizations such as the NCAI and the Indian Rights Association, the conference was intended to "bring a widely representative number of Indian persons to Washington . . . to secure cooperative national leadership" on the issue of Indian poverty and "to define the role of education in a program against poverty among American Indians within the broader context of health, housing, employment and community mobilization." The timing was not accidental. The conference was held in May in order to pressure lawmakers to include Indians in the nation's war on poverty and to influence the legislation then before Congress. Although he declined, Sargent Shriver had been invited to give the opening address.[18]

On 9 May, the opening night of the conference, Senate Majority Whip Hubert Humphrey served as the keynote speaker, offering a speech entitled "Poverty in Our National Life." Claiming that the "critical economic condition of the American Indian is a mirror of the poverty problem the United States faces," Humphrey declared that Indian reservations must be a "prime target" in the war on poverty. Robert Burnette followed Humphrey with a speech titled "Poverty in American Indian Life," in which he urged President Johnson to visit several reservations to see firsthand "the almost indescribable poverty." Jack T. Conway, a member of Shriver's task force, then delineated the specifics of the pending legislation and its relevance to Native Americans to the audience, which one newspaper estimated at two hundred and fifty people.[19]

The following day had been declared American Indian Sunday at the Washington Cathedral. Vine V. Deloria, a Standing Rock Sioux and father of activist Vine Deloria, Jr., led the morning service. In keeping with the theme of the day, a Navajo choir accompanied by drums then performed. During the afternoon conference delegates visited an exhibit of Indian art at the Department of Interior offices, where both Stewart Udall and Philleo Nash greeted them. The day's activities closed with an Evensong service, at which BIA Deputy Commissioner John Crow read Bible verses and Secretary Udall spoke.[20]

Udall claimed that the administration's antipoverty proposals marked "the first time in our history" that Americans had tackled the longstanding problem of Indian poverty. In addition to hailing the president's legislative initiative, Udall declared that the nation as a whole could benefit from recognizing "that our Indian people have much to teach us." Calling Native Americans "a proud people with a complex culture," Udall maintained that "all Americans can learn" about ideals such as conservation and individualism from examining Indian values. Although these remarks indicated a respect for and appreciation of Indian cultures, Udall then commented that the country might be approaching "the last and triumphant phase in the relationship of the American Indian to American society," a phrase that might have startled those Indians who feared that termination remained the goal of federal Indian policy.[21]

Melvin Thom, a Northern Paiute and president of the National Indian Youth Council (NIYC), reminded the conference of the goals of many Native Americans. Declaring that "we do not want to be pushed into the mainstream of American society," Thom rejected cultural assimilation on the grounds that "we want to remember that we are Indians. We want to remain Indian people." However, he also asserted that Indians "do not want to be freed from our special relationship with the Federal Government. We only want our relationship . . . to be one of good working relationship [sic]." Thom called for Indian participation "at the grassroots level" and urged Indians "to cooperate and learn to work together." Although some Native Americans regarded the NIYC as a radical organization—Thom was nicknamed "Mao-Tse Thom"—the speech captured the spirit and sentiment of Indian self-determination.[22]

On the following day delegates attended a reception held at the Capitol Building, where they met with a number of legislators. Burnette remembered that "Indians had the opportunity to impress these lawmakers with the dire needs that exist on every reservation." He believed that "there was probably more communication that afternoon between American Indians and American lawmakers than had taken place in the world's history." The Capital Conference thus provided Native American leaders the opportunity to lobby for Indian participation in the poverty program in the very halls of the nation's capitol.[23]

Throughout the conference delegates attended workshops on topics such as education, health, employment, housing, and community mobilization. The final reports of each workshop were compiled and presented as the Conference Findings and Recommendations. The conference supported passage of the Economic Opportunity Act with some minor revisions, including the appointment of a deputy director "responsible for the development of programs for Indians," because many tribes "will be unaware of the benefits and possibilities of this act." The final report also offered twenty-four separate educational reforms, among them the recommendation that "all educational programs be designed to include traditional tribal values, and [that] the greater appreciation of the American Indian culture be reflected in educational materials." Health and housing suggestions called for increased federal funding and expanded services. While recognizing the "responsibility of Indians to achieve legislative goals" and "the ability of Indians to act independently," the conference did not reject technical or voluntary assistance from non-Indians; rather, it merely asked that non-Indians "be educated to know the Indian." The report did not directly address the issue of termination, but its calls for increased federal funding and direct tribal-federal relations bypassing state and local governments indicated continued opposition to that policy.[24]

In a speech given at the conference's final session, Philleo Nash offered comments on the Findings and Recommendations. Although Nash agreed that Indian poverty was an enormous problem, he took a defensive attitude when it came to the work of the BIA. He argued that "Indians are better off than Southern Negroes chiefly because of the work of the much criticized Bureau of Indian Affairs. As poor as the Indian people are, the rural nonwhites are much poorer." Nash pointed to recent improvements in Indian health, housing, and economic development as evidence that government programs worked. His remarks caught the audience by surprise. The *Amerindian* reported that he "threw a 'block buster,'" and in fact Nash was incorrect in his assertions. Many African Americans in both the north and south indeed endured wretched living conditions well below those of most whites, but Native Americans remained the most impoverished Americans during the 1960s.[25]

At the conclusion of the conference, the Steering Committee announced that the meeting had "succeeded beyond all anticipation," a statement that was not an exaggeration. Robert Burnette later recalled that the conference "really made an impression on the political system of this country." The American Indian Capital Conference on Poverty was intended to draw attention to the issues and problems that confronted Native Americans; and it did so, garnering press coverage in both the *New York Times* and the *Washington Post*. Most important, the Capital Conference received attention from prominent government officials such as Hubert Humphrey, a leading liberal who would be elected vice president before year's end, and Jack T. Conway, director of the Community Action Program, and, for a brief time in 1965, deputy director of OEO. In addition, Stewart Udall had publicly committed himself to ensuring that Native Americans would participate in the administration's poverty programs.[26]

The 1964 American Indian Capital Conference on Poverty was similar to the 1961 American Indian Chicago Conference but with one important difference. By the mid-1960s, Native American leadership had grown increasingly capable of making its demands heard in the corridors of power. Politically astute, pragmatic in its requests and moderate in tone, the 1964 conference evidenced a greater familiarity with the ways of Washington and represented a shrewd effort to influence the policy process through the establishment of political connections and no small degree of public pressure.

The BIA, the EOA, and OEO

Indian poverty was very much on Secretary Udall's mind at the BIA Conference of Superintendents held in Santa Fe, New Mexico, in June 1964. Don Carmichael, a member of the Shriver task force, attended the conference, as did ARA director William Batt and Public Housing Commissioner Marie McGuire. In his remarks at the opening session, Udall declared that "the purpose of this conference . . . is to raise our sights to the heights pointed to by the President" in the war on poverty. He told the BIA officials that "we are here to plan how to integrate our

Indian programs and Indian problems and Indian opportunities into the war on poverty." Udall defined human and resource development as the primary mission of the BIA, and claimed that the "Economic Opportunity Act can help." Enthusiasm had replaced Interior's slow start with the antipoverty bill, and Udall's support for the legislation reflected his department's ongoing effort to extend the benefits of other government projects to American Indians.[27]

The same week of the Santa Fe meeting, the Senate began hearings on S. 2642, the Senate version of the antipoverty bill. Testifying on 17 June, Sargent Shriver noted in his prepared statement that "the subject of poverty among Indian Americans has been brought into sharp focus in recent weeks," both by the Capital Conference and the superintendents meeting. Lee Metcalf, again serving as an advocate for Indian interests, told Shriver that "you want to be sure this program takes care of the American Indians," and questioned him about Indian participation in the projected poverty programs. Metcalf ascertained that tribal governments qualified as communities under the terms of the legislation and received Shriver's assurance that local and state officials desirous of funding would be unable to block Indian reservations from receiving funds. Satisfied with the task force director's responses, Metcalf thanked Shriver for preparing a statement that "would be very important in alleviating some of the needs of these unfortunate people." Although the brief exchange constituted the only substantive discussion of Native Americans during the hearings, the attention that Indian poverty had received recently assured Metcalf and his colleagues that Indians would benefit from the administration's antipoverty efforts.[28]

Two months later, on 20 August 1964, President Johnson signed the Economic Opportunity Act into law. However, the inclusion of Indians in the war on poverty did not offer a panacea for Native American ills. In early May 1964, Philleo Nash and Stewart Udall had discussed the BIA budget vis-à-vis the planned war on poverty. In a follow-up memo written on 18 May, Nash estimated that Indians would receive approximately fifteen million dollars for educational programs, perhaps two million dollars for community action programs, assistance from seven hundred volunteers, and grants and loans for three thousand families. Nash argued that these benefits constituted a "limited amount in the face of need on Indian reservations." He also noted that the EOA "has little or nothing to offer in the public works sector of the reservation economy." The commissioner believed that the "imbalance between appropriations for education, welfare, and other related Community Service items; as compared with monies appropriated for resource development" contributed to the ongoing poverty of Indians. He favored increasing appropriations for economic development as the key to ending Indian poverty. Nash had a point. The heart of the administration's Indian policy lay in development, not merely in the expansion of community services, however desperately needed. To that end, he suggested that Udall push for an increase in the BIA budget for the coming fiscal year.[29]

During the Santa Fe conference in June, Nash noted that the war on poverty "may . . . stimulate us to review, appraise, and revise our own ideas" concerning assistance to Indians. Far from acknowledging OEO programs as a positive stimulus to BIA planners, Nash's statement implied a lack of enthusiasm for OEO and reflected a bureaucratic aversion to competition from other government agencies. Nash approved of federal programs focusing on economic development, but he resented projects intruding upon the BIA's custodial duties, which he regarded as "social services . . . best funded in the Indian Bureau program." During the 1965 appropriations hearings, Nash struggled to convince Congress that OEO would not supplant any BIA operations. He argued that OEO would benefit only urban Indians who did not qualify for BIA programs, claiming that an Indian "living on the reservation . . . is going to be coming to us, not to the Office of Economic Opportunity." In the coming years this sense of territoriality would lead to "turf wars" between BIA and OEO officials at all levels in the two agencies.[30]

Stewart Udall remembered that "Indian Bureau people didn't particularly like the OEO programs because they were not supervising them," and James Officer recalled that conflict between the OEO and BIA was "more pronounced than that between BIA employees and colleagues in other federal agencies." He maintained that OEO employees often dismissed BIA workers as "anti-Indian, unimaginative, and overly paternalistic." Officer was correct. Sanford Kravitz, who was involved in drafting the EOA in 1964, recalled "a general lack of sympathy among the program planners for the Bureau of Indian Affairs." A 1965 story in the OEO publication *Communities in Action* illustrated some of the ongoing quarrels between the agencies. Upon discovering that Emma Old Bear, an elderly Sioux woman suffering from malnutrition, had money in an account "with a local Federal agency," two CAP workers had a "heated conversation" with an "official" who refused to approve monthly cash allotments until threatened with legal action. Although the agency and official were never identified, the BIA was clearly the culprit in this tale that portrayed CAP workers as sensitive and dedicated and BIA employees as heartless bureaucrats.[31]

Peter MacDonald, director of the Office of Navajo Economic Opportunity (ONEO), discovered that BIA officials resented the OEO programs and refused to offer support and assistance. He recalled that "the attacks against us were constant." Navajo requests to use BIA facilities and supplies were automatically denied. When the Indian Health Service threatened to close a preschool food program, only the threat of unfavorable publicity saved the project. Despite such obstacles, ONEO proved to be a successful agency, earning MacDonald the attention and popularity necessary to run successfully for tribal chairman in 1970. Thus, BIA intransigence was more a nuisance than an obstacle to the operation of OEO programs on the Navajo Reservation.[32]

Tensions between the BIA and OEO reached the highest levels. In November 1965 Sargent Shriver addressed the members of the NCAI at a meeting in Scottsdale, Arizona, and in his speech he quoted a member of his staff, a Sioux Indian, who allegedly said, "I would like to see the day when an Indian can withdraw $10 of his own money from his own bank account . . . without having to lie to the government official that he needed the money for shoes or food," and "the day when the tribal council has a real say in the makeup of a tribal government." Shriver also claimed that experts—which he implied were BIA officials—had argued that most tribes would not respond positively to OEO programs. Although Shriver intended for his speech to promote Indian participation in administration poverty programs, the Native Americans in the audience could not have missed the criticism of BIA policies and practices.[33]

Nor did Interior officials miss the import of Shriver's speech. In a memo to Secretary Udall, James Officer complained that Shriver's remarks constituted "a mixture of facts without explanations and half-truths," which were "rather typical of the sort of thing that the Office of Economic Opportunity representatives have been saying for quite some time." Officer did not blame Shriver, instead claiming that disgruntled former BIA employees who had moved to OEO were the source of the poor attitudes. Although he believed that "we are getting along very well" with OEO employees on the reservations and "have only a minimum of differences with them here in Washington," Officer nonetheless urged Udall to meet with Shriver to iron out disagreements between the agencies.[34]

Despite these squabbles, Stewart Udall remained committed to OEO involvement in Indian affairs. Lady Bird Johnson recalled seeing the interior secretary at a 1965 White House meeting of the poverty program's advisory council. In 1967, when OEO had become an embattled agency with numerous opponents in Congress, Udall defended the war on poverty. During congressional hearings he stated that "the effort to help the poor through the Office of Economic Opportunity needs to be continued" because it was "a vital force that has already improved the lives of the poor and renewed hope for many." Udall saw OEO as "instrumental in renewing efforts to help Indians and broadening resources available to them." Although he acknowledged that "there are probably people in my Department that regard the OEO people as a gadfly," he claimed that "we have needed a gadfly organization." The interior secretary dismissed the OEO-BIA conflicts because "in this initial period, it was inevitable that there would be some friction and some sort of pulling and hauling when it came to getting the new programs going."[35]

Udall's positive assessment of OEO and its importance to poor American Indians was accurate. Interagency conflicts were to be expected in Washington, D.C., and on the reservations, and the quarreling between the BIA and OEO did not have a significant impact on the reservation programs. In many cases, BIA officials actively supported OEO programs. In early 1965, Assistant Commissioner Selene Gifford informed the superintendents that Head Start was "a valuable supplement to the [BIA's] present programs." Whatever the attitudes of the BIA, Indians responded enthusiastically to the EOA provisions. By the end of FY 1965, fifty-five Indian communities had applied for Youth Corps funds, twenty had requested Head Start programs, and sixty-one had submitted grants for community action programs. Although some BIA workers were dismayed, many Indians developed a beneficial and productive relationship with the Office of Economic Opportunity.[36]

THE OFFICE OF ECONOMIC OPPORTUNITY AND NATIVE AMERICANS

Concerned that Indians might be unable to take advantage of the poverty programs, OEO established a task force to assess their ability to draft grant proposals and create effective CAPs. After the task force concluded that Native Americans possessed the skills necessary to develop appropriate programs, OEO representatives visited sixteen reservations to build interest in and support for CAPs. Each of these reservations soon filed grant proposals, all of which OEO rejected because they "were not within the legal purview of OEO," or "were not practicable in the light of fiscal realities." Although Native Americans were well aware of the problems their communities faced and were eager to participate in the resolution of those problems, they lacked the bureaucratic expertise necessary to craft their proposals according to OEO directives.[37]

The experience of the Rosebud Sioux, as described in the administrative history of the OEO housed in the Johnson Presidential Library, offers insight into the difficulties of creating programs on the reservations. In early 1965 the Christian Social Action Committee, which included Rosebud Sioux tribal members, submitted a grant application to OEO. Because regulations recognized only tribal governments as grantees, OEO rejected the initial application, which the Rosebud Sioux Tribal Council then agreed to sponsor. OEO's Office of Civil Rights noted that allowing the tribal council to serve as grantee excluded poor whites who lived on reservation land from participating in program administration. After "a great deal of persuasion" from OEO officials, the tribal council created the Rosebud Economic Opportunity Commission, a branch of the tribal government designed to permit white participation in the CAP. Only then did OEO approve the grant to the Rosebud Reservation.[38]

The difficulties faced by Indian communities such as the Rosebud Sioux prompted OEO officials to offer technical assistance in designing and implementing projects. In 1965, assistance was provided on a regional basis through three universities—Arizona State, the University of Utah, and the University of South Dakota. Three years later OEO expanded the assistance program to include Bemidji State College in Minnesota, the University of Montana, and the University of New Mexico. To reduce the complexity of the grant process, OEO created an Indian Division within the Office of Special Field programs, allowing Native Americans "direct contact with a special office in Washington staffed by persons with experience in the special problems of Indians, many of them Indians themselves." As Vine Deloria, Jr., noted during Senate testimony in 1967, the OEO organization meant that "Indian people were not required to go to a State office, then a regional office, then a district office, then finally a national office simply to get a program." The creation of an Indian Division served OEO's Indian clients so well that it functioned as a model for other federal departments, including HEW and Labor, which later established their own Indian desks.[39]

OEO funding for Indians rose dramatically between 1965 and 1967 and then leveled off. The 1965 expenditures for community action programs was $3.6 million; by 1967 it grew to $20.1 million, increasing slightly in 1968 to $22.3 million. (These figures do not include additional OEO funds for programs such as VISTA that did not pass through the Indian Division.) Although OEO expenditures could not possibly solve the problem of poverty on the reservations, Indians availed themselves of the new federal funds and the possibilities for change that OEO programs brought to their communities. By 1968 OEO claimed that it served 323,000 Indians, or eighty percent of the U.S. Indian population on reservations, through CAPs on 129 reservations.[40]

AMERICAN INDIANS AND OEO

American Indians throughout the United States responded with zeal to the administration's poverty programs. At a 1967 Senate hearing on the effectiveness of the war on poverty held in Albuquerque, New Mexico, Indians from several tribes offered testimony favorable to OEO. NCAI executive director Vine Deloria, Jr., maintained that "if nothing else the poverty programs have brought a sense of dignity, responsibility, enthusiasm, and desire to people who were almost completely without hope." Domingo Montoya, representing the Pueblos, stated that "my Indian people . . . have benefited tremendously from the programs instituted through the war on poverty," and Ronnie Lupe, White Mountain Apache, called OEO "a godsend." While these leaders were critical of many aspects of OEO administration and offered numerous recommendations for improving performance and efficiency, they remained overwhelmingly supportive of OEO and the war on poverty.[41]

In later years many Native Americans looked back with satisfaction at the impact OEO had on Indian life. They considered the Office of Economic Opportunity projects as the most beneficial federal programs available to Indians at that time. Philip S. Deloria claimed that "the 1960s was above all else an Office of Economic Opportunity decade." "I will stand up and defend OEO as long as I live," declared LaDonna Harris, Comanche, in 1983. Russell Means, a Yankton Sioux who became the most well-known Indian activist in the United States in the early 1970s, later claimed that "OEO was the best thing ever to hit Indian reservations." Phillip Martin, surveying the achievements of the Choctaw in Mississippi in the 1990s, regarded a $15,000 community action grant received by the tribe in the mid-1960s as "the key to all the changes that came afterward."[42]

American Indian enthusiasm for OEO stemmed from five benefits that its poverty programs brought to their communities. The most important benefit Native Americans received from OEO was the opportunity to devise and operate their own programs. The 1961 *Declaration of Indian Purpose* had pointed to the "desire on the part of Indians to participate in developing their own programs with help and guidance as needed and requested." The Lummis in western Washington state used a 1966 CAP to create a full-time position for a Lummi Indian for the first time in their tribe's history and to staff their business council. Similar incidents occurred on reservations throughout the United States. While many Americans might consider such changes inconsequential, Native American communities exulted in the opportunity to manage their own affairs. Thus, OEO was the first federal program created in the 1960s supporting the principle of Indian self-determination, an ideal recognized by Udall and Nash but which they had been unable to make a reality.[43]

The next two benefits derived directly from Native American participation in the policy process. First, OEO provided valuable training in administrative and bureaucratic procedures to Native Americans who hoped to run tribal governments and business enterprises. From grant writing to recordkeeping to personnel training, OEO programs gave Indians the opportunity to acquire the skills needed for the successful management of their interests. Second, OEO offered young and ambitious Native Americans new leadership opportunities, and a future generation of tribal chairmen and activists started as OEO directors and employees. Peter MacDonald and Peterson Zah of the Navajo Nation serve as two examples of chairmen with OEO backgrounds. Alfonso Ortiz, an anthropologist from the San Juan Pueblo, noted that these new leaders were "not intimidated by bureaucratic procedures" and were more willing to seek assistance outside the confines of the BIA than an earlier generation of leaders had been.[44]

Indians also appreciated the establishment of OEO as an entity separate from the Bureau of Indian Affairs and other governmental agencies. As a 1966 study concluded, "Indians wanted this program for themselves, and they wanted this badly enough to turn their backs on traditional external sources of help." Native Americans regarded the BIA and many other government departments with a suspicion born of years of conflict and misguided policies. The establishment of an Indian desk and the access to funding made Indians who were typically distrustful of the federal government supporters of the Office of Economic Opportunity. In 1967 OEO's congressional opponents hoped to dismantle OEO and distribute its operations to the existing Cabinet departments, a proposal Native Americans rejected. Vine Deloria, Jr., believed that dissolving OEO "would scuttle the Indian war on poverty," because Indians would again have to deal with Washington bureaucrats unwilling or unable to make necessary decisions. Peter MacDonald feared that other government departments would fund state rather than Indian programs, because "when the shortage of fund [sic] comes, the Indian gets left out." During House hearings held in 1967, LaDonna Harris, president of Oklahomans for Indian Opportunity and wife of Sen. Fred Harris (D.-Okla.), proclaimed her "strong conviction that OEO must be continued as a separate agency of the Government."[45]

The expansion of much-needed social services on the reservations provided the fifth and final benefit. Head Start provided medical and dental care and educational programs for preschoolers. It also promoted parental involvement in children's education. In fiscal years 1967 and 1968, fifty year-round and seventeen summer Head Start programs served an estimated ten thousand children, about a third of the preschool Indian population. Alvina Greybear, Standing Rock Sioux, claimed that Head Start was "the first time that, where Indian people themselves have gotten involved in these [educational] programs." Legal Services offered assistance in the form of legal aid and advice in both criminal and civil matters. OEO estimated that 30,000 people made use of legal service programs in 1968. The Dinebeiina Nahiilna Be Agaditahe, the legal services agency established by ONEO on the Navajo reservation, assisted nearly eight thousand clients in 1967, handling cases involving issues such as wage claims, divorces, child adoption, and criminal misdemeanors. The Home Improvement Program offered training in the construction trades while upgrading the quality of existing reservation housing. These and other such programs made essential social services available to Indians under their own management, disproving Philleo Nash's contention that the BIA was the agency most capable of providing custodial services on the reservations.[46]

OEO programs also had unintended consequences. As Vine Deloria, Jr., later noted, "OEO was a whole new . . . power base" on the reservations. On the Papago reservation, the CAP created in 1965 offered free transportation, which on an extensive and remote reservation was a valuable service to those who did not own cars or trucks. The transportation program shifted power away from the more affluent Papago tribal members who had been previously the only people able to move about the reservation freely. The Passamaquoddy, a tribe in Maine that did not have federal recognition and received no BIA assistance, organized a CAP in the mid-1960s. The experience proved to be so positive that it emboldened the tribe to pursue legislation to protect its interests in the state of Maine. In addition, OEO programs allowed Passamaquoddy tribal leaders who had previously taken off-reservation employment the opportunity to remain on the reservation, thus allowing them more contact with tribal members. For the Passamaquoddies, OEO was a path to development, empowerment, and activism.[47]

OEO also transformed the status of women on some reservations. The Salt River Pima-Maricopa Indian Community formed a CAA in

1965 and received its first grant that same year. By 1969 the community was receiving about a quarter million dollars in OEO funds. Women, many of whom possessed clerical skills, made up a large percentage of the OEO employees. Their OEO experience led to an expanded role for women in community affairs and increased participation in tribal government.[48]

However, OEO had a negative impact on several reservations. Robert Burnette of the Rosebud Sioux later maintained that "Indians had seen corruption, but the Johnson administration programs overshadowed anything in the past." Burnette pointed to a "tidal wave of theft, embezzlement, graft and corruption," and asserted that "tribal chairmen all too often followed the only example of leadership—the BIA—and got rich on everything that crossed their desks." Locked in an ongoing, bitter battle with Rosebud tribal chairman Cato Vallandra, Burnette accused Vallandra of nepotism and charged that the tribal government used OEO funds to reduce "the number of potential discontents in the tribe" by offering jobs to those "who might testify about the scandals on the reservation." On the White Earth Reservation located in Minnesota, twenty percent of the CAP employees were relatives of tribal council members. These abuses revealed the tensions between the traditional paternalistic policies and efforts to foster Indian self-determination. Decades of government paternalism had stunted the development of Native American institutions capable of managing increasingly complex tribal affairs. Self-determination projects such as those sponsored by the OEO could not immediately overcome the crippling dependency that plagued Native American communities; and some degree of corruption, fraud and incompetence was one unfortunate consequence of the transition toward self-determination.[49]

Increased opportunities for corruption were not the only change OEO brought to tribal governments. OEO funds sometimes altered or at least complicated reservation politics. Most tribal councils served as the reservation CAA—one OEO official declared that "we could count the tribal councils on the fingers of one hand that have decided that they would prefer another group" to serve as the CAA. The

Passamaquoddies experienced divisive debates and confrontations between the tribal council and the CAA, a body distinct from the council. The conflict led the council to insist that it be designated as the CAA, a demand OEO administrators at first rejected but to which they finally assented. Although having the tribal chairman serve as the CAP director increased the efficiency of the CAP program, it also concentrated a great deal of power in the hands of one individual. On the Papago reservation, one Indian complained that OEO had wrought significant changes in the operations of the tribal government, empowering committees at the expense of the communal process that had been the historical method of decision making. On the Navajo reservation, ONEO director Peter MacDonald struggled to keep the agency out of the hands of the tribal council members; as a result, some tribal officials sided with the BIA against OEO, thereby contributing to an already intense factionalism existing on the Navajo reservation.[50]

OEO funding also raised the issue of continued Indian dependency, a problem that worried Hank Adams, an Assiniboine Sioux and board member of the National Indian Youth Council. Adams was one of the most dedicated, intelligent, and skilled of the Indian activists of the 1960s and 1970s. Employing tactics successfully used by African Americans in their civil rights struggles, Adams organized "fish-ins" to protest treaty violations in the Pacific Northwest. He was shot in the stomach at the site of one such protest. A tough critic of the federal government, he was nonetheless willing to work with government officials in order to achieve his goals. During the 1972 BIA building occupation and the 1973 siege at Wounded Knee, Adams served as a negotiator between the protesters and Nixon aide Leonard Garment, who remembered Adams as "a slender, dark, nervously tentative young man," who was "highly intelligent" and "knew every negotiating trick in the book." When Adams turned his attention to OEO, he understood that, despite the good intentions of the war on poverty, continued dependency might be one of its outcomes.[51]

Adams expressed his concerns in a prepared statement submitted to the Senate Committee on Labor and Public Welfare. He praised OEO for achieving "a great deal for the amount of funds available to it," but argued that "few of OEO's overall accomplishments would survive a termination of the program." A 1966 study conducted for OEO had reached a similar conclusion, noting that "without external support these [OEO] programs would come to a complete halt." Adams believed that although OEO had "stimulated better service activity," it had failed at "creating employment on a permanent basis for heads of families." He pointed to Neighborhood Youth Corps programs that were "little more than meaningless activities or time-clock leisure," as an example of funding that created no real improvements in reservation economies.[52]

Adams concluded that "congressional concern should not be focused on how Indians are faring in the present 'war' on poverty with the ally OEO—but should review in close examination the entire scope of federal Indian programming." The direct benefits Indians derived from OEO were contingent upon continued federal funding of its programs, a dangerous reliance given that congressional critics of the war on poverty were becoming more strident in their opposition. Thus, Adams held a view similar to that of Philleo Nash—an increase in custodial services, however desirable, could not replace the need for long-term economic development of the reservations.[53]

Adams's fears were well founded. OEO programs furthered Indian dependency in at least one area of the United States. Don Mitchell of the Alaska Federation of Natives believed that access to OEO monies destroyed the traditional subsistence economy and left many Native Alaskans dependent upon continued federal funding, a dangerous circumstance given the pendulum swings of federal policy. While Mitchell acknowledged the many benefits of government programs, including much needed improvements in housing, he decried the replacement of a limited but dependable subsistence economy with an unstable dependency on federal largesse.[54]

In addition to worries about dependency, some Native Americans feared that OEO would promote assimilation. Although it was never an overt goal of the war on poverty—the 1966 study of OEO's reservation programs found "no attendant clear conceptualization of ultimate outcomes," which indicated that OEO never considered assimilation either as an end or as a consequence to be avoided—Native Americans were nonetheless alert for any threat to their cultural values. Given the commitment to community action it would seem unlikely that the poverty programs could contribute directly to the destruction of Native cultures. One of Peter MacDonald's primary goals for ONEO was the founding of a cultural center to serve as a "source of history, education, and pride for the Navajo people," and such a center opened in 1966. Leaders such as Domingo Montoya, Sandia Pueblo, saw Head Start as an opportunity for Indian children to learn about tribal culture, history, and language, knowledge that would serve them well as they interacted with non-Indians.[55]

Yet the new employment opportunities and the educational emphasis of many OEO programs nonetheless created at least the potential for continued assimilation. Robert Burnette later maintained that "OEO diverted the attention of the Indian people from their sacred land" as they "ran over each other to get jobs at $2.50 an hour" and "forgot all the things that they had learned as Indian people." The 1966 study argued that "Head Start . . . when properly implemented and fully accepted by and for reservation children, is in reality a first step toward assimilation." The report then added that Indians "appear to be aware of the unstated bias toward assimilation of a number of CAP components, and . . . reject them as anything other than a temporary source of funds or diversion." Thus, Native Americans recognized the potential threat of assimilation posed by some programs. They regarded the need for those OEO programs that offered income and promoted cultural preservation as outweighing "the unstated bias toward assimilation" perceived in some programs, a bias that they could readily identify and counter in their management of the CAPs.[56]

ASSESSING THE WAR ON POVERTY

Lyndon Johnson's war on poverty had a significant effect on American Indians, offering opportunities for self-determination (with all the problems that goal entailed), coupled with the risks of deepening an already crippling economic dependency and continuing the cultural erosion that Native Americans had fought for so long. That Indian communities across the nation willingly accepted those risks cannot be dismissed as grasping for increased funding by impoverished people. Although American Indians recognized the advantages that OEO spending brought to their lives, the desire for self-determination was the driving force behind Indian enthusiasm for OEO. In the memories of those individuals who participated in its programs, the most enduring legacies of the war on poverty were the experience it provided and the confidence it engendered. As LaDonna Harris recalled, "OEO taught us to use our imagination and to look forward to the future as an exciting adventure."[57]

However, for all the effects both good and ill OEO had on Native American communities, it failed to achieve its primary goal, the reduction of poverty on the reservations. OEO programs were chronically underfunded and could not meet the needs of the hundreds of thousands of impoverished Native Americans. When the Pine Ridge Reservation created a Ranger Corps, it received 127 applications for ten positions; another reservation program received 150 applications for five positions. Between 1965 and 1967, OEO spending on reservations increased eleven percent while the number of communities participating in such programs grew nearly five hundred percent. In 1968 total OEO expenditures for Indians came to $35 million, less than ten percent of that year's total federal spending on Native Americans. Although OEO mounted a laudable effort to improve the lives of American Indians, poverty remained a cruel reality for most Indians both on and off reservations at the end of the 1960s.[58]

Officials in the Interior Department, however, had not abandoned the economic development plans developed earlier in the decade. A new federal program that sailed through the 89th Congress in 1965 guaranteed continued funding for development, and the BIA pressed ahead with its projects for the industrialization of Indian reservations.

THE PUBLIC WORKS AND ECONOMIC DEVELOPMENT ACT OF 1965

Although the Area Redevelopment Administration had scored many successes since its creation in 1961, by the middle of the decade it suffered from an image "tarnished by mistakes and unrealized expectations." However, the purpose behind the ARA, providing stimulus in the form of grants and loans to economically stagnant regions in the United States, remained popular with both the White House and Congress. In 1965, senators Paul Douglas and Patrick V. McNamara (D.-Mich.) introduced S. 1648, legislation to create the Economic Development Administration (EDA). The new agency was to have a mission similar to that of the ARA, the stimulation of economic development in distressed areas through loans and grants for technical assistance, public works, and the establishment of private business interests. Like the Area Redevelopment Act of 1961, S. 1648 explicitly included American Indians in its provisions, stating that "Federal or State Indian reservations which the Secretary [of Commerce], after consultation with the Secretary of the Interior, determines manifest the greatest degree of economic distress," qualified for assistance under the terms of the act.[59]

Given the considerable financial benefits Native Americans received from the ARA and the Public Works Acceleration Act, and Philleo Nash's concern that economic development remain at the forefront of the administration's Indian policy, Interior Department officials should have shown interest in the creation of the EDA. However, when the subcommittee of the Senate Committee on Banking and Currency held hearings on the bill during the first week of May, no one from the Interior Department testified in favor of the bill; nor did any representatives from tribes or Indian organizations appear to lend support to the legislation. Only NCAI executive director Vine Deloria, Jr., sent a telegram calling for passage of the bill. Noting that "too often legislation has asked the American Indian to jump from the stone age to the computer age in a matter of generations," Deloria argued that this bill allowed Indians "a better understanding of what makes your culture work without destroying the values we have held sacred for so long." During the hearings, Sen. Walter F. Mondale (D.-Minn.) made the only references to the needs of Native Americans. The lack of support for the bill from Interior officials and Indians continued the following week when the House Committee on Public Works held its hearings. The only extended discussion concerning Indians came from Donald Greve, the owner of an Oklahoma carpet factory who made a point of hiring Native Americans.[60]

Interior Department indifference to the hearings might have been the result of the overwhelming support that S. 1648 had garnered in the Senate. One week after Douglas and McNamara introduced their bill, thirty-five senators joined as cosponsors. During the floor debates on the bill, Joseph Montoya (D.-N. Mex.) noted that the "Acoma, Isleta, Laguna, Jemez, Jicarilla, Mescalero, Ramah, Santo Domingo, Zuni, Santa Clara, and Navajo" were among the several Indian communities in his state that stood to benefit from the passage of S. 1648. Walter Mondale declared that he was "most happy that the bill specifically provides for relief and assistance to those living in substandard and poverty conditions on Indian reservations in the United States," conditions he condemned as "a pathetic circumstance of incalculable proportions in the midst of the richest nation in the world." Cognizant of the harsh realities of Indian life in their home states and determined to see that American Indians received needed assistance from the federal government, liberals such as Montoya and Mondale considered the inclusion of Native Americans in the bill's provisions as an additional reason to support the legislation. On 1 June 1965, the Senate passed the Economic Development Act by a vote of 71 to 12. The House vote on 12 August was closer, but the bill still passed by a large margin.

The liberal Democratic majority of the 89th Congress had scored a major success for its ranks, for the administration, and for the Indians who would receive funds from EDA programs in the coming years.[61]

The first year of EDA operations brought few benefits to Indians. Created on 26 August 1965, when President Johnson signed S. 1648 into law, the Economic Development Administration had only ten months left in Fiscal Year 1966 in which to organize, assess program applications, and commit nearly a third of a billion dollars in funds appropriated by Congress. In the resulting rush, Native Americans received little attention. Although fifty-four reservations had been designated as areas qualifying for assistance, projects slated for Indian communities totaled only $3.2 million, less than one percent of EDA expenditures for the fiscal year.[62]

Recognizing the substantial difficulties inherent in developing Indian reservations, EDA officials made two important decisions in 1967. First, they created an Indian Desk in the Office of Policy Coordination. Staffed in part by Native Americans, the Indian Desk worked with state and local agencies and private businesses in creating and implementing programs for reservations. Second, and most important, the EDA initiated the Selected Indian Reservation Program (SIRP) in order to bring "about the maximum return for the Federal dollar invested, in terms of both immediate and long-range benefits." To achieve this end, EDA officials worked jointly with the Office of Economic Opportunity to coordinate activities on the selected reservations. Under the terms of the SIRP, fifteen reservations regarded as having "high potential for economic growth" were placed on an Action List so that they would receive the "most intensive efforts and a large share of Federal Indian-assistance funds." Reservations were chosen "on the basis of tribal leadership's interest in the program, available manpower skills, educational facilities, raw materials and transportation, and nearness to regional growth centers." During fiscal years 1967–1969 Indian reservations received a total of $52.9 million, of which Action List reservations received almost $30 million, or slightly more than half of all EDA funds for Indians.[63]

In addition to reservation programs, EDA officials also worked with OEO and the NCAI to attract industry to the reservations. In 1968 these organizations sponsored two trade shows, one in Los Angeles and one in New York, touting the advantages reservations offered as industrial sites. Booths displayed the products already manufactured on reservations while tribal representatives discussed the specific benefits that their reservations offered. The EDA estimated that three hundred industrialists attended each show and credited these conferences with General Dynamics's decision to build a plant on the Navajo reservation.[64]

The EDA faced significant and at times insurmountable obstacles in its efforts to promote reservation development, so much so that a 1972 study concluded that "the results on reservations are not encouraging." Events on the Red Lake Reservation of the Chippewa Tribe illustrated some of the difficulties. In 1967 the EDA approved a $981,000 business loan to Eisen Brothers, a furniture manufacturer, for the construction of a manufacturing plant on the reservation. The plan collapsed when the firm backed out of the project. The EDA had more success with a $184,000 business loan to rebuild the tribal sawmill, which had been destroyed in a fire. However, project analysts concluded that EDA participation, while appreciated, had been unnecessary because the tribe had access to other loan sources. In 1967 the EDA approved a $187,924 grant/loan combination for the creation of an industrial park. The tribe received many indirect benefits from the construction project, including a new sewage system and improvements to the roads and the water supply. However, as of 1972 not a single business had opened at the park. Nor did a 1968 planning grant of $35,900 yield any appreciable results, in part because intratribal disputes led to the demise of the study. Although EDA expenditures had assisted the Chippewas in many small ways, EDA had failed to meet its goal of economic development. Reservation isolation, conflicts within the tribe, and the fear among the Chippewas that recreational and tourist development would lead to the destruction of their culture contributed to the EDA's failures on the Red Lake Reservation during the 1960s.[65]

The 1972 evaluation of EDA performance on reservations did not paint a bright picture. Benefits received on the Blackfeet reservation were "less than expected," while on the Rosebud Sioux reservation the "direct impact of jobs and income from these [EDA] projects" was "minor." The Lower Brule gained only nine jobs through EDA projects. However, the administration scored some successes. The Metlakatla Indian Community on Annette Island benefited from the construction of an EDA-financed dock and loading ramp that allowed the Indians to expand their timber industry. On the Navajo reservation EDA projects created over six hundred jobs by 1972, and contributed to the creation of several water and sewage projects. The Mescalero Apaches used EDA funds to finance a cattle fencing project that led to a significant increase in herd size and the employment of fifteen cattle hands.[66]

The Economic Development Administration increased the amount of capital available to advance the BIA's program of reservation economic development. Although officials hoped that the EDA would attract businesses through loans, planning grants, and working capital guarantees, the bulk of EDA's reservation expenditures went to public works such as infrastructure development necessary to create an environment amenable to business and industry. These public works programs provided jobs and, as in the case of the Red Lake Reservation, an improved standard of living for some reservation residents. However, low funding levels and the EDA's understandable decision to concentrate its limited resources on selected reservations meant that most Native American communities did not realize significant benefits from EDA programs.[67]

THE ELEMENTARY AND SECONDARY EDUCATION ACT OF 1965

The Elementary and Secondary Education Act (ESEA) represented another longstanding liberal goal, federal aid to education, realized during the 89th Congress. Previous attempts to pass such legislation had foundered on the issues of funding parochial schools and the expansion of federal power into an area considered by many Americans to be a local concern. White House aide Joseph Califano recalled that Johnson "tapped all his persuasive and political skills" to achieve passage of the act; and the president scored yet another major legislative victory when Congress approved the ESEA on 9 April 1965. Two days later, with an eye for drama and good press, Johnson signed the bill in the schoolhouse he had attended as a child, his first teacher seated next to him, declaring that "no law I have signed or will sign means more to the future of America." The ESEA provided over a billion dollars to "local education" agencies throughout the nation according to the number of poor children within the school district. It also contained provisions for library resources and textbook purchases, generous provisions that almost warranted Johnson's characteristic hyperbole.[68]

However, the ESEA contained no explicit guarantees that Indians would receive any of its benefits. Those Indian students who attended public and parochial schools, about 91,000 children constituting sixty percent of the total Indian school-age population, would count toward total ESEA funding that school districts received; but no mechanism ensured that any of those monies would be spent directly on Indian students. If they so desired, school districts could use the federal funds for general expenditures, ignoring the special educational needs of their Indian pupils. Moreover, the ESEA made no reference to the 48,000 students attending BIA operated institutions.[69]

Interior officials had assumed that the ESEA's provisions covered the BIA schools, but to their dismay they discovered that this was not the case. In 1966 Udall admitted to a congressional committee that the BIA believed it would receive ESEA funds "simply by asking for money to qualify our children under our regular appropriation." However, the Bureau of the Budget rejected this approach, informing the Interior Department that additional legislation would be necessary to qualify BIA students. Although Congress approved legislation to include BIA schools in 1966, the damage was already done. As Udall noted in his testimony, "we have already lost 1 year under this program," a year that

Native American students could ill afford to lose. The BIA assumption was a grave error, and, given the poor state of Indian education, an inexcusable one.[70]

BIA LEADERSHIP DURING THE GREAT SOCIETY'S EARLY YEARS

The failure to safeguard the interests of Indian students was not mere oversight. By 1965 the Bureau of Indian Affairs was in disarray, which may also explain why the BIA did not actively support the EDA legislation that year. In December 1965, Nash confided to a friend that "it has been most unpleasant for the past ten months." Tensions between Udall and his commissioner had been building since early 1964, and by late the following year had reached a breaking point. As a result, during the years that Great Society programs offered new opportunities to Native Americans, the agency charged with Indian affairs offered little leadership and showed no initiative. Great Society successes such as the Economic Opportunity Act and the Economic Development Act could not outweigh BIA failures. Issues such as trusteeship, treaty obligations, and cultural preservation did not fall under the pale of Great Society responsibilities; such issues were the province of the Interior Department and fell upon Stewart Udall, Philleo Nash, and their employees. In an era of continuing congressional pressure for termination, overwhelming deficiencies in Indian education, and ongoing battles over the meaning of trust and treaty obligations, American Indians needed a strong bureau in the hands of a capable commissioner. During the years 1964 and 1965 they had neither.[71]

CHAPTER FOUR

The Nash Resignation

During the early years of the Johnson administration the Bureau of Indian Affairs suffered from internal tensions, and these disputes and disagreements ultimately led to Philleo Nash's resignation in March 1966. As differences between Udall and Nash grew increasingly acrimonious, bureau operations suffered, and Native Americans received little support or guidance from the agency charged with their welfare. To compound the turmoil that marked those years, the Senate Interior Committee pressed the termination policy with renewed vigor. Through various means, including withholding judgment funds and exploiting tribal factionalism, Sens. Clinton Anderson, Frank Church, and Henry Jackson sought to force the withdrawal of federal services from several Indian tribes. For American Indians, the continued threat of termination tempered the optimism that Great Society programs brought to the reservations during the mid-1960s.

NASH AND UDALL

"I decided along in '64 that I wanted to replace Nash," recalled Stewart Udall in a 1969 interview. Nash had not been Udall's first choice to serve as Indian commissioner, and relations between the two men had never been warm. Nash did not offer the "kind of drive and dynamism" that Udall desired in Indian affairs. For his part, Nash contended that the dispute between him and Udall "started on January 20, 1961," because "Udall's a know-it-all and I'm a know-it-all and there is no way in which the two of us would ever get along personally." Aside from their clashing personalities, Nash believed that Udall inappropriately applied his understanding of Southwestern Native Americans to other tribes and regions, areas "which quite frankly Stewart Udall didn't know anything about in Indian affairs." Personality and policy differences led to a worsening relationship, and after a time Nash proved unable to combine the sympathetic leadership that marked his tenure in office with the force and vision that Udall demanded.[1]

Nash's administrative style served as one source of tension between the commissioner and the secretary. Nash disliked confrontation and the direct exercise of his authority, preferring instead to create an atmosphere of trust in which subordinates resolved conflict through discussion and compromise. This approach brought many benefits—James Officer recalled that "Nash's even-handedness with both Indians and BIA employees resulted eventually in a much better working relationship between the two"—but it also created difficulties within the BIA. Corinne Locker, an AAIA attorney, observed that Nash "refuses to believe that the motivations—to say nothing of the capabilities—of those under him are anything but the best," a humane but naive position for an administrator to take.[2]

Richard Schifter addressed the problems that such a management style can cause in a 1963 letter to AAIA president Oliver La Farge. Schifter complained about "Philleo's inadequacy in coping" with a split between old-style BIA administrators and the new personnel that Nash had brought in. Bob Vaughn, a BIA employee whom Richard Schifter regarded as "a valuable ally," had several disagreements with Deputy Commissioner John Crow. Nash counseled Vaughn to work out his problems with Crow on his own, a solution that Schifter noted "reliev[ed] the Commissioner of the need to make a decision." Vaughn contended that Nash was "acting as if he were running for office, trying to curry favor" with old-line bureau staffers such as Crow, and he requested a transfer out of the BIA, which he received. Udall, who was "deeply shocked" at Vaughn's move, "promptly called in Philleo and gave him hell."[3]

The commissioner's unwillingness to take a hard line with his employees when necessary displeased Udall, who sought strong leadership of a sort that Nash could not provide. By early 1964, the differences between the secretary and the commissioner had become open and obvious. At the superintendents conference held in Santa Fe that June, Corinne Locker observed "a sense of jealous rivalry that Dr. Nash seems to feel toward the higher echelons in the Department." Nash publicly boasted that he and Udall had disagreed over the import of the pending Economic Opportunity Act for Indian affairs, a display Locker perceived as evidence of the "petty jealousy" Nash felt toward Udall.[4]

During the conference Udall requested the formulation of ten-year plans for the various agencies, allowing the superintendents three months to prepare their proposals. At the close of the conference Nash belittled Udall's suggestion, arguing that it constituted "nothing new to the Bureau," and informing the superintendents that they had only one month to complete their plans. Locker saw Nash's behavior as "a slap at the Secretary, almost a sneer." More important, Nash's poor attitude would affect Indian policy because his one-month deadline was "an irresponsible administrative order that will put unreasonable strain on the agencies, interfere inordinately with their regular operations, and result in hastily prepared plans." As Locker realized, rising tensions between Udall and Nash threatened to have an adverse impact on the Native Americans whom the Interior Department served.[5]

NASH AND THE SENATE INTERIOR COMMITTEE

In addition to his conflicts with Udall, Nash suffered from increasingly poor relations with members of the Senate Interior Committee. Despite a change in leadership, the committee was still committed to terminating the tribes. In 1963 Clinton Anderson had left his position as Interior Committee chairman to head the Senate Aeronautical and Space Science Committee, but the New Mexico senator retained influence over Interior matters. Jerry T. Verkler, a personal aide to Anderson who served as the Interior Committee staff director from 1963 to 1974, recalled that "as a senior member and a former chairman of the Interior Committee, there wouldn't be anything on Interior that he [Anderson] wanted that he couldn't get." Moreover, Anderson's successor as chairman, Henry Jackson, was so concerned with reelection and other Senate matters that "during the year [sic] of '63 and '64, Clint Anderson was still virtually running the committee," chairing "most of the meetings and markups." John Carver recalled that Anderson was "such a gray eminence in this field . . . that it took a year or two for that to shake down, for everybody to remember that Anderson wasn't still the chairman." According to Richard Schifter, as late as October 1964 "Clinton Anderson remains the most powerful figure" on the committee. Anderson met with no conflict from Jackson, who held attitudes similar to his own in the field of Indian affairs. The liberalism sweeping the United States Congress in the mid-1960s was not in evidence on the Senate Interior Committee, at least not in regard to Indian policy.[6]

Anderson was a determined Nash foe, as the contents of a 1964 letter to Senate committee staffer Stewart French revealed. Referring to Joseph McCarthy's 1953 allegation that Nash had communist ties, the New Mexico senator maintained that "there were dubious matters in his record which were overlooked and then we proceeded to confirm him." Anderson's real complaint against Nash was more substantive. The New Mexico senator opposed the creation of schools on the Navajo reservation, advocating instead "integrating his children [Nash's Indian students] with the white children" in public school districts. Because of this and other Nash policies, Anderson asserted that "if I had known he would work against everything I favor . . . I would not have supported him and worked to confirm him." Complaining that Nash "works at cross purposes with the members of Congress from states with heavy Indian populations," Anderson noted that "the day will come when he will need a friend and then he may take a different viewpoint of people in Congress."[7]

BIA OPERATIONS

Nash's increasing difficulties with Udall and the Senate Interior Committee affected BIA operations. In his opening address at the 1964 Santa Fe conference, Stewart Udall told the superintendents that "we need creative thinking. We need big plans, not little plans. We need solid plans." However, the feuding between Udall and Nash stifled creativity because tensions at the highest levels did not create an environment conducive to innovation. Reflecting upon his last years in the Interior Department, Nash concluded that internal controversies caused employees "to draw into their shells and become protective," because "they don't know which way the cat's going to jump so they don't make any decisions at all if they don't have to—it gets to be a pretty bad bureau."[8]

In addition to the bureaucratic withdrawal from risk taking, budgeting issues also rendered "big plans" unlikely. President Johnson had instituted an economy program, and the Interior Department drafted a 1965 appropriations request Udall referred to as "basically a hold-the-line budget." Nash found the minimal increases in BIA funds troubling, and he told Udall that "a special appeal should be made to the Budget Bureau and the President on behalf of an over ceiling increase for Indian Bureau operations." However, the following year Udall offered yet another "tight budget" to Congress, leading Richard Schifter to report that the BIA and the Indian Health Division would have to "continue their operations without significant change in scope." Schifter noted that "increases in operating funds for both agencies were . . . sufficient merely to absorb routine increases in the cost of operations without allowing for program expansion." Limited funds reduced opportunities for new approaches to Indian affairs, a reality reflected in bureau operations during that period.[9]

The paucity of new ideas was apparent at a three-day conference on Indian affairs held shortly after the presidential election in November 1964. Assistant Secretary John Carver, Commissioner Nash, and other Interior officials attended, but the paternalistic tradition ensured that no Native Americans were present at discussions concerning their future. Nash informed Udall that "the conference was more successful in identifying major problem areas than it was in reaching agreement on solutions," and another participant reported that "no major changes or new goals were suggested." The group decided to retain the 1961 task force report "as the continuing charter for the Bureau," while taking "into account three basic elements of President Johnson's policy—the attack on poverty, the concept of the Great Society, and the need for frugality." Of the seven conference proposals Nash forwarded to Udall, two called for "studies," and one recommended a "review." The remaining four proposals were trivial ("encourage Indian tribes to establish their own information programs . . . for such activities as producing motion pictures, books, etc.") or vague ("work with the State of Alaska in getting the natives [sic] title to some of the lands which they claim").[10]

As was the case during the Kennedy years, the bureau shied away from offering important legislative initiatives. The November conference attendees regarded one proposal, "to seek a way of setting up an Indian Development Loan Bank with the wealthier tribes investing their funds in this endeavor," as the "Number One legislative goal" in the coming years. Yet they "agreed that the first step [in achieving this goal] should be a study by a foundation or consulting firm on this proposal," hardly a decisive course of action. Lacking both ideas and funds, and facing a hostile Senate committee, Nash did not seek possible legislative avenues to improving the lives of Native Americans.

In 1966 Richard Schifter noted that "only one major item of specifically Indian legislation was enacted during 1965," a bill that increased annual authorization ceilings for the BIA's adult vocational program from $12 million to $15 million.[11]

The BIA and the Navajo Reservation

While the bureau's operations in general faltered during this period, its activities on the Navajo reservation came to a dead halt. Covering territory in Arizona, Utah, and New Mexico, the reservation was larger than the state of West Virginia and constituted, in the words of Philleo Nash, "1/7th of all the Indian Commissioner's responsibilities," duties Nash came to neglect or avoid.[12]

Nash proved unable to offer any solutions to an ongoing controversy between the Navajos and the Hopis, which constituted the most troubling intratribal conflict in the country. In 1882, President Chester A. Arthur issued an executive order creating a reservation for the Hopis "and other such Indians as the Secretary of the Interior may see fit to settle thereon" in northwestern Arizona. At that time a small number of Navajos resided within the 2.472-million-acre rectangle of land set aside for the reservation, but over the years the Navajo population boomed and the tribes quarreled over land ownership.[13]

Stewart Udall later admitted that as the area's congressional representative during the 1950s he had thought "that this was like a quiet title dispute only in a large scale," but the intratribal conflicts grew increasingly acrimonious. In 1958 Congress passed legislation permitting the tribes to seek a court settlement. Four years later a three-judge panel decided in the case of *Healing v. Jones* that the Hopis had exclusive right to an area known as District 6, but that both tribes had "joint, undivided and equal rights" to the remainder of the reservation, which was to be managed as the Joint Use Area (JUA). In a comment that surely dismayed the BIA, the court left it to "the tribes and government officials to determine whether . . . the area outside District 6 can and should be fairly administered as a joint reservation."[14]

Udall later recalled that "the court didn't really resolve" the Navajo-Hopi land dispute, which "really came back to the Bureau as a question [as to] how we solved [it] administratively in terms of [the] court['s] decision." The ruling placed Philleo Nash in the unenviable position of mediating a bitter, eighty-year-old dispute between two tribes over territory BIA employees soon dubbed the "No Hope Area." Nash met with representatives from both tribes in a hotel in Scottsdale, Arizona, in early August 1963 to try to iron out an agreement for the joint use of the land, announcing that "I would not like to be the commissioner who is found timid or wanting, unable to recognize the duty and the power of the federal government in this case."[15]

However, Nash met with intransigence from both tribes, neither of which had any interest in sharing the JUA. To complicate matters, John Boyden, attorney for the Hopis, requested that the BIA immediately end Navajo overgrazing in the JUA, a demand that raised memories of John Collier's stock reduction program on the Navajo reservation. The Navajos maintained an enduring bitterness toward the BIA because of that program, and no one in the BIA had any desire to repeat that experience. The conference ended without producing any results. After a second meeting held in September also failed to move talks forward, Nash abandoned the problem. Although attendees at the November 1964 BIA planning conference discussed "the need . . . for settlement of the Navajo-Hopi controversy over administration of the joint ownership area," the BIA did not resolve the Navajo-Hopi land dispute during the remaining six years that Udall served as interior secretary.[16]

LITTELL V. UDALL

The legacy of the forced stock reduction programs and Interior's inability to resolve the JUA conflict complicated relations between the government and the Navajos. To make matter worse, the tribal government was in turmoil for the most of the 1960s. In 1963 Raymond Nakai, a Navy veteran who had served during World War II, won election as Navajo tribal chairman on his third attempt. According to Nash, Stewart Udall had hoped for a Nakai victory, in part because the new chairman was a Democrat. However, a faction ardently opposed to Nakai dominated the tribal council. Known as the "old guard," this group vigorously opposed almost all of Nakai's initiatives, resulting in "the most divisive factionalism in all of Navajo political history." When Udall intervened in this volatile atmosphere in 1963, he initiated a controversy that would result in legal battles lasting for over three years. In a move Nash later condemned as "the most idiotic thing which he [Udall] ever did in Indian affairs," the interior secretary "tangle[d] with the Navaho [sic] tribal government" in an ugly dispute concerning Norman Littell, the tribal attorney.[17]

A Rhodes Scholar who entered private practice after leaving the Justice Department in 1944, Littell had little experience with Native American legal issues. During his tenure as assistant attorney general, Littell had terminated the Indian Law Survey, a project under the direction of Felix Cohen, possibly because he feared that the survey's results would aid Native Americans in their land claims against other western interests. (Cohen completed the project, which resulted in the highly acclaimed *Handbook of Federal Indian Law*, under the auspices of the Interior Department.) In 1947 the Navajos retained Littell as general counsel because they needed an attorney to file claims with the Indian Claims Commission.[18]

As a proponent of reservation development and a harsh critic of the BIA's stock reduction program, Littell quickly earned the admiration of many Navajo leaders and, according to the *Navajo Times*, became "the sparkplug of tribal development." However, by the late 1950s Littell's prominent position in tribal affairs and his failure to secure a favorable judgment from the Indian Claims Commission had earned him many enemies, among them Raymond Nakai, whose 1963 campaign platform included a pledge to fire Littell. The old guard, who "held him [Littell] in great respect," defended the attorney and blocked Nakai's attempts to oust him. The debate over terminating Littell's contract stood at the center of the factional disputes that defined Navajo tribal politics at that time.[19]

According to the terms of his 1957 contract, terminating the attorney required the approval of the Navajo tribal council. Philleo Nash, always an admirer of political skill, took a dim view of Nakai's talents as chairman, maintaining that "when it came to lining up the votes to deal with the Tribal Attorney who was an enemy of his, he [Nakai] didn't know how to get them." When Nakai could not build the necessary majority on the council, he turned to Udall for assistance. In a meeting held with several of Littell's opponents in his office on 19 June 1963, Udall recommended that the Navajo Advisory Committee, a body composed of the chairman's appointees, request an investigation of Littell. Less than a week later the advisory committee passed a resolution headed as follows: "Requesting Secretary of the Interior to Investigate, Audit and Terminate Norman M. Littell's General Counsel and Claims Attorney Contract with the Navajo Indian Tribe."[20]

At first the resolution was "handled in a routine fashion," but after Nakai pressed for an immediate investigation in August, Secretary Udall asked Frank J. Barry, department solicitor, to investigate the matter. On 1 November Barry sent Udall two memos examining the advisory committee's request. Noting that a "thorough investigation, fair to all parties," would "necessarily take a great deal of time," Barry limited the scope of his first memo to technical questions regarding Littell's payment for work done on the *Healing v. Jones* claims case. The second memo, which Barry marked confidential, stated that Littell "has often taken unfair advantage of the Tribe's confidence in him to serve his own interest," and concluded that "Mr. Littell's conduct must be characterized as contrary to and inconsistent with his responsibilities as the Tribe's attorney." Barry pointed to significant increases in Littell's retainer and demands for contingency fees in the claims case as evidence that Littell "used his position as the tribal attorney to advance his own personal interest." Barry recommended that Udall suspend Littell's contract immediately, and "that unless our conclusion is proved to be in error, his contract be terminated on December 1, 1963."[21]

Following Barry's suggestion, Udall suspended Littell's contract on 1 November, provided the attorney with copies of both memos, and gave him thirty days to "explain away the implications suggested by the record." Littell responded in mid-November with a lawsuit charging that the interior secretary did not have the authority to terminate his contract. On 29 November, two days before the deadline Udall imposed, a judge issued a preliminary injunction that prevented the interior secretary from suspending or terminating Littell's contract. Udall found himself involved in a legal battle and, far worse, embroiled in a heated factional conflict within the largest Indian tribe that his department served.[22]

Although Nash believed that Udall possessed the "power to do what he did" when he terminated the Littell contract, he doubted "the wisdom of it," later calling it "the wrong thing to do" and "an abuse of power." He maintained that Udall's intervention may have "set back the Navaho's [sic] political development maybe a generation." Fearing that his disagreement with Udall would become public and worsen the situation, Nash elected to sit out the controversy and stay away from the Navajo reservation. Thus, the Littell incident reduced Nash's effectiveness in his relations with one of the largest Indian communities in the country. In addition, Nash claimed that his refusal to become actively involved in the dispute widened the rift between him and Udall and contributed to the secretary's growing dissatisfaction with his commissioner.[23]

The preliminary injunction did not calm the turmoil on the Navajo reservation, and battles between the Nakai faction and the old guard continued. The situation on the Navajo reservation worsened to the point that one Interior Department official claimed in 1965 that "almost the only business conducted by the Tribe since Mr. Nakai's accession as Chairman has been the dispute between him and Littell." In response to the advisory committee's 1963 resolution, the tribal council created a new advisory committee in September 1964, which, old guard members maintained, would "no longer rubber stamp what Nakai, with Udall-Nash support, asks for." On 14 December 1964 a group of Nakai supporters used a tribal council meeting to publicly denounce the old guard, the newly constituted advisory committee, and Norman Littell. The following week the tribal council appointed J. Maurice McCabe, who had aspired to the position of commissioner of Indian affairs in 1960, as director of administration. Because this newly created position, which oversaw the tribe's finances, answered to the tribal council and not the chairman, the McCabe appointment constituted another attempt to undermine Nakai's authority. Governing the Navajo reservation had degenerated into a power struggle.[24]

Because of Udall's involvement in the Littell case, the old guard directed a great deal of their animosity toward him and the Interior Department. Orren Beaty, special assistant to the interior secretary, noted that "since the lawsuit was filed, the [old guard] faction in the Navajo Tribal Council has made Secretary Udall, Solicitor Barry and Commissioner Nash targets of abuse." A letter to President Johnson from Annie D. Wauneka, a member of the old guard on the tribal council, revealed the anger that many Navajos felt toward Udall. Wauneka raised allegations of corruption and scandal regarding tribal finances and blamed Udall for the chaotic state of tribal affairs, contending that "no one can adequately measure the damages to the Navajo Tribal organization caused by Udall, or to our Navajo confidence in the Department of the Interior." She claimed that the secretary had "brutally abused this 'stewardship' [his trust obligations] for his own and others' purposes," and closed her letter with a reference to Albert Fall, the interior secretary who served prison time for his involvement in the Teapot Dome scandal of the 1920s.[25]

Although her letter was clearly biased and contained several errors (at one point she charged that "Udall wants to be appointed to your Cabinet"), Wauneka was a prominent figure on the Navajo reservation whom the administration could not ignore. She commanded great respect from many Navajos, several of whom knew her from work on the council's health committee and from her hospital visits to tuberculosis patients. In December 1963, in the company of notables such as Marian Anderson and Felix Frankfurter, Wauneka had received the Medal of Freedom from President Johnson for "her long crusade for improved health programs," which "dramatically lessened the menace of disease" on the Navajo reservation. The following year she received an invitation to Johnson's 1965 inaugural ceremonies.[26]

However, Wauneka was also a controversial figure on the reservation. Peter MacDonald (a Nakai supporter) remembered her as "viciously divisive and needlessly hurtful," and as someone who "would rather focus on politics than on the mutual concerns" of tribal members. He maintained that she "prove[d] to be the enemy of every [tribal] chairman."[27]

Wauneka's charges constituted a troubling and potentially embarrassing development for the Interior Department and the administration. The White House routed Wauneka's letter to Orren Beaty, who drafted a reply that he then forwarded to Lee White, Associate Special Counsel to President Johnson. Beaty responded to Wauneka's allegations point by point, dismissing her accusations against Udall as "complete fabrication," but admitting that "with respect to the charge of mishandling of Navajo tribal funds, our investigations have disclosed that this was a matter which should be looked into." However, Beaty believed that any financial misconduct had occurred during the administration of Paul Jones, Nakai's predecessor as tribal chairman. Rather than respond in detail to Wauneka, White chose to write a guarded reply, maintaining that the "pendency of litigation" prevented him from responding at length to her charges. Thus, White fended off attacks from Wauneka at least until the release of a court ruling on the issue of a permanent injunction.[28]

The court's decision did not please the administration. On 26 May 1965, U.S. District Court Judge John J. Sirica granted a permanent injunction against Udall. Nicknamed "Maximum John" for his behavior on the bench, Sirica, who would later rise to fame during the Watergate affair in the 1970s, ruled that "once the 1957 contract, with its termination clause, was approved by the Interior Department, the secretary lost his administrative power to terminate this contract." According to Sirica, the power to remove Littell resided exclusively in the tribal council. He found that the advisory committee's 1963 request for an investigation of Littell constituted "an attempt . . . to eliminate Littell with the guise of legitimacy by getting a resolution passed by Nakai's hand-picked puppet committee." Moreover, Sirica decided that Littell "did not have unclean hands" in his dealings with the Navajo tribe, thus determining that Udall lacked not only the administrative authority but any compelling reason to terminate the attorney's contract.[29]

Sirica was also highly critical of the Interior Department, maintaining that Littell "was entitled to better treatment and consideration by those in a position of authority than he received," treatment that Sirica condemned as "brutal and shabby." Udall received the lion's share of the judge's wrath. Charging that the secretary's decision to terminate the contract "was not motivated by a recognition of any existing legal power" but by the "desire to 'get rid of Littell,'" Sirica claimed that "this whole controversy could have been averted by the secretary" had he referred it to "the Tribal Council rather than by handling it in the manner that he did."[30]

Sirica went beyond reproaching Udall and the Interior Department for their handling of the Littell dispute. Noting that "it has been the policy of the federal government to foster and encourage self-government for the Indians," and arguing that the "Tribal Council has the ability, knowledge, and intelligence to handle its own affairs," Sirica rejected the Interior Department's claim that it had merely fulfilled its trust obligations in attempting to remove Littell. The judge's contention that "Indian self-government should be a meaningful goal rather than an empty phrase" was a strong criticism of Udall's conduct of Indian affairs in general. Thus, Udall had not only failed in his efforts to terminate Littell's contract; he had received a stinging rebuke from a federal court that questioned his commitment to Indian self-sufficiency, one of the major goals of Indian policy as identified in the 1961 task force report.[31]

Response to Sirica's ruling was immediate. On 28 May, Lee White contacted Udall to see "if there is anything the Administration should or could do about this matter." That same day Udall announced his intention to appeal, a decision that was not surprising given the tone of the judge's ruling. Annie Wauneka, who had refrained from pressing her case against Udall to administration officials, forwarded a copy of Sirica's opinion to Lee White and in a letter dated 10 June reminded him that Johnson "has made it clear that he will not tolerate corruption in his government," and asked "what, then, does he intend to do about Udall?"[32]

The old guard also used the ruling to engage in public attacks on Udall's authority. On 9 June Udall informed the Navajos that he had scheduled a meeting for the following week to "discuss plans for . . . Navajo economic development." Two days later the advisory committee, which the old guard now controlled, voted 12 to 0 to reject Udall's invitation. Wauneka and eight other tribal council members sent Udall a lengthy telegram informing him that the items on the meeting's announced agenda were already under consideration "by the properly constituted authorities within the Navajo tribal organization." Claiming that the Navajo people had come to a "complete loss of confidence in you," they argued that "we have been solving these [economic] problems for the last seventeen years, and can continue to do so. These are our resources, not yours." Wauneka released the telegram to the press, and on Sunday, 13 June, the *Albuquerque Journal* ran a front page story entitled "Navajo Group Renews Feud With Udall."[33]

The administration responded in a low-key fashion. Referring to Wauneka as a "wild woman," Udall suggested that White offer no reply to her letter. White sent Wauneka a brief and condescending letter assuring her that "we are aware of the very deep emotions . . . involved in this troublesome matter and will continue to follow it closely." However, White could not so easily dismiss Sen. William Proxmire (D.-Wis.), who had also become interested in the Littell case. Proxmire told White that he was "greatly concerned" about the conflict between the Interior Department and the Navajos. Calling Sirica's opinion and finding of fact "devastating," and noting that "it is not often that a member of the President's cabinet is permanently enjoined by a Federal Court," Proxmire called for a "thorough review by the executive branch to determine if such conduct can be tolerated by the highest of our officials." With reference to the *Albuquerque Journal* article, Proxmire concluded that "the court case will not end the problems which precipitated it."[34]

Although Proxmire had not threatened a congressional investigation, the administration did not relish any "thorough review" of a Cabinet member's actions. White attempted to calm Proxmire with the vague promise that the Littell case would "continue to receive the attention of the Administration," but Proxmire was not satisfied. On 23 June he requested "a more precise description of the attention the Administration is giving to the actions taken by the Secretary of the Interior and his subordinates." Orren Beaty counseled a brief response to Proxmire's request instead of offering "a lengthy detailed description of the bitter controversy which has gone on for over two years." After delaying for over a month, White sent another guarded reply, assuring Proxmire that "there will be no violation of any Federal Court injunction." This communication ended the correspondence between Proxmire and White on the Littell matter, indicating that both sides awaited the results of Udall's appeal.[35]

The U.S. Court of Appeals heard the Littell case on 18 April 1966 and offered its decision on 2 September. Asserting that "the broad authority vested by Congress in the Secretary to oversee Indian affairs . . . includes the power to cancel contracts between a tribe and its attorneys for cause by appropriate administrative action," the court reversed Sirica's decision and lifted the permanent injunction on Udall. The court also concluded that Littell's "unauthorized use of Tribal staff attorneys on claims cases constituted adequate grounds for cancelling his contract as General Counsel." Thus, Udall had both administrative authority and compelling cause to terminate Littell's contract. The ruling undoubtedly cheered Udall and the administration, but Annie Wauneka complained that the decision could "put us back to the days of Fort Sumner where the

Secretary and the Indian Agent told us what to do and we had no voice in the matter."[36]

The Littell case came to an end in early 1967. In January the U.S. Supreme Court refused to grant a writ of *certiorari*, and the following month it denied Littell a rehearing. The attorney immediately resigned from his position as general counsel. In the meantime Nakai had won reelection as tribal chairman in November 1966. Although quite close, the victory allowed Nakai to regain control over the advisory committee. Navajo tribal politics remained factional and divisive, but the conclusion of the Littell dispute offered hope that the factionalism might abate in the future.[37]

Udall's involvement in the Littell controversy illustrated the problems that the secretary faced in promoting Indian self-determination. Although committed to a policy of increasing Native American self-sufficiency, Udall also had trust responsibilities. In the interests of self-determination he might have left the decision to retain or terminate Littell to the tribal council; however, given the concerns over the attorney's handling of Navajo affairs, Udall had to act on his obligation to protect tribal assets and concerns. Because the tribe's legal counsel "play[ed] a critical role affecting the allocation of Navajo land resources" and "the promotion of Navajo employment," he had no choice but to fire Littell when it became apparent that the attorney had ignored the tribe's needs in favor of personal gain. However, because the position of legal counsel also served as an "affirmation of Navajo direction in their own affairs" and worked for "the protection of Navajo sovereignty," Udall's actions conflicted with the move toward self-determination. In addition, the secretary's close friendship and political relationship with Raymond Nakai ensured that his intervention in tribal affairs would only exacerbate the factionalism that rendered Navajo government dysfunctional and increase bitterness toward the BIA among some groups on the reservation.[38]

Two attorneys affiliated with the Navajos later claimed that Udall had contemplated "taking over the administration of the Navajo Tribal Government for some time if he deemed it necessary." Such a drastic move would have proven disastrous, alienating not only the Navajos but

Native Americans throughout the country who were dedicated to the cause of self-determination. Udall was wise to allow the tribal government to continue its operations. By steering a moderate course and weathering the unpleasant consequences, Udall fulfilled his trust responsibilities while allowing the Navajo people to struggle with the problems that self-determination brought to their government.[39]

JAMES HALEY AND INDIAN AFFAIRS

During the era of disarray in the BIA and conflict on the Navajo reservation, James Haley, the Florida congressman who chaired the House Subcommittee on Indian Affairs, proved to be a champion of American Indian interests. While Haley agreed that Indians should "participate to a greater degree in the [policy] planning process," he did not advocate self-determination. He maintained that "the right of self-determination is in the Congress as a representative of all the people— not in the tribe." However, as a Southern gentleman Haley believed that the government had obligations to the tribes that it must fulfill, commitments that included protecting Indian assets and honoring treaty provisions. This attitude led him to block long-term leasing legislation Stewart Udall actively supported and to fight for a generous settlement for the Senecas displaced by the construction of the Kinzua Dam. Haley's position on these issues earned him the high regard of many Native Americans and illustrated the differences between the House and Senate Interior Committees concerning Indian affairs.[40]

LONG-TERM LEASING

Legal limitations imposed on leasing Indian lands posed an obstacle to industrial development on the reservations. A 1955 act set the maximum length of a lease at twenty-five years, with an optional renewal period of an additional twenty-five years. However, business leaders, bankers, and insurers expressed a reluctance to invest the capital necessary to launch industrial enterprises on reservations without the security of a much longer lease period. Udall saw opportunity in extending the lease period and took a personal interest in the issue—notes from the first meeting of the 1961 task force state that "the Secretary is particularly interested in this [long-term leases] because of lease income possibilities of Arizona Indian lands."[41]

Although its final report did not mention the subject, the task force drafted a memo recommending that "the Department request legislation to permit 99-year leases in exceptional cases in which longer terms are necessary or desirable," though it cautioned that "this authority . . . be used sparingly, for a 99-year lease is in the nature of a conveyance of the land." The task force also recommended that any legislation include provisions for periodic renegotiation of lease terms, right of recapture, and continuation of trust status during the lease period in order to protect Indian title to the land.[42]

Congress proved willing to extended leases on specific reservations through amendment to the 1955 act or through special legislation, but Udall wanted the authority to approve long-term leases without congressional action. In 1963 the Senate passed legislation extending the lease period to fifty-five years (with no renewal option), significantly shorter than the ninety-nine years the secretary desired but, in the eyes of the Interior Department, an acceptable improvement nonetheless. Rep. Morris K. Udall (D.-Az.), Secretary Udall's brother, introduced a companion bill in the House that immediately met with opposition from Haley, who informed the Arizona legislator he was "not opposed to a longer term leasing of Indian lands" but that he preferred continuing on a case-by-case basis "so that we might give the Tribe the benefit of our counsel and advice and, as far as possible, see that Indians' rights were fully protected." Because of Haley's doubts concerning long-term leasing, the House Indian Affairs Subcommittee did not report out the Udall bill in 1963.[43]

Morris Udall introduced the legislation again in 1964, but comments offered at a February 1964 hearing indicated that the House subcommittee remained adamant in its opposition. Wayne Aspinall, always intent upon protecting congressional authority, objected to expanding the powers of the executive branch, "where the growth of dictator operations and autocratic government automatically asserts itself." He complained that "when they [the Interior Department] are once given a general policy in a particular matter, then it is no time before they begin to trespass upon it as far as Congressional consideration is concerned." Haley contended that "it is the duty of this committee . . . and the best thing for the Indian tribes as a whole, to look over each individual proposition, because . . . one error in judgment could put a tribe in a position where their entire economic base could be entirely destroyed."[44]

Two months after the subcommittee hearing, Barry Goldwater, a cosponsor of the Senate long-term leasing bill, informed Sterling Mahone, chairman of the Hualapai Tribal Council, that he was "hopeful . . . this bill will receive favorable action in the House this session," and recommended that Mahone "get in touch with the House members, especially those who are on the House Interior Committee, to urge enactment of the bill." Goldwater was far too optimistic. In August 1965, Lloyd Meeds (D.-Wa.) correctly informed a constituent that "legislation of this nature has little chance of being enacted by the House," noting that "it was the Committee's policy that legislation of this nature must be specific in regard to the tribe and to the contract." Haley's opposition ensured that Congress would never pass a general long-term leasing bill. The Florida congressman's careful attention to Indian affairs led him to stop legislation later deemed by two scholars to be "in effect a sale of the reservation because it meant heavy investment by non-Indian developers with the almost certain result that the lease would be renewed a century later."[45]

The Seneca Nation Relocation and Termination

James Haley killed the leasing bill by refusing to report it out of his subcommittee. He could not employ this strategy in his efforts to assist the Seneca Nation as it struggled with the consequences of the Kinzua Dam project, a circumstance some western senators hoped to exploit in their efforts to revive the termination policy.

In August 1961, President Kennedy had promised that the "departments and agencies of the Federal Government would take every action within their authority to assist the Seneca Nation and its members who must be relocated" because of the Kinzua Dam project. The two agencies directly involved, the Army Corps of Engineers and the Bureau of Indian Affairs, made plans to comply with the president's directive. On 4 October 1961, Philleo Nash and Lt. Gen. W. K. Wilson of the Corps met in the White House office of Lee White to coordinate their efforts. The following week Nash and several representatives from the Corps met with Basil Williams, the president of the Seneca Nation, members of the tribal council, and the tribe's attorney to discuss plans for assisting the Senecas. On 5 November roughly sixty-five tribal members attended a public meeting held on the reservation to discuss their future with Corps and BIA officials. In order to prepare for relocation, the Senecas formed the Kinzua Planning Committee, and in March 1962 the BIA assigned Sidney Carney, Choctaw, to the reservation to aid the Senecas.[46]

Despite the planning sessions and ongoing communications among the tribe, the BIA, and the Corps, negotiations over compensation for damages and the creation of projects for reservation development proceeded slowly. As of early 1963 the Senecas had yet to receive any funds or relocation assistance even though the dam was nearing completion. D. C. Lindholm of the Bureau of the Budget determined that "there appears to have been little, if any, [Interior] departmental followup or guidance on what was required to comply with the Presidential directive." He concluded that "the initiative for bringing about a settlement seems to have been lost by Interior with the result that the final settlement will be more costly."[47]

The Seneca Nation and members of Congress sympathetic to their cause had taken the initiative in the form of legislation introduced in January 1963. Attorney Arthur Lazarus drafted a proposal introduced by James Haley as H.R. 1794 (not coincidentally the year the treaty was signed), a bill to "authorize . . . payment for a flowage easement and rights-of-way" on Seneca lands and "to provide for the relocation, rehabilitation, [and] social and economic development of the members of the Seneca Nation." Pennsylvania congressman John Saylor, the only Pennsylvania lawmaker who had opposed the dam's construction, introduced an identical bill, designated H.R. 3343.[48]

Generous in its all its measures, H.R. 1794 authorized payments for damages both to the tribe and to individuals who lost property. It protected the Senecas' claim to any mineral rights (except for sand and gravel) in the flowage easement and rights-of-way. It also required the secretary of the Army to "relocate and reestablish . . . such Indian cemeteries, tribal monuments, graves and shrines inside the taking area as the Seneca Nation . . . shall select and designate," a matter of great concern to the Senecas because several graves, including that of the revered Gaiantwaka, would soon be underwater. H.R. 1794 also authorized funds for a rehabilitation program including the development of commercial, recreational, and industrial projects, the acquisition of lieu lands, and the creation of a scholarship program. The bill did not detail any specific sums because the total cost of the proposed programs had yet to be assessed, but any monies the tribe received under the act were to be exempt from state and local taxes.[49]

At the first hearing on the bill, held on 18 May 1963 in Salamanca, New York, Haley made clear the cost of the Kinzua project to the Seneca Nation. He stated, "I wonder if it is really progress when I see homes, villages, cemeteries destroyed, families uprooted and forced to scatter, all ties disrupted and American citizens forced to be relocated." Referring to the 1794 treaty, Haley argued that "it was a horrible tragedy, a horribly tragic thing that our powerful Nation would break a solemn and binding obligation between two nations." Although he contended that "when it comes to spending tax money, I am considered to be to the right of [Barry] Goldwater," Haley announced that he intended to "press for liberal payments from the Federal Government" to the Seneca Nation and its members.[50]

Determined to assist the Senecas, Haley held hearings on the Kinzua Dam project throughout 1963. In a prepared statement presented at a hearing held on 12 August 1963, Philleo Nash outlined the BIA's position on the Haley bill. He favored most of its proposals but balked at the reservation development program. While he agreed with the goals of the program, he noted that it would be economically "marginal" unless Congress authorized a $29 million grant. Realizing that BIA support for an expenditure that large would antagonize terminationists, Nash cautiously stated that "only Congress itself can determine whether such a sum is a proper disbursement of public funds." Once again the persistence of termination sentiment within Congress, especially on the Senate Interior Committee, prevented Nash from offering his full support to a measure that would greatly benefit Native Americans.[51]

The House Subcommittee on Indian Affairs finished its work on the Seneca relocation legislation in early December. In his determination to "press for liberal payments," Haley had crafted legislation that authorized expenditures far beyond the minimums demanded in a typical compensation case. The final draft paid the Seneca Nation and individual tribal members over three million dollars in compensation for direct and indirect damages caused by the Kinzua Dam project. Section 4, which contained provisions for the rehabilitation program, authorized $16.9 million for "assistance designed to improve the economic, social, and educational conditions of enrolled members of the Seneca Nation." The total cost of H.R. 1794 came to $20.1 million. Despite the considerable expense, the House unanimously passed H.R. 1794 on 7 February 1964.[52]

The Haley bill's generous terms met with opposition from several sources, including the Bureau of the Budget (BOB) and the Senate Interior Committee. In response to a request from Henry Jackson, Phillip S. Hughes, BOB's assistant director for legislative reference, detailed his department's views on the bill. Hughes compared the proposed Seneca bill with a 1962 bill compensating the Creek and Lower Brule Sioux Indians for damages resulting from a flood control project in the Missouri River Basin. In that settlement, Congress had authorized compensation equal to a per capita distribution of $2,250 for the enrolled members of those tribes. Using that figure, Hughes noted that the Seneca compensation came to only $2.5 million if applied to the number of Senecas in the affected area, or $9.3 million if applied to all enrolled members of the Seneca Nation. He also argued that the proposed industrial development would have a negligible impact on Seneca employment. In conclusion, Hughes urged the Senate Interior Committee "to consider the limited economic effect of the project on the Senecas and the relationship of this settlement to previous ones" in determining compensation for the Senecas.[53]

The Hughes letter influenced the Senate Interior Committee's handling of the Seneca relocation legislation, which Sen. Jacob K. Javits (R.-N.Y.) sponsored in the Senate as S. 1836. On 2 March, the Senate Subcommittee on Indian Affairs held hearings on the legislation. In contrast to the House hearings, which were held intermittently throughout 1963, the Senate subcommittee completed its business in one day, in part because the pressing need for a settlement prevented a drawn-out inquiry, and because the civil rights bill then before the Senate dominated everyone's attention. However, the Seneca legislation was not ignored, and an impressive number of senators either appeared to testify or sent communications to the committee. Javits declared that "H.R. 1794 is acceptable to me and . . . to my cosponsors," and five other senators also urged the committee to report out the House version of the bill.[54]

However, not all the subcommittee's members supported the Haley bill. Chairman Frank Church and Peter Dominick (R-Co.) questioned both the need for and the expense of the rehabilitation program. Insisting that "I am not a bit sure I want to set up a fund this large," Dominick grilled Commissioner Nash on the reasons for establishing a rehabilitation program. Dominick claimed that the Senecas had been "emancipated" from federal supervision, and that Section 4 would "recreate a tribal situation tending to pull them back from this emancipated position." Following the line of argument presented by Phillip Hughes, Dominick asked Nash to compare the Seneca compensation package to that which the Creeks and Lower Brules had received two years earlier. Frank Church also drew comparisons to the 1962 settlement, and then argued that the rehabilitation program would only encourage other tribes "to point to this as a special precedent for extended and preferential treatment for themselves." Thus, both Dominick and Church ignored the implications of the treaty abrogation that had motivated James Haley and other House members. The senators sought a limited settlement in order to avoid setting any precedent for expanding government assistance to Indian communities, thus evincing the attitude toward Native American issues prevailing among key members of the Senate Interior Committee during the 1960s—that of providing minimal assistance with the goal of eventually terminating all federal services to the tribes.[55]

Church and Dominick won out over Javits, McGovern, and other senators who pressed for Senate passage of H.R. 1794. They reported out a bill that reduced compensation for indirect damages from $1,033,275 to $824,273, the sum recommended by the Army Corps of Engineers. Funding for the rehabilitation program was slashed from $16.9 million to $6.1 million. To arrive at that figure the committee had authorized $2,250 (the per capita amount of the Creek and Lower Brule settlement) for each Seneca tribal member who would be relocated, and $1,200 (the per capita amount in a 1957 settlement for the Standing Rock Sioux) for every other member of the Seneca Nation.[56]

More important, the Senate bill went far beyond merely reducing the expenditures in the Haley bill. The senators added a new provision, Section 18, which required the Seneca Nation to design a termination program within two years, and directed the interior secretary to submit legislation based on that program within ninety days of receiving it. The terminationists on the Senate Interior Committee had turned the House bill, which Haley had intended to be a partial remedy for the treaty abrogation, into a vehicle for the continuation of the termination policy.[57]

The Senate passed the Church version of the Seneca bill on 30 March 1964. Because the Kinzua Dam project was approaching completion and a relief bill was necessary, Javits and other Senate supporters of the Haley bill voted for the amended version but hoped that a conference committee would increase the appropriations. As expected, the House rejected the Senate version and named a conference committee consisting of Representatives Aspinall, Haley, John Saylor, Ed Edmondson (D.-Okla.), and Charlotte T. Reid (R.-Ill.). The Senate appointed Church, Dominick, McGovern, Clinton Anderson, and Milward L. Simpson (R.-Wyo.) to serve on the conference committee. The committee thus contained terminationists such as Dominick, Church, and Anderson; the liberal George McGovern; and congressmen including Haley, Saylor, and Aspinall, who could not be considered liberal but who advocated a generous settlement for the Senecas, all in all a combination of viewpoints offering little hope of a compromise.[58]

The conflict over the Seneca relocation bill caused consternation in the Interior Department, which regarded "the House bill as reflecting legislative approval of the results achieved in pursuance of President Kennedy's instructions." In a memorandum to Lee White, John Carver noted that the "Senate's unwillingness to join with the House . . . faces us with a number of unpleasant possibilities." Carver outlined three specific problems. Referring to the upcoming presidential election, he noted that it was "a particularly unfortunate year for this symbolically important Administration measure to be left unfinished." Second, the delay in passing any legislation meant that Seneca families might have to leave their homes without any federal assistance in relocating. Finally, Carver stated that "termination without consent of the Indians is strongly opposed by the tribes and the Indian organizations," and passage of Section 18 would "be handing our opponents an effective moral issue." Carver concluded that "in addition to Chairman Church and Chairman Haley, it may be considered desirable to discuss the matter with Senator Anderson," an observation that again revealed Anderson's continued importance in Indian affairs even though he no longer chaired the Senate Interior Committee.[59]

Lee White agreed that Anderson "is the key to this." He perceived the impasse over the Seneca bill as "a very difficult and sticky moral issue which we should do our best to terminate," and noted that failure to resolve the disagreement between the House and Senate would leave the White House "with the difficult question of whether to close the dam gates before the Senecas are adequately relocated," which he called "an alternative that gives me the shakes."[60]

White's concerns were not unfounded. On 15 July 1964, Philleo Nash notified him that "some 31 Seneca families living on the lowest ground in the area to be flooded will be in some danger of rising water this fall." Nash feared that the "work still to be done by the Conference Committee will go past the point where a serious problem is presented." The delay in arriving at a compromise would constitute a significant failure for the administration and, given the press coverage the Kinzua project had received over the years, a public relations disaster.[61]

White informed Major General Jackson Graham, Director of Civil Works of the Army Corps of Engineers, that "any decisions on the closing date [of the dam] be checked very carefully" with the White House. Graham, with the lack of sympathy and understanding that marked Corps attitudes towards the Seneca's problem, replied that though the Indians' "inclination to await further gratuitous legislative assistance is understandable, their problems could be resolved . . . by prompt and decisive action, which only they can take." Graham maintained that the Seneca Nation had adequate resources to care for the dislocated families, although he added in a handwritten note that "we are sensitive to the over-all situation."[62]

The conference committee reached a compromise after five meetings. Released on 17 August 1964, its final report set indirect damages at $945,573 and appropriated $12,128,917 for the rehabilitation program. The House conferees were able to increase the sums set for the Seneca relocation program, but their success came at a price. The final bill contained a provision that forbade the interior secretary from expanding services to the tribe and required the secretary to submit termination legislation for the Seneca Nation within three years. Lee White had believed that "the termination provision . . . was included for bargaining purposes," but in fact the Senate terminationists considered that section an essential part of the legislation and had refused to abandon it. The Seneca Nation's supporters had been able only to delay the termination plan for one additional year. The Senate passed the compromise Seneca bill on 17 August, and the House approved the legislation the following day. President Johnson signed the measure into law on 31 August 1964.[63]

Preparations for the disbursement of funds began before the president signed the bill. On August 25 Acting Commissioner of Indian Affairs John Crow informed Lee White that "everything is being done without delay so that it may be possible to provide funds to the tribe and the members in danger of being relocated." Two months later Major General Jackson Graham noted that houses for four of the relocated families "are nearing completion" and twelve houses "are in various stages of construction." Jackson claimed that "there is no real possibility that progress on the dam . . . would subject the twenty-two Seneca families [still living in the reservoir area] to flooding" before the relocation could be completed. Graham Holmes of the BIA agreed, stating in a 29 October memo that "it appears beyond any reasonable doubt that the Indians will be relocated before the land is flooded." As far as the federal government was concerned, the Kinzua Dam controversy had ended.[64]

The settlement constituted both a loss and a victory for the Seneca Nation. No sum of money, no matter how large, could compensate for the loss of tribal homelands, and the Senecas struggled for decades with the consequences of relocation. Adding insult to injury, Congress had required the Seneca Nation to prepare a plan for the termination of its relationship with the federal government. However, the rehabilitation program offered the Seneca community substantial financial assistance in rebuilding their communities, credit for which belonged to the tenacious James Haley, who was determined to right the wrong of the treaty violation. During his testimony before the Senate Interior Subcommittee, Philleo Nash confessed that "Chairman Haley exhorted me in very definite and commanding terms . . . to insist on the Indian right in future matters of this kind." The House Interior Committee's report on the original Haley bill concluded with a statement recognizing "the patience and understanding shown by representative James A. Haley . . . in pursuing the cause of justice for the Seneca Indians" and "his undeviating perseverance in achieving a fair settlement." During debate on the bill, John Saylor noted that Haley had made Seneca relocation a "personal crusade," and Wayne Aspinall responded that Haley and Saylor both deserved "commendation" for their commitment to the Seneca's cause. Most important, the Seneca Nation recognized Haley's efforts, later naming a community center after him.[65]

Although Haley played the critical role, two other factors assisted the Senecas in their struggle. First, the press had paid careful attention to the matter. Philleo Nash claimed that the Senecas' cause was "extraordinary in the degree of public interest that is involved." No one in the federal government relished the negative publicity that would ensue if the Senecas were forced to relocate before the passage of favorable legislation. Second, the recently slain President Kennedy had promised the Senecas "our cooperation," and that promise carried great weight with several officials in the government. In his appeal for Senate passage of the Haley bill, Jacob Javits reminded the Senate subcommittee of "the words of our beloved and unhappily deceased President in respect to this matter." Commissioner Nash stated that the BIA sought to bring about "the consequences desired by the President in his letter to Basil Williams" because "to do less than that would not be to honor the directive in the President's letter." American Indians had seen the federal government break many promises over the years, but in this instance Kennedy's statement served to ensure that the Senecas had support within the government.[66]

THE PERSISTENCE OF TERMINATION

The battle over the Seneca relocation bill revealed the larger tensions within Congress over the direction of federal Indian policy. Party lines were largely irrelevant. Frank Church and Clinton Anderson, both Democrats, allied with a Republican, Peter Dominick, to oppose a generous settlement, and in so doing gained the support of Joseph S. Clark, a Pennsylvania Democrat. Seneca supporters included Democrats James Haley and George McGovern and Republicans such as Jacob Javits and John Saylor. Nor did ideology play a major role. Seneca backers George S. McGovern and James Haley were at opposite ends of the political spectrum—the South Dakota senator was a leading liberal, while the Florida congressman exemplified the tradition of southern conservatism.

Rather than a partisan or ideological conflict, the disagreements over federal Indian policy were regional and institutional. During the dispute between the House and Senate over the terms of the Seneca bill, Charles Goodell (R.-N.Y.) complained that "the Senate having knocked the insides right out of the House bill, there is probably a minimum of justice for them [the Senecas]," and asked Richard Schifter if he had "any influence over some of these western Senators." Goodell was correct in recognizing the role of the western senators in the Seneca controversy and in Indian affairs in general. It was this small but powerful group of men who dominated the Senate Interior Committee, which continued to press for a termination policy, even as support for that policy waned in the Congress as a whole during the late 1950s and early 1960s.[67]

Three Senate Interior Committee members, all westerners and all members of the majority party, vigorously supported termination: Frank Church, Clinton Anderson, and Henry Jackson. John Carver recalled that "Church was the one that was most outraged about it [the Haley bill]." During the Senate debate, Joseph Clark, who had originally supported passage of the Haley bill, credited Frank Church with convincing him that the "amount requested [in the House version] was substantially in excess of what could be logically justified, or even justified on compassionate grounds." However, Church's role in Indian affairs would diminish greatly after 1964. Frustrated by his inability to achieve notable results, especially in the area of heirship legislation, he resigned his position as chair of the Indian Affairs Subcommittee at the end of that year.[68]

Church's departure from the subcommittee made little difference because many of his colleagues remained staunch proponents of termination. Clinton Anderson, who was in John Carver's words, "critically important to the Department's [Indian] program," had not abandoned termination as the goal of federal Indian policy. Although he was no longer the committee chairman, Anderson nonetheless wielded power behind the scenes, as Lee White's assumption that Anderson was behind the Seneca termination provision indicated. Interior Committee chair Henry Jackson played no direct role in the Seneca legislation, but he was in accord with Church's and Anderson's views on Indian policy. Jackson became the most prominent terminationist for the remainder of the decade, and he played a leading role in the drive to terminate two tribes in his home state of Washington.[69]

THE COLVILLE RESERVATION JUDGMENT MONIES

Jackson's involvement with the ultimately unsuccessful move to terminate the Colville Reservation lasted almost the entire decade of the 1960s. The Confederated Tribes of the Colville Reservation included members from several Native American communities, including the Colvilles, Nepselems, and others, all of whom shared a reservation in northeastern Washington established by executive order in 1872. The diversity of the population contributed to an intensely factional environment within the community, a situation further complicated by the fact that in 1960 less than half of the community's members lived on the reservation. Tribal trust lands encompassed over one million acres, nearly three-fourths of which were covered by timberlands with considerable commercial value. The lack of tribal unity, the dispersion of Colville members throughout the United States (at least one member lived in Guam), the possibility of substantial personal gain following the liquidation of tribal assets, and a weariness with BIA paternalism combined to create a powerful force for termination within the tribe during the late 1950s and 1960s.[70]

In addition to its significant land and timber holdings, the Colville Tribe also had nearly one million dollars in an account with the federal government, the result of a judgment issued by the Indian Claims Commission in 1960. The disbursement of these funds became entangled in the termination movement and led to an ugly conflict between Jackson and Commissioner Nash. In the 1961 Senate Interior Committee report that accompanied the judgment monies appropriation legislation, Henry Jackson declared, "[I]t is the committee's recommendation that . . . the Secretary of the Interior take steps to provide for a per capita payment to the Indians from the funds covered by the legislation." In keeping with the goal of economic and industrial development of the reservations, both Udall and Nash opposed any per capita distributions, and the Interior Department ignored Jackson's recommendation. Philleo Nash later recalled that "I simply adopted the view that I would do what I was required to do by law . . . and follow the policies of the Secretary and the President and the Executive Branch generally," a decision that infuriated the Washington senator and turned him against Nash.[71]

In 1956 the U.S. Congress passed a law returning unceded lands to the Colville reservation that also required the tribe to submit termination legislation within five years. The Interior Department objected to Colville termination legislation introduced in 1962 on the grounds that the bill was poorly written and at points self-contradictory. Philleo Nash noted that the bill "in effect liquidates the principal tribal assets . . . yet it does not in effect terminate the entire Federal trust," thus continuing "all the problems of trusteeship without the economic footing . . . to manage these residual trust activities." The following year

Senator Jackson introduced two bills regarding the Colville reservation. The first, S. 1442, closed the tribal rolls "preparatory to the submission of proposed legislation for the termination of federal supervision" of the reservation. The second, S. 1169, provided for a per capita distribution of $350 from the judgment monies, which at that time stood at over $1.5 million because of interest.[72]

The Interior Department recommended the enactment of S. 1442 with some amendments, but remained opposed to the distribution of judgment funds. At hearings on the Jackson bills held in Washington state in October 1963, the tribe was divided over the issue of termination but strongly supported the per capita payment. The support for a distribution of funds from both the Senate Interior Committee and the Colvilles led Nash to compromise, and the BIA announced a per capita distribution of $150 on 13 November 1963. However, the compromise was not enough, and one week later Graham Holmes had to defend the bureau's smaller sum in hearings before Frank Church and the Indian Affairs Subcommittee.[73]

Holmes maintained that distributing $350 to each tribal member would deplete the judgment monies, funds that he argued the tribe should use "in planning for their future development, and possibly for their future termination." He believed that the desire for a distribution of tribal assets was a case of "killing the goose that laid the golden egg." Church disagreed, claiming that the tribe wanted to "expedite the termination procedure, and not to hold money for investment on a reservation that is destined to be terminated anyhow." Jackson eventually won out—in August 1964 Congress passed S. 1169 authorizing a $350 per capita distribution—but Nash maintained that Jackson blamed him personally for forcing "the Chairman of the Senate Committee and future candidate for President of the United States to do what he didn't want to do and that was pass a law—instead of running the Executive Branch from his committee."[74]

The animosity Jackson held toward Nash was apparent at Colville termination hearings held in April 1965. Jackson first attacked the BIA, complaining that a bureau report was "inconsistent," and arguing that "when a termination bill comes up, or when we obtain a judgment that we must distribute to the Indians . . . suddenly the Bureau gets very concerned about the welfare of the Indians." Jackson then focused his ire on Nash, referring to some of Nash's public remarks regarding Colville termination as "really most unfortunate," and accusing the commissioner of painting the Interior Committee as irresponsible for pursuing the termination of the Colville reservation. The dispute over the per capita distributions had poisoned relations between the two men, and Nash later recalled that Jackson "never forgave me." Nash avoided future conflicts with the Interior Committee chairman, as his limited role in the Kalispel termination battle evidenced.[75]

TERMINATING THE KALISPELS

The Kalispels (also known as the Lower Pend d'Oreilles) lived on a small reservation in Washington. They had adopted a constitution and incorporated under the terms of the Indian Reorganization Act in 1938, but received few benefits and little assistance from the Bureau of Indian Affairs. The Kalispels were poor—a 1952 BIA survey noted that only five out of eighteen Kalispel families did not require welfare assistance, and a 1960 study reported that they had the lowest wage income of any tribe in Washington. Beset by poverty, the tribe's hopes for the future rested on a petition filed with the Indian Claims Commission in 1951 for compensation for lost tribal lands. The legal proceedings dragged on for over a decade, but in March 1963 the Indian Claims Commission finally awarded the Kalispels $3 million minus attorney's fees, a sum the tribe's attorney believed was "the largest judgment on a per capita basis of any tribe in the United States." Two months later Congress passed the legislation needed to appropriate the funds. However, elation turned to dismay when the Kalispels learned they were required to submit a plan for disposition of the funds that would also require legislative approval before they could receive any of the judgment monies.[76]

The Kalispels submitted a plan that included a scholarship program, construction of a community center, and a payment of $7,000 to each Kalispel family for home purchases or improvements. Because the tribe believed that the proposal "was completely uncontroversial and would slide through in good fashion," no tribal representatives appeared before the Senate subcommittee, which held a hearing on the Kalispel legislation on 27 May 1964. However, the hearing degenerated into a heated debate between Senator Church, who expressed anger over the BIA's failure to pursue termination, and BIA representative Graham Holmes, who attempted to explain to the subcommittee chairman the reasons the bureau opposed terminating the Kalispels. As a result, the "uncontroversial" hearings resulted in a deadlock, and the Kalispels faced not only another delay in receiving their judgment money but also the possibility of termination.[77]

Church dominated the hearing. Pointing out that the judgment equaled a $77,000 per capita distribution, he proclaimed that "if we can't take an opportunity of this kind, it is so much money for so few, to launch these people, to emancipation from the wardship . . . then there will never be a time that we can do it." Church wanted to designate a private trustee to oversee the operation of the tribe's plan so that federal services could be withdrawn from the Kalispels. Holmes defended the Kalispel's proposal, but Church argued that it "leaves the land in government control, still leaves its disposition subject to the direction of the Indian Bureau, still leaves the wardship intact, still makes these people dependent upon unending government jurisdiction and government control." He insisted that the omission of "any provision of final termination of government jurisdiction and direction of the land and property of these Indian people seems to me to be inexcusable." When Holmes reminded the senator that termination had become "a bad word," Church agreed but retorted that "there are several reasons why this happened, not the least of which is the attitude of the Indian Bureau itself."[78]

Holmes explained that in the case of the Kalispels a termination provision might lead the tribe to "listen to the people trying to persuade them to demand a full per capita payment at one time." Merchants who would benefit from the infusion of cash into the depressed local economy hoped for just such a distribution, and the BIA feared that the relatively unsophisticated Kalispels would be cheated and duped. More important, economic development would stall if the funds were distributed to individuals, who would be inclined to spend the money, instead of the tribe, which would concentrate on investment, educational programs, and health and housing issues. The 1961 task force had regarded Indian claims as a "potential source of capital for resource development," and had declared that "every effort should be made to see that this [judgment] money is not dissipated on a per capita basis to tribal members." However, Church dismissed Holmes's concerns and recommended that the BIA reconsider its support of the Kalispel program.[79]

Two months after the hearing Henry Jackson sent Robert Dellwo, the tribe's attorney, a transcript, and the Kalispels learned that once again the government had delayed release of the judgment funds. Dellwo told Jackson that he "saw two Indian mothers weep" when they heard the news, and then he complained that the Kalispels "faced . . . what appears to be an ultimatum from the Chairman of the Sub-Committee on Indian Affairs that this tribe can't get a dime of its judgment monies until it agrees to some plan of termination." However, the Kalispels had not given up. They sent telegrams to Church and Jackson urging them to pass the Kalispel legislation in its original form. They received assistance from the tribal council of the Coeur d'Alenes, a neighboring tribe, which passed a resolution calling for passage of the bill. They also received support from the House of Representatives. On 16 June the House Interior Committee approved the Kalispel plan and reported out the bill without amendment. The House passed the legislation on 21 July.[80]

The week after the House vote Jackson responded to the tribe's request and reported out legislation that did not require a termination plan, which the Senate passed and the president signed into law on 10 August. However, the Kalispels had to endure further delay before receiving any funds. Despite legislative approval of the Kalispel program, Jackson had not abandoned the goal of terminating the tribe. He included remarks in the committee report declaring that "it is the sense of this committee . . . that the Kalispel Tribe should be moved toward termination." The committee directed the BIA "to furnish a report . . . on the practicality of placing the administration of this [disposition] program in the hands of a private trustee," and "to recommend at the earliest possible time legislation to accomplish" the termination of the Kalispel Tribe. Through the reference to a private trustee the Senate Interior Committee indicated that the BIA should not release any funds until it devised a Kalispel termination plan.[81]

Jackson was not merely interested in the terminating the Kalispels—he wanted termination recognized as the goal of federal Indian policy, and like Frank Church he blamed the BIA for ignoring the will of Congress. The report stated that the Interior Committee was "deeply concerned about the failure of the Bureau of Indian Affairs to carry out the intent of House Concurrent Resolution 108, 83rd Congress, relating to termination programs for tribes," and promised that "the committee plans to hold hearings on this subject, and the manner in which the Bureau has performed its responsibilities pursuant to the 1953 concurrent resolution." Through the comments in the Kalispel report, Jackson and Church sent a clear message to the BIA to proceed with termination of the Kalispels and other Indian tribes, or face an unpleasant investigation from the Senate Interior Committee.[82]

Jackson and Church placed Interior Department officials in an awkward position, as the Kalispels had voted unanimously against termination and the department had stated publicly that termination would not proceed without tribal consent. The BIA did not release the funds, but it did not draft termination legislation either. The tribe continued to lobby for the release of funds and in December Dellwo and the tribal chairman met with Frank Church. In his final month as a member of the Indian Affairs Subcommittee and weary of Indian affairs, Church agreed to an immediate per capita distribution of $400 from interest earned on the claim settlement. However, Jackson remained adamant, and the judgment monies remained in an account through the summer of 1965 as the BIA, the Interior Committee, and the Kalispels wrangled over a solution to the deadlock.[83]

Frustrated at Jackson's intransigence, Dellwo requested assistance from John Carver in May 1965. Carver assigned Richmond F. Allan, an attorney in the Interior Department's Office of the Solicitor, to look into the matter. In the meantime the tribe's supporters organized a publicity campaign to halt the termination movement. In response, Jackson agreed to release approximately half the judgment monies for housing and sanitation programs operated under BIA supervision, but insisted that a private trust administer the remaining $1.37 million. Jackson's offer placed the Kalispels in a difficult position. They badly needed the money for housing, but they realized that accepting a private trust constituted the first step toward termination.[84]

Hoping to secure support from the BIA to continue the fight against termination, Dellwo appealed to Nash for help. Unwilling to antagonize Jackson and the other members of the Interior Committee, Nash offered Dellwo little comfort, informing him that "unless the Tribe expressed an unconditional acceptance" of Jackson's offer, the BIA would refuse to administer any part of the program. In early October the Kalispels reluctantly agreed to the Jackson plan. Less than two weeks later, however, the Kalispels received good news. On 12 October Interior Department attorney Richmond Allan informed Robert Dellwo that he had ordered the BIA to release all the Kalispel judgment funds. Allan noted that the committee's report had no force of law, and he correctly surmised that Jackson did not want to suffer from any negative publicity. The Kalispels received $2.7 million in October 1965, fourteen years after they first filed their suit and over a year after Congress had approved the legislation authorizing the disposition of the funds.[85]

Frank Church had deemed the omission of a termination provision "inexcusable," but the real tragedy in this instance was the Interior Committee's willingness to block judgment funds to a tribe in desperate need. A county health officer had described Kalispel housing as "deplorable—beyond description." Less than half the houses had running water, and none had indoor toilets. Given the substandard living conditions and shocking poverty of the Kalispels, the committee's decision to play politics with the judgment monies evidenced a mindless determination to advance termination at any cost. Although Nash had offered no leadership, the Department of Interior had shown considerable resolve in confronting the Senate Interior Committee on the Kalispel legislation. Rather than bow to the demands of two very influential senators, both Graham Holmes and Richmond Allan acted in the interests of the Kalispels.[86]

The resolution of the Kalispel claim only exacerbated tensions between the Senate Interior Committee and the Bureau of Indian Affairs. Though the committee and the Interior Department held different philosophies regarding Indian policy, the senators regarded Commissioner Nash as the culprit, and were determined to see him removed from office.

THE BVD FACTORY

It was yet another incident involving the Navajo reservation that led to the final break between Udall and Nash and to Nash's resignation from the office of commissioner in March 1966. In 1965 Udall pushed for the opening of a BVD apparel factory in Winslow, Arizona, outside the Navajo reservation. Peter MacDonald believed that Udall had taken a special interest in this particular development project, because "it was unusual for the secretary of the interior to handle such a task [of negotiating directly with industry leaders]." MacDonald cited Udall's actions as another example of paternalism, claiming that "the Navajos were told nothing about it [the BVD project] until after Udall assured BVD that the Indians were giving it full support."[87]

Despite Udall's personal involvement, the project met with opposition from two sources. The firm expected the Navajos to sponsor the construction of the factory, but the Navajo Tribal Council rejected the project because the proposed plant was not located on the reservation. MacDonald recalled that Udall "was livid with us." He remembered Udall telling Chairman Nakai that he had "worked . . . very hard, very long, and got them [BVD] to agree to come to Winslow so they could employ your people," and that the tribal council's vote "made a liar out me."[88]

Udall was also angry with Philleo Nash, another opponent of the BVD project. Nash had met with members of the Amalgamated Clothing Workers Union and the International Ladies Garment Workers Union who argued that BVD sought to "run away" to Arizona so that it could circumvent the unions—the construction of the plant in Arizona would mean a loss of union jobs in New York. A union representative later maintained that "there was every indication that these runaway shops would exploit the Indians." Interior Department officials were familiar with this problem—John Carver recalled that "you'd get these runaway industries who were interested really in just taking those grant funds for the training," and in "get[ting] away from the labor problems that they might have where they were." In fact, garment industries had a bad reputation among many Native Americans for offering low wages and poor working conditions.[89]

In addition to pointing out problems the BVD plant would pose for both union workers and Indians, the union representatives threatened Nash, claiming that if "you go through with this, we'll fight you and we haven't lost one yet." Nash took the union objections and threats seriously. He feared that if he spent funds from the BIA's Adult Vocational Training Program to train workers for the BVD project, pro-union members of Congress might retaliate and reduce funding for vocational training programs in the future. Faced with union opposition and possible congressional backlash, Nash informed John Carver that he would not approve the training contract with BVD. Upon hearing the news, Udall reportedly "blew up" and accused the commissioner of "letting the unions run my [Nash's] business and his business." He was also angry that Nash had told Carver and not him personally. Nash's recollection that "I didn't feel that I could talk to him about it" reflected the low level to which the relationship between the two men had sunk. Nash remembered this dispute as the "straw that broke the camel's back" and prompted Udall to actively seek Nash's resignation from the office of Indian commissioner.[90]

THE NASH RESIGNATION

On 2 September, Lee White and John Macy, the president's adviser on appointments, informed President Johnson about the worsening relationship between Nash and Udall. Macy and White reported that "there is not a close working relationship between these two men despite their four years [of] association." They pointed to Udall's desire "to establish himself as the important personality in Indian affairs," and "to strengthen and improve the Indian programs" as "basic elements of difficulty" between the secretary and his commissioner. They agreed with Udall's contention that "Nash's relationships with Anderson, Jackson and Aspinall are very bad and that a change of Commissioners would improve the situation tremendously."[91]

The president's advisers also noted that "Nash likes his job and is unwilling to walk away from it." Nash argued that he had "superb relations with many other Senators and Congressmen," and blamed his poor relations with the members on the House and Senate Interior Committees on differences over the conduct of Indian policy, with Nash promoting "a strong Indian program," and the members of Congress desiring "a program as small as possible." Macy and White recognized that the Nash-Udall split could cause political problems, with "considerable displeasure on the part of the Indian tribes," and "severe criticism from some Congressional quarters" if Nash were forced to resign as commissioner. Despite "the very understandable desire of the Secretary to have as Bureau heads individuals with whom he can work and in whom he has confidence," Macy and Lee argued that the administration "cannot afford such an explosion [between the two men] at this time," and urged Johnson to "tell Udall . . . that he ought to make every effort to work with Nash or at least give it a six-month trial."[92]

Udall proved unwilling to wait six months. In October he transferred Robert Bennett, his choice to succeed Nash, from Alaska to Washington to serve as acting deputy commissioner, a move that clearly signaled to BIA employees that Nash's departure was imminent. In a November memorandum to the president, he "strongly recommend[ed]" that Johnson approve the transfer of Nash from the BIA to the governorship of Samoa. Udall complained that Nash "has been a disappointment," whose "congressional relations have been the worst in my whole department." For his part, Nash still hoped that he would survive Udall's attack. In a 10 December letter to a supporter, he claimed that "White House staff, lesser officials in the Department, and various friends in Government, including the Vice-President, have urged me to stand firm."[93]

However, Udall's determination to replace Nash had undermined support for the commissioner. Less than a week after Nash wrote his letter, John Macy composed a draft memorandum to Johnson concluding that efforts "to bring about a compatible arrangement" between Udall and Nash "have been in vain," and recommended that Nash be appointed as high commissioner of the Trust Territory of the Pacific. The day before Christmas, Hubert Humphrey told Nash that "it is my considered judgment that because of the situation in Interior, you ought to make a move." Although he still had powerful supporters, including Sen. Joseph Montoya of New Mexico, Nash realized that he had little choice but to resign. Soon after the New Year he informed a friend that "I fought this battle in-house and appear to have lost."[94]

Nonetheless, Nash met with the secretary and demanded to know Udall's reasons for requesting his resignation. After Udall offered "his list of complaints," Nash reminded him that "you ought to recognize that the Indians in this Country feel that this is the best administration they've ever had," and declared that he had "less enemies among the Indians than John Collier had." Unmoved, Udall sent Nash to discuss the matter with Lee White, who conferred with President Johnson. White informed Nash that Johnson (who never fired an employee during his administration) refused to become involved in the conflict. Nash had lost all support, and after "lengthy negotiations" with White and John Macy, he rejected a transfer within the Interior Department but agreed to resign as commissioner of Indian affairs effective 15 March 1966. As a presidential appointee, Nash submitted his resignation to Johnson, who "signed it and returned it within 45 minutes," which he later remembered with some bitterness as the "fastest Presidential action I've ever seen!"[95]

ASSESSING COMMISSIONER NASH

In a 1969 oral history interview, John Carver called Nash "a great commissioner," but then added, "I guess he couldn't be a great commissioner, paradoxical as that might seem." Three weaknesses marked (and marred) Nash's tenure as commissioner. First, his nonconfrontational administrative style pleased American Indians and many BIA employees, but it prevented him from making the hard choices often necessary in a leadership position. Nash lacked the single-mindedness and toughness necessary to reorganize the bureau so that it efficiently met the needs and demands of Native Americans. He should have "cleaned house" in the education division, replacing the old-line employees committed to assimilation with a dynamic and progressive administration seeking to meet the educational needs of Native American children. Instead, he did nothing, a decision that rendered the education program, which by all accounts was central to the future of Indian communities, irrelevant and useless to many Indians.[96]

Nash's second weakness stemmed from his differences with Udall. As Carver noted, Nash "didn't have that good a relationship with the Secretary, and you have to really eventually if you're going to succeed as commissioner." Without Udall's support and confidence, Nash could not hope to succeed. Rather than appease Udall, Nash instead made their disagreements public, a serious breach of protocol that could only have negative consequences. At the same time he avoided Udall, working instead with John Carver. Nash admitted that he "relied very heavily on John Carver . . . for advice, for support, for consultation," and Carver recalled that "Philleo and I worked [together] so well that it was just bound to be that the Secretary would sometimes feel left out of it." Udall remembered that Nash had the "idea that he didn't want to disturb the secretary. And I wanted to be distrubed [*sic*], and I was damn mad about it in the end." And in the end, Udall insisted that Nash resign.[97]

Nash's third weakness, and perhaps the most important, was his poor relationship with Congress, which was the main source of Udall's unhappiness with his commissioner and the primary reason for Nash's departure from the BIA. In 1969, Udall stated that "the thing that made him [Nash] a weak commissioner was that he completely lost contact with the important Congressmen, Senators on the Hill." Noting that "[in] making dramatic or rapid progress with Indian affairs the obstacle has always been the Congress," Udall complained that Nash "concentrated on wooing the Indians so much that he neglected ever to establish very good relations" with Congress, which "increasingly meant that legislation that we proposed would move at a sluggish pace." Udall's frustrations were understandable. Congress played the central role in the conduct of federal Indian policy, and Nash's inability to work with the Congress, especially the Senate Interior Committee, limited his effectiveness as commissioner.[98]

Nash's failure to mollify men such as Clinton Anderson and Henry Jackson stemmed from a fundamental misunderstanding of the ways in which Congress worked, from Nash's personal dislike of confrontation, and from policy differences between the executive branch and the legislative branch. John Carver maintained that "some people just don't understand the Congress" and argued that Nash erred in not having a staff member to "respond to the Indian problems of the members in their districts fast enough so that they never had to face head-on . . . the situation of fighting with the Indians." Had Nash pleased congressmen such as Wayne Aspinall, who were not firmly committed to termination, he might have developed better relations and stronger support on Capitol Hill that would have benefited Native Americans and his career as commissioner.[99]

For Philleo Nash, Congress represented a confrontational and hostile environment from his earliest days in the Kennedy administration. He never regained his balance after his confirmation hearings, which he remembered as a "battle" and a "humbling experience." Rather than working to improve his image he chose to avoid Congress, admitting that he "kept out of the individual senators and congressmen's hair." Udall claimed that "he [Nash] was almost persona non grata to those people [in Congress]." As was the case with Udall, Nash's contacts with Congress were thus limited to conflicts and disagreements, without any positive exchanges of the sort John Carver later discussed. Had Nash overcome his reluctance to work closely with Congress, he might have mitigated the bad feelings that existed between him and men such as Anderson and Jackson.[100]

Nash contended that the real source of congressional dissatisfaction with his performance issued from differences over Indian policy, specifically the continuation of termination. Arguing that "the commissioner is the one that congressional committees go after," Nash saw his defense of Interior Department policies, especially the slow pace of termination planning, as the ultimate cause of his departure from the BIA. He maintained that the "Chairmen of . . . [the] two [Interior] Committees," were responsible for Udall's decision to remove him from office. He claimed that Henry Jackson "demanded my resignation and at one point, I'm pretty sure somebody was saying that there would be no more National Parks built—no more Wild life refugees [sic]—until Udall got Nash;" and in 1986 he wrote that "I was asked to leave the BIA because my presence had become an embarassment [sic] . . . with those parts of the [Interior] Department that depend on Congress for appropriations" in areas other than Indian affairs.[101]

Nash also recognized the regional makeup of the Interior Committee's membership played a role in the its actions. He claimed that in Indian affairs "you immediately find you have to get into a fight with the ranchers or the miners—in other words, your western [sic], the settlers are looking for cheap land, cheap water, cheap timber, cheap grass, cheap minerals, and . . . they're not in favor of a strong pro-Indian program." In October 1966, just seven months after leaving office, he blamed the "rancher, the cowboy and his friends in Congress" for his departure from the BIA.[102]

Nash was correct in asserting that congressional opposition to BIA programs and procedures earned him the ill will of western senators such as Anderson and Jackson; however, he overstated his own public opposition to termination during the early 1960s. "I went up the political ladder fighting Termination and I went out the same way," he wrote in 1986, but he was never so forthright while in office. Although Nash did not actively support termination, and later vigorously denounced it, he muted his opposition while in office. During his years as commissioner he offered no serious opposition to Jackson's Colville termination legislation and provided no assistance to the Kalispels during that tribe's fight against termination in 1964 and 1965. Given the attitude of the Senate Interior Committee his reticence concerning termination was politically astute; however, in his final months as commissioner, when it became clear that he had alienated Congress and Udall and that his time in office was limited, Nash might have more ardently opposed the Colville bill, defended the Kalispels, and made public statements to bolster the confidence of Native Americans who actively opposed termination.[103]

Nash had his weaknesses, but he also had strengths, leading Vine Deloria, Jr., to conclude in 1995 that Nash was "the last person to hold the commissioner of Indian affairs position . . . who had any understanding of the job." When compared to Dillon S. Myer and Glenn Emmons, his immediate predecessors in the office of Indian commissioner, he fares well. Myer and Emmons carried out the termination policy with enthusiasm and without regard for its effects on Native Americans and their communities. Nash reached out to Native Americans in a sympathetic and friendly manner long absent from the conduct of federal Indian policy. Mike Mansfield declared that Nash "should be commended for his effort in restoring Indian confidence in the Federal Government. He excelled in his personal relationship with

Indians." The NCAI *Sentinel* called Nash "one of the two outstanding commissioners in American history," and praised the "unspectacular but steady progress" Indians realized during his tenure in office.[104]

Nash believed his primary responsibility as commissioner was the restoration of "confidence on the part of the Indians in the integrity on the part of the U.S. GOVERNMENT [*sic*] in their dealings with them and I was successful in that." Indeed he was. Although the economic and human resource development programs had met with only limited success by the mid-1960s, the gains that had been made must be in part credited to Nash's leadership. In 1961, when Nash took office, many Native Americans suspected that every federal program was instituted with the goal of termination in mind. Nash's reassurances to the contrary created an environment of cooperation and persuaded many Native American communities to avail themselves of new federal programs. Thus, Nash's achievements as commissioner resulted from his ability to work closely with Native Americans.[105]

However, the BIA offered little assistance or guidance to American Indians during the final years of the Nash administration. The BIA appeared unwilling or unable to stop the Senate Interior Committee in its vigorous pursuit of tribal termination, and with Nash's resignation, many Native Americans feared that they had lost their strongest if not their only advocate within the federal government. Divisions within the Native American community also contributed to a growing sense of crisis in Indian affairs, as some communities such as the Confederated Tribes of the Colville Reservation experienced wrenching internal divisions over the possibility of tribal termination. However, Indians did not respond passively to the renewed attacks on their tribal sovereignty and their continued existence as a separate group within American society. The fight against the Church heirship bill and the success of the American Indian Capitol Conference had revealed the impact of organized political activity and the influence Native Americans could exert over the policy process, and in the years following Nash's departure Native Americans would strive to end paternalism while maintaining their special relationship with the federal government.

CHAPTER FIVE

THE INDIAN RESOURCES DEVELOPMENT ACT

Secretary Udall used Philleo Nash's departure as an opportunity to reinvigorate his department's handling of Indian affairs. Although he replaced Nash with a shrewd and capable commissioner, Udall personally took charge of Indian policy issues after he made the dramatic move of proposing what he called "landmark" legislation in early 1966. For the next two years the secretary struggled to build support for his legislative proposal, but he discovered that Native Americans were unwilling to support legislation in which they had no hand in creating. He also found that Congress, which for the most part turned away from the termination policy, nonetheless retained specific ideas concerning the conduct of Indian policy. For American Indians, the years 1966 and 1967 marked a transition from quiet political activity to a more aggressive and confrontational politics that included the public rejection of administration policies and increased demands for Indian participation in the policy process.

COMMISSIONER BENNETT

In keeping with his desire to set a new direction in Indian affairs, Udall sought "imaginative new leadership for our Indian programs." He chose Robert LaFollette Bennett, a member of the Oneida Tribe and a career BIA official, to replace Nash as commissioner. Born on 16 November 1912 on the Oneida reservation in Wisconsin, Bennett "knew the pangs of living in two worlds." His mother was a full-blooded Oneida, while his father was Pennsylvania Dutch. Bennett never learned the Oneida language. He graduated from the Haskell Institute in Lawrence, Kansas, with a business degree in 1931. He joined the BIA in 1933, working on the Ute reservation in Utah until 1938, when he transferred to the BIA's central offices in Washington, D.C. While there he earned a law degree at the Southeastern University School of Law. In 1943 Bennett was assigned to the Navajo reservation, where he remained until enlisting in the U.S. Marine Corps in 1944. After World War II Bennett directed a training program for Indian veterans operated under the auspices of the Veteran's Administration. In 1949 he returned to BIA service and climbed the bureaucratic ladder.

During the course of his career, Bennett had the opportunity to hold many positions in different parts of the United States, thus familiarizing him with the variety of needs to which the BIA had to respond. He served as a job placement officer in South Dakota, an assistant on tribal development programs at BIA headquarters, superintendent of the Consolidated Ute Indian Agency in Colorado, and as an assistant area director in South Dakota before being appointed area director for the Juneau Area Office in 1962.[1]

A short and stocky man with a pleasant personality—Robert Burnette remembered him as "a man of considerable charm" who "played the piano very well and was always a genial host"—Bennett adhered to the administration's policy of reservation development. In a 1963 article, he advocated "build[ing] industries and tribal enterprises through the development of reservation resources" as an effective way for Native Americans to "achieve economic security." He proved to be a competent and capable area director, and his performance caught Secretary's Udall's attention. At the 1964 superintendents conference he praised "the tremendous job that Bob Bennett has done." Significantly, Udall claimed that Bennett was "the sort of guy who doesn't mind getting into debates with members of a Legislature [sic]," a character trait that Philleo Nash did not possess. AAIA attorney Corinne Locker noted that "Bennett was the only field man so praised, and repeated joshing references were made to it throughout the rest of the conference."[2]

When Udall finally decided to replace Nash, he turned immediately to Bennett, appointing him deputy commissioner as of 1 November 1965, with the intent of offering Bennett the top job upon receiving Nash's resignation. Udall's decision to nominate Bennett for the position of commissioner was a shrewd one. Because Bennett, like Nash, was from Wisconsin, Udall did not have to fear any opposition from that state's senators. In addition, Udall knew that many Native Americans admired Nash, and he sought to mute their protest over Nash's departure by nominating a Native American to take his place. As Udall later recalled, "the best way to do this [remove Nash] was to pick the best Indian that I could find to be Commissioner." Bennett's record proved that he was among the best—Udall remembered him as the "ablest career bureaucrat in the Indian Bureau"—and indicated that he could handle the responsibilities of the position.[3]

Despite the political advantages inherent in the Bennett nomination, in at least one way Bennett was an odd choice for commissioner. Udall's frustration with the BIA centered on its lack of initiative and creativity. Nominating a career bureaucrat, no matter how capable, risked a continuation of old patterns of thinking, old ways of approaching Indian policy. With the exception of his military service and his stint with the Veteran's Administration, Bennett had been a BIA employee for thirty-three years at the time of his nomination. Udall desired "a fresh look at new policy with the sort of dynamism and new ideas exciting the country" during the 1960s; an official with a third of a century's service in an agency Udall condemned as "very sluggish, very deep in the groove, and not very flexible" was not necessarily the best place to seek innovation. Udall later defended his decision to go within the BIA for his commissioner, maintaining, "I wanted somebody who had been tested in the fires. . . . Everybody was pretty high on Bob Bennett."[4]

BENNETT AND THE SENATE INTERIOR COMMITTEE

Udall hoped that Bennett's bureaucratic background would enable him to deal skillfully with the Congress. However, Bennett had a run-in with Clinton Anderson almost immediately after being named acting commissioner in March 1966. Bennett angered Anderson in two ways, one a minor breach in protocol, the other in a decision regarding a proposed Indian high school in Albuquerque, New Mexico. When Bennett sent Rep. Thomas Morris (D.-N. Mex.) a letter regarding the school, he forwarded a copy to Anderson's office. Anderson considered receiving a copy (rather than a personal communication) an affront, and he telephoned Bennett to remind him that the senior senator from New Mexico merited more respect.[5]

The issue of the school itself was far more important. Under Nash's direction, the BIA had planned to build a vocational school devoted to meeting the needs of Indian students living in the Albuquerque area. The controversial project elicited charges of segregation from the local community. Thus, Bennett inherited an already volatile situation that he worsened when he approved a plan whereby BIA employees and local public school officials "coordinated" the expenditure of BIA funds for the project. Corinne Locker reported that Anderson, who objected to the involvement of local officials in the administration of a federally funded project, "hit the ceiling" when he learned of Bennett's decision. Realizing that Anderson might well block his confirmation hearing, Bennett (and Tom Morris, who supported Bennett's decision) backed down and revised the appropriations bill for the project to meet Anderson's demands.[6]

Anderson had used the Albuquerque school controversy to remind the acting commissioner that the Senate Interior Committee paid close attention to Indian affairs, a lesson the entire committee impressed upon Bennett on 1 April 1966, when it convened for hearings on his nomination. Bennett received support from several congressmen who attended the hearing. Edward L. Bartlett (D.-Alaska) stated that Bennett had "the dedication, the devotion, the intelligence, and the ability" to serve as commissioner, while his colleague Ernest Gruening "consider[ed] his choice for the commissionership an excellent one." Gaylord Nelson (D.-Wis.), George McGovern, Karl Mundt (D.-S. Dak.), and Rep. Benjamin Reifel (R.-S. Dak.), Rosebud Sioux, offered similar words of praise for the nominee.[7]

Although no Native American communities sent representatives to the hearing, many Indian groups sent telegrams and letters to the committee recommending Bennett's confirmation. Francis Wyasket of the Ute Tribal Business Committee noted that Bennett was "well qualified by previous experience to make an outstanding contribution to the Indians of the United States," and the All-Indian Pueblo Council considered the Bennett nomination "a wise and judicious choice." Bennett also received endorsements from the Metlakalta Indian Community, the Tyonek Village Council, and the Rosebud Sioux Tribe. The Navajos did not oppose the Bennett confirmation but asked for a postponement of the hearing so that a tribal representative could attend, a request the committee did not honor. In addition to support from Native American communities, Bennett also received the backing of the Alaska Native Brotherhood and the Indian Rights Association.[8]

However, support for Bennett did not necessarily translate into approval for the conduct of Indian policy, so Bennett kept his opening statement brief, studiously avoiding any controversial matters. He argued that the "destructive effects of paternalism must be overcome" and that "Indian leadership must be developed as a positive force." He called for the creation of an "atmosphere of free choice," in which Indians "have the experience of making those decisions which affect their everyday life," but he wisely avoided making any specific policy statements. Upon the conclusion of Bennett's statement the hearings began in earnest, with Chairman Jackson and other pro-terminationists grilling Bennett on BIA operations. The Kalispels' attorney Robert Dellwo, who attended the hearing, recalled that Jackson and his colleagues asked Bennett "loaded questions." However, the senators did not direct their hostility at the nominee, whom they all agreed possessed the qualifications necessary for the position; rather, they used the hearing as a forum to condemn the Bureau of Indian Affairs.[9]

Henry Jackson led the attack. Referring to recent news stories regarding Indian poverty, he charged that "either the Bureau is not doing its job within its organization, or they are not calling upon the other departments of the Government to assist." Len B. Jordan (R.-Idaho) followed suit. After assuring Bennett that he would vote for confirmation, Jordan expressed "grave apprehension about the Bureau of Indian Affairs, and the course that has been pursued throughout the years." He complained that the government was not "getting much for our money" in the field of Indian affairs. He also asked Bennett about setting target dates for tribal termination. Bennett replied that "the inability to forecast or project over too long a period of time what changes in the economy and other changes in situation will occur" made forecasting termination dates difficult. When Jordan asked about tribes with high per capita wealth, Bennett still rejected termination, instead proposing managed programs allowing Native American communities to become "a part of the business community . . . in the regular economy and business affairs of the country."[10]

Clinton Anderson queried Bennett on the Colvilles, which had a sizable membership requesting termination. Bennett replied that the Interior Department would support appropriate legislation when a tribe requested termination as evidenced by a referendum. Thus, while catering to the demands of committee members who advocated termination, Bennett adhered strictly to the policy Interior Secretary Fred Seaton had announced in 1958, that of proceeding with termination only after securing tribal consent. When Frank Church pressed the issue, Bennett held his ground, stating that "the time has come when Indian people make decisions that we should accept and be ready to live with the consequences of their decisions." While this hardly constituted an endorsement of termination, Church accepted it as a willingness to pursue the policy under certain circumstances.[11]

Following the confirmation hearing, the committee took the unusual step of "departing from customary Senate practice" by filing a written report on the Bennett nomination. The report was "not to be construed as a reflection on Commissioner Bennett," whose nomination the committee unanimously favored. Instead, it "reflect[ed] the committee's dissatisfaction with the pace of progress in elevating the American Indian to a level of parity with other citizens of the country," and placed the blame for this state of affairs squarely on the Bureau of Indian Affairs.[12]

The committee declared that the goal of federal Indian policy was to "raise the educational and social well-being of the Indians, assist in developing their assets, and encourage them to handle their . . . affairs so that they may all eventually become self-sufficient citizens of our American society." However, because the BIA had "tenaciously held onto its wards, without whom it would have no reason to exist," these goals had not been met. The "Bureau had paid virtually no attention to nor performed services" for the Kalispels until the tribe had won its claims settlement; it had only "given lip service" to heirship legislation; it had operated economic development programs that had "proved very questionable"; and it was "more interested in perpetuating its hold on Indians and their property than in bringing them into the mainstream of American life." Pointing to Indian poverty as "a clear indictment of past programs and policies pursued by the Bureau," the committee "expected that these long-standing problems will be attacked vigorously by executive action fully utilizing existing programs and, where needed, through legislation."[13]

The committee detailed specific areas for immediate bureau action. Seeking to use judgment funds "to assist the Indians in planning complete independence from further Bureau stewardship," it requested that the BIA "furnish up-to-date reports on all tribes whose judgment distribution bills are now before Congress, and provide Bureau appraisals of the capacity of these tribes and their individual members to manage their own affairs." It asked the bureau to "submit at an early date proposed [heirship] legislation that will effectively and seriously meet this issue." The senators rejected the proposed reservation development program, instead calling for the expansion of "special Indian relocation and vocational training programs which have been enthusiastically expanded." The committee expected Bennett to respond to these issues, and it instructed him to report "the steps he has taken to meet the problems outlined herein" within ninety days of his confirmation.[14]

The Interior Committee's condemnation of bureau operations did not affect Bennett's confirmation, and the Senate unanimously approved his nomination on 13 April 1966. He was sworn in as commissioner in the East Room of the White House on 27 April 1966. Bennett and his wife, Udall, Anderson, and Jackson were present as President Johnson grandiosely predicted that Bennett would "be one of the great Indian Commissioners the United States of America has ever known." After mentioning that Bennett began his BIA service in Utah, the president declared that "most people from the great state of Utah have a rare dedication to their Government." (The fact that Bennett was not from Utah and had not worked there since 1938 indicated the depth of Johnson's familiarity with his new commissioner.) As he had during the 1964 meeting with NCAI leaders, Johnson "deviate[d] just a moment" and used the ceremony as an opportunity to address the assembled members of Congress on matters unrelated to Indian affairs. He then returned to the matter at hand and called for a "sound, realistic, progressive, adventuresome and farsighted" program in Indian affairs.[15]

BENNETT'S RESPONSE TO SENATE EXECUTIVE REPORT NO. 1

Johnson put little (or no) thought into his comments at the swearing-in ceremony. Nonetheless, a president's remarks can carry great weight, and in the report that Bennett submitted to Jackson on 11 July 1966, the new commissioner reminded the senator that the president had pledged "the support of the entire Executive Branch of the Federal Government" in "meet[ing] the challenges of the unresolved Indian problems outlined in the Committee report." He then argued that "large scale financial commitments are necessary" to bring about "permanent rehabilitation of adults and education of the young for useful and full social and economic contribution." These statements revealed Bennett's bureaucratic skills. After reminding Jackson that he had the support of the White House, Bennett charged Congress with the responsibility for appropriating the necessary funds to bring about improvements in American Indian welfare. Jackson wanted to diminish and eventually eliminate the BIA; but Bennett advocated an increase in bureau funding in order to satisfy the demands of the Senate Interior Committee.[16]

The remainder of the report adroitly rejected the Senate Interior Committee's goals. Jackson and Anderson wanted the bureau to promote termination. However, Bennett argued that requiring the BIA "to both define the criteria which constitute Government termination policy and at the same time evaluate the tribes as to their fitness under those criteria" undermined the bureau's effectiveness. He noted that an "adversary [sic] relationship is often created between the Bureau and the Indian people when discontinuance of Bureau services is discussed," a "relationship [that] is most unfortunate in that it destroys meaningful communication and mutual confidence that must exist if the Bureau is to perform its functions effectively and the Indian people are to benefit." Instead, Bennett called for "a tutorial or advisory relationship in which the Indian people exercise maximum options as to the goals they wish to pursue," with the BIA providing "services and advice," a suggestion remarkably similar to those advanced by Native Americans in the 1961 *Declaration of Indian Purpose*. Bennett proposed that Congress and the BIA design termination criteria, but allow each tribe to take "the initiative in breaking its special ties with the Government." Thus, Bennett's response to Senate Executive Report No. 1 constituted a repudiation of the Indian policy the terminationists desired.[17]

THE DECLINE OF THE SENATE INTERIOR COMMITTEE'S INFLUENCE

Bennett was able to submit such a report because Jackson and his colleagues exercised a waning influence on Indian affairs. Had the senators been more careful (and honest) in their assessment of Indian policy, they would have recognized the overwhelming truth that termination was a discredited policy with few supporters. As the *Newark Evening News* noted, the "Senate Interior Committee looked no further than to bureaucratic bumbling in fixing the fault for the pathetic conditions which prevail among . . . reservation Indians." The senators refused to consider the weaknesses of tribal termination, flaws that had become apparent to all other parties involved in the conduct of Indian policy. Instead, they blamed an agency in the executive branch of the government for the persistence of poverty and suffering on the reservations, an agency they could bully and threaten.[18]

Commissioner Bennett recognized the demise of termination as a credible Indian policy and stood fast, politely but firmly refusing to follow the committee's lead. He knew that the termination policy had lost support in the Senate, had few backers in the House of Representatives, and most important, had virtually no advocates among American Indians, a shift in the political landscape that Jackson and his colleagues had failed to acknowledge.

While Jackson and Anderson demanded the withdrawal of federal services to Indians, many of their fellow senators desired a new direction in Indian affairs. Sen. Fred Harris (D.-Okla.) articulated this attitude in a speech delivered on 21 April 1966. Instead of condemning the BIA, Harris pointed to a "new sense of purpose, direction, and urgency" within the bureau, and noted that BIA employees were "mostly good people . . . who fervently want to do the right thing." He argued for an expansion of bureau operations to include services for Native Americans living off the reservation, a policy position far different from that of senators who hoped to dismantle the bureau. Finally, Harris called for greater Indian participation in the policy process, declaring that "our undertakings . . . have too often imposed solutions and synthetic leadership from the outside. We have been doing things to Indians, rather than with them." Although Harris retained a commitment to assimilation—he perceived "helping the American Indian become a full-fledged citizen, able to move with ease into the mainstream of the American economy and culture," as the goal of federal Indian policy—he never once mentioned termination.[19]

Many of Harris's colleagues lauded his pronouncements on Indian affairs. Sens. Mansfield, Mondale, Daniel Inouye (D.-Hawaii), and A. S. "Mike" Monroney (D.-Okla.) all commended Harris for his "outstanding" speech that was "long overdue." The speech prompted NCAI president Wendell Chino to inform Harris that the "depth of your understanding and thoroughness of your analysis of Indian problems greatly impresses me," words of praise that no Indian leader offered to Henry Jackson in 1966. As Harris's remarks revealed, the Senate Interior Committee's position on Indian policy did not reflect the views of the Senate as a whole.[20]

The committee's terminationists even had opponents in their midst. On 12 April 1966, Udall reported to Johnson that "the Senate report . . . is a one-sided document. It does not accurately reflect the temper of the Senate Interior Committee." Udall was correct, as a letter written by Lee Metcalf in August 1966 revealed. Serving as Church's replacement as chairman of the Indian Affairs Subcommittee, Metcalf informed tribal leaders of his "firm opposition to proposals calling for the reintroduction of termination as a general Indian policy of our government." He also dedicated himself to Indian self-determination, pledging to "continue to influence and shape the kind of Indian policy that Indian people consider in their best interests," a position not in step with the Interior Committee's leadership.[21]

Nor did the Senate executive report represent prevailing attitudes in the House of Representatives. The House Interior Committee had consistently blocked termination legislation and other bills that would have diminished the role of the federal government in Indian affairs. It had never held hearings on Church's last heirship bill and had never reported out long-term leasing legislation. James Haley had worked tirelessly to prevent the inclusion of a termination provision in the Seneca compensation bill, surrendering only because the Seneca Nation needed the rehabilitation funds immediately. Although Henry Jackson had opposed the release of the Kalispel judgment funds without a termination plan, the House nonetheless had voted to release the monies. Jackson and Church blamed the BIA for failing to advance the termination of the Colvilles, but as Sen. Quentin Burdick noted in 1967, the "House did not take favorable action" on the issue either. While House members did not articulate a new direction in Indian policy, they clearly rejected termination.[22]

Senate Interior Committee members also ignored the growing influence that Native Americans exerted on Indian affairs. Their leaders had become sophisticated in the ways of Washington, and had effectively used political pressure and publicity to block the heirship bill and to guarantee Indian inclusion in the war on poverty. Most tribes opposed the withdrawal of federal services, but the paternalistic tradition rendered the senators blind to the fact that Indian affairs could no longer be conducted without Indian participation. However, Native Americans were cognizant of the role Jackson and his colleagues played in the persistence of the termination policy. Mel Thom of the NIYC voiced the Indian response to the Interior Committee's report when he maintained that "Indians need help in developing resources on their own reservations" but "it appears that the United States Senate wants to create . . . urban ghettos [similar to Watts] filled with uneducated, unprepared Indians." The Washington State Project of the NIYC informed Jackson of its "strong dissent" to the executive report and warned the senator that "any Senate attempts to alter or terminate federal treaties unilaterally will . . . be strongly opposed." In the past Native Americans had few options but to endure the policies imposed upon them; but by the mid-1960s, Indian activism, though still limited in scope, was a reality.[23]

Thus, the terminationists on the Interior Committee stood virtually alone in their continued call for tribal termination, and the executive report proved to be the last hurrah for the champions of that failed policy. Jackson pressed for the termination of the Colvilles for the remainder of the decade, but his efforts met with no success. Nor did Congress act on the 1967 termination proposal submitted by the Seneca Nation in accordance with the provisions of the 1965 compensation. Although the federal government would withdraw services from several California tribes already scheduled for termination through 1970, Congress never again passed legislation terminating a Native American community.

However, the threat of termination was very much alive in 1966, and it remained the focus of Indian concerns. Native Americans had good cause to view the federal government with suspicion. In the previous five years Congress had approved a termination program for the Poncas and had forced the Seneca Nation to accept termination in the near future in order to receive federal funds. The Kalispels had narrowly avoided the planned withdrawal of federal services, and internal divisions over the possibility of termination had disrupted life on the Colville reservation. Although Native Americans had found allies in James Haley, George McGovern, and other lawmakers, Henry Jackson and Clinton Anderson remained forceful proponents of the termination policy. Philleo Nash, a bureaucrat sympathetic to Native American concerns, had resigned in part because of conflicts with these powerful senators. American Indians could not help but perceive the potential for termination behind each official pronouncement and within every government program.

Thus when Bennett took office American Indians had little reason to believe that a new era in Indian affairs had commenced. Terminationists clamored loudly for the revival of a policy many Indians hoped had become moribund. The stifling paternalism that had been the hallmark of federal Indian policy throughout the twentieth century still limited Indian participation in the policy process. In fact, however, a new era had dawned, one in which Native Americans used their burgeoning political and organizational abilities to decisively affect Indian affairs. Unfortunately, Stewart Udall underestimated the importance of Native American activism. He learned just how skilled Native Americans had become in the arena of public affairs when he took the lead in the nation's Indian policy in 1966 and 1967.

THE SANTA FE CONFERENCE

In an effort to inspire bureau employees in the weeks after Nash's resignation, Stewart Udall became a visible presence in Indian affairs. On 22 March he called for "a new period in the history of the Bureau of Indian Affairs" at a meeting held in the BIA auditorium, urging the assembled BIA employees to "react quicker, be more sympathetic and show better insight into Indian problems" and asking for their suggestions for improving bureau operations. After admitting that "I don't think our leadership has been good enough," the secretary promised a reorganization of the bureau "at the top level." Udall announced that reorganization plans and a discussion of Indian problems would be the subject of a BIA conference to be held in Santa Fe, New Mexico, the following month.[24]

Concerned that the Interior Department hoped to transfer operating authority for OEO programs from the tribes to BIA officials, the National Congress of American Indians announced plans for an emergency meeting to coincide with the upcoming BIA conference. On 13 April approximately two hundred Native American leaders including NCAI executive director Vine Deloria, Jr., Rosebud Sioux tribal chairman Cato Vallandra, NIYC leader Mel Thom, and Udall's nemesis from the Navajo Tribal Council, Annie Wauneka, met in Santa Fe. Much to their consternation and outrage, they were not admitted to the BIA conference. Udall had ordered the meeting closed to outsiders, including the Indians whose futures were under discussion.[25]

From an administrative standpoint, Udall's decision made sense. He closed the BIA sessions in order to encourage his employees to offer candid criticisms and to recommend unusual and innovative suggestions for improving Indian affairs. However, Udall erred in barring Indians from the conference, a move hardly "more sympathetic" to or revealing "better insight" into Native American needs. He compounded the error of prohibiting Indian participation when he permitted an AAIA representative and delegates from church organizations to attend the meeting. His actions indicated that the paternalistic ethos still guided the creation and formulation of Indian policy. Bureaucrats behind locked doors debated the fate of Native Americans while Indian leaders stood in the street. The symbolism of the moment was potent, and naturally garnered media attention. The *New York Times* opened its story on the conference by noting that "Indians were turned away from a meeting of the Bureau of Indian Affairs," surely not the sort of publicity Udall desired for his "new period in the history" of the BIA.[26]

Robert Bennett attempted to mollify NCAI representatives, but to no effect. The NCAI leadership discussed holding a silent vigil outside the Episcopal church where the conference was being held. Faced with a public relations crisis, Udall had no choice but to compromise. He met with the NCAI and promised to consult with tribal leaders on the proposed reorganization of the BIA. He also agreed to allow two Indian delegates to observe the conference proceedings. However, the damage had been done. Udall had missed an opportunity to establish a new bond of trust with Native Americans. Despite his sincere desire to redefine Indian policy, he could not envision allowing Indians any significant role in crafting policy. The legacy of paternalism stifled not only Native Americans; it also limited well-meaning federal officials who could not see beyond the narrow confines that it imposed upon their understanding of federal Indian policy.[27]

Although the actual gains were slight—Udall made few concessions—Vine Deloria, Jr., recalled Santa Fe as "a major victory for its time. Indians had forced the Interior Department to consult with them and allow them to attend a planning meeting for the first time in history." The Indian protests against BIA paternalism signaled a new assertiveness in Native American efforts to enter the policy process. As far as Indian leaders were concerned, self-determination would become a reality either with government cooperation or in response to government intransigence. If the Interior Department refused to include Indians in the formulation of policy initiatives, Indians would prove unwilling to support those initiatives.[28]

Santa Fe also marked the emergence of Vine Deloria, Jr., as a leading Native American spokesman. The great-grandson of a medicine man and the son of an Episcopal archdeacon, Deloria had served in the U.S. Marines and had studied theology at the Augustana Lutheran Seminary. His 1964 election to the directorship of the NCAI evidenced the growing influence of young Native Americans in the area of pan-tribal activism. An astute and pragmatic advocate of Indian concerns, Deloria was willing to work closely with government officials to achieve his goals. However, as events in the coming year would reveal, he could also be a determined and effective opponent of policy developments that he deemed inimical to Indian interests.[29]

Udall's "Foundation Indian Legislation"

Despite the conflict over Native American inclusion, most BIA employees responded enthusiastically to Udall's demand for a vigorous new approach to Indian affairs. As one participant recalled, the "air was electric with portents of change." In his comments at a morning session held on 15 April, Udall declared that "yesterday was one of the most productive days I have spent in the last five years." His remarks at that session revealed his intentions regarding the future of Indian policy. He urged the BIA employees to "really work intensively in the next 8–9 months" to design "a whole new approach, particularly relating to economic development." After referring to the 1934 Indian Reorganization Act as "significant when it was passed, but . . . really a rather simple idea, logical at that point in history," Udall challenged the conference attendees to "put together a piece of foundation Indian legislation that would be the most important piece of Indian legislation ever written," a bill that would "strike the shackles off in the whole field of Indian economic development."[30]

Udall's comments revealed his ambition to submit legislation that was nothing less than historic, a goal Udall had not discussed publicly but which had been on his mind for some time before 1966. After Nash resigned Udall realized that the moment for his foundation legislation had arrived, and it became the focus of his Indian policy initiatives for the next year. It was an effort doomed from the start because it was calculated to please Congress and thus philosophically out of step with Indian demands, and strategically bungled from the outset.[31]

A LEGISLATIVE OUTLINE

In hindsight, Udall's presentation at the 15 April morning session revealed the weaknesses of his legislative plan. He called for "the greatest historic piece of landmark legislation of all time," during a conference from which Indians initially had been excluded. For assistance in drafting the bill, he wanted to "bring the best brains of the Congress and the Department together—bring in some of the outside people that can be brought in from the business community." Conspicuous in its absence was consultation with Indian leaders. In his enthusiasm for a "new approach," Udall had completely missed the import of the NCAI emergency meeting. Udall went further, outlining an economic development program that relied upon "the biggest businessman—the best economists—the best university people." Again, Udall did not mention the "best Indians," a flaw born of paternalism that would prove fatal to the future of his foundation legislation.[32]

American Indians heard in Udall's speech a continuation of past policies in which "experts" would create solutions for the "Indian problem." As D'Arcy McNickle noted in an article published five months after the Santa Fe conference, the "Secretary wants more involvement by outsiders who would know what to do with Indian resources." Novelist, former BIA employee, and cofounder of the NCAI, McNickle had played an important role in organizing the American Indian Chicago Conference and had written the first draft of what would become the *Declaration of Indian Purpose.* The seasoned activist argued that "the circumstances and personalities involved lend themselves to hurried decisions and hurried methods which, if Indian consent is not forthcoming, will prevail in the absence of consent." Native Americans desired expert assistance and advice, not outside leadership, a reality to which Udall did not give sufficient weight.[33]

Paternalism partially explained Udall's position, but he also had his eye on the congressional response. During his remarks he quoted from a letter by Clinton Anderson in which the senator claimed that "it might be quite useful to create an advisory committee of men knowledgeable in business and economic development to consult the tribes and the BIA." Udall then told his employees that "we should give thought to Senator Anderson's idea of bringing in leaders from the business community." He was playing to the powerful New Mexico senator, and it worked. Anderson, who attended some of the conference meetings, later told reporters that he was "very pleased" with Udall's proposals, which would bring "better days" for the nation's Indians. Udall knew he needed congressional support; however, in this instance it came at the cost of alienating Native Americans, thereby ensuring their opposition to the proposed legislation.[34]

A specific policy recommendation, one which stood at the heart of Udall's foundation legislation, constituted the interior secretary's most grievous error. He proposed enabling "the Indian people to deal with their property in terms of mortgaging" in order "raise funds for investment," with "some kind of mortgage insurance scheme so that in those few instances where you get a bad bargain you could pick it up." If for no other reason, American Indians opposed the Udall legislation because of the proposed mortgage provisions. Over the centuries Native Americans had seen their land base inexorably eroded through government policy, fraud, and deception. Any legislation offering the possibility of further alienation of Indian land was doomed, as Stewart

Udall would have known had he consulted with American Indian leaders. Udall considered the mortgage provision to be the "heart of the matter"; but in fact it was the flaw that would ultimately kill his "landmark legislation."[35]

Udall offered more information regarding the bill at two press conferences, the first in Santa Fe on 15 April and the second in Washington D.C. one week later. He recommended the creation of economic development boards independent of the tribal councils. Although these boards would have Indian majorities, he suggested that Indians "could invite . . . leading businessmen of the country" to serve as board members. It was these boards that would have the authority to mortgage Indian lands in order to raise capital.[36]

Development boards were one topic of discussion at an Interior Department "all hands on deck" meeting held in Udall's office on 28 April 1966, the day after Bennett's swearing-in ceremony. Udall, Bennett, and other Interior Department officials considered proposals for the Omnibus Bill, as it was now known, including loan guarantees and, at Senator Anderson's insistence, an "art-of-the-possible heirship bill." Udall set a 1 July deadline for the completion of a draft of the legislative program that would serve as the basis for "discussions with Congress, the Indians, Indian Tribal attorneys and other interested parties." He hoped for consultations to be conducted through late August so that the legislation would be ready "by December 15 for inclusion in appropriate Presidential messages to Congress."[37]

However, the drafting process took far longer than Udall had anticipated. Planning sessions were held on 4 July and 15 August. In late August, the projected date for completing the consultation process, Assistant Secretary Harry R. Anderson informed Udall that "it will be at least another month before it is ready to expose to the Indians" and that a full consultation with Native Americans would push the bill back "until early spring." Anderson advised "spending about a month consulting with key tribal leaders, Indian attorneys and interest groups." He noted that "while this would not be entirely satisfactory to them, nor would it give us a consensus, it would permit us to have something ready by the time of the [January 1967] State of the Union address."[38]

Anderson's comments regarding the consultation process outlined the role Indians were to play in creating the Omnibus Bill. The department intended to furnish interested parties with a completed draft for their comments and recommendations. However, Native Americans had arrived at a very different conclusion regarding their participation, one in which they played the central role in drafting the bill. The differences between the process envisioned by the Interior Department and demanded by Native Americans led to a bitter falling-out between the two parties that contributed to the demise of the Omnibus Bill.

NATIVE AMERICAN OPPOSITION

Initial Indian response to the plans Udall presented at the Santa Fe conference in April was cautious. At the conclusion of the conference, Vine Deloria, Jr., warned that "if we start seeing the old bureaucrats showing up on the reservations again with Indian programs all mapped out—no dice." He later recalled that "everyone left Santa Fe keeping a wary eye on everyone else." Udall had promised to consult with Indians on the proposed legislation, but he had not welcomed the NCAI's offer of an Indian advisory committee to work with the BIA on drafting the bill. By late summer many Native Americans became suspicious as "rumors began to filter out that Udall had already commissioned people to draw up the legislation, without any consultation with the tribes." Their suspicions were confirmed in late summer when NCAI members procured a draft prepared by E. Reeseman Fryer of the BIA.[39]

For Native Americans, the Fryer draft was evidence of betrayal on the part of Secretary Udall, the Interior Department, and, by extension, the federal government. Bennett later claimed he had disliked the Fryer draft and so allowed the NCAI to kill it. However, the situation was not nearly so simple, because Bennett was responsible for building support for an administration bill that now served as another example of government paternalism and perfidy. At a series of regional meetings held in October and November, he discovered that Indian opposition to any legislation had hardened following the release of the Fryer draft.[40]

At this point Bennett made a tactical error. Alvin Josephy, Jr., an historian affiliated with the AAIA, complained that "Rob Bennett is not only *not* putting the [Fryer] paper on the table for frank discussion and revisions, he is denying its importance." Rather than using the Fryer draft as a talking paper the tribal delegates could use as a starting point, Bennett and other BIA officials insisted "that no formal draft of the omnibus bill exists." This claim was hardly credible given that NCAI delegates were handing out copies of the Fryer draft in the hallway outside the first regional meeting. In addition to raising doubts about his trustworthiness, Bennett risked the possibility of losing Indian support for any major legislation by refusing to admit the obvious—the administration had worked on the legislation before consulting with Native Americans.[41]

In an 18 October letter to AAIA attorney Corinne Locker, Josephy declared that "a situation of great potential danger is building up." He feared that "the stage seems set for exactly what the Secretary and President Johnson do not want—the roof falling in after the bill goes to Congress." In her reply, Locker agreed that "the situation looks bad with respect to the omnibus bill." Highly critical of the administration's performance, she claimed that the format of the regional meetings was "obviously designed to steer clear of comment on BIA and Departmental thinking." Tribal representatives were asked to prepare reports and statements that the commissioner would then collect, allowing for little discussion of the actual contents of any proposed legislation. Locker also criticized Bennett's performance, complaining that he "has made no commitment to submit to the tribes for comment any proposed legislation before it is introduced in Congress," leaving unclear whether Native Americans would have opportunities to critique administration proposals before Congress held hearings.[42]

Thus, Indians had no reason to support any bill. At the 1966 NCAI convention held in Oklahoma City in November, delegates criticized the legislation (the specifics of which remained unknown) as the Anonymous Bill and the Ambush Bill. Seeking to improve relations with the tribes and to revive the fortunes of his foundation legislation, Udall informed Wendell Chino, NCAI president, that preliminary drafts of the proposed legislation would be sent to tribal chairmen for their perusal. After Indian communities had an opportunity to formulate recommendations, their leaders would attend a conference in Washington, D.C., to discuss the bill. The preliminary drafts were mailed on 27 December 1966, and the recipients were given until 23 January 1967 (a deadline soon extended by one week to 30 January) to prepare their assessments of the draft.[43]

The decision to forward preliminary drafts of the Omnibus Bill to the tribes was intended to repair Interior's relations with Native Americans. However, instead of creating a sense of partnership, Udall further alienated them and crippled his already fragile "landmark legislation." For months Bennett and his employees had insisted that no such draft existed; yet Indians were now receiving a draft prepared without their assistance. The inclusion of a proposed letter of transmittal for the secretary to the Speaker of the House only heightened the suspicion that the draft was in fact a completed bill. Moreover, they were expected to respond to the legislative proposals in a little over a month. Realizing that delays might prevent Congress from acting on the bill in the upcoming congressional session, Udall wanted the bill submitted to Congress as quickly as possible. However, Native Americans perceived Udall's sense of urgency as a disregard for their opinions.[44]

Vine Deloria, Jr., detailed the Indian response to Udall's initiative in a 20 January 1967 letter. He declared that "the mood of the tribes is now one of solid opposition because they were promised at the area meetings that they would have their ideas incorporated into any legislation and this [new draft] is basically the same as the one we had in October." Maintaining that most tribal leaders regarded the drafting of the bill as "a bitter betrayal," Deloria noted that they might oppose the bill "in favor of additional funds for the Poverty programs and more housing."[45]

As the new year began, the Interior Department faced a nearly impossible situation, charged with building support for a bill not yet completed among Native Americans who, because of failed departmental strategies, were not open to any new legislation. To make matters worse, Udall wanted the bill submitted to Congress as quickly as possible, a task made all the more difficult because the annual appropriations hearings, scheduled to begin in February, put a tremendous strain on BIA employees. In the midst of the pressure and confusion surrounding the Omnibus Bill, Udall and his staff encountered yet another crisis, this time from a totally unexpected quarter, a presidential task force on American Indians.

THE 1966 TASK FORCE ON AMERICAN INDIANS

Lyndon Johnson often used task forces, created both from agencies within the administration and individuals outside the government, as sources of policy recommendations. He insisted that task force policy proposals remain secret, informing his cabinet in 1964 that "they will operate without publicity. It is very important this not become a public operation. The purpose of these task forces is to come up with ideas, not to sell those ideas to the public." Of the more than one hundred task forces organized during the Johnson administration, two—the 1966 President's Task Force on American Indians and the 1967 Task Force on American Indians—researched Native American issues, probably prompting Vine Deloria's 1969 complaint that "we are TASK FORCED to death."[46]

The 1966 task force had its origins in a White House meeting on Indian affairs held on 25 August. Presidential aide Joseph Califano "suggested an off-record White House task force" assigned to examine Native American issues. According to a synopsis of the meeting, Udall was "initially opposed to the idea," but eventually "seemed to agree that it would be a good idea." Udall's reluctance was understandable. He had little to gain from a White House task force assembled to make policy recommendations to his department. If the task force approved of the current Indian policy, Interior would receive little benefit, because, as Udall later asserted, the White House "substantially left it [Indian affairs] in my hands" and already offered "pretty thorough going support" for Interior Department initiatives in that area. However, if the task force criticized the new direction in Indian affairs, Udall might face increased White House intervention in his departmental activities, an unpleasant circumstance for any cabinet officer. Thus, Udall "seemed to agree" to the formation of the task force, hardly an enthusiastic endorsement. However, Califano was close to the president and Udall could not dismiss his suggestion.[47]

The White House quickly assembled the task force, which held its first meeting a mere six weeks after Califano had proposed its creation. Academics and businessmen composed the membership of the President's Task Force on American Indians. Dr. Walsh McDermott, who chaired the task force, was the chairman of the Department of Public Health and Preventive Medicine at Cornell University Medical College. Other members included an insurance company executive, a professor who worked for Union Carbide, and a professor of political science from MIT. Four members had played important roles in Native American affairs in the past decade. William W. Keeler, the only Indian on the committee, had served on Udall's 1961 task force; AAIA attorney Richard Schifter had been a powerful voice for Indian concerns; Dr. Richard Roessel directed the Rough Rock Navajo Demonstration School; and Dr. Sol Tax had organized the American Indian Chicago Conference in 1961.[48]

After its first meeting on 11 October 1966, the group went about collecting information for its final report. In addition to interviewing officials from numerous government agencies providing services to American Indians, task force members visited the Navajo and Laguna reservations and met with tribal representatives attending a conference on Indian education. Four members held a one-day meeting with

Indian leaders, including Wendell Chino, Raymond Nakai, Domingo Montoya, and Cato Vallandra. Two members observed the BIA's Oklahoma City regional conference on the omnibus legislation. The task force convened for the last time on 11 December, and submitted its final report, "A Free Choice Program For American Indians," to the White House on 23 December 1966.[49]

THE TRANSFER PROPOSAL

The task force made several general policy recommendations, including a "complete disavowal of 'termination' as a governmental policy or goal." Specific suggestions included the usual plans for developing reservation economies and improving Indian health and education, all of which required increased appropriations. The task force also wanted to transfer the BIA "from Interior to HEW and reorganize and upgrade it into [the] Indian Affairs Administration," a proposal that constituted a significant change in the conduct of Indian affairs. The study group maintained that a transfer to HEW "would place executive branch responsibility in the department best equipped to develop effective programs to meet the needs of the Indian people, because it is the department responsible for related programs for the general public." Task force members did not reach a consensus on this recommendation—two members, W. W. Keeler and Lewis Douglas, an executive from Mutual Insurance of New York, opposed the transfer. Keeler was not "unalterably opposed," but favored "a careful study of all of the implications for the Departments" before giving his approval.[50]

A precedent for an interdepartmental transfer of responsibilities existed within the Johnson administration, ironically at the hands of Stewart Udall. In a 1965 memorandum, Udall had urged the president to approve a transfer of air and water pollution programs from HEW to Interior. In his determination to acquire these programs, Udall offered a quid pro quo with the promise "to determine whether I should not also recommend to the President that the responsibility for Indian education be transferred from Interior to HEW." Although air pollution remained under the auspices of HEW, Udall succeeded in having water pollution moved to his department in 1966.[51]

As his memo to President Johnson indicated, Udall did not oppose transferring some BIA operations, specifically education, out of the Interior Department. He envisioned reorganizing the Department of Interior into a Department of Conservation, with authority over the nation's natural resources. Under such a plan, Indian education would be administered by some other agency. However, Udall wanted most BIA functions to remain in Interior. He later maintained that Indians "were not resource problems except in an important way they were . . . because they own land. They have two percent of the American land . . . and that land is a resource and has to be managed." In Udall's mind, trust responsibility for native lands properly belonged in his department.[52]

In an early January meeting with Califano and HEW Secretary John Gardner, Udall argued against the task force's transfer proposal on the grounds that his new Indian program was just getting underway. He also claimed that the proposal would create "some Congressional trouble." Joseph Califano and HEW Secretary Gardner, both of whom supported the transfer recommendations, argued that congressional opposition "could be tested and should be tested in the context of a full Indian program." When Udall proposed moving only the bureau's educational operations to HEW, he was told that "education was two-thirds of the budget and people of the Indian Bureau and that if you transferred education, you might as well transfer the whole Bureau." In the end, Udall agreed to "abide by any Presidential decision in this area and wholeheartedly support it."[53]

Udall's political instincts regarding congressional response to the transfer proved superior to Califano's. Whatever the merits of the proposal, congressmen on the Interior Committees, especially those who represented western states, had no interest in losing control over a policy area. Unbeknownst to Interior officials, word of the secret task force proposals had leaked, and Wayne Aspinall was not pleased. In a late January hearing on Indian affairs conducted by the House Interior Committee, Wayne Aspinall surprised Commissioner Bennett and Harry R. Anderson, assistant secretary of land management, when he opened the hearing with the announcement that the transfer proposal "has come to my knowledge from various channels." Anderson replied that "at this time we prefer not to get into this area," but Aspinall would not be deterred. He told Anderson that "I will be very definite in my statement. Just as soon as anybody in the United States decides to place Indians in the same position as other beneficiaries of HEW, then I'm opposed to it." James Haley agreed with the committee chairman, declaring that Aspinall had "pretty much expressed the views of the [Indian affairs] subcommittee." Haley added that "HEW hasn't done too good a job on that [welfare] with the money they've had."[54]

Given Aspinall's opposition, the transfer was a dead issue, but Interior officials refused to recognize this fact. In a report on the meeting, Charles Luce noted that "the Chairman's reaction to the proposed transfer was predictable," and recommended that Gardner "talk with the Committee and Subcommittee Chairmen of both the House and Senate Interior Committees as quickly as possible," a suggestion that indicated Luce had misinterpreted the force of the committee chairman's objection.[55]

The task force report was now a matter of public record—a New York Times reporter had covered the Interior Committee meeting and quoted both Aspinall and Haley. American Indians learned that once again the administration was pondering a major policy shift regarding their future before conferring with tribal leaders. Secretary Gardner noted that "some [Indians] are disgruntled because they have not yet been consulted," another setback for proponents of the transfer. Nonetheless, administration officials continued to promote the transfer. In early February, Secretary Gardner requested White House permission to discuss the transfer at a meeting with Indian leaders to be held in Kansas City on 17 February. Califano agreed with Gardner, informing President Johnson that "we can benefit from discussing this and it will give Secretary Gardner a fair chance to sell his program as well as work any bugs out of it before we go to the Hill." Johnson approved the plan, and Gardner journeyed to Kansas City to persuade Indian leaders that the transfer was in their best interests.[56]

Once again, Califano and Gardner evidenced a lack of familiarity with Indian affairs. Vine Deloria, Jr., who believed the transfer proposal had some merit, wanted HEW to present the idea to small groups of selected tribal leaders who in turn would build support for the transfer. Instead, as Deloria recalled, HEW "insisted on presenting the idea to the entire group of assembled tribes—cold." The tribal representatives did not know that Gardner would speak until the night before his appearance. Although Native Americans had no great love for the BIA, they perceived the transfer proposal as the first step toward dissolution of the bureau and termination of federal services. When Gardner insisted that treaty rights would remain intact and that the transfer constituted no significant change in government policy, one Indian leader present asked the obvious question: "Why, if there are to be no changes at all, do you want to transfer the Bureau to HEW?" After Gardner's presentation, the Indian leaders unanimously approved a motion to allow "tribal governing bodies . . . an opportunity to study what benefits it [the transfer] will have."[57]

Native Americans responded quickly to the news that the White House was seriously considering the transfer. In a 1 March letter to White House Assistant James Jones, Earl Boyd Pierce, general counsel for the Cherokee Nation, complained that "Indians have not been consulted" and worried that "the President does not know all the facts pertaining to the suggested transfer." On 2 March, the Inter-Tribal Council of the Five Civilized Tribes adopted a resolution requesting a public hearing so that "the Indian leaders of this Nation [can] be given a full and free opportunity to express their views on the entire subject, including the source of the proposal." They sent a copy of the resolution to Congressman Carl Albert (D.-Okla.), who informed them that he "share[d] the Council's feeling that the Department of the Interior is better fitted" to provide services to the tribes, and agreed that "this responsibility should not be transferred to any other Department without the Indians' knowledge and consent."[58]

Native American objections to the transfer were capably presented in a statement sent by the Oglala Sioux Tribal Council to the White House on 17 March 1967. After noting that the tribe had no knowledge of the White House "study group," and had learned of the transfer proposal from the *New York Times* article, the tribe discussed its reasons for opposing the transfer. First and foremost, "DHEW has never been involved with land problems of the landowners and would therefore only prolong our efforts to solve urgent and immediate problems of tribal land consolidation and the heirship problem." The statement then listed problems that the tribe had experienced with HEW's operation of the Public Health Service. Finally, the Oglala Sioux argued that "a harmonious relationship has been developing between the Tribe and the Bureau of Indian Affairs" marked by a "better understanding of their mutual interests." A transfer of services would "result in the necessity of rebuilding a new relationship between the government and Indians." This statement indicated that to some degree the Interior Department's efforts during the decade had succeeded, and at least one Indian tribe was willing to defend the Bureau of Indian Affairs.[59]

Ultimately, the transfer proposal came to naught. On 22 March, Gardner sent President Johnson a memo in which he noted that "there are very serious obstacles in the way of moving the Bureau of Indian Affairs to HEW," including "Congressional and Indian objections." In addition, Gardner complained that "I simply do not have time to engage in extensive campaigning to win over Indian tribal leaders." (Gardner neglected to mention that employees in the HEW's Office of Education were not enthusiastic about taking responsibility for Indian schools.) Instead of a transfer, Gardner suggested that he "offer Stu Udall all the assistance and resources that HEW can provide to help him in doing a better job under the present organizational structure." Gardner's suggestion became policy, and in July Udall was able to inform Sen. Mike Mansfield that "a reorganization plan is not receiving serious consideration within the Administration at this time."[60]

THE VALUE OF SECRET TASK FORCES

The short life of the transfer proposal indicated that President Johnson's requirement that task force policy proposals remain secret had some justification. Task force recommendations presented the administration with a variety of policy options, but premature release of potentially controversial proposals galvanized opposition, prevented the White House from building support, and effectively killed the proposal. Such was the case with the BIA transfer. Both Congress and Native American leaders immediately opposed the transfer in part because it was created without their input. The recommendation was never open to discussion or debate and was thus never judged on its merits.

The task force members had recognized the need to cultivate congressional approval for the measure. After noting that "attitudes toward organizational change of the several cognizant congressional committees are important," the task force claimed that "these attitudes . . . are likely to be affected both by the substance of any proposed changes and by the way it is presented." The transfer proposal was "presented" to Wayne Aspinall as a leak from a secret White House study group examining a policy area overseen by his committee, and his attitude was thoroughly negative.[61]

In addition, the task force stated that "there are clear indications that if suddenly confronted with this proposal, the Indian leaders will regard it as being linked in some way with the termination 'policy,'" and warned that "if mentioned out of context prematurely in the press, [the transfer proposal] could cause serious harm in terms of Indian acceptance of *any* proposed new programs." Therein laid the true impact of the transfer proposal—it increased American Indian distrust of the federal government and made passage of Udall's Omnibus Bill all the less likely.[62]

THE INDIAN RESOURCES DEVELOPMENT ACT OF 1967

Only two days after the *New York Times* reported the existence of a White House task force on Indian affairs and the proposed transfer of the BIA to HEW, Commissioner Bennett met with Indian leaders in an effort to secure their support for the Omnibus Bill. In a letter to President Johnson drafted on 2 February 1967, the Native Americans who attended the conference set forth their views on the proposed legislation. The Indians first requested "an extension of time so that copies of this most important legislation can be sent to all tribal leaders with sufficient time thereafter for their constructive consideration and comments." The policy statement then noted that "certain major titles and provisions thereof were rigorously opposed and unanimously rejected upon the grounds that they are inimical to and uncongruous [*sic*] with the present needs, capabilities and conditions of the American Indians," an assessment that did not bode well for Udall's bill.[63]

The objections to the legislation revealed the centrality of land ownership to Native American culture and society. The land mortgage proposal generated the greatest concern. The Indian leaders argued that "certain of the managerial techniques . . . effecting mortgage, hypothecation and sale of Indian lands, would render the Indian people immediately vulnerable to subversive economic forces" leading to "the prompt erosion and demise of the social and economic culture of the American Indian." They also criticized an heirship provision that did not include "truly effective preferential rights of owners and tribes to purchase such lands."[64]

Despite these criticisms, the Indians found provisions of value buried in the "41 page opus and its 21 page explanation." They praised sections regarding loan guarantees, increases in the revolving loan fund, and the extension of authority to tribal governments to condemn land. However, they questioned the strategy of including these desirable provisions in a "legislative 'package' in which you have a Hobson's choice of having to accept bad legislation or legislation without adequate review to get the good or desperately needed legislation."[65]

The legislation's reception did not improve in the weeks that followed. In a 19 February letter, the Council of the Pueblo of Acoma informed Sen. Joseph Montoya that "the introduction of the proposed Omnibus Bill is another aggressive act against Indian people." Reminding the senator that "American Indian people in New Mexico means over 10,000 votes," the council called upon Montoya to "support our efforts in opposing" the legislation. Robert Bennett later noted that Gardner's Kansas City meeting in February 1967 "increased and aggravated their [Indian] suspicions" regarding the Omnibus Bill. During the months of April and May, "the proposal was considerably modified including several deletions and amendments, which satisfied many of the negative reactions of the Indian people to the proposal," but in early May, just days before Udall sent the bill to Congress, Charles Luce noted that it would "receive a mixed reception from Indian organizations."[66]

Although they lacked significant Indian backing, Interior officials believed that they had congressional support. Luce informed Joseph Califano that "the bill will be favorably received by the Interior Committees," and Udall cited "overwhelming [congressional] support for the legislation." Califano told President Johnson that "the program will be controversial and there will be some Indian opposition," but recommended that the legislation be sent to Congress. Johnson agreed, and Udall transmitted the bill—now entitled the Indian Resources Development Act of 1967—to Congress on 16 May 1967.[67]

The bill, which Interior recognized was "long and complex," was not the broad-based foundation legislation Udall desired. It contained almost no provisions regarding education, health, or welfare, and only touched upon the heirship problem. As its title suggested, the Indian Resources Development Act concentrated upon mechanisms to promote economic growth on the reservations, specifically through the expansion of available credit and the formation of Indian corporations.[68]

Title I of the bill called for the creation of an Indian Loan Guaranty and Insurance Fund and an expansion of the already-existing revolving loan fund. The new fund would allow Indians to pursue private sources of capital, while the revolving fund would back projects for which no private loans could be secured. Requested appropriations for these two funds totaled $500 million, a sum exceeding total federal expenditures on Indian affairs by more than ten percent. Title I also allowed the tribes to issue tax-exempt bonds as another source of capital. Title II permitted tribes to organize corporations separate from tribal governments that possessed authority over specific tribal assets. Title III allowed the tribes limited authority "to sell, mortgage, invest, or otherwise use, pledge, or dispose of trust or restricted property including tribal funds deposited in the U.S. Treasury." Title IV contained miscellaneous provisions, including a section allowing Indians to receive compensation upon the voluntary withdrawal of tribal membership. This measure was intended to resolve conflicts of the type that had divided the Colvilles, in which some members supported termination and the division of tribal assets while others vigorously opposed such a move.[69]

Participation in any of the bill's programs was voluntary. As Udall pointed out, "no single Indian tribe or group . . . has to avail themselves of the provisions of this legislation." In addition, the bill contained numerous safeguards intended to prevent the unnecessary alienation of Indian land. The provisions in Title III required secretarial approval and authorization either in the tribe's constitution or through a tribal referendum.[70]

CONGRESSIONAL RESPONSE

Udall's contention that the bill had "overwhelming support" was born of optimism or enthusiasm, for in reality he was wrong. He had overestimated the extent of the bill's support in Congress. An Interior Department Committee checklist had reported that Henry Jackson "will be one of the strongest supporters on the Hill," and claimed that

"Secretary Udall has paved the way with Rep. Aspinall and is convinced that the Committee will give priority attention" to the bill. In addition, Interior officials believed that twelve Senate Interior Committee members and twenty-one House Committee members were favorably disposed toward the legislation. However, not a single congressman agreed to sponsor the bill. Instead, both Jackson and Aspinall introduced it by request, which meant that "we aren't for it and we're not against it," as Aspinall explained to a reporter.[71]

The coolness in Congress toward the Omnibus Bill stemmed from two sources: its cost and the omission of an heirship provision. When Aspinall saw the bill's price tag, "a soft whistle escaped his pursed lips." The *Christian Science Monitor* reported that the size of the appropriations troubled members of the Senate Interior Committee, with an anonymous committee source declaring that "whether funds could be used in a better way is a question on which honest men will differ." Some congressmen also expressed consternation because the bill did not address the heirship problem in depth. Aspinall complained that "those fellows downtown [Interior officials] know I wanted an heirship provision." Senate staffers also voiced their concerns about the bill's failure to address the heirship issue.[72]

An Interior Department account of the bill's history notes that it "received unenthusiastic preliminary hearings in the House and Senate." The Senate Interior Committee held its hearings on 11 July, and the House Indian Affairs Subcommittee convened later that same week. Interior Department officials Stewart Udall, Robert Bennett and Charles Luce were the only witnesses at both hearings. In his opening statement, Udall headed off complaints about the missing heirship section when he informed the subcommittee that the Interior Department had submitted "a separate bill that will deal with the fractionated-land problems" to the Bureau of the Budget for commentary.[73]

Many committee members expressed frustration with provisions that required secretarial approval. After noting that the stated purpose of the act was "to permit them [Indians] to exercise great initiative and self-determination," Wayne Aspinall claimed that the bill contained twenty different provisions requiring secretarial approval. He asked, "[A]re we kidding ourselves that we are giving them more self-government, or are we being honest with them and giving them some additional advantages, but perhaps the control is still left with the Secretary?" John Saylor followed Aspinall's lead, arguing that the bill "reminds me of saying to the Indian that you are going to give him a horse, a blanket, and a job, but put a noose around his neck when you give it to him. The noose is in the hands of the Secretary." He charged that "if you do not do the job the way the Secretary likes it, the Secretary is going to yank that and pull you right down off the horse."[74]

Questions about specific provisions consumed most of the hearing. Although few members of Congress were as openly hostile as John Saylor, no committee member expressed outright approval for the measure. Even Ed Edmondson (D.-Okla.), who praised the bill as "one of the most conscientious, one of the most statesmanlike efforts to do something on a really broad scale and constructive scale to meet some of the pressing needs of our Indian people," offered numerous objections to various sections. In the end, the House hearings indicated that Congress had little interest in promoting the Indian Resources Development Act.[75]

Indian opposition played a role in the tepid congressional response. During the hearings, James Haley noted that "many of the Indians are disturbed about this particular bill because some of them have the idea that it could well be classed as 'the termination bill of 1967.'" Native Americans were forthright in their condemnation of the legislation. Vine Deloria, Jr., later recalled that "we just beat it to death." Lewis Zadoka, chairman of the Wichita Indian Tribe, informed Udall that the bill "IS NOT ACCEPTABLE" [sic]. Mad Bear, chairman of the Tuscarora General Council, forwarded to the White House a resolution from several tribes arguing that the bill "does not in any wise [sic] represent the views or suggestions or sanction of our Indian Nations." Richard Roessel of the 1966 task force reported that "the Navaho [sic] tribe, which has not been known for any unanimous action in recent years, had only one dissenting vote when it went on record in opposition to the proposed bill."[76]

A few tribes did support the act. The Osage Tribal Council approved the measure "subject to the proviso that the Osage mineral estate be excluded entirely from the operation and effect of the legislation." Representatives from eleven tribes in Eastern Oklahoma, including the Cherokees, the Chickasaws, and the Choctaws, "unanimously agreed in general with the provisions of the proposed legislation," and "urge[d] that it be enacted into law." Despite such statements of support, Native Americans were on the whole opposed to the bill.[77]

The negative congressional and Indian responses did not dismay Udall, who told Forrest J. Gerard, his congressional relations officer, that the Indian Resources Development Act remained "the Department's priority Indian legislation proposal before the 90th Congress." Udall instructed Gerard to press the Indian Affairs Subcommittee chairmen for field hearings. George McGovern, the current chair of the Senate subcommittee, told Gerard that other commitments made it "virtually impossible" to schedule hearings in 1967. James Haley was much more amenable to the idea, but Gerard reported that Wayne Aspinall "has reportedly taken the position that none of his Subcommittees would conduct field hearings following adjournment." Gerard concluded that "there appears to be serious questions whether field hearings can be conducted by the House Subcommittee."[78]

Despite Gerard's gloomy assessment, BIA officials still took "every opportunity and . . . expended considerable time and effort in explaining the provisions of the bill to the Indian people." Delegates at the NCAI convention held in Portland, Oregon, in October 1967 adopted a resolution opposing passage of the bill, but they also included a paragraph calling for "additional studies and hearings in the hope that acceptable, comprehensive legislation can be drafted in consultation with the Indian tribes which will retain the good features of the [existing] legislation." Commissioner Bennett told James Officer, who had left the BIA for the position of assistant to the secretary, that the resolution was evidence of "a definite softening in the attitude of many Indian leaders who were originally opposed to the proposal."[79]

Bennett was putting a positive spin on a complicated circumstance.

The apparent "softening in attitude" was a move calculated to satisfy Congress; most Native Americans still opposed most of the provisions found in the legislation. Sen. Lee Metcalf had informed an attorney for the Blackfeet that aggressive opposition to the act might jeopardize other Indian legislation pending before Congress, so the NCAI delegates had added the moderating paragraph to the resolution on the advice of tribal attorneys.[80]

Toward the end of 1967 Udall declared that the bill "will be one of the Department's priority legislative items next year," but in fact the Indian Resources Development Act was dead. Without substantial Native American backing, Interior Department officials could not hope to persuade members of the Interior Committees to act on the proposal. The Senate Interior Committee held a field hearing in May 1968, but by this time the administration had admitted defeat and abandoned the bill.

"Tactics Rather Than Intentions"

In an article published shortly after he left office in 1969, Udall contended that "tactics rather than intentions were at fault in our failure to secure passage of the Indian Resources Development Act of 1967." In his mind, the failure to build Indian support was the primary reason that the legislation died. He admitted that "we did not discuss the specifics of the bill soon enough or thoroughly enough with the Indian leadership," and also noted that "the bill contained several proposals upon which the Indians had relatively little opportunity to express their views." Udall concluded that the bill's failure "demonstrates that the Indians themselves must be fully in accord before we can even begin to lay the necessary legal foundation for economic growth on the reservations."[81]

The secretary's assessment was honest but missed the point. By 1966 Indians had no desire to "discuss the specifics" of or "express their views" on legislative proposals; they demanded the right to participate in the formulation of the legislation from the outset. Udall perceived consultation as the process of building a consensus in support of the administration's initiative, while Native Americans understood consultation to mean Indian involvement in the policy process, or, even more desirable, Indian leadership in that process. Like many other government officials, Udall recognized and even welcomed the growing activism of Native Americans; however, he did not fully realize the extent to which Indians had rejected the paternalistic tradition that had long dominated federal Indian policy.

In claiming that tactics killed the bill, Udall allowed himself to believe that its specific proposals had merit. Had he engaged in a full consultation with Native Americans, he would have learned that the mortgage and sale provisions, though optional, were completely unacceptable. Native American communities had experienced the loss of their lands for centuries. Any measure, no matter how well intentioned, which raised the possibility of further dispossession of Indian lands was anathema. Clumsy tactics ensured the death of the act, but the mortgage and sale provisions would also have proven fatal.

Alienating American Indian leaders was not Udall's only error. He also handled Congress poorly. Interior officials had spent nearly a year drafting and revising the proposed legislation, but never laid the groundwork with influential congressmen. Not a single legislator expressed enthusiasm when the measure was submitted to Congress in May 1967. Excluding heirship provisions from the act was a wise move—Frank Church's frustrating experience with that issue indicated that the resources bill would become mired in a fight over heirship proposals—but Udall should have informed both Interior Committee chairmen that heirship would be addressed in separate legislation. Instead, they learned of the omission of heirship provisions when they received a copy of the act, which upset them and created doubts about the legislation.

Stewart Udall was responsible for the bill's short life. It was Udall's initiative, drafted according to his suggestions, and presented to Native Americans and Congress under his guidance. Bennett and other BIA officials followed his lead. The failure of his bid for greatness in Indian policy might have soured him on Native American issues, but Udall maintained an active interest in Indian affairs for the remainder of his tenure in office. In December 1967, he informed President Johnson of his intention to "make and implement a maximum of pro-Indian decisions during my remaining time as Secretary." During the coming year Udall would succeed in putting "a pro-Indian stamp on this administration," but he would also be in for a surprise in April when the 90th Congress passed landmark Indian legislation of a far different sort than he had envisioned.[82]

A NATIVE AMERICAN VICTORY

The defeat of the Indian Resources Development Act constituted a major victory for Native Americans. They had successfully opposed a bill proposed by the interior secretary and backed by the White House, an achievement that evidenced the effectiveness of pan-tribal organization and communication in influencing the actions of the federal government.

Vine Deloria, Jr., considered the battle over the Omnibus Bill to be a major advancement for Indian leadership and for the National Congress of American Indians. Deloria noted that "for many years the N.C.A.I. was dominated by old line conservatives and passed extremely conservative resolutions that advocated the status quo." He regarded the organization's handling of the Omnibus Bill as proof that "younger leaders have taken hold of the reins of leadership nationally."[83]

Throughout the early 1960s, Native Americans had used unified political action, publicity, and pressure on Congress and the administration to achieve their goals. The 1961 American Indian Chicago Conference, the defeat of the heirship bill in 1963, and the 1964 Capital Conference on Poverty all revealed the increasing political power of Native Americans. However, the public protest at the 1966 Santa Fe conference marked a turning point. The forceful request that Native

American representatives be permitted to attend the superintendents meeting indicated that the weariness with paternalism had reached the breaking point. The subsequent battle against the Indian Resources Development Act revealed Indians' determination to wrest control of their fate from Washington bureaucrats. However, in 1968 they would again face another major legislative proposal originating in Washington, D.C., one which was much more ambiguous in its impact and therefore difficult to evaluate and even harder to oppose.

CHAPTER SIX

BENNETT AND UDALL

Whether his experience with Philleo Nash soured him on the office of commissioner or his desire for progress prompted him to take a leadership role, Stewart Udall never allowed Robert Bennett to take full command of Indian affairs. This was unfortunate. Bennett brought considerable talents to his office. He possessed the legislative savvy to work with Congress, the background and personality to communicate with American Indians, and the bureaucratic skills to manage the BIA. Because he was dedicated to achieving the goal of Indian self-determination, he was in tune with the demands and concerns of the nation's Indians.

Nonetheless, Udall failed to make adequate use of his new commissioner. Although their relationship was never acrimonious, Udall later expressed disappointment in Bennett's performance. In an oral history interview conducted in July 1969, he complained that Bennett "wasn't radical enough." Although he admitted that Bennett "did get support from Congressmen on the Hill that [Philleo] Nash did not get," Udall maintained that Bennett "was too much a prisoner of the bureaucracy, too much a creature, having worked in it twenty-five years, of the whole process." In assessing the Bennett years, Udall concluded that "we had a great difficulty in developing the kind of new initiatives and new policies that I would like to have seen."[1]

COMMISSIONER BENNETT

Bennett was a far more effective commissioner than Udall gave him credit for. In evaluating Bennett's performance, Udall underestimated the skills Bennett brought to his office. Bennett's style would never impress any observer as radical—Robert Burnette remembered him as "too nice a guy to rock the boat or bring about any meaningful change"—but he worked to end the paternalism dominating the conduct of Indian policy. He consistently advocated policies and programs that promoted self-determination. In addition, he used his bureaucratic skills to sidetrack efforts to continue tribal termination. Thus, Bennett offered Native Americans the kind of Indian policy they had requested for years.[2]

Udall also ignored the liabilities under which Bennett labored, one of which was Udall's increased involvement in Indian affairs. Promoting Udall's Indian Resource Development Act consumed nearly two years of Bennett's thirty-seven months in office and limited opportunities to promote new legislative initiatives. Moreover, Udall played a leading role in issues regarding Indian lands, and Bennett had no choice but to follow the secretary's lead. Bennett also had to contend with pressures from the Senate Interior Committee to continue the withdrawal of federal services from the tribes. He resisted these pressures, but in so doing he had to limit his activities in other areas so as not to anger Henry Jackson and others of his persuasion.

As a result of these limitations, Bennett exercised a quiet style of leadership that did not capture much attention. His performance in

Indian affairs was overshadowed by two important events in 1968, the release of a presidential message on Indian affairs and the passage of the Indian Civil Rights Act. Because both of these initiatives emanated from outside the BIA, Bennett did not play a significant role in either. Nonetheless, Bennett brought important changes to the BIA during the closing years of the Johnson administration.

BENNETT AND INDIAN AFFAIRS

Bennett's support of the Indian Resources Development Act, which most Native Americans opposed, did not damage his relations with Indian leaders or their communities. Some Indians even claimed that Bennett covertly opposed the act. The newsletter of the League of Nations Pan.-Am. Indians alleged that Bennett told Chief Frank Ducheneaux "they are going to do it anyway, I can delay it, stall, do anything to slow it up. If I quit in protest, they'll just put somebody in who will rob us fast. Maybe if I stall long enough a miracle will happen." Although one tribe, the Comanches, told Bennett that they were "deeply disappointed that you are lending your support and the prestige of your good office to the sponsorship and passage" of the Omnibus Bill, many Native Americans assumed that Bennett had no choice but to promote Udall's initiative. In Vine Deloria, Jr.'s account of the legislation's history, he asserted that "Bennett . . . was given the thankless task" of building support for the bill.[3]

American Indian willingness to consider Bennett as an ally was based on his attitude concerning the federal government's responsibilities to Native Americans. At a congressional hearing held in January 1967, Bennett argued that the "time is ripe for us to recast the trusteeship relationship between Indians and the Federal Government so that life and conditions on the reservation can be structured by the Indian people, with the help of the Federal Government." Thus, he perceived the BIA's role as that of assisting Native Americans rather than leading them, a position articulated in the 1961 *Declaration of Indian Purpose* and numerous other Indian pronouncements throughout the decade.[4]

In early 1969 Bennett revealed a specific plan regarding bureau operations, informing a congressional subcommittee that he hoped to convert the BIA "into a strictly professional organization known as the American Indian Development and Professional Service Agency." Under the terms of the plan, all "nonprofessional services [provided by the BIA]" and professional services "wherever capability" existed, would be "contracted to individual Indians, groups of Indians, or tribes." In addition, "all existing Bureau installations" would "be turned over to tribes or tribal housing authorities." After receiving tribal approval, local school boards would receive authority over bureau schools. Although the conversion plan was never realized, in part because Bennett resigned from office several weeks after making it public, it revealed much about Bennett's intentions and goals during his tenure as commissioner.[5]

Bennett's desire to turn BIA services over to Indian communities did not mean that he envisioned the eventual abolition of the BIA. The 1969 conversion proposal actually called for the expansion of BIA services to include "Indians anywhere who are found to be neglected," meaning that Native Americans who had relocated to urban areas would become eligible for BIA benefits. Bennett explained his support for the BIA in 1967, when he declared, "[T]he property protection and social services now provided by the Bureau must continue as a baserock from which local development can occur without the shockwaves of abrupt change or undue risk." Rather than abolish the BIA, he wanted Indian communities to provide the services currently offered by federal employees, thus promoting both self-determination and economic opportunity on the reservations.[6]

BUREAU ORGANIZATION AND PERSONNEL

In order to improve the quality of bureau services, Bennett made several changes within the BIA, including a reorganization of the bureau's administrative structure "to give more flexibility to every operation" and "to speed services to the Indian." Because "the Indian people need to be brought face to face with their problems and to have an understanding of them so we can get their contribution" to federal Indian policy, Bennett created the Office of Community Development. This office was responsible for helping Indians "develop the kinds of organization, leadership ability, communication skills and motivation to focus their own resources and the resources of other groups and organizations toward the realization of their goals." However, the community development program did not appeal to the appropriations committees in Congress, and in 1969 its director admitted that it was a "very limited program."[7]

The most important organizational change occurred in the area of education. In 1950 Commissioner Dillon S. Myer had created eleven area offices, each having the authority to override directives from the Branch of Education, and thus limiting the effectiveness, and even the possibility, of innovation in Indian education. In 1966 Bennett "elevated our education program to division status with an Assistant Commissioner over it." This move gave the director of education line authority over educational personnel, eliminating direct interference from the area directors and creating an atmosphere conducive to experimentation in Indian schools.[8]

Bennett was not successful in reorganizing all aspects of bureau operations. Over the years the BIA had found itself in constant conflict with the solicitor's office in the Interior Department—Philleo Nash remembered his relationship with Frank Barry of that office as one of "vigorous disagreement." In 1968 Bennett asked Udall to create a solicitor's office within the BIA or to allow him authority over department attorneys involved with Indian affairs. Udall rejected these requests, but did inform the solicitor's office to take a more "pro-Indian" stance in the future.[9]

Reorganization efforts meant little without an accompanying change in personnel—Nash's failure to remove ineffective personnel from the ranks of the BIA had hampered the effectiveness of his administration— so Bennett and Udall brought new people into top bureau positions.

Udall later recalled that "whereas Nash had gone along with the old career education people who were very unimaginative, Bennett and I reached out and got some of what we felt were the best educators in the country." Dr. Carl Marburger, a professional educator who had served as a consultant to the U.S. Office of Education, became the new assistant commissioner for education. Dr. William R. Carmack, former director of the University of Oklahoma's Human Relations Center, took the position of assistant commissioner of community services. Udall, who considered the new personnel to be "highly capable people," informed President Johnson that the appointments were "key steps in making the Bureau more responsive to the needs of the Indian people." That these appointments came "from outside the circle of bureaucracy," evidenced the desire of Bennett and Udall to bring fresh perspectives to the conduct of Indian affairs. They would need these new viewpoints as they worked to resolve pressing problems in Indian affairs, especially in the field of education.[10]

LEGISLATION

Like his predecessor, Bennett did not advocate any significant legislative measures during his tenure in office. He spent 1966 and 1967 working for passage of Udall's Indian Resources Development Act. In addition to the limitations that the uncertainty surrounding that bill brought to Indian affairs, Bennett faced additional problems with Congress that stifled legislative initiatives.

Bennett detailed the "several basic problems affecting Indian legislation . . . which have, as in the past, adversely affected our relationship with Congress and the prospects of the enactment of certain types of desirable Indian legislation" in a January 1968 memo to Stewart Udall. Bennett admitted that "most of the problems . . . are of long-standing duration with little prospect of solution." He noted that the "divergent positions of the Senate and House Committees" made passage of a long-term leasing bill unlikely. A split between the two committees also prevented the enactment of a plan to increase the Indian land base by conveying "public lands and property not needed by the United States to Indian tribes." The Senate committee wanted the lands transferred in fee status, while the House favored the Interior Department's desire to convey the lands in trust status. Bennett also pointed to the continued congressional demands for an heirship bill as another "perennially pressing legislative issue" that seemed to have no solution. Problems such as these prevented Bennett from offering any substantive legislation. Instead, he turned his attention to obstructing the passage of termination legislation and to improving the quality of BIA services.[11]

TERMINATION

In 1967, George McGovern assumed the position of chairman of the Indian Affairs Subcommittee, a move that promised much for the conduct of Indian policy within Congress. The previous year McGovern had introduced a resolution to the Senate declaring that "American Indian and Alaska Native communities should be given the freedom and encouragement to develop their maximum potential." Moreover, McGovern called upon Congress to "support a policy of developing the necessary programs to bring Indians and Alaska Natives to a desirable social and economic level." In remarks made while offering the resolution, McGovern opposed "any general arbitrary policy of termination for the groups whose social and economic conditions require long-range Federal assistance."[12]

McGovern had high hopes for his subcommittee. In January 1968 he informed Robert Kennedy of his intention "as Chairman of the Subcommittee on Indian Affairs to launch in the near future a thorough and complete investigation of all matters pertaining to the problems of our Indian citizens." However, Henry Jackson, who remained the leading proponent of termination, maintained tight control over the subcommittee and prevented McGovern from achieving any of his goals. Fred Harris recalled that "McGovern . . . didn't want to stand up too much to Jackson, his chairman, and [Clinton] Anderson." In 1969 McGovern admitted that "we really haven't rolled on the Indian Affairs Subcommittee."[13]

Jackson's ability to dominate the Interior Committee did not translate into success for the termination policy. Bennett skillfully opposed termination, as his efforts to prevent the slated termination of the Senecas in 1967 evidenced. The Seneca rehabilitation package required the introduction of a termination plan to Congress by 31 August 1967. In July of that year Bennett traveled to the Seneca Nation to discuss tribal termination. To the surprise of the Senecas, he asked them to prepare their own termination plan. He also told them that any proposed legislation would include a provision requiring a tribal referendum to approve termination. On 18 August he met with a tribal delegation and presented them with a BIA draft of legislation, informing the Senecas that this plan "should not be considered final."[14]

At this point Bennett evidenced the familiarity with legislative practices that had prompted Udall to advance him to the position of commissioner. Realizing that Wayne Aspinall would refuse to schedule any hearings after 1 September, Bennett delayed submitting the proposed bill until 31 August, thus meeting the deadline but preventing congressional action on the bill. The commissioner had given the Senecas another year to fight the proposed termination, and he recommended that they pressure their congressional delegation to oppose any such legislation.[15]

Bennett had assisted the Senecas, but Jackson and some members of the Senate committee pushed for the termination of several other tribes. Jackson still demanded the termination of the Colvilles in his home state, but the House Interior Committee's refusal to take action on that issue had effectively blocked the tribe's termination. As of early 1968 the committee had "required by instructions in various Committee reports" termination legislation for seven tribes. Bennett had no choice but to comply with the committee's demands, but he applied "three basic principles" to the drafting of termination bills. First, he wanted every bill to include provisions for tribal consent. Second, each bill was to provide for "continued recognition of the tribe as an entity by the Federal Government." Finally, Bennett wanted the tribes to retain eligibility "to negotiate as an entity for services from other Federal, State and private agencies."[16]

The application of these principles would not merely limit the nature of termination proceedings, they would end them. Bennett knew that by 1968 not a single tribe would consent to a termination bill. The draft legislation for terminating the Eastern Shawnee Tribe of Oklahoma included a consent provision; however, Bennett had a letter from Shawnee Chief Julian B. BlueJacket that stated the tribe's opposition to termination. Thus, the inclusion of the consent provision ensured that the tribe would not be terminated. Bennett's insistence upon obtaining consent ensured that no new termination legislation passed Congress during his years in office. However, despite his resistance to tribal termination, the issue still troubled Native Americans and weakened their support for federal programs promoting self-determination.[17]

EDUCATION

Rather than pursue legislative avenues to create new programs, Bennett attempted to upgrade the quality of existing projects. Improving educational services was a priority and a problem throughout Bennett's term in office. However, bureau reorganization and personnel changes could not provide a quick fix to problems resulting from years of poor administration. Frustrated by disputes with area directors, Assistant Commissioner Carl Marburger resigned after only one year in office. Charles Zellers, an expert in business administration who worked in the U.S. Office of Education, filled the vacant slot and remained in office through early 1970, when he too resigned.[18]

Educational services did not improve dramatically during this period, but important changes did occur. In 1967 the BIA hired an outside consultant to develop "a course of study to help Indian students understand the strengths and origins of their Indian culture." The following year Bennett reported that "teaching of Indian languages is being encouraged as rapidly as possible." These measures showed Bennett's desire to end the forced assimilation of Indians into American society through attacks on their culture, long the policy of the federal government. In keeping with his commitment to Indian self-determination, Bennett established the National Indian Advisory Committee on Education, a panel that included "tribal leaders from across the Nation."[19]

One education project, the Rough Rock Demonstration School, garnered favorable media attention. Sponsored by both the BIA and OEO, the school opened on the Navajo Reservation in 1966. An experiment in community control, Rough Rock had local residents on its school board and Navajo parents serving as dormitory attendants. The curriculum included studies in Navajo history and culture. The school received positive media coverage, which pleased bureau administrators, but in fact Rough Rock was an unusual case that proved hard to repeat. Because the school received funds from two government agencies, it had twice the budget of schools of comparable size. Despite its uniqueness, Rough Rock served as an example of the benefits that innovation and Indian inclusion could bring to the BIA's education division.[20]

Rough Rock was an exception in more ways than one. It was one of the few Indian education programs that was not condemned by critics of Indian education, the most prominent of whom was Robert F. Kennedy. While serving as the junior senator from New York (and while planning a run for the presidency in 1968), Kennedy had developed an interest in the problems of poor and minority Americans, including Indians. Sen. Fred Harris recalled that "Robert spent a lot of time talking to LaDonna [Harris, the senator's wife and Cherokee] about that subject [Native American issues]." In July 1967 Kennedy assumed the chairmanship of the newly created Special Subcommittee on Indian Education, which provided him a forum from which to censure the nation's treatment of Native Americans.[21]

As subcommittee chairman, Kennedy engaged in scathing attacks on Indian education that received national attention. At hearings held on 14 December 1967, he called the education programs "a major failure," and the living conditions endured by Native Americans "a national tragedy and a national disgrace." He condemned the boarding school system as "barbaric," a remark reported in the *New York Times*. In early January 1968 Kennedy complained that "we've again betrayed our Indian people in not preparing them for the world. I'm distressed and shocked by our inattention to the Indian problem."[22]

The Indian education system deserved the criticism that Kennedy leveled against it; however, in the eyes of the Johnson administration (and most Americans), Robert Kennedy was not merely a concerned observer. Lyndon Johnson considered Kennedy to be his main political rival. Thus, the White House perceived Kennedy's effort in terms of their political impact. This viewpoint would play a role in the release of a presidential message on Indian affairs in March 1968.[23]

LAND ISSUES

In addition to the problems with educational services, conflicts concerning the management and ownership of native lands constituted a major concern for the Interior Department during the Bennett years. Because management issues were entangled with other Interior responsibilities such as reclamation, and land claims were politically volatile, Stewart Udall made the major decisions regarding native lands during the second half of the 1960s. Udall offered inconsistent leadership in this area, at times betraying the Indians' best interests and at other times championing their cause.

THE NAVAJO-HOPI LAND DISPUTE

The unresolved conflicts on the Navajo reservation remained a pressing problem for the BIA when Robert Bennett took office. Philleo Nash had been unable to bring about meaningful negotiations between the Navajos and the Hopis regarding the lands in the Joint Use Area (JUA), and the dispute poisoned relations between the tribes. In December 1965, the Hopis served eviction notices to two Navajo families living in District Six, the zone that a 1962 court ruling had determined belonged exclusively to the Hopis. In response, the Navajos considered evicting Hopi families living at Moenkopi, a village located in another disputed area outside the JUA known as the 1934 reservation. Because an attempt to oust the Moenkopi families would undoubtedly result in another long, bitter legal battle between the tribes, Commissioner Bennett traveled to the Navajo reservation to address the crisis on 20 April 1966, only a week after his Senate confirmation. He asked the Navajo tribal attorneys not to serve the eviction notice to the Hopis until he had an opportunity to study the problem. Two days later the Navajo Tribal Council voted to mount a legal battle against the eviction of the Navajo families instead of moving against the Moenkopi Hopis. Though Bennett's request probably played a role in the tribal council's decision, in all likelihood the tribe's attorneys had advised against an eviction because it would result in a court case for which they were not prepared.[24]

Had Bennett pursued a moderate and impartial course regarding the land disputes, he might have improved relations between the Navajos and the BIA. However, on 8 July 1966 he issued an administrative order that resulted in further conflict. The order placed restrictions on development in the more than 1.5 million acres of the 1934 reservation (similar restrictions were already in place on the JUA). The "Bennett Freeze," as it came to be known, required "formal action by the Hopi as well as the Navajo Tribe on all those cases which hypothecate the surface or subsurface resources for exploration, mining, rights-of-way, traders, or other use or occupancy authorized by permit, lease or license." In other words, development programs would require the approval of both tribal councils. Furthermore, "all moneys derived from the use and management of the surface and subsurface resources therein" would be placed in a "special deposit account" pending judgment of the Hopis' interest in the 1934 reservation. Finally, "neither tribe should be permitted unilaterally to take actions within the said area that trespass on the rights of the other," a provision that precluded the eviction of the Hopis living in Moenkopi.[25]

Given that the Hopis had rejected most projects within the JUA, the Bennett Freeze ended development within the designated area. The order noted that the Freeze would "place a financial hardship on both tribes," but this was not correct. Although the region included the Hopi village of Moenkopi, Navajos, who dominated the cities of Tuba City, Cameron, and Page in the Freeze area, bore the brunt of the order's impact. Peter MacDonald later argued that the Freeze "was part of Stewart Udall's revenge against the Navajo," coming as it did only two months after the tribal council had rejected Udall's proposal for the construction of the BVD factory. He also believed that Udall issued the order in order to force the Hopis and Navajos to resolve the land claim disputes, a more likely explanation. The order had stated that "the period of hardships . . . would be shortened materially by a friendly confrontation of the tribes, to the end that in face-to-face talks they agreeably negotiate" a conclusion to the land dispute.[26]

Bennett informed the Navajo Tribal Council that the Freeze was intended to prevent further legal battles between the Navajos and Hopis. The Navajos had recently granted a right-of-way through the disputed area, a move that John Boyden, attorney for the Hopis, had protested. The Freeze, Bennett explained, would head off another lawsuit over disputed lands. However, the Navajo Tribal Council took Bennett's explanation as evidence of collusion between Udall and Boyden, a friend and fellow Mormon. The council voted 52 to 2 to condemn the order and accused Udall of issuing it to aid Boyden.[27]

Such a vote could not have surprised Udall, who was still at odds with the tribal council over the contract of attorney Norman Littell.

However, Udall was incorrect if he thought that the Freeze would bring about a quick resolution of the decades-old conflict. Instead, it worsened the situation. Because the impact of the order was lopsided, with Navajos bearing a far greater burden, the Hopis had little reason to approve any development projects. BIA officials assured the Navajos that the Hopis would grant approval for projects such as a school and hospital planned for Tuba City, but the Hopis saw the Freeze as an opportunity to wring concessions from the Navajos in the intermittent negotiations concerning the JUA and the 1934 reservation and refused to sanction those plans. Life for the Navajos living in the Freeze area grew harder, and they rightfully blamed the BIA and the Hopis. Far from prodding the tribes to negotiate a settlement, the Freeze only exacerbated tensions between the tribes and made the Navajos even angrier at Udall and the BIA.[28]

Negotiations over the disputed areas deadlocked and the Freeze remained in place. Bennett made sincere attempts to bring about a settlement between the two tribes, acting as a mediator at meetings of the Navajo and Hopi negotiating committees held in 1967 and 1968. In keeping with his commitment to Indian self-determination, he allowed the tribal delegates to conduct the actual business of hammering out an agreement. David M. Brugge, an attorney with the Navajo, admired Bennett's "reasonableness" and his "skills as a mediator in a dispute between Indians." However, despite Bennett's efforts, the tribes could not resolve their differences. Both tribes hoped to gain the upper hand and receive the largest share of the disputed areas. The Freeze itself had become part of the maneuvering for advantage. At an October 1967 meeting, Navajo tribal delegates told Bennett that the Freeze limited their ability to negotiate and asked him to revoke or modify it. The Hopis wanted Bennett to extend the Freeze over the entire Navajo reservation. Recognizing that discussions had reached an impasse, Bennett announced that he would modify the Freeze to allow certain public works projects (such as the Tuba City school and hospital) to proceed on his authority, but that apart from these exceptions the Freeze would remain in effect.[29]

Bennett told Navajo Area Director Graham Holmes that the Freeze was merely a temporary measure. However, Bennett never lifted the Freeze, which remained in effect until 1992, when a U.S. District Court rejected most of the Hopis' land claims and partially rescinded the Freeze. A 1972 amendment to Bennett's original order exempted Tuba City and Moenkopi, which improved the lives of the residents of those cities but also excluded Hopis from the effects of the Freeze. In 1980 Congress transformed the Bennett Freeze into law and widened it to include a ban on private construction projects, which prevented the Navajos on the 1934 reservation from completing housing improvements. As Peter MacDonald recalled, the Navajos in the Freeze area "lived in squalor," with "elderly people whose wells had run dry but who could not legally dig a new well" and "handicapped people who could not build a wheelchair ramp onto the front of their homes."[30]

In a 1993 Senate hearing on the impact of Bennett Freeze, Navajo Nation President Peterson Zah complained that "we could not allow people for the last 27 years to climb on top of their roof and re-roof their house." He called the Freeze area "the land where time stood still," noting that "the economic infrastructure of this area has not improved for over 26 years. No new roads, no new power lines, no new water lines, no new housing, no new schools, and no new community facilities. Nothing." The Bennett Freeze condemned some 2,500 Navajo families to lives of misery and poverty for over a quarter century.[31]

The damage the Freeze caused went beyond mere economic disruption. Relations between Navajos and the Hopis, already poor because of the land claims, worsened, and even after the Freeze was lifted both sides remained resentful. At the 1993 Senate hearing, Herb Yazzie, Navajo, called the Freeze "the weapon . . . that was handed to the Hopi people . . . to stifle and to punish Navajo people." At the same hearing Vernon Masayesva, Hopi tribal chairman, argued that the Freeze was "the only mechanism available to the Hopis to protect what rights they had from a surrounding Navajo population."[32]

The 1966 decision to implement the Freeze was therefore both irresponsible and cruel. The Interior Department sought to pressure the tribes to resolve a land dispute by denying tribal members economic opportunities and an improved standard of living, the very goals of the department's Indian policy. Although Bennett later claimed that Udall and E. Reeseman Fryer had drafted the Freeze order, and that he had signed it without even reading it, both he and Udall bear responsibility for the freeze. They implemented an administrative order that continued as government policy for twenty-six years, a policy that intentionally increased the suffering of a people who were already among the most impoverished in the nation.[33]

BLACK MESA

The Bennett Freeze was a mistake, but not the only one Udall made with regard to the Navajos and Hopis. In 1966 he approved a leasing agreement that raised suspicions about his ties to industrial concerns, his commitment to the environment, and his trusteeship of Native American lands.

Black Mesa, a 3,300-square-mile plateau in northeastern Arizona, straddled the Navajo reservation and the JUA. Geological surveys conducted in the early twentieth century revealed that Black Mesa contained sizable deposits of soft, bituminous, low-sulfur coal. The presence of this coal fit into two aspects of Udall's agenda as interior secretary. First, Udall wanted to promote the economic development of the reservations, and the lease or sale of the coal could provide capital to both the Navajos and Hopis. Second, Udall committed himself to the growth of the American Southwest in general and his home state of Arizona in particular. The coal could fuel the power plants necessary to support this growth.[34]

In 1964 the Navajos signed a lease allowing the Peabody Coal Mining Company to strip mine 40,000 acres of Black Mesa within the Navajo reservation. Udall hailed the leasing arrangement as "a giant step forward in the development of a formula for joint public and private resource development in the Colorado Basin that will become a model for the Nation." It would bring "new jobs, large tax benefits, [and] tremendous economic advantages not only in royalties and jobs for two Indian tribes but also for the entire Southwest." Udall's enthusiasm for the project led him to support Peabody Coal's efforts to expand its operations into the JUA, a move that would require joint permission from the Navajos and the Hopis and a deal for the tribal water necessary to process and transport the coal.[35]

The Peabody Company's request for water was among the topics Udall planned to discuss with Navajo leaders at a June 1965 meeting. Although Udall met with Nakai and other tribal representatives, old guard members of the tribal council boycotted the meeting, which was scheduled to take place only two weeks after Judge John Sirica had issued his order barring Udall from firing tribal attorney Norman Littell. In a letter to Udall, the old guard recommended that Udall "ad vise [sic] your friends in the Peabody Coal Company to take their problems on the Navajo Reservation to the properly constituted authority, the Navajo Advisory Committee or Council."[36]

Despite this response, Udall continued to work for the expansion of coal mining operations. In late 1965 he created a task force that included then-Deputy Commissioner Robert Bennett to coordinate energy development issues with the Navajo tribe. Meanwhile Norman Littell conducted negotiations with Peabody Coal, the Hopi tribe, and Interior Department officials in order to craft a lease for the JUA coal deposits. Drafted during the winter months of 1965, the proposed lease included provisions for the construction of a slurry pipeline to transport the coal, a project requiring large amounts of tribal water. On 17 February 1966 Littell presented a draft of a lease agreement to the Navajo Tribal Council. Graham Holmes remembered Littell "walking up the Council aisle, waving papers for the Council to approve, like the Saviour had returned."[37]

The tribal council had no expertise in the area of coal leasing and little accurate information regarding the Black Mesa deposits. Moreover, council members believed that they had no time to investigate the matter because they "were told fossil fuel wouldn't be worth a tinker's damn" in the coming years because nuclear power would make coal power plants obsolete. Faced with the opportunity to increase tribal income and employment, the tribal council approved the lease the following day by a vote of 53 to 1.[38]

Tribal Councilman Keith Smith later claimed that "the Council never had a good discussion" of the lease and was "asked, in effect, to say yes or no to the proposal." Interviews conducted several years later revealed that many council members had not understood the terms of the leasing agreement. The discussion that had taken place focused on positives such as job creation rather than the potential negative consequences of the mining including community disruption and environmental degradation. The Navajos agreed to the lease because of its promised financial rewards and because Littell and Interior Department officials enthusiastically supported the deal.[39]

Because the proposed mine was located in the JUA, it required the approval of the Hopi Tribal Council. As was the case with the Navajos, the tribal attorney, John Boyden, pressed for the council's endorsement of the lease. On 16 May 1966 the Hopi Tribal Council voted 10 to 0 to approve the lease, a vote that did not accurately indicate Hopi attitudes toward the mining of Black Mesa. Hopi society was divided between members committed to traditional values and those identified with modernization and economic development. The latter group controlled the tribal council and favored the lease.[40]

The Hopis believed that Black Mesa was included within a sacred site known as "Tukunavi . . . part of the heart of our Mother Earth." In a 1949 letter to President Harry Truman, traditional Hopi leaders asserted their opposition to mineral leasing on the "sacred home of the Hopi people"; ten years later they repeated that message in a letter to BIA Commissioner Glenn Emmons. Given the sacredness of the mesa, most Hopis would have opposed the lease had they known of it. However, as Richard O. Clemmer, an anthropologist who worked with the Hopis and protested the mining operations during the 1970s, later noted, "there had been no open hearings, no community discussion, no administrative disclosures by either their own tribal government or the Bureau of Indian Affairs" regarding the Peabody lease. The tribal council that approved the coal lease in 1966 did so quietly, with no fanfare, because it did not have the support of most Hopis.[41]

The tribal council was originally created under the terms of the 1934 Indian Reorganization Act, which the Hopis had accepted in an election marred by controversy. Alien to Hopi social and political organization, the tribal council disbanded in 1943 but was revived in 1951 at the insistence of the BIA. In 1955 the federal government recognized the council as the official governing body of the Hopi people. Although the Hopi constitution did not empower the council to approve leases, in early 1961 the Interior Department gave it that authority, a decision of questionable legality.[42]

Most Hopis ignored the federal government's recognition of the council and rejected its authority, looking instead to the Kikmongwi, the traditional village leaders, for guidance. As a result, in May 1966 only eleven of the council's seventeen seats were filled. Moreover, only six of the eleven council members had been certified by the Kikmongwi, a requirement spelled out in the tribal constitution. Thus, the council that approved the Peabody lease not only lacked the confidence of the Hopi people; its status as a legally constituted body was in doubt, as well as its legal authority to sanction any leases. Nonetheless, the Interior Department accepted the council's vote of 16 May and certified the lease in early June.[43]

According to the terms of the leases (the Navajos had renegotiated their 1964 lease), both tribes received royalties on the mining operations of 3.35%, which meant that the Navajos would earn some $58.5 million over the thirty-five years the leases were in effect, and the Hopis approximately $14 million. Peabody Coal's profits from the Black Mesa strip mine were estimated at $750 million. In addition, the Navajos agreed to sell water to the company for $5.00 per acre-foot. The Hopis had struck a poorer bargain, receiving only $1.67 per acre-foot. Beyond reseeding the mined areas at company expense, Peabody had no obligations other than to surrender the land "upon the termination of this lease, in as good condition as received, except for the ordinary wear, tear and depletion incident to mining operations," a troubling provision because the "scalping and decapitation [of strip mining] give the land the look of the surface of the moon," according to one critic.[44]

The leases protected neither the Indians' land nor their economic interests, as later events would show. All but ignored during the lease negotiations, the environmental degradation the strip mining caused garnered national media attention during the early 1970s, and Black Mesa became a rallying symbol for environmental activists. Renegotiations of the original leases in 1987 revealed just how poor the original royalty rates of the original leases had been. Under the new leases, the tribes received 12.5% of the coal's value, and $300 per acre-foot for the first 2800 acre-feet of water, and $600 per acre-foot for all water used thereafter.[45]

With regard to the Black Mesa coal mining operations, Stewart Udall failed to act as the trustee for Indian interests. In his opposition to the proposed transfer of the BIA to HEW, Udall had argued that his department was most able to oversee Indian land. However, the Interior Department also furthered the exploitation of resources, a mission that led to a fundamental conflict of interest within the department. In the case of Black Mesa, responsibility for protecting Indian lands and economic concerns lost out to the mining of coal to operate power plants that would serve the citizens of the Southwest.

Both the leases and the council votes should have come under the close scrutiny of the Interior Department. The leases contained no provisions protecting the environment and no enforcement mechanisms to police violations. The royalty rates for the coal and fees for the water were far below industry norms. The 1966 tribal council votes approving the coal leases were both suspect. The Navajos did not have sufficient information to make an informed decision, and the Hopi Tribal Council might not have been a legally constituted body. In neither case did the councils consult or confer with tribal members to discuss their views of the mining operations. All these issues should have raised concerns within the Interior Department, but in his determination to promote the economic development of the American Southwest Udall ignored his responsibilities as trustee.

Land Claims

Udall's failure to protect Native American interests at Black Mesa did not reflect his administration's position regarding Indian lands in general. Under his direction, the Interior Department defended the claims of Native Alaskans against competing claims brought by the state government during the 1960s.

Confusion and disagreement over Native Alaskan land claims dated back to the 1884 Organic Act, which created a civil government for the Alaska territory. The act did not grant title or recognize any specific rights, but did guarantee that Native Alaskans "shall not be disturbed in the possession of any lands actually in their use or occupation or now claimed by them." The act left the final determination regarding Native land claims to "future legislation by Congress." Over seventy years later Congress considered native land claims when it debated the terms under which Alaska would be admitted as a state. However, far from resolving the issue, the 1958 Alaska Statehood Act further complicated the conflicts over Native Alaskan land claims.[46]

The act required that the state of Alaska "disclaim all right and title . . . to any lands or other property (including fishing rights), the right or title to which may be held by any Indians, Eskimos, or Aleuts . . . or is held by the United States in trust for said natives." The act also permitted the state to select up to "one hundred and two million five hundred and fifty thousand acres from the public lands of the United States in Alaska which are vacant, unappropriated, and unreserved." Because Congress failed to provide any mechanism for recognizing native title, the state's land selection process inevitably conflicted with the claims of Native Alaskans.[47]

The Interior Department was fully aware of these conflicts and other problems that Native Alaskans faced. The 1961 task force had concluded that "because of its location, its pattern of settlement, and its traditional and actual relationship with the Federal Government, Alaska requires a separate, detailed study." In brief remarks concerning land claims, the task force stated that "natives in all areas [of Alaska] are deeply concerned that the lands which they believe to be theirs will be taken by the State through the authority in the enabling act which permits it to select more than a hundred million acres of Federal land" and urged the Interior Department to "renew its efforts to obtain satisfactory legislation" aimed at ending the land claims issue.[48]

Udall responded to the task force recommendations and organized a task force on Alaska Native affairs in 1962. Two task force members, W. W. Keeler and James Officer, had served on the 1961 task force. The Alaska task force conducted field work in June 1962 and submitted its final report the following December. The task force made several suggestions regarding land claims. It argued for the "need for more effective implementation of the existing legislation toward conveying land title to individual natives," a reference to the Native Allotment Act of 1906, which granted individual Native Alaskans restricted title to a 160-acre lot, and to the Native Townsite Act of 1926, which granted title to small lots in villages. The task force also recommended the creation of "subsistence use areas" in which Native Alaskans would have a "continuing privileged claim to the harvest of . . . natural products" such as berries.[49]

In the end, the report recognized the role of Congress in resolving the land claims. It pointed to the "need for Congress to elucidate the aboriginal rights of the native and if necessary to establish a forum in which their claims can be heard." The task force also responded to the pressures that the state of Alaska exerted on the situation, declaring that "Congress should enact a statute of limitations in any provision for deferral of state selection, so as not to hold it up indefinitely."[50]

Native Alaskans rejected the task force recommendations, which they claimed ignored both native mineral rights and cash settlements for lost lands. Another objection, the most important, highlighted misperceptions regarding native subsistence economies. Most Americans perceived Alaska as a vast and empty wilderness, but Native Alaskans required the use of literally millions of acres in order to thrive in the harsh northern climate. As an Alaskan newspaper noted, "natives have steadfastly maintained that they need large areas for hunting, fishing and trapping." The small plots of land available through the Allotment and Townsite acts were inappropriate for survival and success in Alaska. Native Alaskans also had an eye on their future, recognizing the central role land would play for "development of resources later as their economy changes."[51]

The Alaskan congressional delegation favored the continuation of the state's land selection and the extinguishment of native land claims either through legislation awarding a cash settlement or through the action of the Indian Claims Commission. Native Alaskans feared both these alternatives, neither of which would grant them title to the lands they desired. In 1963 Native Alaskans from twenty-four villages asked Udall to impose a freeze on all land transfers in disputed areas, a request echoed by the National Council on Indian Affairs. Udall took no action at that time, but Alaskan land claims remained a problem that Interior officials knew would eventually require their attention. At a 1964 policy planning session, they discussed the "need for settling the land problems of the Alaskan natives," although the only proposal made to that effect was "to work with the State of Alaska in getting the natives title to some of the lands which they claim."[52]

Sen. Ernest Gruening of Alaska raised the land claims issue during Robert Bennett's confirmation hearing in April 1966. Gruening opposed granting title to large land claims, arguing that economically depressed villages "in their despair, have been advised by lawyers and others who are concerned to try and seek large areas of land set aside for them." He dismissed contentions that Native Alaskans needed the land to support their subsistence economies, claiming that the "land . . . will no longer support the game it once did when there were fewer people to harvest it." Gruening tried to pin Bennett down on this issue, asking him if he believed that "reserving large tracts of land for each native village would be a proper solution." Bennett offered an evasive reply, declaring that he did not believe that "land in and of itself is a solution to the problems of the native people."[53]

Gruening let Bennett's remark pass, but he did not abandon the land claims issue. He appended a statement concerning the Alaska situation to the Senate executive report released the week after the confirmation hearing. In his comments, Gruening declared that the "single most difficult problem in Alaska . . . related to the policies of the Bureau of Indian Affairs is the existence of native protests to State land selections and other claims to land on dubious grounds of aboriginal rights." He noted that as of 1966 the Interior Department had not resolved native protests concerning fifteen million acres that the state desired. Gruening claimed that the "practical effect of the Department's refusal to act one way or another, either approving them or dismissing these native protests, has been to paralyze the land selection program" leading to the "withdrawal of 15 million acres of Alaska from eligibility for selection."[54]

Gruening was correct in his assertions. Unbeknownst to him and the other members of the Senate Interior Committee, Newton Edwards, special assistant to John Carver, effectively placed an unofficial bureaucratic freeze on the state's land selection process. Realizing that the native protests would probably be rejected, the sympathetic Edwards literally filed the native protests away in a drawer in his office, where they sat for years. Attorney Arthur Lazarus later remembered Edwards as an "unsung hero" for his actions, which slowed the state's acquisition of public lands and thus offered natives additional time to mount a defense of the lands they claimed.[55]

Gruening's complaints drew attention to the land claims issue, which was a topic of discussion at a 28 April 1966 BIA planning session that both Udall and Bennett attended. In a memorandum written the following day, Udall reminded his commissioner that they had agreed to "tackle the native land claims issue [in Alaska] head-on." However, the Interior Department took no action until later that year, after a group of Native Alaskans met in October 1966 to discuss the situation.

Approximately two hundred and fifty people attended the three-day conference, which led to the founding of the Alaska Federation of Natives (AFN). The conference approved recommendations including a freeze on all federal lands pending the settlement of native claims and consultation with Native Alaskans before Congress acted to resolve the matter.[56]

Udall responded to the conference's demand for action on the land claims issue, announcing on 1 December 1966 that the scheduled sale of oil and gas leases in the northwest Arctic "will be suspended pending further consideration of protests which have been received" in regard to native title. Because the suspension order raised doubts about title to the land, it served in effect as a land freeze. Native Alaskans recognized the opportunity the suspension provided, and by May 1967 native groups filed thirty-nine protests concerning 380 million acres of land, thus preventing any action, include state land selection, from taking place.[57]

Emil Notti, president of the AFN, stated that "my sympathies are with Mr. Udall and the land freeze," and argued that Udall "should maintain the freeze until positive action is taken for the settlement of the claims." The reactions of officials within the state government were not so favorable. Because the state received ninety percent of the revenue generated by the sales and leases, the suspension affected the state's income. Walter J. Hickel, the newly elected Republican governor, claimed that Udall was playing politics, punishing Alaskans for electing Republicans to high office in the November 1966 election. Edgar Paul Boyko, Hickel's nominee for the position of state attorney general, declared that the state "could conceivably be bankrupt in four to six years if the freeze continues." In his defense, Udall informed Hickel that he "could not in good conscience allow title to pass into others' hands," especially because "to permit others to acquire title to the lands the Natives are occupying would create an adversary against whom the Natives would not have the means of protecting themselves."[58]

While state officials complained about the land freeze, members of the Alaskan congressional delegation pressed the Interior Department to "take the initiative in proposing a solution to the Alaskan native claims."

As Undersecretary Charles Luce noted in a January 1967 memorandum, the legislators refused to draft legislation because "approximately 20 percent of the voters of Alaska are Indians or Eskimos," a considerable constituency no congressman dared offend. Ernest Gruening wanted legislation that would "provide for compensation of such claims from funds in the Federal Treasury in lieu of awards of real property," but in June 1967 he introduced by request an Interior Department bill authorizing the interior secretary to grant native villages land not exceeding 50,000 acres. In addition, the bill permitted "the State to initiate an action in the Court of Claims on behalf of all Natives, as a single group, to recover from the United States the value of the additional lands to which the Natives have a valid use and occupancy claim."[59]

Udall defended the bill on the grounds that it "would put Alaska natives on equal footing with the Indian people of the other 49 states" in that it provided them with clear title to some lands and the opportunity to pursue a cash settlement for lands to which they had lost title. The AFN opposed the Interior bill because it deemed the eight to ten million acres that Native Alaskans would receive under its provisions to be insufficient. In addition, the AFN did not want the granted lands to be held in trust status for twenty-five years as the Interior bill required. The AFN persuaded Sen. Edward Louis "Bob" Bartlett (D.-Alaska) to introduce another proposal to Congress, a bill that gave the Court of Claims jurisdiction over Native Alaskan claims. The AFN proposal allowed the court to "award the natives of Alaska a judgment of ownership" to disputed lands to which the United States still retained title. As for lands to which title had already been granted to non-native interests, the court was permitted to "render judgment on behalf of the natives of Alaska for such amount as the court shall find to be the fair market value." In a report to President Johnson, Stewart Udall pointed out the most serious flaw in the AFN proposal, noting that it would "undoubtedly take 15–20 years for a judgment to be rendered" if the dispute went through the courts.[60]

In November 1967, Udall met with Native Alaskan leaders in Anchorage, Alaska, to discuss compromise solutions to the land claims issue. He informed President Johnson that the event was "one of the most satisfying public meetings I have participated in during my seven years as Secretary." At this meeting, which Governor Hickel attended, Udall "threw out the idea of a three-point compromise settlement." In addition to land grants for each village and a "modest, immediate payment" of anywhere from seven to fifteen million dollars, Udall recommended legislation "giving the natives of Alaska a permanent percentage interest in all oil and gas revenues realized by the U.S. government from the Alaska continental shelf," an idea that had come to him during the plane flight to Alaska. Because he could not guarantee administration support for his suggestion, he told his listeners that "I'm not making a proposal. I'm tossing out an idea."[61]

Despite its off-the-cuff nature, Udall's suggestions had merit. As he later told President Johnson, the proposal would offer Native Alaskans "a quick compromise rather than the long delays of litigation," although it did "involve a gamble by the native people" because "the oil and gas potential" of the shelf was unknown. He also maintained that this solution would "have the enthusiastic support of the Governor and the Alaska congressional delegation."[62]

Udall's contention that both Native Alaskans and the state government would prove receptive to his idea was correct. In February 1968, Emil Notti told members of the Senate Interior Committee that the "proposal has caught the support of the native groups because we see in it the possibility of a settlement that can be implemented in the near future." At the same hearing Governor Hickel declared that "the idea is good and I think that it is important." However, some congressmen balked at the idea. Lee Metcalf complained that the total revenues from the continental shelf were as yet unknown, and that in the event they proved substantial "there are places that that [revenue] could be very well used in the government [other than settling the land claims]."[63]

Budget concerns such as those Metcalf expressed killed Udall's revenue-sharing proposal, which did not appear in new legislation that Interior submitted in April 1968. At hearings on this bill, S. 3586, Metcalf praised Udall "for abandoning that Outer Continental Shelf program" because "it might have been too little or it might have made some of these natives the most affluent members of our society." Udall made no mention of his 1967 proposal, but did state that "the Bureau of the Budget is noted for looking hard at things of this kind [settlement proposals]," which suggested that Udall had found little support for his idea within the administration.[64]

S. 3586 retained the provision allowing each village a land grant not to exceed 50,000 acres. In addition, it allowed Native Alaskans to use land owned by the United States for "aboriginal use," including "hunting, fishing, trapping, and berrypicking" for a period of fifty years. Finally the bill included a settlement for the Alaskan land claims in the form of a $180 million payment to a special account established for Native Alaskans. Villages would receive annual payments from the account according to their populations. The Bureau of the Budget had arrived at the $180 million figure by allowing $3,000 for each of the estimated 60,000 Native Alaskans. Udall told the Senate Interior Committee that "the way essentially that we persuaded them [BOB] to go along with the $3,000 was to argue that we should not be less liberal with the natives that we have neglected for so long than we were with the Senecas." Thus, the 1965 compromise over the Kinzua Dam settlement for the Seneca Nation played a role in attempts to resolve the Alaska land claims conflict three years later.[65]

Despite well-intentioned efforts from all parties involved, the 90th Congress did not pass legislation concluding the land claims dispute. Native Alaskans opposed the Interior bill, asking instead for 40 million acres of land and a $500 million settlement. During the hearings, Udall announced his intention to keep the land freeze in place because "this holds everybody's feet to the fire and we tend toward a solution." However, the 1968 presidential election forced Udall to change his plans. Fearing that the incoming Republican administration would lift the freeze, Udall announced on 11 December 1968 that he would withdraw all unreserved lands in Alaska from settlement. That this announcement came on the same day that President-elect Richard Nixon's intention to nominate Hickel for the post of interior secretary became public was no accident. The formal withdrawal order, which Udall did not impose until 17 January 1969, three days before he left office, stated that "subject to valid existing rights, and subject to the conditions hereinafter set forth, all public lands in Alaska . . . are hereby withdrawn from all forms of appropriation and disposition . . . including selection by the state of Alaska." The public lands were to be "reserved under the jurisdiction of the Secretary of the Interior for the determination of the rights of the native Aleuts, Eskimos, and Indians of Alaska." With this order, on which Udall placed a two-year time limit, the informal freeze now had the force of law.[66]

In response to the withdrawal order, Walter Hickel announced that "what Udall can do by executive order I can undo." However, Hickel needed to build support for his nomination as interior secretary, and in exchange for an endorsement from the AFN, Hickel agreed to allow the freeze to remain in place. Far from being a short-lived, last-minute move on the part of Udall, the withdrawal order played a continuing role in attempts to resolve the land claims dispute, which ended in 1971 with the passage of the Alaska Native Claims Settlement Act (ANCSA).[67]

Udall had taken advantage of a unique situation to protect Native Alaskan interests. From a political perspective, Udall operated in Alaska with a free hand. Because Native Alaskans composed a sizable percentage of the electorate in that state (approximately twenty-five percent), their demands carried weight that members of the Alaskan congressional delegation could not ignore. Well aware of the risks that taking a leadership role in resolving the land claims issue would create, Ernest Gruening left the matter in the hands of the Interior Department. Senator Bartlett, who was sympathetic to the native cause, was in ill health and died in 1968. Finally, the Republican victory in the 1966 gubernatorial election allowed Udall to act without concern for the needs and preferences of a Democratic administration.[68]

In an interview conducted six months after Udall left office, he declared that "one of the other things that I took most satisfaction in the last two years . . . was in championing the cause of the Alaskan natives and their desire to have land in Alaska." He claimed that "what I was doing essentially was saying, 'Well, we've made all these mistakes in the past.' The one area where we still have an opportunity to come up with the right policies was in Alaska, and at least we were going to try and achieve that." As evidenced by the size of the land grants the Interior Department legislation offered, Udall never completely understood the needs of the Native Alaskans. However, his freeze and withdrawal orders protected their interests and their bargaining position during the years it took to forge a settlement of the claims disputes. Unlike the Black Mesa affair, in the case of Native Alaskans Udall fulfilled his obligations as the trustee of Native American interests.[69]

INDIAN AFFAIRS OUTSIDE THE INTERIOR DEPARTMENT

Although Interior Department activities stood at the center of the nation's Indian affairs, other federal agencies such as the Office of Economic Opportunity and the Economic Development Association played important roles in providing services to Native Americans during the late 1960s. During the final year of the Johnson administration, two unusual sources influenced the direction of Indian policy. In March 1968 the White House, which had taken a "hands-off" attitude toward Udall's management of Indian affairs, sent a special message regarding American Indians to the Congress. The following month Sam Ervin, a segregationist who did not sit on the Interior Committee, shepherded a bill concerning the constitutional rights of Indians through Congress.

THE 1967 TASK FORCE ON AMERICAN INDIANS

The president's special message on American Indians had its origins in a 1967 White House task force. In a memorandum of 19 August 1967,

Joseph Califano informed Lee White, now chairman of the Federal Power Commission, that he was to head a presidential task force on American Indians. Unlike the 1966 task force, which had relied upon experts from outside the government, White's group was to consist of "representatives from the Departments of Interior, Health, Education, and Welfare, Commerce, Labor, Housing and Urban Development, Treasury, the Office of Economic Opportunity and the Bureau of the Budget." Rather than offering a broad policy statement, Califano charged the new task force with developing "a strong and imaginative program for consideration by the second session of the 90th Congress."[70]

Califano's decision to organize the task force reflected the administration's "deep concern for the problems now facing the American Indians," and, in all likelihood, was a response to the failure of Udall's Indian Resources Development Act to make any headway in Congress. Because Califano expected the task force to offer realistic proposals for the administration's 1968 legislative package, program costs were of particular concern. Califano asked White to include "costs and benefits of implementation" for all task force proposals, and in September he told White that "a pricing of the individual program proposals" was necessary "to obtain the explicit judgment of your Task Force on program priorities."[71]

The task force, which included Udall and HEW Secretary John Gardner as members, submitted its final report to Califano's office on 23 October 1967. That same day Lee White sent Califano a memo summarizing the main points of the study. He admitted that the task force's suggestions were "pretty much in line" with the 1966 task force's final report, which he regarded as a "bit bolder" but "quite a bit more expensive" in its proposals. Both budget concerns and an awareness of political realities limited the scope of the task force's recommendations, but White's desire to build a consensus among the task force members also prevented them from being "radical and far-reaching." White told Califano that "we could have indulged our instinct for the jugular where the BIA is concerned only at the cost of the pretty solid consensus we now have." The result was a report that was lackluster and unimaginative, contributing no interesting or useful concepts for the improvement of federal Indian policy.[72]

White reported "a general agreement (at least, outside of Interior) that the Bureau of Indian Affairs has done a lousy job," but rejected the transfer of the BIA as a solution. A transfer proposal would "start a real political donny-brook, with violent consequences from Congress" and in any case would not solve the problem of "mediocre and uninspired leadership," which White believed was the "primary difficulty" with the government's management of Indian affairs. Because the task force concluded that the "answer [to improving Indian affairs] is where the action is in the field, in the dedication and industry of BIA's staff," it recommended only "legislative odds and ends . . . which hardly add up to an LBJ Indian program." The Indian Resources Development Act, which was still before Congress, also limited the administration's action in regard to promoting reservation development. As White noted, "I don't see how the President could submit a brand new proposal at this time."[73]

Because the task force did not see the need for a major legislative initiative, it offered instead a number of policy and program proposals, many of which had been heard in Washington for years. Specific recommendations included an increase in the number of new homes built for Indians; expansion of Head Start, kindergarten and higher education programs; additional financial support for the BIA's community development operations; and more "flexibility in managing Indian assets." However, two proposals were of significance. First, in order to "give highest visibility to a 'people oriented philosophy,'" the task force recommended combining the BIA with the Office of Territories under an assistant secretary of the interior for Indian and territorial affairs. Second, the study group called for "a Presidential message on American Indians," which would "acknowledge the Indian's right to maintain his unique identity, avow the government's intention not to pursue a policy of accelerated or coerced termination and pledge support for full Indian participation" in federal programs involving Indians.[74]

Response within the administration toward the final report was mixed. White reported that Udall "seemed aware that the 'half of a loaf' he did get—namely, the recommendation to leave BIA in Interior—was the best he could hope for." One BOB staffer complained that health recommendations in the report were "fairly pedestrian and unimaginative" and at times were "misleading and contradictory." Earl Darrah, another BOB employee, declared that "the Task Force has done a good job of defining the problems and developing responsive recommendations." Although the suggestion that the president offer a special message on Indians was not new—Stewart Udall had been pushing for a White House statement since Kennedy was in the White House—it was this proposal that received the most attention. In late 1967 administration officials in the White House began preparing such a message.[75]

THE PRESIDENT'S SPECIAL MESSAGE ON INDIAN AFFAIRS

Because the administration had no legislation to push, no new programs to tout, drafting "the Indian Message" proved difficult. Ervin Duggan, one of the White House staffers who worked on the message, complained about "the thinness of the program and the general lack of imagination in the program." Moreover, the White House had to craft the text carefully so as not to inadvertently make promises that would not be kept. Lee White argued for the removal of the phrase "lands are inviolate" from the draft because it "could even be considered to inhibit any Federal water project taking [of] Indian lands." In addition, White wanted specific figures regarding off-reservation Indians deleted because "the area is such a policy thicket," which is "calculated to touch sore nerves." Ervin Duggan described the completed message as "primarily one of policy rather than program."[76]

Despite the weaknesses of the proposed message, advance congressional responses were positive. Udall reported that Sens. Jackson, McGovern, Harris, and Metcalf all reacted favorably, and though House members proved "less enthusiastic" they agreed to most of the message's content. With congressional support guaranteed, the White House had to choose the most auspicious time to release the message.[77]

Udall and Bennett, who considered the message "the most positive statement ever made by a President about the Indians," wanted it released on Tuesday 5 March, to coincide with the meeting of the executive council of the NCAI in Washington, D.C., that day. For reasons not clear, the message was not released on 5 March, but that same day Joseph Califano informed Johnson that Robert Kennedy was preparing "a major Indian speech for Friday [8 March]." Califano suggested that the message be released before then "because otherwise he will probably include a lot of what is in our message in his speech." The White House sent the statement to Congress the next day, 6 March 1968. Although the message was not written to steal Robert Kennedy's thunder on the issue of Indian policy, Lyndon Johnson put it to that purpose when the opportunity arose.[78]

The message declared a new goal [in federal policy] "that erases old attitudes of paternalism and promotes partnership." Johnson recognized the Indian "right to freedom of choice and self-determination" and called for a federal policy "with new emphasis on Indian self-help and with respect for Indian culture." These pronouncements articulated the direction Indian affairs had taken during Bennett's tenure as commissioner, and evidenced the changes in Indian affairs since the 1953 promulgation of HCR 108, which had called for the termination of federal services to the tribes.[79]

Stewart Udall later claimed that the 1968 message "really laid it on the line and laid the basis for the kind of action that was needed," an enthusiastic overstatement. As Ervin Duggan had realized, the message was "thin" on program. Johnson declared that his administration sought to "promote Indian development by improving health and education, encouraging long-term economic growth, and strengthening community institutions," essentially the direction federal Indian policy had taken in the seven years since Udall took office. To achieve these ends, the president requested a ten percent increase in appropriations for "programs targeted at the American Indian." Because Johnson had rejected the proposal to create a new assistant secretary position at Interior, the only new idea in the message was the establishment of the National Council on Indian Opportunity. Intended to bring "the problems of the Indians to the highest levels of Government," the council would be chaired by the vice president and would "include a cross section of Indians leaders . . . and high government officials who have programs in this field."[80]

Native Americans responded enthusiastically to the recognition that the message brought to their circumstances. Richard Halfmoon, chairman of the Nez Perce Tribal Executive Committee, informed Udall that the Nez Perce were "deeply grateful for the contents of the message." W. W. Keeler told Johnson that the message "was very stimulating," but he was also cautious, noting that the "Indian people will respond if the Congress will make legislation calculated to achieve your goals." Initial congressional response proved promising—Udall recalled that in Congress the message "was received surprisingly well"—indicating that lawmakers might take action in the field of Indian affairs.[81]

Sen. Fred Harris deemed the president's statement to be "the greatest Indian message ever given by any president in history," a remark that reveals more about presidential involvement in Indian affairs than it does the content of Johnson's message. It was historic because, as Robert Bennett noted, it was "the only special message that has ever gone to the Congress on American Indians by a President of the United States." However, the message lacked an essential ingredient necessary for "greatness" at that point in Indian affairs. What Indians needed most from President Johnson was an explicit repudiation of the termination policy; instead, Johnson asserted that his "new goal . . . ends the old debate about 'termination' of Indian programs and stresses self-determination." For Native Americans, the "old debate" would not be over until the president officially declared the demise of termination in any form as a goal of federal policy.[82]

An anticipated negative congressional response prevented the White House from explicitly abandoning termination. After the 1966 task force had recommended a "complete disavowal of 'termination' as a governmental policy or goal," a White House review of the task force suggestions determined that such a move "will be strongly opposed by congressional committees, especially in the Senate." The White House did not change this evaluation in the ensuing year. In October 1967 Lee White reminded Joseph Califano that "some Congressional critics— probably Senator Anderson, for example—would like to 'terminate' governmental responsibility for Indians," and argued that these opponents "might resist any Presidential avowal of a strengthened governmental commitment."[83]

Although their power was in decline, the terminationists on the Senate Interior Committee had again determined the boundaries of the nation's Indian policy. In Udall's assessment of congressional reactions taken before the release of the message, he noted that Henry Jackson "commended the political desirability of summarizing current programs in a Presidential Message," which in a nutshell captured the real extent of Johnson's statement. As one critic in the press asked, "is there anything new here, other than further action-displacing sympathy that has bred a skepticism into most Indians long resigned to poverty in perpetuity?" This was an overly harsh assessment, but it did point to the lack of daring and creativity that marked the president's message.[84]

The Indian Civil Rights Act of 1968

Despite its limitations, Johnson's presidential message constituted a new high for federal recognition of the difficulties that American Indians faced. Nonetheless, it was not the most significant action taken by the government during 1968. A little more than a month after releasing the message, Johnson signed into law a civil rights bill that had profound implications for both individual Native Americans and the sovereignty of tribal governments.

The Indian Civil Rights Act came from a source not usually associated with Indian affairs. In 1961, Sen. Sam Ervin (D.-N.C.), chairman of the Subcommittee on Constitutional Rights of the Senate Judiciary Committee, opened hearings on the constitutional rights of American Indians. His motivations for doing so remain obscure. He may have acted at the urging of Helen Maynor Scheirbeck, a Lumbee from North Carolina, whose concern "about termination and the problems they [tribal leaders] faced under Public Law 280," led her "to get a job on Capitol Hill to see if I could help Indian people." Ervin offered her a position on the subcommittee staff, and she later recalled "talking about this [Indian affairs] in the subcommittee."[85]

However, Ervin was also a dedicated segregationist and a determined foe of all civil rights initiatives. In 1957 he had signed the Southern Manifesto in protest against the drive to desegregate school systems in the South. While his opposition to civil rights measures did not preclude an interest in Native American affairs—James Haley held similar views—it did raise fears that Ervin hoped to use the issue of Indian rights to muddy the ongoing debates over the civil rights initiatives concerning African Americans.[86]

While Ervin's intentions were suspect, there was no doubt that the issue of Indian rights merited attention. The 1961 report of the United States Commission on Civil Rights concluded that "the denial of equal protection of the laws to Indians appears to be widespread" and noted that "denials . . . stem at least in part from the unique legal and political status of Indians." The commission complained that "the Indian wears three legal 'masks,' tribal, citizen, and 'ward' and bears relationships to three legal authorities, Federal, State and tribal," a reality that made the issue of Indian rights "complex and not always uniform." While drawing attention to the racism Native Americans endured as a minority in American society, the commission also pointed out that "while neither Congress nor the States may infringe the basic civil rights of Indians . . . Indians are not so protected against the actions of tribal governments."[87]

The commission was correct in its final assertion. The Bill of Rights did not apply to Native Americans in their relations with tribal government. In a 1961 letter to Ervin's subcommittee, Attorney General Robert Kennedy admitted that "it is not entirely clear to what extent constitutional restrictions applicable to the Federal Government . . . and the State governments are applicable to the tribal governments." However, Kennedy noted, "decided cases indicate that there are large areas in which such restrictions are not applicable." The extension of the Bill of Rights to prevent tribal governments from violating rights guaranteed to other U.S. citizens under the Constitution would become the center of Ervin's subcommittee's investigations.[88]

In 1964 Ervin introduced several pieces of legislation to Congress reflecting this concern, although Indian testimony before the subcommittee had focused on discrimination, not constitutional safeguards against tribal governments. The bills were introduced too late in the session for congressional action, so Ervin reintroduced them in February 1965. One bill responded directly to the issue of Bill of Rights guarantees. Designated S. 961, this measure declared that "any Indian tribe . . . shall be subject to the same limitations and restraints as those which are imposed on the Government of the United States by the United States Constitution." Two bills addressed specific areas of existing law, one allowing Indians to appeal criminal convictions to state or federal courts, the other requiring the Attorney General to respond to complaints of civil rights violations received from Indians. Two of the proposed acts sought to clarify Indian law, authorizing the interior secretary to develop "a model code governing the administration of justice" for use on reservations and to "prepare and revise certain materials related to Indian affairs" including a compilation of "treaties, laws, Executive orders, regulations, and other pertinent documents which appertain to Indians."[89]

Two bills responded directly to Native American concerns. In response to complaints that state governments rarely policed relations between non-Indians on the reservations over which the tribal governments had no legal authority, S. 965 granted the "United States jurisdiction concurrent with the States over offenses committed by non-Indians against non-Indians in Indian country." The second bill, S. 966, modified Public Law 280, the 1953 act that permitted the states to assume civil and criminal jurisdiction over Indian reservations unilaterally. The Ervin bill required the states to acquire Indian consent before assuming jurisdiction, though it did not contain any provisions for the retrocession of jurisdictions some states had already assumed.[90]

Hearings on the Ervin bills opened on 22 June 1965. Native Americans' testimony at the hearings revealed mixed feelings toward this raft of legislation. Witnesses supported S. 966, which fulfilled the long-desired goal of repealing the unpopular PL-280. Vine Deloria, Jr., called for an amendment allowing periodic revisions of any jurisdictional agreements, but otherwise considered that bill to be "a good constructive beginning and . . . the application of the first principle of government—the consent of the governed." Cato Vallandra declared that the United Sioux Tribes "heartily" endorsed S. 966. However, the other bills, especially S. 961, met with several objections. Deloria pointed out that "many tribes have written a basic bill of rights into their tribal constitution based upon the provisions of the U.S. Constitution," thus rendering S. 961 unnecessary. Domingo Montoya presented a statement from the All-Pueblo Council of New Mexico rejecting S. 961, S. 962, and S. 963, arguing that the bills would "bar the effective administration of the tribal government." The All-Pueblo Council maintained that "the traditional means of tribal justice should be continued" rather than bringing new standards of justice to Indian Country. Thus, Native Americans favored S. 966, but had serious doubts about the other bills, especially S. 961.[91]

At the time that he had submitted his proposed legislation, Ervin declared that "these bills should not be considered as final solutions . . . the language in some of these proposals may be revised and concepts clarified as the Senate deliberates these matters." The senator was true to his word, and he used the hearings to gather recommendations for revisions. In 1966 his subcommittee released a summary report detailing some of the proposed changes. The summary report concluded that S. 961 should be amended "to indicate in more specific terms the constitutional protections the American Indian possesses in relation to his tribe." The revised S. 966 "should be amended to provide for piecemeal assumption of jurisdiction by the States," rather than requiring states to assume complete civil and criminal jurisdiction after securing tribal consent.[92]

Ervin introduced his revised bills on 23 May 1967. At this point the Indian bills became entangled in a heated battle over an administration civil rights bill that included provisions banning discrimination in housing. Ervin had played a role in the Senate defeat of the open housing bill in 1966, and he hoped to see the measure fail again. The House version of the open housing act, H.R. 2516, was sent to Ervin's subcommittee. At this point Ervin began an elaborate legislative game. Believing that the "House [Interior] Committee was adamantly opposed to the Indian Bill of Rights," Ervin sought to bypass that committee by offering a substitute bill that combined the open housing act with his Indian civil rights bills. He knew that the addition of the controversial Indian provisions might overburden the open housing act and lead to its defeat, in which case he would have succeeded in killing the administration's civil rights initiative. On the other hand, if Congress agreed to the amended bill, he would succeed in securing his Indian Bill of Rights, which would mitigate his loss over the open housing bill. In either circumstance, Ervin stood to gain. The subcommittee approved Ervin's substitute bill, but the Judiciary Committee rejected it, sending the original H.R. 2516 to the Senate for consideration. Undeterred, Ervin combined his Indian bills into one piece of legislation, S. 1843, which the Senate passed on 7 December 1967.[93]

Native American response to the comprehensive bill was mixed. Although they disliked many provisions in the bill, they saw its passage as the only way to secure revision of PL-280. Wendell Chino, NCAI president, was especially enthusiastic about the amendment to PL-280, because "as far as the American Indians are concerned it [PL-280] is a despicable law." As a result, he offered his support to S. 1843, declaring that "passage of a [sic] legislation ensuring the civil and individual rights of our Indian people is much desired and long overdue." Although the All-Pueblo Council approved the bill's "provision . . .

modifying Public Law 280" it refused to support the legislation. Thomas Olson, the council's attorney, stated that the council regarded much of the bill as "another invasion of their sovereignty."[94]

While many Indians expressed doubts, the administration offered its support to the Ervin bill. In his special message President Johnson called upon Congress "to complete action on that Bill of Rights in the current session." On 6 March 1968 Ervin praised Johnson's support for his bill, declaring, "I hope his call will be heeded, and that S. 1843 will not be allowed to die this session." Two days later Ervin returned to the strategy he had used the previous October, offering his bill as an amendment to H.R. 2516, the open housing bill then under Senate consideration.[95]

Ervin defended his action on the grounds that the House Interior Committee would never report out S. 1843; however, he knew full well that his amendment threatened the survival of the open housing bill. Senate Majority Leader Mike Mansfield, who had struggled with the administration bill for over two years, asked Ervin to withdraw the amendment. In return, Mansfield promised to secure a promise from the House committee to hold hearings on Indian civil rights immediately. Ervin rejected this offer, complaining, "I did not think anybody supporting a bill to secure constitutional rights to black people would be opposed to giving constitutional rights to red people. But apparently I am mistaken." The Senate approved Ervin's amendment by a vote of 81 to 0. On 11 March the Senate approved the civil rights bill, which was then sent back to the House.[96]

James Officer believed that "Ervin hoped that tacking the Indian caboose onto the Civil Rights train would wreck the railroad," and for a time it looked as if Officer's fears would be realized. Wayne Aspinall, who opposed the Indian civil rights bill, announced that he would hold hearings on S. 1843. Officer believed that Aspinall and James Haley planned to pack the hearings with Pueblo witnesses antagonistic to the bill. This would "permit Haley and others who oppose the broader Civil Rights legislation to oppose it on the floor on the grounds that the Indians oppose the Indian rider." Officer maintained that the Pueblos "are the perfect pawns here to shoot down both the Indian bill and the broader one." In fact, the issue of Indian rights was now merely a pawn in the struggle to prevent passage of open housing legislation.[97]

Aspinall held his hearing on 29 March, and it went much as Officer predicted it would. However, the strategy came to naught when the civil rights bill was sent to the House Judiciary Committee, which reported on the bill favorably. The House accepted the Senate version on 10 April, and President Johnson signed it into law the following day. In his remarks during the signing ceremony, Johnson made not a single reference to the Indian provisions in the bill.[98]

The passage of the Indian Civil Rights Act only a month after President Johnson's message hailing self-determination revealed the paternalism still present in federal Indian affairs. Sam Ervin believed that "all the laws ought to be applied to all the people just alike," and sought to provide the constitutional protections most American citizens enjoyed to Native Americans. However, the extension of those constitutional guarantees conflicted with the goal of self-determination, which demanded that tribal governments determine which rights their people had. In 1983, Helen Maynor Scheirbeck lauded the "opportunity [Ervin offered] in that subcommittee to hold hearings for five years at the local community level," but Ervin was far more interested in constitutional issues than in the testimony that American Indians offered regarding discrimination and abuse. Indians assented to the passage of the act because it modified the hated PL-280, not because they recognized the need for protection from their own governments.[99]

The act was clearly significant, but as Robert Bennett admitted in November 1968, "we do not know what the full effects of this legislation will be." Its impact was realized through later court decisions. For the first decade after the passage of the act, it appeared as if it would constitute a threat to tribal sovereignty. In the 1969 case of *Dodge v. Nakai*, an Arizona federal court determined that it had jurisdiction over a dispute involving the Navajo Tribal Council because the Indian civil rights act made "substantial changes in the manner in which Indian tribes could exercise their quasi-sovereign powers." The ruling resulted in a flood of suits against tribal governments that subsided only after the 1978 U.S. Supreme Court decision in *Santa Clara Pueblo v. Martinez*, which declared that a writ of habeas corpus was the only appeal remedy available under the terms of the 1968 act.[100]

TRANSITION 1969

Congress passed the Indian Civil Rights Act less than two weeks after Lyndon Johnson announced that he would not seek reelection to the White House. Stewart Udall realized that with Johnson's departure his tenure in the Interior Department would come to an end, but Robert Bennett had hopes of remaining in his position. In September 1968, the NCAI passed a resolution that "urge[d] the retention of Robert L. Bennett as Commissioner of Indian Affairs upon the change of administration in January next." However, when President-elect Richard Nixon announced that Alaska Governor Walter J. Hickel was his choice for interior secretary, Bennett, who had his share of run-ins with Hickel, knew that his days in the BIA were numbered. Rather than wait for Nixon to request his departure, Bennett resigned from office effective 31 May 1969.[101]

In office a little over three years, Bennett had few opportunities to exercise significant influence over the nation's Indian affairs. Udall's intervention in Indian affairs in 1966 and 1967 forced Bennett to play a supporting role and prevented him from offering any major initiatives of his own. This was unfortunate. The commissioner's dealings with Congress revealed a shrewdness that his predecessor, Philleo Nash, lacked. Bennett managed to avoid complying with their demands for continued termination without antagonizing them, a feat that required considerable skill. Instead, he promoted Indian self-determination, serving as an advocate for Indian interests and concerns. Both American Indians and President Nixon would have been well-served had Bennett been allowed to continue as commissioner, especially given the poor performance of Bennett's successor, Louis Rook Bruce.[102]

CONCLUSION

On 8 July 1970, President Richard Nixon sent a special message on Indian affairs to the U.S. Congress. In the message, Nixon declared that "forced termination is wrong, in my judgment, for a number of reasons." Claiming that "the special relationship between Indians and the Federal government is the result . . . of solemn obligations which have been entered into by the United States government," he argued that "to terminate this relationship would be no more appropriate than to terminate the citizenship rights of any other American." Moreover, "the practical results have been clearly harmful in the few instances in which termination actually has been tried." Finally, Nixon maintained that the threat of termination "has created a great deal of apprehension among Indian groups and this apprehension, in turn, has had a blighting effect on tribal progress."[1]

Nixon concluded that "termination is morally and legally unacceptable, because it produces bad practical results, and because the mere threat of termination tends to discourage greater self-sufficiency among Indian groups." He urged Congress "to expressly renounce, repudiate and repeal the termination policy," replacing it with a resolution that "would explicitly confirm the integrity and right to continued existence of all Indian tribes and Alaska native governments, recognizing that cultural pluralism is a source of national strength." Nixon then asked Congress to "guarantee that whenever Indian groups decided to assume control or responsibility for government service programs, they could do so and still receive adequate Federal financial support."[2]

Although Congress did not follow Nixon's recommendation to formally repudiate HCR 108, during the 1970s it enacted several measures intended to further Indian self-determination, including the 1972 Indian Education Act and the 1975 Indian Self-Determination and Education Assistance Act. Congress also began restoring to trust status tribes that had been terminated. The Menominees, who had struggled with grinding poverty during the 1960s, were restored in 1973, establishing a precedent for restoration that would serve other tribes such as the Klamaths in the coming years.[3]

White House aide Leonard Garment attributed the Nixon administration's achievements in Indian affairs to "a rare combination of political circumstances, a sympathetic atmosphere, an absence of internal competition, and an unobstructed policy shot." Garment did not specifically mention Congress, but it was the collapse of terminationist sentiment in Congress that allowed for Nixon's successes in Indian affairs. It was the threat of termination emanating from the Senate Interior Committee that distorted Indian affairs during the Kennedy and Johnson years.[4]

In crafting the 1961 task force report, the document that served as the blueprint for federal Indian policy for most of the 1960s, Interior Department officials consistently limited their initiatives to coincide with committee concerns. Committee hostility prevented the pro-Indian Philleo Nash from taking a more forceful stance regarding the operations of the Bureau of Indian Affairs. Robert Bennett advocated programs that promoted self-determination, but he did so quietly and with an eye to reactions on the Interior Committee.

The threat of termination made many Native Americans wary of self-determination. They feared that self-determination might ultimately lead to termination. In 1966, Earl Old Person, Blackfeet, claimed that trying to promote Indian participation in development programs while simultaneously supporting termination was like "trying to cook a meal in your tipi when someone is standing outside trying to burn the tipi down." Robert Bennett echoed Old Person's comments in a 1968 memo. He noted that "cutting across the broad field of Indian legislation as well as the administration of Indian affairs in general is the Indians' fear of termination of Federal trusteeship and services." He claimed that "positive attempts to bring about the development of the Indian people" were met "with outright suspicision [sic] by the Indian people" because they saw the threat of termination implicit in programs intended to promote self-development. Bennett placed the blame for this situation on the Senate Interior Committee, which "still relied upon [HCR 108] . . . as the official Congressional Indian policy."[5]

However, during the final years of the Johnson presidency, the terminationists on the Senate Interior Committee were a beleaguered group that had lost the support of their colleagues as the negative impacts of termination on tribes such as the Menominee became readily apparent. The three key supporters of termination, Frank Church, Clinton Anderson, and Henry Jackson, eventually proved unwilling or unable to pursue their goals in Indian policy. Frustrated and fatigued by the battles over heirship legislation, Church simply lost interest in Indian affairs. The aging and infirm Anderson (who died two years after retiring in 1973) lacked the energy to fight for termination.

Henry Jackson's position on Indian policy proved to be one of cynicism and self-promotion. The Washington senator was the source of termination efforts in the late 1960s, consistently demanding termination legislation, especially for the Colvilles in his home state. However, sometime after 1970 Jackson became an enthusiastic advocate of self-determination. It was Jackson who in 1972 introduced a bill intended to "promote maximum Indian participation in the government of the Indian people by providing for the full participation of Indian tribes in certain programs," quite a departure from termination. His conversion to the goal of self-determination was a product of Jackson's political ambitions. A Senate Interior Committee staffer later recalled that "some of his later actions in the early 70s clouded the Scoop Jackson that we knew in the '60s," because "what he did was calculated, and was measured against what he could gain from the standpoint of that old 1600 Pennsylvania Avenue position." Thus, Jackson's new attitude toward Indian affairs was a part of his bid for the White House rather than a sincere response to Native American needs.[6]

The persistence of termination sentiment during the 1960s on the Interior Committee reflected the regional makeup of the committee membership. Anderson, Church, Jackson, Allott, and many other committee members were all westerners seeking to meet constituent needs. They served the interests of developers, ranchers, and farmers whose support was essential to the senators on the committee. For these senators, the persistence of Indian communities presented an obstacle to western development. Each of these westerners perceived Indian affairs as a demanding and time-consuming endeavor that offered few political rewards. For these westerners, Indians and their communities were a liability, one which termination promised to eliminate.[7]

The insensitivity to Indian demands also reflected the marginal influence that Native Americans had on American politics. Relegated to isolated areas, impoverished, and not given to political participation because of ignorance, cultural standards, or obstruction on the part of state officials (Indians in New Mexico could not vote until 1948), "the Indian did not muster some of the political clout that he might have had," as Udall later recalled. Lacking "political clout," Native Americans had limited influence over the committee's conduct of Indian policy. Jackson believed that he could ignore Indian concerns—he declared in 1964, "hell, they don't vote." Over the course of the decade, Indian activism and political participation increased, and Indians gained more influence over the policy process. It was no coincidence that the western senators who advocated a more progressive policy from the floor of the Senate during the 1960s, George McGovern and Fred

Harris, both came from states where Robert Bennett maintained that "the Indian vote is critical to the reelection of Democratic incumbents in the United States Senate" in 1968. However, Indians never exerted any political power over Anderson and his terminationist colleagues during this period.[8]

Unfortunately, support for termination extended beyond the Senate Interior Committee. It was that group's insistence on immediate termination which set it apart from officials who perceived a gradual process of withdrawal of services as the means to achieve the eventual severing of relations between the federal government and the tribes. Stewart Udall was the foremost advocate of such a process. As late as 1967 the interior secretary declared that "I am a gradualist—gradual termination." When Wayne Aspinall quizzed Udall on the impact of the Indian Resources Development Act, Udall admitted that "the ultimate end result" would be the end of Indian reservations. Although he never explicitly discussed a time frame for this gradual process, in an April 1966 press conference he stated that "if you give us five or ten years, discussion of termination will disappear. Tribes of their own volition will say 'Get out of our way.'" Five to ten years was an optimistic and unrealistic expectation regarding the resolution of difficulties literally centuries in the making, even when applied to the wealthier and more sophisticated tribes.[9]

Udall's actions, attitudes, and abilities were central to the conduct of Indian policy during the Kennedy-Johnson administrations, in part because neither President Kennedy nor President Johnson displayed any real concern in that area, a lack of interest that remains the norm for the modern presidency. In a 1990 interview, James Officer declared that "I can't think of a single person in Kennedy's office who, in my opinion, was very much involved or interested in becoming involved in Indian affairs." President Kennedy's concern did not extend beyond the public relations liability that the construction of the Kinzua Dam caused. President Johnson intentionally distanced himself from the activities of the Interior Department—Udall later recalled that "he substantially left it [Indian affairs] in my hands," which resulted in "a heavy delegation [of] responsibility" but with "thorough going support" from the White House for Udall's initiatives.[10]

Shortly before he left office, Udall expressed the hope that "the trend toward diminishing the high degree of Federal paternalism in Indian affairs has been so well set in recent years that it will prove difficult to reverse," a trend that can be understood as the move toward Indian self-determination. Udall's greatest achievement in federal Indian affairs was his support for projects that promoted self-determination. Instead of denying or resisting the trend toward greater Indian involvement in policy formulation and implementation, Udall became an enthusiastic defender of war on poverty programs, so much so that he hoped to model BIA efforts along the same lines. As such, Udall must be credited with "diminishing the high degree of Federal paternalism in Indian affairs."[11]

However, the credit he receives must be limited, because his commitment to Indian self-determination was not complete. In 1969, Vine Deloria, Jr. called Udall "a tremendous disappointment," faulting him because "too many times he was unresponsive to Indian proposals." Udall's failure to respond to many Indian demands stemmed from his commitment to gradual termination; from the need to satisfy congressmen including Anderson and Jackson who were hostile to an expansion of federal services to the tribes; and from conflicts arising from his roles as trustee of Indian lands and as the cabinet official responsible for the development of the nation's natural resources. The interior secretary complicated matters by taking an intermittent but intense interest in Indian affairs. Because he was not constantly in touch with Indian leaders, he was not fully aware of the growth of Indian activism and the commitment to self-determination. Thus, during those periods when he did assume leadership of Indian affairs, his proposals did not adequately reflect the needs of Native Americans.[12]

Udall's advocacy of gradual termination weakened his commitment to a policy of self-determination because it defined the federal-Indian relationship as one of economic assistance to the impoverished, thereby ignoring issues such as treaty rights, tribal sovereignty, land ownership, and cultural integrity. He and other government officials regarded economic advancement as synonymous with self-determination. Thus, they showed little interest in defining or increasing the authority of the tribes in areas unrelated to economic advancement. Programs conducted under the auspices of the Office of Economic Opportunity, the Area Redevelopment Administration, and the Economic Development Administration bolstered tribal sovereignty to some degree because tribal governments received recognition as qualifying public institutions. However, the existence of the treaties that gave Indians a different legal status in American society remained problematic for the Democratic administrations, as the conflict over the Kinzua Dam revealed.

Udall's statements and actions also indicated that government paternalism served as another obstacle to Indian self-determination. Critics have charged that the paternalism present in the Democratic administrations of the 1960s reflects a continuity with the older paternalistic approaches that had fostered dependency and promoted the assimilation of Native Americans into the wider culture. However, the Indian policy of the era must be regarded as a departure from previous patterns of administrative attitudes and behaviors. Nash's consultations with Indian leaders and Bennett's efforts to turn programs over to the tribes constituted a new and enlightened approach to Indian affairs, one that recognized the importance of Indian participation in the development of successful programs. Paternalism did not disappear during the 1960s, but both commissioners recognized its insidious impact on Indian policy and tried to mitigate its effects by providing Native Americans a greater say in policy formulation and implementation. While their conduct of Indian affairs did not end government paternalism, it furthered its erosion during a period when Native Americans demanded the leading role in Indian policies and programs.[13]

The Kennedy-Johnson administrations inherited the problem of dependency within American Indian communities; by the end of the 1960s these communities were still dependent, if not more so, because of their reliance upon federal funding for employment and program operations. However, assessing the administrations' performance is not so easy as merely determining that Indians remained dependent during this period. No administration, no policy, no program could solve the problem of Indian dependency in a decade. Rather than blame the Kennedy-Johnson administrations for increasing Indian dependency, critics must consider the reasons for that increase within the context of specific policy goals.

The terminationists believed that they could end dependency with a simple stroke to eliminate all federal assistance, thus forcing the Indians to take control of their lives and futures. The Kennedy-Johnson administrations adopted the more humane (and just) approach of promoting economic development, a method that would bring long-term rather than immediate benefits. The process of developing the reservations' physical and human resources required greater expenditures on physical plants and education. In addition, most Native Americans were in dire need of expanded social services. This influx of money targeted at improving the standard of living and the opportunities available on the reservations inevitably created a greater reliance on the federal government. However, policymakers intended for this short-term dependency to increase self-reliance and opportunities that would lead to a diminution of federal assistance and a move away from dependency. That this did not occur is a measure of the desperate conditions Native Americans endured rather than a flaw in the federal policy. The administrations cannot be faulted for spending more money on the most impoverished Americans.

Assimilation, the incorporation of Native Americans into the wider society and culture, had been a recurring feature in federal Indian policies. At times the hostility toward Indian culture was overt, as when the BIA banned certain traditional dances during the 1920s. The position of the Kennedy-Johnson officials was far more complex. By the 1960s, the narrow nationalism that had predominated during the early years of the Cold War had given way to a greater appreciation of cultural pluralism. Udall and his commissioners expressed an admiration for Indian cultures. In 1969 he argued that Americans had often "overlooked what the Indian, with his own history and his own culture, what he could add as an extra element, extra dimension to our society" and asserted that "we ought to be big enough as a country" to permit "the Indian who wanted to cling to his values and his culture and his art" to do so.[14]

Although they were not hostile to Indian culture, Interior Department officials considered the preservation of that culture to be a choice and responsibility left to Native Americans. Policy pronouncements of the era make little reference to preserving Indian culture. The creation of educational programs in the late 1960s that inculcated pride in Indian heritage served as one of the few official programs aimed at the retention of native cultural values. Policymakers were far more concerned with the economic development of the reservations, and focused their attentions on this area.

This emphasis on economic development, with the attempts to train Native Americans in industrial jobs and to bring factories and businesses to the reservations, also raised questions concerning assimilation. Again, critics have charged that this development process posed a great threat to Indian culture and rendered the policies of the day as assimilative in intent as past policies. Policymakers were aware of the conflict between Indian values and those of modern industrial America. Economic development required that Native Americans be taught many Euroamerican values, especially regarding time management. In 1962, one task force member admitted that "making him [the Indian] a more effective American does not necessarily imply making him *not an Indian*, but making him less Indian may to some extent be involved."[15]

However, to infer that this aspect of Indian policy indicated a hostility toward Indian cultures ignores the fact that many Native Americans saw economic development as a desirable goal. The 1961 *Declaration of Indian Purpose* called for the "establishment upon Indian reservations of industries and other activities which will provide employment and otherwise improve the economic status of Indians." In 1967, Indian leaders attending the Conference on Policy and Legislation requested loan funds "to provide prompt rapid economic growth in the underdeveloped areas of our own country," and maintained that "to do less is to deny our own first Americans assistance in social and economic development that we are now providing others world wide." These policy statements indicated that American Indians placed a premium on economic development. Well aware of the pressures to assimilate that such development would bring, Native Americans appeared confident that cultures which had survived nearly five hundred years of disease, decimation, and paternalism could still thrive and prosper.[16]

The impact of the assimilative features of the economic development programs was also limited because those programs resulted in minimal gains during the 1960s. From the outset the isolation of the reservations, the low level of training among the Native American workforce, cultural resistance to the norms of industrialized life, and unwelcome obstacles such as union opposition to the relocation of industries to Indian country combined to thwart efforts in this area. The disastrous coal mining operations at Black Mesa revealed the problems surrounding the exploitation of natural resources. Development remained the centerpiece of federal policy during the Kennedy-Johnson years; for the most part, it was a failure, or, more charitably, a learning experience and a foundation for future efforts in that area.[17]

Nor could the officials involved in Indian policy claim any striking achievements in raising the Indian standard of living. In 1970, as in 1960, Native Americans were the poorest and least educated people in the United States. In 1970 the median income for Native American men age sixteen and over was $3,509, and for women, $1,697. The 1970 census reported that the median income for all American men over age seventeen stood at $6,783, and for women, $2,480, both sums considerably higher than that which Indians earned. Nearly forty percent of Indian families lived below the poverty level. Only one-third of Native Americans over age twenty-five had high school diplomas. These figures indicated an improvement over the conditions that prevailed in 1960, but policymakers could not claim success in tackling the problem of Indian poverty.[18]

Despite the minimal gains and his lack of personal interest in Native Americans, Lyndon Johnson had a positive impact on Indian affairs, one which stemmed from his general concern for minority issues and his specific desire to combat poverty in America. Although it was not intentionally designed with Indian needs in mind, the Community Action Program constituted a move toward greater Indian control over their lives and communities. The war on poverty programs did bring new problems to the reservations, prompting Robert Burnette to claim that Johnson's "treatment of the Indians will never win his memory any laurel wreaths," a negative assessment derived from Burnette's concern over the corruption that he argued federal monies brought to the tribal governments. Corruption was indeed a problem, but Burnette ignored the fact that Johnson's war on poverty programs brought funds and increased opportunities for tribal control over finances, both of which Native Americans desired during this period. More than any other federal effort initiated before the 1970s, the war on poverty programs promoted Indian self-determination.[19]

The underfunding of OEO programs, the persistence of terminationist sentiment in the Senate Interior Committee, Udall's belief in gradual termination, and the difficulties inherent in promoting economic development on the reservations combined to mitigate the positive aspects of the Indian policy that executive branch officials advocated during the 1960s. Thus, the era marked a transition between the extremes of the termination efforts of the 1950s and the expanded government commitment to self-determination in the 1970s. The transitional nature of this era was also reflected in Native American efforts to exert control over the conduct of federal Indian policy. Continuing paternalism in Washington, D.C., prevented administration officials from undertaking efforts to include Indians in the formulation and implementation of that policy. The rhetoric of self-sufficiency was never matched by administrative mechanisms designed to incorporate Indian participation at the highest levels. Thus, Native American influence over the direction of federal policy was usually limited to blocking the passage of legislation that Indian leaders and their advisers deemed harmful to their interests.

The difficulties Native Americans faced in their attempts to enter the policy process were not only the product of bureaucratic opposition. In 1969 Udall maintained that "the Indian leaders of the 1960s tended to be more the quiescent types who were looking primarily towards their own politics of staying in power, rather than reach the country or to influence the country or to dramatize Indian injustice." Vine Deloria, Jr., offered a more trenchant assessment in 1999 when he complained of "old dictatorial chairmen that had been in office twenty years. . . . and they weren't going to give up control." These observations illuminated the tentative nature of pan-tribal efforts to exert political influence over national policy in the 1960s. Native Americans retained a sense of loyalty to their own communities that conflicted with efforts to organize across tribal lines. During the conflict over the Omnibus Bill, Deloria noted that "Indians were easily turned against each other by clever lawyers, dissident individuals, and bureaucrats." To compound the problem, disagreements within the NCAI and between the NCAI and younger Indian activists associated with the NIYC also hampered moves toward unity.[20]

Despite such difficulties, American Indians grew increasingly sophisticated in their efforts to attract attention to their proposals and to pressure Congress to support their goals. The 1961 American Indian Chicago Conference and the 1964 Capital Conference on American Indian Poverty garnered national press attention and issued policy proposals that executive branch officials studied. Native Americans organized to defeat the heirship bills and the Indian Resource Development Act, both of which would have had significant (and negative) impacts on their lives. Although they often turned to Euroamerican attorneys sympathetic to their causes for advice and assistance, Native Americans looked toward their own organizations, especially the NCAI, for direction and leadership, evidence that self-determination had become a reality during the 1960s.

NOTES

INTRODUCTION

1. For "eras" in Indian policy, see Vine Deloria, Jr., and Clifford M. Lytle, *American Indians, American Justice* (Austin: University of Texas Press, 1983), 1–24. The first two quotations are from Francis Paul Prucha, *The Great Father: The United States Government and the American Indians* (Lincoln: University of Nebraska Press, 1984) 2:1087; third quotation from Donald Parman, *Indians and the American West in the Twentieth Century* (Bloomington: Indiana University Press, 1994), 148; fourth quotation from Donald Fixico, *Termination and Relocation: Federal Indian Policy, 1945–1960* (Albuquerque: University of New Mexico Press, 1980), 200; fifth quotation from Vine Deloria, Jr., and Clifford M. Lytle, *The Nations Within: The Past and Future of American Indian Sovereignty* (New York: Pantheon Books, 1984), 183, 195–96; sixth quotation from M. Annette Jaimes, "The Hollow Icon: An American Indian Analysis of the Kennedy Myth and Federal Indian Policy," *Wicazo Sa Review* 4 (spring 1990): 34–44; and seventh quotation from Rebecca L. Robbins, "The Forgotten American: A Foundation for Contemporary American Indian Self-Determination," *Wicazo Sa Review* 4 (spring 1990): 32–33. For a comprehensive historiography of Johnson's Indian policy, see Christopher Riggs, "Indians, Liberalism, and Lyndon Johnson's Great Society, 1963–1969" (Ph.D. diss., University of Colorado, 1997), 3–12.

2. At this writing, the only monograph that examines federal Indian policy during the 1960s in any detail is George Castile, *To Show Heart: Native American Self-Determination and Federal Indian Policy, 1960–1975* (Tucson: University of Arizona Press, 1998).

3. For a discussion of paternalism as a paradigm for understanding federal Indian policy, see Francis Paul Prucha, *The Indian in American Society: From the Revolutionary War to the Present* (Berkeley: University of California Press, 1985), 10–11, ff. For a challenge to Prucha's argument, see Laurence M. Hauptman, *Tribes and Tribulations: Misconceptions About American Indians and Their Histories* (Albuquerque: University of New Mexico Press, 1995), 63–79.

CHAPTER ONE

1. First quotation from *Gallup Navajo Times,* 19 April 1961; quoted in Dorothy R. Parker, *Singing An Indian Song: A Biography of D'Arcy McNickle* (Lincoln: University of Nebraska Press, 1992), 189. Dozier is quoted in Nancy Oestreich Lurie, "The Voice of the American Indian: Report on the American Indian Chicago Conference," *Current Anthropology* 2 (December 1961): 489–90, 494.

2. D'Arcy McNickle, *Native American Tribalism: Indian Survivals and Renewals* (New York: Oxford University Press, 1973), 117.

3. U.S. Bureau of the Census, *U.S. Census of Population: 1960. Subject Reports. Nonwhite Population by Race. Final Report PC(2)-1C* (Washington D.C.: GPO, 1963), x, xi, 2. Prior to 1960, census enumerators determined a respondent's racial identity. Eskimos, Aleuts, and native Hawaiians were included in an "All Other" racial category. Some figures presented here have been rounded to the nearest percentage point.

4. U.S. Bureau of the Census, *Nonwhite Population,* 12, 26, 104. National median income information from U.S. Bureau of the Census, *U.S. Census of Population: 1960. General and Social Economic Characteristics, United States Summary. Final Report PC(11)-1C* (Washington D.C.: GPO, 1963), xxxix–xl. Additional information regarding education is found in Margaret Szasz, *Education and the American Indian: The Road to Self-Determination, 1928–1973* (Albuquerque: University of New Mexico Press, 1974), 126, 134. Crow Dog quotations are from Mary Crow Dog and Richard Erdoes, *Lakota Woman* (New York: Grove Weidenfeld, 1990), 20, 26.

5. Robert Burnette, *The Tortured Americans* (Englewood Cliffs, N.J.: Prentice-Hall, Inc., 1971), 22; U.S. Department of Health, Education, and Welfare,

Public Health Service, Bureau of Medical Services, Division of Indian Health, "Indian Health Highlights," n.p., November, 1961, cited in William A. Brophy and Sophie D. Aberle, comps., *The Indian: America's Unfinished Business* (Norman: University of Oklahoma Press, 1966), 163; U.S. Department of Health, Education, and Welfare, Public Health Service, "Illness Among Indians," n.p., 1961, cited in Brophy and Aberle, *Unfinished Business,* 164–65; U.S. Public Health Service, "Indian Health Trends and Services," n.p., 1969, 8, 31, 32, cited in Alan L. Sorkin, *American Indians and Federal Aid* (Washington, D.C.: Brookings Institution, 1971), 53, 54.

6. For a brief but useful discussion of trust responsibilities, see Kirke Kickingbird, "Trust Responsibilities and Trust Funds," in *Native America in the Twentieth Century: An Encyclopedia,* ed. Mary B. Davis (New York: Garland Publishing, 1994), 658–59.

7. Bureau of Indian Affairs, "United States Indian Population and Land, 1960–1961," n.p., 1961, cited in Brophy and Aberle, *Unfinished Business,* 215–17 (see also p. 11). Some tribes, such as the Alabama and Coushatta in Texas, received limited services after termination.

8. In 1977 the position of assistant secretary for Indian affairs was created to supersede the commissioner's office. However, a commissioner was appointed in 1978, although since 1980 deputy secretaries have carried out the duties once assigned to the commissioner. See Robert M. Kvasnicka and Herman J. Viola, eds., *The Commissioners of Indian Affairs, 1824–1977* (Lincoln: University of Nebraska Press, 1979), xiii–xvii, quotation from xiv; and Theodore W. Taylor, *The Bureau of Indian Affairs* (Boulder: Westview Press, 1984), 39–41.

9. Philleo Nash, "Science, Politics, and Human Values: A Memoir," *Human Organization* 45 (fall 1986): 195.

10. Nash, "Human Values," 195; Richard F. Fenno, Jr., *Congressmen in Committees* (Boston: Little, Brown and Co., 1973), 5; Clinton P. Anderson, *Outsider in the Senate: Senator Clinton Anderson's Memoirs* (New York: World Publishing Co., 1970), 227–28. For a brief discussion of the role of these committees and insights on members, see Edward S. Cahn, ed., *Our Brother's Keepers: The Indian in White America* (New York: World Publishing Co., 1969), 163–73.

11. Aspinall quotation from Transcript, Aspinall Oral History, 15 February 1979, by Nancy Whistler, 19–20, Manuscripts Division, Library of Congress, Washington, D.C. (hereinafter cited as LOC).

12. Fixico, *Termination,* 14, 15, 16, 18; Alison R. Bernstein, *American Indians*

and World War II: Toward a New Era in Indian Affairs (Norman: University of Oklahoma Press, 1991), 157.

13. Larry W. Burt, *Tribalism in Crisis: Federal Indian Policy, 1953–1961* (Albuquerque: University of New Mexico Press, 1982), 4–5, 19–21; and Parman, *Indians and the American West,* 123; Prucha, *Indians in American Society,* 69.

14. Kenneth R. Philp, "Termination: A Legacy of the Indian New Deal" *Western Historical Quarterly* 14 (April 1983): 165–80; Kenneth R. Philp, *Termination Revisited: American Indians on the Trail to Self-Determination, 1933–1953* (Lincoln: University of Nebraska Press, 1999), 1–15.

15. Fixico, *Termination,* 25–29. For quotation, see Arthur V. Watkins, "Termination of Federal Supervision of Indians: The Removal of Restrictions Over Indian Property and Person," in *Annals of the American Academy of Political and Social Science* 311 (May 1957): 50.

16. *Congressional Quarterly's Guide to Congress,* 4th ed. (Washington, D.C.: Congressional Quarterly Inc., 1991), 420; and Fixico, *Termination,* 93–99; *Statutes at Large,* 67 B132.

17. The term "liquidation" previously had been used by some BIA officials, but the term fell into disuse because of its unpleasant connotations. See John R. Wunder, *"Retained by the People": A History of the American Indians and the Bill of Rights* (New York: Oxford University Press, 1994), 98; James E. Officer, "Termination as Federal Policy: An Overview," in *Indian Self-Rule: First-Hand Accounts of Indian-White Relations from Roosevelt to Reagan,* Current Issues in the American West series, vol. IV, ed. Kenneth R. Philp (Salt Lake City: Howe Brothers, 1986), 124; Burt, *Tribalism in Crisis,* 24–25; and "Indian, State jurisdiction over criminal and civil offenses," in *United States Statutes at Large,* vol. 67, (Washington, D.C.: GPO, 1953), chap. 505, 588–90. For Eisenhower quotation, see Eisenhower, *Public Papers of the Presidents of the United States, Dwight D. Eisenhower, 1953* (Washington, D.C.: GPO, 1960), 564. The five states named in PL 280 were California, Minnesota, Nebraska, Oregon, and Wisconsin. Some reservations in those states were exempted from the law's provisions.

18. *United States Statutes at Large,* 67: B132; and Watkins, "Termination of Federal Supervision," 49, 55. For second quotation, see p. 48 in Watkins.

19. Fixico, *Termination,* 134–57; and Burt, *Tribalism,* 53–58.

20. Burt, *Tribalism in Crisis,* 49–51, 70–72, 85–89.

21. Ibid., 29–47.

22. Thomas W. Cowger, *The National Congress of American Indians: The Founding Years* (Lawrence: University of Nebraska Press, 1999), 99–125.

23. Memo, J. L. Taylor to Rep. James A. Haley, 26 September 1958, "Indian Affairs Correspondence Misc. 1958," James A. Haley Papers, Florida Southern College Library, Lakeland, Florida (hereinafter cited as JHP).

24. Parman, *Indians and the American West,* 141; for La Farge quotation, see Oliver La Farge, "Termination of Federal Supervision: Disintegration and the American Indians," in *Annals of the American Academy of Political and Social Science* 311 (May 1957): 46; for Collier quotation, see John Collier, "The American Indian," in *Understanding Minority Groups,* ed. Joseph B. Gittler (New York: John Wiley & Sons, 1956), 50; Burt, *Tribalism,* 67; Parman, *Indians and the American West,* 141–42; Richard D. Warden, *Metcalf of Montana: How a Senator Makes Government Work* (Washington, D.C.: Acropolis Books, 1965), 89; Jerry Kammer, *The Second Long Walk: The Navajo-Hopi Land Dispute* (Albuquerque: University of New Mexico Press, 1980), 124–25. For first Metcalf quotation, see Lee Metcalf, "The Need for Revision of Federal Policy in Indian Affairs," in *Indian Truth* 35 (January–March 1958): 2; and second quotation, Memo, J. L. Taylor to Rep. James A. Haley, 26 September 1958, JHP.

25. Seaton speech reprinted in Congress, Senate, *Federal Responsibility Toward Indians,* 86th Cong., 1st sess., *Congressional Record* (2 March 1959), vol. 105, pt. 3, 3105–6.

26. Prucha, *Great Father,* 2:1048, 1058–59.

27. Donald Bruce Johnson and Kirk H. Porter, *National Party Platforms, 1840–1972* (Urbana: University of Illinois Press, 1973), 597, 617; Cowger, *Founding Years,* 130.

28. Memorandum, Frank Sieverts to Mike Feldman, n.d., "Briefing Papers Government Information—NDEA and Disclaimer," 1960 Campaign Files, Pre-Presidential Papers, microfilm edition.

29. Press Release, 6 August 1960, "Area Director's Conference, Oklahoma City, Oklahoma, March 5–7, 1962—Miscellaneous Notes," Box 150, Philleo Nash Papers, Harry S. Truman Library, Independence, Missouri (hereinafter cited as PNP).

30. "Statement by Vice President Nixon to the Association on American Indian Affairs," reprinted in *Freedom of Communications: The Joint Appearances of Senator John F. Kennedy and Vice-President Richard M. Nixon, Presidential Campaign of 1960* (Washington D.C.: GPO, 1961), 529–31.

31. "Letter on Indian Affairs from Senator John F. Kennedy to Mr. Oliver La Farge, President, Association of American Indian Affairs, October 28, 1960," reprinted in *Freedom of Communications: The Speeches of Senator John F. Kennedy, Presidential Campaign of 1960* (Washington D.C.: GPO, 1961), 800–803.

32. Letter, Richard Schifter to author, 19 August 1998, author's collection; see also Transcript, Philleo Nash Oral History, 26 February 1971, interviewed by William M. Moss, Interview no. 3, 8, John F. Kennedy Library, Boston, Massachusetts (hereinafter cited as JFKL). Schifter made certain that Kennedy's reply was included in a Bureau of the Budget collection of Kennedy's campaign promises.

33. Commission on the Rights, Liberties, and Responsibilities of the American Indian, *A Program For Indian Citizens: A Summary Report, January, 1961*, n.p., ii–iv. A copy may be found in "A Program For Indian Citizens: A Summary Report, January 1961," Box 78, William A. Brophy Papers, Harry S. Truman Library, Independence, Missouri (hereinafter cited as WBP). Excerpts may be found in Francis Paul Prucha, ed., *Documents of United States Indian History*, 2d ed. (Lincoln: University of Nebraska Press, 1984), 242–44. A revised and expanded version of the report was published in 1966 as *The Indian: American's Unfinished Business*. For a critical discussion of the Ford Foundation and the Commission, see Guy B. Senese, *Self-Determination and the Social Education of Native Americans* (New York: Praeger, 1991), 46–53.

34. Commission, *Program*, 1–14.

35. Ibid., 15–21.

36. Ibid., 22–29.

37. Ibid., 30–45.

38. Ibid., 1.

39. Lurie, "The Voice," 481–82, 489; and Carl Tjerandsen, *Education for Citizenship: A Foundation's Experience* (Santa Cruz, Calif.: Emil Schwartzhaupt Foundation, Inc., 1980), 64, 65. See also Lawrence M. Hauptman and Jack Campisi, "The Voice of Eastern Indians: The American Chicago Conference and the Movement for Federal Recognition," *Proceedings of the American Philosophical Society* 132 (December 1988): 316–29. This article is reprinted in Hauptman, *Tribes and Tribulations*, 95–108.

40. Tjerandsen, *Education*, 66; Hauptman and Campisi, "Voice of Eastern Indians," 326; D'Arcy McNickle, *Native American Tribalism*, 117; and

American Indian Chicago Conference, *Declaration of Indian Purpose* (Chicago: American Indian Chicago Conference, 1961), 5, 20. A copy of the declaration can also be found in Appendix D, "Task Force Three: Federal Administration and Structure of Indian Affairs," *Final Report to the American Indian Policy Review Commission* (Washington D.C.: GPO, 1976).

41. AICC, *Declaration,* 6–8. The forced account method required contractors to institute preferential hiring for Indian workers.

42. Ibid., 9–11.

43. Ibid., 11–13.

44. Ibid., 13–16. The problem of fractionated land ownership stemmed from the government policy of allotment, which was instituted during the nineteenth century and continued until 1934. By the 1960s a large number of heirs might share ownership of the original allotment, resulting in legal complications that often prevented the land from being used productively.

45. Ibid., 6, 20.

46. *New York Times,* 8 December 1960, 1, 27; Stan Opotowsky, *The Kennedy Government* (London: George G. Harrap & Co., 1961), 142; Transcript, Stewart Udall Oral History Interview, 18 April 1969, by Joe B. Frantz, Interview no. 1, 13, Lyndon B. Johnson Library, Austin, Texas (hereinafter cited as LBJL).

47. "Udall, Stewart Lee," in Charles Moritz, ed., *Current Biography Yearbook, 1961* (New York: H. W. Wilson Company, 1961), 464–66; "Udall, Stewart Lee," in *Biographical Directory of the United States Congress, 1774–1989,* Bicentennial Edition (Washington D.C.: GPO, 1991), 1966; *New York Times,* 8 December 1960, 27; Barbara Laverne Blythe LeUnes, "The Conservation Philosophy of Stewart L. Udall, 1961–1968" (Ph.D. diss., Texas A&M University, 1977); and *Washington Post,* 24 June 1969, A18.

48. Burt, *Tribalism,* 74–75; Congress, House, *Remarks on Indian Affairs,* 84th Cong., 2d sess., *Congressional Record* (28 March 1956), vol. 102, pt. 3, 5779; second quotation from Charlotte Buchen, "Rhodes, Udall Give Hope to Indians," *Arizona Republic,* 10 December 1959; and third quotation from "Udall Raps Policy on Indians," *Tucson Star,* 10 December 1959.

49. *New York Times,* 8 December 1960, 34. Udall immediately regretted his remark about serving as his own Indian affairs commissioner. Kennedy previously had stated that he might serve as his own secretary of state, and Udall believed he had been arrogant in drawing a parallel between himself and the president-elect. See Journal Notes, 10 December 1961, "S.L.U.

Notes and Thoughts on Appointment, Aug.–Dec. 1960," Box 80, Stewart L. Udall Papers, Special Collections, University of Arizona, Tucson, Arizona (hereinafter cited as SUP). He later condemned the remark as "very foolish"; see Transcript, Stewart Lee Udall Oral History Interview, 29 July 1969, by Joe B. Frantz, Interview no. 3, 1, LBJL.

50. *New York Times,* 8 December 1960, 34; "What Indians Want," *New Republic* 143 (19 December 1960): 7; and Draft Letter, Oliver La Farge to Senator Kennedy, n.d., Oliver La Farge Papers, Humanities Research Center, University of Texas, Austin, Texas.

51. Transcript, Clinton P. Anderson Oral History Interview, 14 April 1967, by John F. Stewart, 37, JFKL; Congress, Senate, Committee on Interior and Insular Affairs, *The Nomination of Stewart L. Udall to be Secretary of the Interior: Hearing Before the Committee on Interior and Insular Affairs,* 87th Cong., 1st sess., 13 January 1961, 5.

52. Committee on Interior and Insular Affairs, *The Nomination of Stewart L. Udall,* 12–13, 14–15; and Congress, Senate, *Nomination of Stewart Lee Udall to be Secretary of the Interior,* 87th Cong., 1st sess., *Congressional Record* (21 January 1961), vol. 107, pt. 1, 1036. The "ringleader" quotation derives from Transcript, Jerry T. Verkler Oral History, 30 January 1992, by Donald A. Ritchie, Interview no. 2, 90, Oral History Collection, Senate Historical Office, Washington, D.C. (hereinafter cited as SHO).

53. Transcript, Phillip S. Hughes Oral History, 7 March 1965, by David McCombs, 29, LBJL; Bernstein, Irving, *Guns or Butter: The Presidency of Lyndon Johnson* (New York: Oxford University Press, 1996), 265–306; and Stewart L. Udall, *The Quiet Crisis* (New York: Holt, Rinehart and Winston, 1963), viii.

54. Transcript, John A. Carver Oral History, 20 September 1968, Interview no. 2, by John Stewart, 32, JFKL.

55. Report, James E. Officer and William S. King, December 1960, "Bureau of Indian Affairs (Comments, Suggestions, Problems)," Box 89, SUP. Officer served in the BIA during both the Kennedy and Johnson administrations.

56. Udall quotation from "Official Report of the Proceedings Before the Department of the Interior in the Matter of Secretary's Meeting on Report of Task Force on Indian Affairs," 9 February 1961, "Bureau of Indian Affairs (Task Force on Indian Affairs)," Box 89, SUP; Nolen Bulloch, "Bartlesville Man to Aid Udall on Indian Affairs," *Tulsa Tribune,* 24 January 1961, 4; and "What Indians Want," 7–8. For a brief discussion of Keeler's role in Oklahoma Indian affairs, see Marjorie W. Lowe, "'Let's Make It

Happen': W. W. Keeler and Cherokee Renewal," *The Chronicles of Oklahoma* 74 (summer 1996): 116–29. This article makes no mention of the task force; Transcript, Nash Oral History, 8 March 1966, Interview no. 2, by Charles T. Morrisey, 37, JFKL; and Castile, *To Show Heart,* 5.

57. Memo, Officer to Udall, 9 February 1961, "Bureau of Indian Affairs (Task Force on Indian Affairs)," Box 89, SUP.

58. All quotations taken from Report of Task Force, 9 February 1961, 2, 4, 5, Box 89, SUP.

59. Ibid., 7.

60. Nash, "Human Values," 196; and Summary, Meeting of Indian Study Task Force, 27 February 1961, and "Memo, Highlights of Comments by Secretary Udall to Bureau of Indian Affairs Area Directors and Superintendents and Members of the Indian Study Task Force," 28 February, "Task Force Minutes of Meetings," Box 149, PNP. For examples of recommendation memorandums offering suggestions on issues of immediate concern, see "Bureau of Indian Affairs (Task Force on Indian Affairs)," Box 89, SUP; for memos relating to policy formulation, "Task Force Recommendation Memo," Box 149, PNP.

61. Summary, Meeting of Indian Task Force, 17 February 1961, "Task Force Minutes of Meetings," Box 149, PNP; Press Release, 10 March 1961, "Task Force—Task Force Trips," Box 149, PNP; "Report to the Secretary of the Interior by the Task Force on Indian Affairs," 10 July 1961 (hereinafter cited as "1961 Task Force Report"). A photocopy of the latter is located in "In/S Gen," IN, Box 4, White House Central Files, Subject Files (hereinafter cited as WHCF), LBJL. The Nash quotation is from Transcript, Nash Oral History, interview no. 3, 66, JFKL; and "1961 Task Force Report," frontispiece (no page number).

Guy B. Senese argues that the task force "established its priorities prior to any consultation with the grass-roots Indian." Noting that Keeler was only one-sixteenth Cherokee, Senese claims that "in choosing Keeler the task force was in search of something other than a grass-roots listening post." Senese fails to place the task force operations in the context of federal policy formulation. Prior to the 1960s, policymakers had shown little inclination to consult with Native Americans (although John Collier held meetings in 1934 in order to gain support for the Indian Reorganization Act). Moreover, the task force's visits to western cities allowed Native Americans who lacked the resources to travel to Washington, D.C., the opportunity to express their opinions. As such, the task force's visits represented a significant departure from previous methods of policy formulation. See Senese, *Self-Determination*, 61–63.

62. Quotations from "1961 Task Force Report," 4.

63. Ibid., 9–19.

64. Ibid., 22–41.

65. Ibid., 42–59.

66. Ibid., 6, 7.

67. Sioux delegation quotation from Meeting of Task Force with delegation of Sioux, 16 February 1961, "Task Force Minutes of Meetings," Box 149, PNP; Fort Berthold community quotation from Summary, Meeting of Indian Task Force, 17 February 1961, "Task Force Minutes of Meetings," Box 149, PNP; task force quotations from "1961 Task Force Report," 5, and frontispiece; Officer, "Termination as Federal Policy," 126.

68. "1961 Task Force Report," 5; and Remarks, Secretary of the Interior to Employees, Bureau of Indian Affairs, 26 September 1961, "S.L.U. Speech at Nash Swearing-In, Sept, 26, 1961," Box 83, SUP.

69. Memo, Officer to Udall, 9 February 1961, Box 89, SUP; Summary, Meeting of Indian Task Force, 21 February 1961, "Task Force Minutes of Meetings," Box 149, Nash Papers, HSTL; and Summary, Meeting of Indian Task Force, 25 February 1961, "Task Force Minutes of Meetings," Box 149, PNP.

70. Report of Task Force, 9 February 1961, 7, Box 89, SUP; Transcript, Nash Oral History, Interview no. 3, 66, JFKL; and Letter, La Farge to Dick (Schifter) and Art (Lazarus), 14 July 1961, Folder 7, Box 74, Association of American Indian Affairs Archives, Seeley G. Mudd Manuscript Library, Princeton University, Princeton, New Jersey (hereinafter cited as AAIAA).

71. First quotation is from Raymond A. Butler, "The Bureau of Indian Affairs: Activities Since 1945," *The Annals of the American Academy of Political and Social Science* 436 (March 1978): 55. Butler, a Blackfeet, served as acting commissioner of Indian affairs for most of 1977. Second quotation is from "1961 Task Force Report," 6, frontispiece (no page number); and third quotation is from William H. Kelly, "Indian Adjustment and the History of Indian Affairs," *Arizona Law Review* 10 (winter 1968): 574.

72. For Udall quotation, see pamphlet titled *Eighteenth Annual Convention of the National Congress of American Indians,* 16, copy in "Memo #167," Box 75, WBP. For discussions of the year 1961 as a turning point and of the three reports, see McNickle, *Native American Tribalism,* 115–16; Alvin M

Josephy, Jr., *The American Indian and the Bureau of Indian Affairs, 1969: A Study with Recommendations* (Toronto: Indian-Eskimo Association, 1960), 13–26; Parman, *Indians of the American West,* 149–50; Prucha, *The Great Father,* 2:1088–90; and Press Release, National Congress of American Indians, 15 February 1961, "American Indian Charter Convention University of Chicago," American Indian File, Western History Collections, University of Oklahoma, Norman, Oklahoma. Larry Burt claims that Udall participated in the Fund for the Republic study, but I have found no evidence of his involvement. See Burt, *Tribalism,* 127–28; Vine Deloria, Jr., ed., *Of Utmost Good Faith* (San Francisco: Straight Arrow Books, 1971), 217.

73. Quotation from "1961 Task Force Report," 77. M. Annette Jaimes wryly notes that the phrase New Frontier was "a rhetorical device not exactly designed to reassure an indigenous population nearly obliterated during the U.S. conquest of its first 'wilderness.'" See Jaimes, "The Hollow Icon," 34.

74. Stewart L. Udall, "The State of the Indian Nation—An Introduction," *Arizona Law Review* 10 (winter 1968): 553; and Transcript, Nash Oral History, Interview no. 3, 59, JFKL.

75. Letter, Goldwater to John F. Kennedy, 3 January 1961, "FG 145–5 Indian Affairs, Bureau of," Box 152, WHCF, JFKL. Udall quotation is from the *Albuquerque Journal,* 20 December 1960. Letters concerning McCabe are found in "Staff, Commissioner of Indian Affairs—Recommendations (Maurice McCabe)," Box 83, SUP; "Navajo Proposed for Indian Commissioner," *The Amerindian* 9 (January–February 1961): 1; and *Phoenix Republic,* 18 December 1960.

Udall had offered W. W. Keeler the position of commissioner in December 1960, but Keeler turned it down, as did William R. Rogers, Jr. Clinton Anderson vigorously opposed the nomination of Maurice McCabe as Indian commissioner. Only after he had received assurances from Udall that McCabe would not be nominated for the position did Anderson give Kennedy his approval for Udall's nomination as interior secretary. See Transcript, Stewart Udall Oral History Interview, 16 February 1970, by W. W. Moss, Interview no. 2, 33, 42, JFKL.

76. Nash, "Human Values," 195–96.

77. Biographical information is found in "Nash, Philleo," in *Current Biography Yearbook, 1962,* ed. Charles Moritz (New York: H. W. Wilson Company, 1962), 315–17; Margaret Connell Szasz, "Philleo Nash," in *The Commissioners,* 313–14; and Fred Eggan, "Philleo Nash: The Education of

an Applied Anthropologist," in *Applied Anthropologist and Public Servant: The Life and Work of Philleo Nash*, ed. Ruth H. Landman and Katherine Spencer Halpern (Washington, D.C.: American Anthropological Association, 1989), 7–8. The quotation is from Transcript, Philleo Nash Oral History, 24 June 1966, by Jerry N. Hess, Interview no. 1, 30, Harry S. Truman Library, Independence, Missouri (hereinafter cited as HSTL).

78. First quotation taken from Francis H. Heller, ed., *The Truman White House: The Administration of the Presidency, 1945–1953* (Lawrence: Regents Press of Kansas, 1980), 53; and Philp, *Indian Self-Rule,* 164–66. Second quotation from Philp, 164; and Transcript, Philleo Nash Oral History, 5 June 1967, by Jerry N. Hess, Interview no. 13, 681–87, HSTL. For Nash's role in writing Executive Order 9981, see Clark Clifford, *Counsel to the President: A Memoir* (New York: Random House, 1991), 210.

79. Szasz, "Philleo Nash," 314; Nash, Philleo, "Anthropologist in the White House," in *Applied Anthropologist and Public Servant: The Life and Work of Philleo Nash*, ed. Ruth H. Landman and Katherine Spencer Halpern (Washington, D.C., American Anthropological Association, 1989), 5; Transcript, Nash Oral History, 7 April 1977, 1, 13, "Writings of Philleo Nash—Oral History Interview—Lyndon B. Johnson Library," Box 208, PNP. This oral history should not be confused with the Truman Library Nash Oral History. Nash was interviewed in 1977 as part of an administrative history of the Johnson administration—see Richard L. Schott and Dagmar S. Hamilton, *People, Positions and Power: The Political Appointments of Lyndon Johnson* (Chicago: University of Chicago Press, 1983). The Nash papers include a copy of this 1977 interview. To avoid confusion, citations refer to this oral history as the 1977 Nash Oral History Interview. Transcript, Nash Oral History, Interview no. 2, 36, 37 JKFL; and Transcript, Nash Oral History, Interview no. 3, 54, JFKL.

80. *New York Times,* 3 August 1961, 22; *Washington Post,* 7 August 1961, A10; James E. Officer, "The Indian Service and Its Evolution," in *The Aggressions of Civilization: Federal Indian Policy Since the 1880s,* ed. Sandra L. Cadwalader and Vine Deloria, Jr. (Philadelphia: Temple University Press, 1984), 83. Udall quotations from Transcript, Udall Oral History, Interview no. 1, 3, LBJL.

81. Nash, "Human Values," 195, 196; Letter, Udall to Haley, 29 June 1961, "I & A: Task Force," JHP.

82. Nash, "Human Values," 196; Transcript, Nash Oral History, Interview no. 3, 67, JFKL; Officer, "Termination as Federal Policy," 127.

83. Congress, Senate, *Announcement of Hearing on Nomination of Philleo Nash to be Commissioner of Indian Affairs,* 87th Cong., 1st sess. *Congressional Record* (9 August 1961), vol. 107, pt. 11, 15218; "Anderson, Clinton Presba," in *Biographical Directory,* 534; and Transcript, John A. Carver Oral History, 25 November 1969, by William W. Moss, Interview no. 8, 85, JFKL.

84. Quotation from Larry J. Hasse, "Termination and Assimilation: Federal Indian Policy, 1943 to 1961" (Ph.D. diss., Washington State University, 1974), 266; Officer, "Termination as Federal Policy," 127; and Comptroller General of the United States, "Review of Certain Aspects of the Program for the Termination of Federal Supervision Over Indian Affairs," March 1961. A copy of the latter report can be found in "FG 145–5 Indian Affairs, Bureau of," Box 152, WHCF, JFKL.

    Nash later noted that Anderson went "right out the roof" at the breakfast when he read the report's summary of events surrounding the Navajo-Hopi Act of 1950, in which Anderson had played a role. Nash recalled that "Anderson attacked that portion of the report and therefore indirectly the whole report." See Transcript, Philleo Nash Oral History, 17 October 1966, by Jerry N. Hess, Interview no. 6, 257–61, HSTL; and "1961 Task Force Report," 67.

85. Transcript, Jerry T. Verkler Oral History, 30 January 1992, by Donald A. Ritchie, Interview no. 1, 28, SHO; Congress, Senate, Committee on Interior and Insular Affairs, *The Nomination of Philleo Nash to be Commissioner of Indian Affairs: Hearings before the Committee on Interior and Insular Affairs,* 87th Cong., 1st sess., 14 and 17 August 1961. The first two quotations are from p. 11, and the final quotation, p. 9. For additional insights on Anderson and Indian affairs, see Cowger, *Founding Years,* 92–97; and Richard Drinnon, *Keeper of the Concentration Camps: Dillon S. Myer and American Racism* (Berkeley: University of California Press, 1987), 209–11.

86. LeRoy Ashby and Rod Gramer, *Fighting the Odds: The Life of Senator Frank Church* (Pullman, Wash.: Washington University Press, 1994), xii, 113–15; and Transcript, Nash Oral History, Interview no. 3, 67, JFKL.

87. Quotations taken from Committee on Interior Affairs, *Nomination of Philleo Nash,* 27–35.

88. Ibid., 27–28, 34–35.

89. Ibid. Gruening quotations from p. 37, and Allott quotations from pp. 47, 48. Nash quotation from Philp, *Indian Self-Rule,* 131.

90. Congress, Senate, *Philleo Nash,* 82d Cong., 2d sess., *Congressional Record* (29 January 1952), vol. 98, pt. 1, 581; Lately Thomas, *When Even Angels*

Wept: The Senator Joseph McCarthy Affair—A Story Without a Hero (New York: William Morrow and Co., 1973), 246; Letter, J. Cordell Moore to Stewart L. Udall, 31 August, 1961, "Staff: Commissioner of Indian Affairs—Philleo Nash I," Box 83, SUP; Letter, J. Edgar Hoover to P. Kenneth O'Donnell, 3 February 1961, "Staff: Commissioner of Indian Affairs—Philleo Nash I," Box 83, SUP; Congress, Senate, Committee on Interior and Insular Affairs, *The Nomination of Philleo Nash to be Commissioner of Indian Affairs, Executive Session Hearing before the Committee on Interior and Insular Affairs,* 87th Cong., 1st sess., 8 September 1961, microfiche.

91. Committee on Interior Affairs, *Nomination of Philleo Nash, Executive Session,* 148; Fixico, *Termination,* 26, 28, 93. Second quotation from Peter J. Ognibene, *Scoop: The Life and Politics of Henry M. Jackson* (New York: Stein and Day, 1975), 134—Vine Deloria, Jr., made the quoted statement.

92. Quotations from Letter, Nash to "Jean," 11 September 1961, "Chrono. File—August and September, 1961," Box 169, PNP; and Letter, Nash to Harry S. Truman, 3 October 1961, "Chrono. File—October, 1961," Box 169, PNP.

93. Congress, Senate, *Commissioner of Indian Affairs,* 87th Cong., 1st sess., *Congressional Record* (20 September 1961), vol. 107, pt. 15, 20427–33.

94. Nash, "Human Values," 196–97.

95. "Aspinall, Wayne N.," in *Biographical Directory,* 552. Udall quotations from Transcript, Stewart L. Udall Oral History, Interview no. 2, by Joe B. Frantz, 10, LBJL; and Fenno, *Congressmen in Committees,* 61, 118–23, 136. Fenno does not provide citations for any of the above quotations. Congressional staff member comment from Transcript, Verkler Oral History, Interview no. 2, 86, SHO. Final quotation from John R. Finger, *Cherokee Americans: The Eastern Band of Cherokees in the Twentieth Century* (Lincoln: University of Nebraska Press, 1991), 135–36.

96. Transcript, John A. Carver Oral History, 18 November 1969, by William W. Moss, Interview no. 7, 63, JFKL. Final quotation from Transcript, Aspinall Oral History, 20, LOC; and Harry A. Kersey, Jr., *An Assumption of Sovereignty: Social and Political Transformation among the Florida Seminoles, 1953–1979* (Lincoln: University of Nebraska Press, 1996), 25–26, 46–47.

97. Haley quotation from Letter, Haley to S. E. Seamans, 28 March 1961, "Indian Affairs Subcommittee Correspondence, 1960–1965," JHP.

98. Letter, Haley to Udall, 6 July 1961, "I & A: Task Force," JHP.

CHAPTER TWO

1. Officer, "Termination as Federal Policy," 127; and Comptroller General, "Review of Certain Aspects," 8–9. The four groups terminated during the 1950s were the Alabama and Coushatta Tribes, the tribes and bands of Western Oregon, the Paiute Bands in Utah, and the Ottawa Tribe. The Wyandotte and Peoria terminations scheduled for 1959 had not been completed because of legal issues involving land claims. Termination dates for the California rancherías, the Choctaws, and the Catawbas had not been scheduled as of early 1961.

2. Fixico, *Termination,* 95; Patricia K. Ourada, *The Menominee Indians: A History* (Norman: University of Oklahoma Press, 1979), 189; Congress, House, *Menominee Tribe of Wisconsin,* 83d Cong., 1st sess., *Congressional Record* (1 August 1953), vol. 99, pt. 8, 10933; also quoted in Nicholas C. Peroff, *Menominee Drums: Tribal Termination and Restoration, 1954–1974* (Norman: University of Oklahoma Press, 1982), 76; and *United States Statutes at Large,* 67: B132.

3. *An Act to provide for a per capita distribution of Menominee tribal funds and authorize the withdrawal of the Menominee Tribe from Federal Jurisdiction, Statutes at Large,* vol. 68, chapter 303, 250–52 (1954); Congress, Senate, Committee on Interior and Insular Affairs, *Amendments to the Menominee Termination Act: Hearings before the Subcommittee on Indian Affairs of the Committee on Interior and Insular Affairs,* 87th Cong., 1st sess., 18, 19, and 24 April 1961, 2–3. For a brief history of the Menominee termination process, see Peroff, *Menominee Drums,* 52–123.

4. Committee on Interior and Insular Affairs, *Amendments to the Menominee Termination Act,* 28: Proxmire quotations from p. 10; Church quotation, pp. 1–2; and *Milwaukee Sentinel* quotation, p. 25.

5. Committee on Interior and Insular Affairs, *Amendments to the Menominee Termination Act,* 28–45.

6. Peroff, *Menominee Drums,* 83–84, 129. By the terms of the termination program and in agreement with the state of Wisconsin, the reservation became a county in Wisconsin. For the disputes between the House and Senate Interior Committees, see AICC, *Declaration,* 34, 35; and Congress, House, *Providing Assistance to Menominee County, Wis.,* 87th Cong., 2d sess., *Congressional Record* (20 March 1962), vol. 108, pt. 4, 4592–93. For the compromise appropriations bill, see *Menominee County, Wis., assistance, Statutes at Large,* 76, 53–54 (1962).

7. Congress, Senate, Committee on Interior and Insular Affairs, *Providing for*

the Division of the Tribal Assets of the Ponca Tribe of Native Americans of Nebraska among the Members of the Tribe, and for other purposes, 87th Cong., 2d sess., 25 June 1962, Senate Report 1623, 1–5. Carver's letter of transmittal is reproduced in this report. See also *Indians. Statutes at Large*, 76, 429–30 (1962).

8. Quotations from Beth Ritter Knoche, "Termination, Self-Determination, and Restoration: The Northern Ponca Case" (master's thesis, University of Nebraska, 1990), 65–66; Prucha, *Great Father*, 2:1048.

9. Department of the Interior, *Annual Report of the Secretary of the Interior, 1962*, 37–38.

10. Adams quotation from Philp, *Indian Self-Rule*, 240.

11. For a brief discussion of the Seneca Nation's battle against the Kinzua Dam, see Alvin Josephy, Jr., *Now That the Buffalo's Gone: A Study of Today's American Indians* (New York: Alfred A. Knopf, 1982), 127–50. Note that the Allegany Reservation and the Allegheny river have different spellings.

12. Arthur E. Morgan, *Dams and Other Disasters: A Century of the Army Corps of Engineers in Civil Works* (Boston: Porter Sargent Publishing, 1971), 310–15; Laurence M. Hauptman, *The Iroquois Struggle for Survival: World War II to Red Power* (Syracuse, N.Y.: Syracuse University Press, 1986), 91–93; and Josephy, *Now That the Buffalo's Gone*, 139.

13. The treaty text is reproduced in Charles J. Kappler, *Indian Treaties, 1778–1883* (New York: Interland Publishing, 1972), 34–36; and Hauptman, *Iroquois Struggle*, 93.

14. First quotation is from Telegram, Sherman P. Voorhees to John P. Saylor, 19 June 1957, "Kinzua Dam Correspondence/Telegram," Box 39, John P. Saylor Papers, Indiana University of Pennsylvania, Indiana, Pennsylvania (hereinafter cited as JSP); and Hauptman, *Iroquois Struggle*, 94–95, 99–101. The Eisenhower quotation is from Hauptman, 109.

15. Hauptman, *Iroquois Struggle*, 111–14; and Morgan, *Dams and Other Disasters*, 315–66.

16. United States v. 21,250 Acres of Land, More or Less, Situate in Cattaraugus County, 161 F. Supp. 376; and Seneca Nation of Indians v. Wilber M. Brucker, 162 F. Supp. 580, 79 S. Ct. 1294.

17. Letter, Saylor to Eisenhower, 16 January 1959, "Kinzua Dam Correspondence/Letters (2)," Box 39, JSP. In recognition of his efforts on behalf of the Senecas, the Nation adopted Saylor as a member in 1962. See Joy A. Bilharz, *The Allegany Senecas and Kinzua Dam: Forced Relocation*

Through Two Generations (Lincoln: University of Nebraska Press, 1998), 65; Hauptman, *Iroquois Struggle*, 120–21, 263 n46; Milton Jacques, "State Braves Take on Indians to Get 'Heap Big' Dam," *The Patriot* (Harrisburg, Pa.), 24 June 1960, 8; and Congress, House, *Public Works Appropriations Bill, 1961*, 86th Cong., 2d sess., *Congressional Record* (25 May 1960), vol. 106, pt. 8, 11061–62.

18. *Freedom of Communications*, 801; Letter, Williams to Kennedy, 22 February 1961, "Resources—Kinzua Dam June 23, 1960–1961," Box 14, General Files, Lee C. White Papers, John F. Kennedy Library, Boston, Massachusetts (hereinafter cited as LWP).

19. Brooks Atkinson, "Proposed Allegheny River Dam Brings to Mind 1794 Treaty With Seneca Indians," 17 February 1961, *New York Times*, 24; "As Long as the River Flows," 22 February 1961, *New York Times*, 24; John F. Kennedy, *Public Papers of the Presidents of the United States, John F. Kennedy, 1961* (Washington, D.C.: GPO, 1962), 157.

20. Quotations from Letter, Elmer B. Staats to Basil Williams, 21 March 1961, "Resources—Kinzua Dam June 23, 1960–1961," Box 14, General Files, LWP; and Louis Fisher, *Presidential Spending Power* (Princeton: Princeton University Press, 1975), 147–48, 163–66.

21. *Washington Post*, 8 April 1961, A8.

22. Memorandum, Sorenson to White, 10 April 1961, "Resources-Kinzua Dam June 23, 1960–1961," Box 14, General Files, LWP; and Letter, Lazarus to White, 10 April 1961, "Resources-Kinzua Dam June 23, 1960–1961," Box 14, General Files, LWP. Lazarus worked for the same Washington, D.C., firm that employed Richard Schifter, author of Kennedy's 1960 letter to the AAIA. For a brief profile of Lazarus, see Edward Lazarus, *Black Hills, White Justice: The Sioux Nation Versus the United States, 1775 to the Present* (New York: HarperCollins, 1991), 217, 225–26; and Letter, Mangan to White, 18 April 1961, "Resources-Kinzua Dam June 23, 1960–1961," Box 14, General Files, LWP.

23. Letter, White to Williams, 7 June 1961, "Resources-Kinzua Dam June 23, 1960–1961," Box 14, General Files, LWP; Letter, Arthur Lazarus to Lee White, 23 June 1961, "Resources-Kinzua Dam June 23, 1960–1961," Box 14, General Files, LWP; and Kennedy, *Public Papers, 1961*, 563.

24. Memorandum, White to the President, 8 August 1961, "Resources-Kinzua Dam June 23, 1960–1961," Box 14, General Files, LWP; and Kennedy, *Public Papers, 1961*, 563.

25. Kennedy, *Public Papers, 1961*, 563.

26. Walter Taylor, "The Treaty We Broke," *Nation* 193 (2 September 1961): 121; and Hauptman, *Iroquois Struggle*, 121. For Kennedy's political debt to Lawrence, see Michael P. Weber, *Don't Call Me Boss: David L. Lawrence, Pittsburgh's Renaissance Mayor* (Pittsburgh: University of Pittsburgh Press, 1988), 365. Nash quotations from Transcript, Nash Oral History, Interview no. 3, 59, JFKL. Udall quotation from Transcript, Stewart Udall Oral History, Interview no. 6, by W. W. Moss, 130, JFKL.

27. Quotation from Vine Deloria, Jr., *We Talk, You Listen: New Tribes, New Turf* (New York: The Macmillan Company, 1970), 97.

28. Nash, "Human Values," 197. First Nash quotation from Transcript, Nash Oral History, Interview no. 3, 61, JFKL; and Transcript, 1998 Udall interview, 1. Second Nash quotation from Transcript, Nash Oral History, Interview no. 2, 42, JFKL.

29. Letter, William Zimmerman, Jr., to Charles Elkus, 26 February 1962, Folder 26, Box 15, William Zimmerman Papers, Center for Southwest Research, University of New Mexico, Albuquerque, New Mexico; and Parker, *Singing an Indian Song*, 200–201.

30. First quotation from Nash, "Human Values," 197; second quotation from "Summary: 'Applied Anthropology and the Concept of Guided Acculturation in Indian Administration,'" 20 November 1970, in "Writings of Philleo Nash—Excerpts of Speeches as Commissioner of Indian Affairs," Box 208, PNP; third quotation from James E. Officer, "Philleo Nash Anthropologist as Administrator," in *Applied Anthropologist and Public Servant: The Life and Work of Philleo Nash*, ed. Ruth H. Landman and Katherine Spencer Halpern (Washington, D.C., American Anthropological Association, 1989), 12; and La Farge quotation from Letter, La Farge to Udall, 16 February 1962, "Correspondence File 1961–1965 'L,'" Box 140, PNP.

31. Transcript, Udall Oral History, Interview no. 2, 40, JFKL.

32. Udall quotation from Remarks, Secretary of the Interior to Employees, Bureau of Indian Affairs, 26 September 1961, "S.L.U. Speech at Nash Swearing-In, Sept. 26, 1961," Box 83, SUP; and "1961 Task Force Report," 47. Nash quotations from Nash, "Human Values," 198; and Officer, "Anthropologist," 11–12.

33. Interior Department, *Annual Report, 1962*, 8–10; "1961 Task Force Report," 47–48; and Officer, "Anthropologist," 11–12. The *Annual Report, 1962* refers to the "new" Division of Economic Employment. However, the division was new only in the sense that it had been reorganized. See

Department of the Interior, Bureau of Indian Affairs, *Developing Indian Employment Opportunities*, by Keith L. Fay (Bureau of Indian Affairs, n.d.), 48–49.

34. First and third quotations from Transcript, Nash Oral History, Interview no. 2, 43, JFKL; and second quotation from Congress, House, Committee on Interior and Insular Affairs, *Policies, Programs, and Activities of the Department of the Interior*, 88th Cong., 1st sess., 31 January through 11 February 1963, 167. The unattributed quotation regarding Nash is from Szasz, "Philleo Nash," 316; and Officer, "Anthropologist," 13.

35. James E. Officer, "The Bureau of Indian Affairs Since 1945: An Assessment," *Annals of the American Academy of Political and Social Science* 436 (March 1978): 65; Letter, Richard Schifter to Oliver La Farge, 20 March 1962, Folder 1, Box 132, AAIAA; Memo, Indian Affairs, Part 1—President's Program Proposals, "Dept. of the Interior (Proposed Legislative Program, 87th Congress, 2d session, Oct. 1961)," Box 88, SUP; Memo, "Indian Affairs, Part 1—President's Program Proposals, Dept. of the Interior (Proposed Legislative Program, 88th Congress, 1st Session, Nov. 1962)," Box 100, SUP; and Memo, "Indians," 1 November 1963, "Notebook—Progress during JFK administration," Box 108, SUP.

36. Estate information is found in Congress, Senate, Committee on Interior and Insular Affairs, *Indian Heirship Land Problem: Hearings before the Subcommittee on Indian Affairs of the Committee on Interior and Insular Affairs*, 87th Cong., 1st sess., 9 and 10 August 1961, 47–48, 50. Numbers regarding total Indian lands with multiple owners are found in Congress, Senate, Committee on Interior and Insular Affairs, *Indian Heirship Land Problem: Hearings before the Subcommittee on Indian Affairs of the Committee on Interior and Insular Affairs*, 87th Cong., 2d sess., 2 and 3 April 1962, 207; and Stephen A. Langore, "The Heirship Land Problem and Its Effect on the Indian, the Tribe, and Effective Utilization," in *Toward Economic Development for Native Communities: A Compendium of Papers*, Congress, Subcommittee on Economy in Government of the Joint Economic Committee, 91st Cong., 1st sess., Joint Committee Print (Washington, D.C.: GPO, 1969): 519.

37. "1961 Task Force Report," 10; Congress, Senate, *Announcement of hearings on S. 1392, Relating to the Indian Heirship Land Problem*, 87th Cong., 1st sess., *Congressional Record* (18 July 1961), vol. 107, pt. 10, 12870; Handwritten note, Legislative: Indians, 29 September 1961, "Bureau of Indian Affairs (Task Force on Indian Affairs)," Box 89, SUP; and Officer, "Anthropologist," 14.

38. Committee on Interior and Insular Affairs, *Indian Heirship,* 1961, 1, 4–6, 21–24.

39. Comptroller General, "Review of Certain Aspects," 21–23; and Committee on Interior and Insular Affairs, *Indian Heirship,* 1961, 6.

40. Committee on Interior and Insular Affairs, *Indian Heirship,* 1961, 7–11, 25. The second Carver quotation is from p. 9, and the third, p. 25. First Carver quotation is from Transcript, Carver Oral History, Interview no. 8, 96, JFKL.

41. Committee on Interior and Insular Affairs, *Indian Heirship,* 1961, 100, 106, 123. Of the many communications received from Indians and Indian organizations, only one, from the obscure Black Hills Treaty and Claims Council, called for the passage of S. 1392 (see p. 153).

42. Ibid., 107, 119.

43. Committee on Interior and Insular Affairs, *Indian Heirship,* 1962, 194, 197–99.

44. Ibid., 199–203, 235.

45. Ibid., 194, 253, 289.

46. Congress, Senate, Committee on Interior and Insular Affairs, *Indian Heirship Land Problem: Hearings before the Subcommittee on Indian Affairs of the Committee on Interior and Insular Affairs,* 88th Cong., 1st sess., 29 and 30 April 1963, 380–83, 386–87.

47. Burnette and Real Bird quotations from Committee on Interior and Insular Affairs, *Indian Heirship Land Problem,* 1963, 419, 455; and Congress, Senate, *Indian Heirship Land Problem,* 88th Cong., 1st sess., *Congressional Record* (11 October 1963), vol. 109, pt. 14, 19371, 19448.

48. Burnette, *Tortured Americans,* 79.

49. Nash quotations from Transcript, Nash Oral History, Interview no. 3, 67, JFKL. First Officer quotation from Officer, "Anthropologist," 14; and second Officer quotation from Officer, "Indian Service," 83. Carver quotation from Transcript, Carver Oral History, Interview no. 8, 97.

50. Officer, "Indian Service," 83. In 1983, Burnette asserted that in 1962 "President Kennedy had that legislation killed. Lee Metcalf . . . told us what had happened." In his 1971 autobiography, Burnette wrote that Kennedy intervened with Senate Interior Committee members twice in 1963 on the issue of heirship, again writing that Metcalf had provided the details about Kennedy's action. Thus, there is some confusion over the dates in the two

accounts, which presumably refer to the same incident. Stewart Udall deemed Kennedy's participation to be "unlikely." See Philp, *Indian Self-Rule*, 211; Burnette, *Tortured Americans*, 77–78; and Transcript, 1998 Udall interview, 7.

51. Letter, Schifter to La Farge, 20 March 1962; and Officer, "An Assessment," 65.

52. Transcript, John A. Carver Oral History, Interview no. 5, by William W. Moss, 28–29, JFKL; Copy, Remarks by Secretary Udall at the Opening Session of the Bureau of Indian Affairs Conference of Superintendents, 16 June 1964, "June 13–16, 1964—Bureau of Indian Affairs Conference of Superintendents (Santa Fe, New Mex.)," Box 119, SUP; and Richard Schifter, "Trends in Federal Indian Administration," *South Dakota Law Review* 15 (winter 1970): 11. Schifter took credit for persuading the PHA to make the regulatory ruling. See Letter, Schifter to author, 19 August 1998; and Transcript, Marie C. McGuire Oral History, by William McHugh, 3 April 1967, 1, 31, 32, 34, 37, JFKL. McGuire recalled meeting with "Commissioner Nash" in "May and certainly not later than June of '61," at which time Nash was not officially an employee of the BIA (Interior Department, *Annual Report, 1962*, 20–22; President, *Public Papers*, John F. Kennedy, 1961, 607).

53. Interior Department, *Annual Report, 1962*, 22; Transcript, McGuire Oral History, 33, JFKL; and Department of the Interior, Bureau of Indian Affairs, *Indian Affairs 1964: A Progress Report from the Commissioner of Indian Affairs*, 12.

54. Lazarus, *Black Hills*, 259–60.

55. Sar A. Levitan, *Federal Aid to Depressed Areas: An Evaluation of the Area Redevelopment Administration* (Baltimore: Johns Hopkins Press, 1964), 1–17; Congress, Senate, Committee on Labor and Public Welfare, *Area Redevelopment: Hearings before the Subcommittee on Labor of the Committee on Labor and Public Welfare*, 84th Cong., 2d sess., 24, 25, and 27 February, 20, 22, 23, 26, 28, and 29 March, and 26 April 1956, 889–90; Congress, Senate, *Unemployment in Certain Economically Depressed Areas*, 84th Cong., 2d sess., *Congressional Record* (26 July 1956), vol. 102, pt. 11, 14641.

56. Levitan, *Federal Aid*, 1–17.

57. Congress, Senate, Committee on Banking and Currency, *Area Redevelopment—1961: Hearings before the Subcommittee of the Committee on Banking and Currency*, 87th Cong., 1st sess., 18, 19, and 26 January and 20 February 1961, 1, 66–68, 81–82.

58. Levitan, *Federal Aid*, 17; Transcript, Oral History Interview, William L. Batt, 26 October 1966, by Larry J. Hackman, 36, JKFL; and Irwin Unger, *Best of Intentions: The Triumphs and Failures of the Great Society Under Kennedy, Johnson, and Nixon* (New York: Doubleday, 1996), 30.

59. Department of Commerce, *Annual Report of the Area Redevelopment Administration of the U.S. Dept. of Commerce, 1962,* 3; *Area Redevelopment Act, Statutes At Large,* 75, 47–63 (1961); Department of the Interior, *Annual Report of the Secretary of the Interior, 1961,* 286; and Interior Department, *Annual Report, 1962,* 10.

60. Transcript, Batt Oral History, 65–66, JFKL; and Interior Department, *Annual Report, 1962,* 8–9, 10–11. For a complete list of approved projects and feasibility studies, see *Area Redevelopment Administration, 1962,* 35–63. Although this report provides a brief description of the approved feasibility studies, it does not offer details on the individual OEDPs. See Department of Commerce, *More Jobs Where Needed: Annual Report of the Area Redevelopment Administration of the U.S. Department of Commerce, 1964,* 29; and Fay, *Developing Opportunities,* 44–45.

61. Officer, "An Assessment," 65; Department of Commerce, *Economic Growth in American Communities: Annual Report of the Area Redevelopment Administration of the United States Department of Commerce, 1963,* 35, 120; Schifter, "Trends," 11; and *Indian Affairs 1964,* 29. For a brief debate about the inclusion of Indians in the Public Works Acceleration Act, see Congress, House, *Loans to Indian Tribes for Public Works or Facilities,* 87th Cong., 2d sess., *Congressional Record* (5 October 1962), vol. 108, pt. 17, 22610; and Transcript, Nash Oral History, Interview no. 2, 39, JFKL.

62. Larry W. Burt, "Western Tribes and Balance Sheets: Business Development Programs in the 1960s and 1970s," *Western Historical Quarterly* 23 (November 1992): 480; and Jennings C. Wise, *The Red Man in the New World Drama: A Politico-Legal Study with a Pageantry of American Indian History,* ed. and rev. by Vine Deloria, Jr. (New York: Macmillan Company, 1971), 381.

63. Burt, *Tribalism,* 128.

64. Interior Department, *Annual Report, 1961,* 296–98; and Fay, *Developing Opportunities,* 168–69.

65. Fay, *Developing Opportunities,* 168–69.

66. Transcript, Carver Oral History, Interview no. 5, 25–26, JFKL. For a brief discussion of the gender issue at the Pine Ridge plant, see Stephen E.

Feraca, *Why Don't They Give Them Guns: The Great American Indian Myth* (Lanham, Md.: University Press of American, 1990), 141–42.

67. Fay, *Developing Opportunities*, 164–65.

68. Henry W. Hough, *Development of Indian Resources* (Denver: World Press, Inc., 1967), 199–202.

69. Interior Department, *Annual Report*, 1962, 22; and Fay, *Developing Opportunities*, 81. Although both Fay and Sorkin rely upon BIA documents, their figures are somewhat different. Sorkin lists fifty openings and different percentage rates for Indian employment for 1961 through 1963, perhaps as a result of different definitions of "industry" located "on or near" reservations. However, both sources reveal the same general trends.

70. Szasz, *Education and the American Indian*, 121–23, 139–40; and Transcript, Udall Oral History, Interview no. 2, 41, JFKL.

71. Transcript, Carver Oral History, Interview no. 5, 23, JFKL; and Congress, House, Committee on Appropriations, *Department of the Interior and Related Agencies Appropriations for 1964: Hearings before the Subcommittee of the Committee on Appropriations*, 88th Cong., 1st sess., 28 January through 21 February 1963, 830. Budget figures do not include supplemental appropriations. See Interior Department, *Annual Report 1961*, 286–87; and Interior Department, *Indian Affairs 1964*, 4.

72. Committee on Appropriations, *Interior Appropriations for 1964*, 895; Szasz, *Education and the American Indian*, 126; and Interior Department, *Indian Affairs 1964*, 8. Construction costs were not part of the education budget.

73. Szasz, *Education and the American Indian*, 129–30, 145–46; Interior Department, *Indian Affairs 1964*, 6; and Transcript, Udall Oral History, Interview no. 2, 41, JFKL.

74. "1961 Task Force Report," 7.

75. Ibid., 7.

76. First and second Nash quotations are from Transcript, 1977 Nash Oral History, 20–21, HSTL. Third Nash quotation is from Transcript, Nash Oral History, Interview no. 2, 43, 48–49, JFKL. Deloria quotation is from Vine Deloria, Jr., *Custer Died For Your Sins: An Indian Manifesto* (New York: Macmillan Company, 1969), 192.

77. Transcript, 1998 Udall interview, 7; and John F. Kennedy, 1962, *Public Papers of the Presidents of the United States* (Washington, D.C.: GPO, 1963), 619–20, and Hauptman and Campisi, "Voice of Eastern Indians," 329.

Nash quotation from Transcript, Philleo Nash Oral History, Interview no. 2, 45, JFKL.

78. Letter, Keeler to Brophy, 27 February 1961, "Keeler, W. W. Jan. 1960 through Dec. 1961," Box 22, WBP.

CHAPTER THREE

1. The final two quotations are from a speech delivered on 22 May 1964. Lyndon B. Johnson, *Public Papers of the Presidents of the United States: Lyndon B. Johnson, 1963–1964,* vol. 1 (Washington, D.C.: GPO, 1965), 114, 704.

2. *Congressional Quarterly's Guide to U.S. Elections,* 3d ed. (Washington, D.C.: Congressional Quarterly Inc., 1994), 403, 461, 595–97; and Joseph A. Califano, Jr., *The Triumph and Tragedy of Lyndon Johnson: The White House Years* (New York: Simon & Schuster, 1991), 149.

3. Johnson, *Public Papers,* 1963–1964, vol. 1, 8–10.

4. Transcript, Udall Oral History, Interview no. 1, 20–21, LBJL.

5. Transcript, Charles K. Boatner Oral History, by Michael L. Gillette, 2 June 1976, Interview no. 4, 20, LBJL. See also Schott and Hamilton, *People, Positions, and Power,* 48–51; Transcript, Udall Oral History, Interview no. 1, 21–22, LBJL; and Transcript, 1977 Nash Oral History, 21, HSTL.

6. *Great Falls Tribune* (Great Falls, Mont.), 28 October 1960; and Daily Diary, 15 August 1962, "Aug., 1962," Box 2, Pre-Presidential Daily Diary, LBJL. For a listing of the House and Senate papers concerning Indian Affairs, see "List of Suggested Materials in the Johnson Library on Indian Policy," May 1987, LBJL.

7. Johnson, *Public Papers,* 1963–1964, vol. 1, 149–52; Memorandum, Secretary of the Interior to the President, 20 January 1964, "11/22/63—2/29/64," EX IN, Box 1, WHCF, LBJL; and Burnette, *Tortured Americans,* 82.

8. Johnson, *Public Papers,* 1963–1964, vol. 1, 149–52; Letter, Indian Rights Association to the President, 13 January 1965, Name File, WHCF, LBJL.

9. Lyndon Baines Johnson, *The Vantage Point: Perspectives of the Presidency, 1963–1969* (New York: Holt, Rinehart and Winston, 1971), 69, 71; and Robert Dallek, *Lone Star Rising: Lyndon Johnson and His Times, 1908–1960* (New York: Oxford University Press, 1991), 77–81, 136–39.

10. Unger, *Best of Intentions,* 80–85; Sar A. Levitan, *The Great Society's Poor Law: A New Approach to Poverty* (Baltimore: Johns Hopkins Press, 1969),

29–37; Congress, House, Committee on Education and Labor, *Economic Opportunity Act of 1964: Hearings before the Subcommittee on the War on Poverty Program of the Committee on Education and Labor,* pt. 1, 88th Cong., 1st sess., 17–20 March, 7–10, 13, and 14 April 1964, 4–18.

11. House, Committee on Education and Labor, *Economic Opportunity Act of 1964,* pt. 1, 8–11; and Unger, *Best of Intentions,* 78–79, 82. For discussion of controversial CAP programs, see Unger, 152–67. For President Johnson's political troubles with OEO and CAPs, see Califano, *Triumph and Tragedy,* 77–80.

12. For a rare mention of poverty planners including Indians in their discussions, see Sanford Kravitz, "The Community Action Program—Past, Present, and Its Future?" in *On Fighting Poverty: Perspectives From Experience,* ed. James L. Sundquist (New York: Basic Books, 1969), 60–62. Irving Bernstein places Udall at planning sessions, but offers no citation. See Bernstein, *Guns or Butter,* 101; "Volume I, Part I, Narrative History," 16, 27, Box 1, Administrative History: Office of Economic Opportunity, LBJL; Levitan, *Great Society's Poor Law,* 17; and Unger, *Best of Intentions,* 80–81. For an example of a document that discusses Indian poverty, see Memo, Walter W. Heller to David L. Hackett, 1 December 1963, 16, 32–33, "CEA Draft History of the War on Poverty (2 of 3)," Box 1, Legislative Background: Economic Opportunity Act of 1964, War on Poverty, LBJL. This document proposed the creation of several task forces, including one dedicated to Indian issues.

13. Unger, *Best of Intentions,* 50.

14. House, Committee on Education and Labor, *Economic Opportunity Act of 1964,* pt. 1, i, 341–50. Nash accompanied Udall to the hearing but did not testify (see p. 362).

15. Unger, *Best of Intentions,* 91; and Committee on Education and Labor, *Economic Opportunity Act of 1964,* pt. 1, 15, 365–66. The final version of the bill did refer to the Department of the Interior in a provision requiring the interior secretary to serve on an Economic Opportunity Council. See *Economic Opportunity Act, Statutes at Large,* 78, 531 (1964).

16. Congress, House, Committee on Education and Labor, *Economic Opportunity Act of 1964: Hearings before the Subcommittee on the War on Poverty Program of the Committee on Education and Labor,* pt. 2, 88th Cong., 1st sess., 15–17, 20, and 21 April, 1964, 1053–68.

17. Committee on Education and Labor, *Economic Opportunity Act of 1964,* pt. 1, 368; Unger, *Best of Intentions,* 91; and Committee on Education and Labor, *Economic Opportunity Act of 1964,* pt. 2, 1066.

18. "To Hold Capitol [sic] Conference on Indian Poverty," *The Amerindian* 12 (March–April 1964): 3; and "American Indian Capital Conference on Poverty," *Indian Truth* 41 (June 1964): 13.

19. Burnette, *Tortured Americans*, 88; "Capitol [sic] Conference on Indian Poverty Sets Forth Needs and Aims," *The Amerindian* 12 (May–June 1964): 1; "American Indian Capital Conference," 13–14; George Eagle, "Poverty of American Indians Called Mirror of U.S. Problem," *Washington Post*, 10 May 1964, A12; and Donald Janson, "U.S. Asked to Ease Poverty of Tribes," *New York Times*, 10 May 1964, 83.

20. "American Indian Capital Conference," 15; "Udall Sees Hope of Anti-Poverty Aid for Indians," *Washington Post*, 11 May 1964, A7.

21. Donald Janson, "Udall Asks Help For Indian Poor," *New York Times*, 11 May 1964, 17; "Udall Sees Hope," A7.

22. Thom's speech is reprinted under the heading "A Statement Made for the Young People," in Congress, Senate, Committee on Labor and Public Welfare, *Economic Opportunity Act of 1964: Hearings before the Select Committee on Poverty of the Committee on Labor and Public Welfare*, 88th Cong., 2d sess., 17, 18, 23, and 25 June 1964, 340–41. Excerpts are available in Alvin M. Josephy, Jr., *Red Power: The American Indians' Fight for Freedom* (Lincoln: University of Nebraska Press, 1971), 54–57; and Paul Chaat Smith and Robert Allen Warrior, *Like a Hurricane: The Indian Movement from Alcatraz to Wounded Knee* (New York: The New Press, 1996), 42.

23. Schedule, American Indian Capital Conference on Poverty, "3/11/64–10/4/64," EX IN, Box 1, WHCF, LBJL; and Burnette, *Tortured Americans*, 88.

24. "American Indian Capital Conference," 14; Committee on Labor and Public Welfare, *Economic Opportunity Act,* 330–44; and "Udall Asks Help," 17.

25. "American Indian Capital Conference," 14; "Needs and Aims," 1.

26. "American Indian Capital Conference," 14. Burnette quotation from Philp, *Indian Self-Rule,* 212; Burnette, *Tortured Americans,* 88; and Schott and Hamilton, *People, Positions and Power,* 116–19. Some historians erroneously contend that the Capital Conference led to the inclusion of Indians in the EOA. This is simply not the case—the final bill contained only the single reference to Indians that appeared in the earliest versions of the legislation printed before the conference. See James J. Rawls, *Chief Red Fox Is Dead: A History of Native Americans Since 1945* (Fort Worth: Harcourt Brace College Publishers, 1996), 57, or Jennings Wise, *New World Drama,* 382, for examples.

27. Remarks by Secretary Udall at the Opening Session of Indian Affairs Conference of Superintendents, "June 13–16, 1964, Bureau of Indian Affairs, Conference of Superintendents (Santa Fe, New Mex.)," Box 115, SUP.

28. Committee on Labor and Public Welfare, *Economic Opportunity Act of 1964,* 137–40.

29. *United States Statutes at Large,* 78, 508; and Memorandum, Commissioner of Indian Affairs to Secretary Udall, 18 May 1964, "Chrono.—April-May-June, 1964," Box 172, PNP.

30. Department of the Interior, Press Release, 18 June 1964, "Indian Affairs 12/63—6/65," Box 34, Federal Records: Department of the Interior, LBJL; Memo, Nash to Udall, 18 May 1964; and Congress, House Committee on Appropriations, *Department of the Interior and Related Agencies Appropriations for 1966: Hearings before a Subcommittee of the Committee on Appropriations,* pt. 1, 89th Cong., 1st sess., 2 February–3 March 1965, 757.
    For a more positive assessment of Nash's attitudes toward OEO, see Castile, *To Show Heart,* 30.

31. Transcript, Udall Oral History, Interview no. 3, 20, LBJL; Officer, "An Assessment," 65–66; Kravitz, "The Community Action Program," 62; and James J. Wilson, "OEO Indian Programs: New Hope for Old Emma," *Communities in Action* 1 (Aug.—Sept. 1965): 24–26.

32. Peter MacDonald and Ted Schwarz, *The Last Warrior: Peter MacDonald and the Navajo Nation* (New York: Orion Books, 1993), 154–57, 164, 166.

33. Address by Sargent Shriver, 5 November 1965, attached to Memo, Associate Commissioner of Indian Affairs to Secretary of the Interior, 16 December 1965, "Dept. of the Interior (Misc. Reports from Various Divisions) II," Box 122, SUP.

34. Memo, 16 December 1965, SUP.

35. Claudia T. Johnson, *Lady Bird: A White House Diary* (New York: Holt, Rinehart and Winston, 1970), 234; Congress, House, Committee on Education and Labor, *Economic Opportunity Act Amendments of 1967: Hearings before the Committee on Education and Labor,* pt. 2, 90th Cong., 1st sess., 19–23, 26, and 28 June, 10 July 1967, 1550, 1555–56, 1560.

36. Address by Sargent Shriver, 5 November 1965, in Department of Interior, Bureau of Indian Affairs, *Indian Affairs 1965: A Progress Report from the Commissioner of Indian Affairs,* Bureau of Indian Affairs, 1965. Gifford quotation from Riggs, "Indians, Liberalism," 309. Note that since the BIA did not provide programs for preschoolers, Head Start did not present any conflicts between OEO and BIA operations.

37. Human Sciences Research, Inc., "A Comprehensive Evaluation of OEO Community Action Programs on Six Selected Indian Reservations," September 1966, reprinted in Congress, House, Committee on Education and Labor, *Economic Opportunity Act Amendments of 1967: Hearings before the Committee on Education and Labor,* Appendix, 90th Cong., 1st sess., 3994.

38. Rosebud Reservation Program, "Vol. II. Documentary Supp. Chapter I (1 of 2)," Box 2, Administrative History: Office of Economic Opportunity, LBJL.

39. Office of Economic Opportunity, *The Quiet Revolution,* 2d Annual Report, 1966, 49; Department of the Interior, Bureau of Indian Affairs, *A History of Indian Policy,* by S. Lyman Tyler, 1973, 208–11; Levitan, *Great Society's Poor Law,* 265; Narrative History, 386, "Vol. I, Part II Narrative History (2 of 3)," Box 1, Administrative History: Office of Economic Opportunity, LBJL; and Butler, "Bureau of Indian Affairs," 55. Deloria quote from Congress, Senate, Committee on Labor and Public Welfare, *Examination of the War on Poverty: Hearings before the Subcommittee on Employment, Manpower, and Poverty of the Committee on Labor and Public Welfare,* pt. 3, 90th Cong., 1st sess., 24 April 1967, 1084. He is also quoted (in a slightly more dramatic form) in Office of Economic Opportunity, *The Tide of Progress,* 3d Annual Report, 1967, 35.

40. Levitan, *Great Society's Poor Law,* 266–68; Sar A. Levitan and Barbara Hetrick, *Big Brother's Indian Programs—With Reservations* (New York: McGraw-Hill, 1971), 92; and Office of Economic Opportunity, *As the Seed is Sown,* 4th Annual Report, 1968, 41, 43.

41. Committee on Labor and Public Welfare, *Examination of the War on Poverty,* pt. 3, 1083, 1114, 1116.

42. Philip S. Deloria, "The Era of Indian Self-Determination," in Philp, *Indian Self-Rule,* 196; Philp, *Indian Self-Rule,* 223; Russell Means and Marvin J. Wolf, *Where White Men Fear to Tread: The Autobiography of Russell Means* (New York: St. Martin's Press, 1995), 137; Fergus M. Bordewich, *Killing the White Man's Indian: Reinventing Native Americans at the End of the Twentieth Century* (New York: Anchor Books, 1996), 307.

43. AICC, *Declaration,* 6; Vine Deloria, Jr., "The Lummi Indian Community: The Fisherman of the Pacific Northwest," in *American Indian Economic Development,* ed. Sam Stanley (The Hague: Mouton Publishers, 1978), 125.

44. Philp, *Indian Self-Rule,* 221; and Ruth Rosenberg, "Zah, Peterson," in *Notable Native Americans,* ed. Sharon Malinowski (New York: Gale Research, Inc., 1995), 474–76.

45. "Comprehensive Evaluation," 3995; Committee on Labor and Public Welfare, *Examination of the War on Poverty,* pt. 3, 1101, 1138; and Congress, House, Committee on Education and Labor, *Economic Opportunity Act Amendments of 1967: Hearings before the Committee on Education and Labor,* pt. 3, 90th Cong., 1st sess., 12–14, 17–19 July 1967, 1759.

46. Means, *White Men,* 137; MacDonald and Schwarz, *The Last Warrior,* 155–56; and Levitan, *Great Society's Poor Law,* 268. Greybear quotation from Committee on Labor and Public Welfare, *Examination of the War on Poverty,* pt. 3, 1103; Peter Iverson, *The Navajo Nation* (Westport, Conn.: Greenwood Press, 1981), 94; and OEO, *As the Seed is Sown,* 23, 41–43. For a thorough discussion of the OEO and other Great Society programs on Indian reservations, see Riggs, "Indians, Liberalism," especially chapters 3 to 6.

47. Transcript, Vine Deloria, Jr., Oral History, 17 July 1999, by Christopher Riggs, 6; Henry F. Manuel, Juliann Ramon, and Bernard L. Fontana, "Dressing for the Window: Papago Indians and Economic Development," in *American Indian Economic Development,* 543; and Susan McCulloch Stevens, "Passamaquoddy Economic Development in Cultural and Historical Perspective," in *American Indian Economic Development,* 318, 322, 348–49. Note that the Papago Tribe returned to its traditional name, Tohono O'odham, in 1986.

48. Paivi H. Hoikkala, "Mothers and Community Builders: Salt River Pima and Maricopa Women in Community Action," in *Negotiators of Change: Historical Perspectives on Native American Women,* ed. Nancy Shoemaker (New York: Routledge, 1995), 214–30.

49. Robert Burnette and John Koster, *The Road to Wounded Knee* (New York: Bantam Books, 1974), 162–63; and Burnette, *Tortured Americans,* 106; "Comprehensive Evaluation," 3978. See also Sorkin, *Federal Aid,* 168.

50. Committee on Education and Labor, *Economic Opportunity Act Amendments of 1967,* pt. 2, 1073; Stevens, "Passamaquoddy," 381, 388; MacDonald and Schwarz, *Last Warrior,* 166–67; and Manuel, et al., "Dressing for the Window," 541–42.

51. Congress, Senate, Committee on Labor and Public Welfare, *Examination of the War on Poverty: Hearings before the Subcommittee on Employment, Manpower, and Poverty of the Committee on Labor and Public Welfare,* pt. 14, Miscellaneous Appendix, 90th Cong., 1st sess., 4419; Smith and Warrior, *Like a Hurricane,* 97–99; and Leonard Garment, *Crazy Rhythm: My Journey from Brooklyn, Jazz, and Wall Street to Nixon's White House, Watergate, and Beyond . . .* (New York: Times Books, 1997), 232.

52. Committee on Labor and Public Welfare, *Examination of the War on Poverty,* pt. 14, 4419; and "Comprehensive Evaluation," 4005.

53. Committee on Labor and Public Welfare, *Examination of the War on Poverty,* pt. 14, 4419.

54. Philp, *Indian Self-Rule,* 219. Mitchell made his observations regarding Alaskan dependency in 1983.

55. "Comprehensive Evaluation," 4007–8; MacDonald and Schwarz, *The Last Warrior,* 156; Riggs, "Indians, Liberalism," 351–52; and Daniel M. Cobb, "Philosophy of an Indian War: Indian Community Action in the Johnson Administration's War on Poverty, 1964–1968," *American Indian Culture and Research Journal* 22, no. 2 (1998), 87.

56. Philp, *Indian Self-Rule,* 226; and "Comprehensive Evaluation," 4007–8.

57. Philp, *Indian Self-Rule,* 224.

58. "Comprehensive Evaluation," 3913, 3920. See also Sorkin, *Federal Aid,* 169; Riggs, "Indians, Liberalism," 233; and Prucha, *The Great Father,* 2:1094–95.

59. Raymond H. Milkman, et al., *Alleviating Economic Distress: Evaluating a Federal Effort* (Lexington Mass.: Lexington Books, 1972), 3–9; and Congress, Senate, *Public Works and Economic Development Act of 1965,* 89th Cong., 1st sess., *Congressional Record* (1 April 1965), vol. 111, pt. 5, 6508, 6513.

60. Congress, Senate, Committee on Banking and Currency, *Public Works and Economic Development: Hearings before the Subcommittee of the Committee on Banking and Currency,* 89th Cong., 1st sess., 4–7 May 1965, 94, 314; and Congress, House, Committee on Public Works, *Public Works and Economic Development Act of 1965: Hearings before the Committee on Public Works,* 89th Cong., 1st sess., 10–14, 18, 19, and 26 May 1965, 117–27.

61. Congress, Senate, *Additional Co-sponsors of Bills,* 89th Cong., 1st sess., *Congressional Record* (7 April 1965), vol. 111, pt. 6, 7270; Congress, Senate, *Public Works and Economic Development Act of 1965,* 89th Cong., 1st sess., *Congressional Record* (1 June 1965), vol. 111, pt. 9, 12154, 12168, 12183; and Congress, House, *Public Works and Economic Development Act of 1965,* 89th Cong., 1st sess., *Congressional Record* (12 August 1965), vol. 111, pt. 15, 20355–56.

62. Milkman, *Alleviating Economic Distress,* 19–28, 293; and Department of Commerce, Economic Development Administration, *Annual Report 1967,* 11.

63. Department of Commerce, Economic Development Administration, *Jobs For America: Economic Development Administration Annual Report, Fiscal 1969*, 35–37; Milkman, *Alleviating Economic Distress*, 293–95; and Department of Commerce, Economic Development Administraion, *1968 Progress Report of the Economic Development Administration*, 28.

64. Commerce Department, *1968 Progress Report*, 28; and Department of Commerce, Economic Development Administration, *Jobs for America: Economic Development Administration Annual Report, Fiscal 1969*, 38.

65. Milkman, *Alleviating Economic Distress*, 314–24, 330; and Boise Cascade Center for Community Development, *Indian Economic Development: An Evaluation of EDA's Selected Indian Reservation Program*, Volume II: *Indian Reservation Reports*, 227–47.

66. Boise Cascade Center, *Indian Reservation Reports*, 14–17, 25, 174, 181, 193–200, 251.

67. Sorkin, *Federal Aid*, 93, 200.

68. For a history of the ESEA, see Hugh Davis Graham, *The Uncertain Triumph: Federal Education Policy in the Kennedy and Johnson Years* (Chapel Hill: University of North Carolina Press, 1984); Califano, *Triumph and Tragedy*, 71; Johnson, *Vantage Point*, 212; and *Elementary and Secondary Education Act of 1965, Statutes at Large*, 79, 27–58 (1965).

69. Bureau of Indian Affairs, *Indian Affairs, 1965*, 3; Helen Maynor Scheirbeck, "Education, Public Policy and the American Indian" (Ph.D. diss., Virginia Polytechnic Institute and State University, 1980), 168–69; and Szasz, *Education and the American Indian*, 183–85.

70. Congress, House, Committee on Education and Labor, *Elementary and Secondary Education Amendments of 1966: Hearings Before the General Subcommittee of the Committee on Education and Labor*, pt. 2, 89th Cong., 2d sess., 15–18, 22, and 23 March 1966, 990.

71. Letter, Nash to Burke, 10 December 1965, "Misc. 1965 Indians," Box 181, PNP.

CHAPTER FOUR

1. Transcript, Udall Oral History, Interview no. 3, 4, LBJL; and Transcript, 1977 Nash Oral History, 21, 23, HSTL.

2. Officer, "Anthropologist as Administrator," 13; Letter, Corinne Locker to Alden Stevens, 30 December 1964, Folder 2, Box 11, Corinne Locker

Papers, Seeley G. Mudd Manuscript Library, Princeton University, Princeton, New Jersey (hereinafter cited as CLP).

3. Letter, Richard Schifter to Oliver La Farge, 26 February 1963, Folder 1, Box 38, AAIAA.

4. Letter, Corinne Locker to Alden Stevens, 26 June 1964, Folder 2, Box 11, CLP.

5. Ibid.

6. Transcript, Verkler Oral History, Interview no. 1, i, 25, 32, SHO; Transcript, Carver Oral History, Interview no. 8, 81, JFKL; and Letter, Richard Schifter to Alden Stevens, 29 October 1964, Folder 2, Box 38, AAIAA.

7. Letter, Clinton Anderson to Stewart French, 9 September 1964, "Interior Department: Indian Affairs," Box 235, Clinton P. Anderson Papers, LOC.

8. Remarks by Secretary Udall, Box 115, SUP; and Transcript, 1977 Nash Oral History, 37, HSTL.

9. Congress, House, Committee on Appropriations, *Department of the Interior and Related Agencies Appropriations for 1965: Hearings before the Subcommittee of the Committee on Appropriations,* 88th Cong., 2d sess., 28 January through 21 February 1964, 25; Memo, Nash to Udall, 18 May 1964; House Subcommittee on Appropriations, *Interior Appropriations for 1966,* pt. 1, 2; and Richard Schifter, "The Legislative Record," *Indian Affairs* 62 (February–April 1966): 2. Copy of the latter is available in "Indian Affairs, 1964–1988," Box 2, AAIAA.

10. Memorandum, Conference on Indian Affairs—November 9, 10, and 11, n.d., "S.L.U. and Staff," Box 115, SUP; and Memorandum, Commissioner of Indian Affairs to Secretary of the Interior, 20 November 1964, "Dept. of the Interior (Misc. Reports from Various Divisions)," Box 116, SUP.

11. Memo, Nash to Udall, 20 November 1964; Memorandum, Commissioner of Indian Affairs to Secretary of the Interior, 3 June 1965, "Chrono. File—May–June 1965," Box 173, PNP; and Schifter, "The Legislative Record," 2.

12. Transcript, 1977 Nash Oral History, 25, HSTL; and Peter Iverson, *The Navajo Nation* (Westport, Conn.: Greenwood Press, 1981), xxiii.

13. For a brief history of the Navajo-Hopi conflict see Catherine Feher-Elston, "Navajo-Hopi Land Controversy," in *Native America in the Twentieth Century,* ed. Davis, 386–89.

14. Udall quotation from Emily Benedek, *The Wind Won't Know Me: A History of the Navajo-Hopi Land Dispute* (New York: Alfred A. Knopf, 1992), 32; and

Feher-Elston, "Navajo-Hopi Land Controversy." The court decision is quoted in Kammer, *Second Long Walk*, 75.

15. Transcript, Udall Oral History, Interview no. 3, 16, LBJL; Kammer, *Second Long Walk*, 75–77; and David M. Brugge, *The Navajo-Hopi Land Dispute: An American Tragedy* (Albuquerque: University of New Mexico Press, 1994), 107–9. Nash quotation from Bureau of Indian Affairs, "Hopi-Navajo Conference, Aug. 6–7, 1963," 5. A copy of the latter available in Folder 31, Box 4, Navajo-Hopi Land Dispute Manuscript Collection, Center for Southwest Research, University of New Mexico, Albuquerque, New Mexico.

16. Kammer, *Second Long Walk*, 75–77; Brugge, *Navajo-Hopi Land Dispute*, 107–9; and Memo, Nash to Udall, 20 November 1964.

   Maintaining that it would be "unfair to accuse Nash . . . of bureaucratic languor," because he faced "a choice between two unpleasant alternatives" (that of reducing the Navajo stock or waiting for further congressional or court initiatives), Kammer excuses Nash's failure to work on the problem.

17. Iverson, *Navajo Nation*, 83–85 (for quotation see p. 85); MacDonald and Schwarz, *Last Warrior*, 134; and Transcript, 1977 Nash Oral History, 22, 23, HSTL.

18. Iverson, *Navajo Nation*, 52–53; Jill E. Martin, "A Year and a Spring of My Existence: Felix Cohen and the *Handbook of Federal Indian Law*," *Western Legal History* 8 (winter/spring 1995): 45–48. An edited version of Littell's correspondence from his tenure at the Justice Department makes scant reference to Indians and never mentions Felix Cohen. See Norman C. Littell, *My Roosevelt Years*, ed. Jonathan Dembo (Seattle: University of Washington Press, 1987).

19. Iverson, *Navajo Nation*, 54–55, 84–85; and *Navajo Times*, 4 November 1965, quoted in Iverson, 55. The "in great respect" quotation from MacDonald and Schwarz, *Last Warrior*, 137. Although he doesn't identify Littell by name, MacDonald discusses his intense dislike for the attorney (see pp. 137–40).

20. Transcript, 1977 Nash Oral History, 24, HSTL; Iverson, *Navajo Nation*, 86; *Littell v. Udall*, 242 F. Supp. 635 (1965); and Memorandum, The Solicitor to the Secretary, 1 November 1963, "IN/Navajo," EX IN, Box 3, WHCF, LBJL.

21. Memorandum, Orren Beaty, Jr., to Lee C. White, 10 February 1965, "IN/Navajo," EX IN, Box 3, WHCF, LBJL; Memo, Solicitor to Secretary, 1 November 1963, 2; and Memorandum (Confidential), The Solicitor to the Secretary, 1 November 1963, "IN/Navajo," EX IN, Box 3, WHCF, LBJL.

22. *Littell v. Udall* (1965).

23. Transcript, 1977 Nash Oral History, 22–25, HSTL.

24. Memo, Beaty to White, 10 February 1965; Letter, Annie D. Wauneka to President Johnson, 31 December 1964, "In/Navajo," EX IN, Box 3, WHCF, LBJL; and Cort Klein, Jr., "Nakai Stripped of Power By Council," *Gallup Independent,* 19 December 1964.

25. Letter, Wauneka to Johnson, 31 December 1964.

26. Ibid.; Robert W. Young, *A Political History of the Navajo Tribe* (Tsaile, Navajo Nation, Ariz.: Navajo Community College Press, 1978), 157; and Johnson, *Public Papers, 1963–1964,* vol. 1, 32.

27. MacDonald and Schwarz, *Last Warrior,* 135.

28. White House Office Route Slip, Lee C. White to Orren Beaty, 8 January 1965, "IN/Navajo," EX IN, Box 3, WHCF, LBJL; Memo, Beaty to White, 10 February 1965; and Letter, Lee C. White to Annie D. Wauneka, 15 February 1965, "IN/Navajo," EX IN, Box 3 WHCF, LBJL.

29. Stanley I. Kutler, *The Wars of Watergate: The Last Crisis of Richard Nixon* (New York: Alfred A. Knopf, 1990), 259; and *Littell v. Udall* (1965). Udall later claimed that "Littell was apparently an old friend of his [Sirica's] from the bar days and so on." See Transcript, 1998 Udall Interview.

30. *Littell v. Udall* (1965).

31. *Littell v. Udall* (1965); and "1961 Task Force Report," 5.

32. Memorandum, Lee C. White to Stewart Udall, 28 May 1965, "IN/Navajo," EX IN, Box 3, WHCF, LBJL; and Letter, Annie D. Wauneka to Lee C. White, 10 June 1965, "IN/Navajo," EX IN, Box 3, WHCF, LBJL.

33. *Albuquerque Journal,* 13 June 1965, 1.

34. White House Office Route Slip, Lee C. White to Orren Beaty, 15 June 1965, "IN/Navajo," EX IN, Box 3 WHCF, LBJL; Letter, Lee C. White to Annie D. Wauneka, 21 June 1965, "IN/Navajo," EX IN, Box 3 WHCF, LBJL; and Letter, William Proxmire to Lee C. White, 17 June 1965, "IN/Navajo," EX IN, Box 3, WHCF, LBJL.

35. Letter, Lee C. White to William Proxmire, 21 June 1965, "IN/Navajo," EX IN, Box 3, WHCF, LBJL; Memorandum, Orren Beaty to Lee C. White, "IN/Navajo," Ex In, Box 3 WHCF, LBJL; and Letter, Lee C. White to William Proxmire, 24 July 1965, "IN/Navajo," EX IN, Box 3, WHCF, LBJL.

36. *Littell v. Udall,* 366 Federal Reporter 2d series, 668. Wauneka quote from Iverson, *Navajo Nation,* 86. In mentioning Fort Sumner, Wauneka referred to the Navajo imprisonment at Bosque Redondo, one of the most

disgraceful abuses Native Americans endured at the hands of the U.S. government in the nineteenth century.

37. *Littell v. Udall*, 87 SCt. 713.

38. Quotations from Peter Iverson, "Legal Counsel and the Navajo Nation Since 1945," *American Indian Quarterly* 3 (spring 1977): 12.

   David M. Brugge, an attorney who worked for the Navajos on the land claims case, did not believe that Udall's relationship with Nakai played an important role in the affair. He maintained that Udall fired Littell because of the tribal attorney's opposition to a partition of the JUA. The Hopis had demanded such a partition, which would have solved the problem of joint administration, but Littell and the Navajos had rejected this solution. See Brugge, *Navajo-Hopi Land Dispute*, 108, 111.

39. Attorneys' quotes from Iverson, *Navajo Nation*, 86.

40. Letter, James A. Haley to Robert W. Kastenmeier, 12 March 1969, "I & A: Miscellaneous, 1960–1972," JHP. Although the quotes are from 1969, they are representative of Haley's attitudes throughout his tenure as subcommittee chairman.

41. *Indians, leasing of restricted land, Statutes at Large*, 69, 539 (1955); and Memorandum, Meeting of Task Force on Indian Affairs, 7 February 1961, "Task Force Minutes of Meeting," Box 149, PNP.

42. Memorandum, Long Term Leasing, 8 May 1961, "Task Force Recommendation Memo," Box 149, PNP. Recapture guaranteed "the right to purchase any improvements on the lease hold."

43. Letter, John Carver to Henry M. Jackson, 12 June 1963, reprinted in Congress, Senate, Committee on Interior and Insular Affairs, "Report No. 461," to accompany S. 48, 26 August 1963, 88th Cong., 1st sess.; Congress, Senate, *Amendment of the Indian Long-Term Leasing Act*, 88th Cong., 1st sess., *Congressional Record* (28 August 1963), vol. 109, pt. 12, 6098; and Transcript, Congress, House, Subcommittee on Indian Affairs of the Committee on Interior and Insular Affairs, *To amend the Indian Long-Term Leasing Act*, 20 September 1963, 88th Cong., 1st sess. A copy of this unpublished hearing is available in "H.R. 7468, 27 April 1965—To Authorize Long-Term Leases on the Papago Indian Reservation," Morris K. Udall Papers, Special Collections, University of Arizona, Tucson, Arizona (hereinafter cited as MUP). At this writing the Morris K. Udall Papers are still being processed, and no box number is available.

   Although an additional five-year lease period seemed to be a short period of time, it made a difference in business financing. As Carver noted in his letter to Jackson, "the minimum unexpired lease period for a construction or a development loan . . . is 50 years from the date the mortgage is executed." The additional five years the Senate bill offered thus allowed businesses "enough time to complete the financial arrangements for the development before the unexpired term of the lease is reduced to less than fifty years."

44. Transcript, Congress, House, Subcommittee on Indian Affairs of the Committee on Interior and Insular Affairs, *H.R. 5002,* 7 February 1964, 88th Cong., 2d sess. A copy is available in "H.R. 7468, 27 April 1965—To Authorize Long-Term Leases on the Papago Indian Reservation," MUP.

45. Letter, Barry Goldwater to Sterling Mahone, 14 April 1964, "Interior and Insular Affairs—Indian Affairs Subcommittee Indian Long-Term Leasing Act," Box 2, 89th Congress, Paul J. Fannin Papers, Arizona Historical Association, Arizona State University, Phoenix, Arizona; and Letter, Lloyd Meeds to Mr. and Mrs. Harry L. Spake, 12 August 1965, "U.S. House Interior and Insular Affairs Committee, Indian Affairs Subcommittee," Box 217, Lloyd Meeds Papers, University of Washington Libraries, University of Washington, Seattle, Washington. Final quotation from Deloria and Lytle, *The Nations Within,* 196.

46. Kennedy, *Public Papers,* 1961, 563; Congress, House, Committee on Interior and Insular Affairs, *Kinzua Dam (Seneca Indian Relocation): Hearings before the Subcommittee on Indian Affairs of the Committee on Interior and Insular Affairs,* 88th Cong., 1st sess., 18 May, 15–16 July, 8, 9, 12, 19, and 20 August, 31 October, 1 November, 9–10 December 1963, 9, 146–61, 297; and Josephy, *Now That the Buffalo's Gone,* 143.

47. Memorandum, Resources and Civil Works Division (D. C. Lindholm) to Phillip S. Hughes, 8 February 1963, "Resources—Kinzua Dam, Jan 21–Oct. 23, 1963 and Undated," Box 14, General Files, LWP.

48. House, Committee on Interior and Insular Affairs, *Kinzua Dam,* 9.

49. Ibid., 9–13, 39–40.

50. Ibid., 20, 25, 40.

51. Ibid., 292–96.

52. Congress, House, Committee on Interior and Insular Affairs, "Report No. 1128," to accompany H.R. 1794, 5 February 1964, 88th Cong., 2d sess.; and Congress, House, *Authorizing Acquisition of and Payment for Flowage Easement and Rights-of-Way Within the Allegany Indian Reservation in New York,* 88th Cong., 2d sess., *Congressional Record* (7 February 1964), vol. 110, pt. 2, 2513–18.

53. Letter, Phillip S. Hughes to Henry M. Jackson, 28 February 1964, "LE/NR 7–1/K-O," EX LE, Box 144, WHCF, LBJL; reprinted in Congress, Senate, Committee on Interior and Insular Affairs, *Kinzua Dam (Seneca Indian Relocation): Hearing before the Subcommittee on Indian Affairs of the Committee on Interior and Insular Affairs,* 88th Cong., 2d sess., 2 March 1964, 24–25. For the Missouri River project, see Mark L. Lawson, *Dammed Indians: The Pick-Sloan Plan and the Missouri River Sioux, 1944–1980* (Norman: University of Oklahoma Press, 1982).

54. Senate, Committee on Interior and Insular Affairs, *Kinzua Dam,* 1, 59, 72, 73–74, 83. The other five senators were Clifford P. Case (R.-N.J.), Joseph S. Clark (D.-Penn.), Samuel J. "Sam" Ervin (D.-N.C.), Kenneth B. Keating (R.-N.Y.), and George S. McGovern.

55. Ibid., 155–71.

56. Congress, Senate, Committee on Interior and Insular Affairs, "Report No. 969," to accompany H.R. 1794, 88th Cong., 2d sess., 20 March 1964, 1, 6–7.

57. Ibid.
    Although eligible, the Seneca Nation did not avail itself of BIA services. The State of New York had criminal and civil jurisdiction on the reservation and provided educational and welfare services. Thus, the termination provision was preventative, intended to ensure that the Senecas did not request federal services in the future. The most important change would be the termination of trust responsibilities over Seneca lands. See Congress, "Report No. 969," 8; and Senate, Committee on Interior and Insular Affairs, *Kinzua Dam,* 154–56.

58. Congress, Senate, *Relocation of the Seneca Nation,* 88th Cong., 2d sess., *Congressional Record* (30 March 1964), vol. 110, pt. 5, 6520–23; Congress, House, *Allegany Indian Reservation—Seneca Nation,* 88th Cong., 2d sess., *Congressional Record* (14 April 1964), vol. 110, pt. 6, 7822; Congress, Senate, *Payments for Flowage Easement and Rights-of-Way Over Lands Within the Allegany Indian Reservation, N.Y.,* 88th Cong., 2d sess., *Congressional Record* (14 April 1964), vol. 110, pt. 6, 8461.

59. Memorandum, John A. Carver to Lee White, 26 May 1964, "LE/NR 7–1/K-O," EX LE, Box 144, WHCF, LBJL.
    This memorandum is revealing of the assistant secretary's attitudes toward Indian affairs. Carver showed more concern for political consider-ations than for the hardships the Senecas might face, and he ignored the fact that termination without consent had not been department policy since Interior Secretary Fred Seaton's 1958 speech on that issue.

60. Memorandum, Lee C. White to Mike Manatos, 15 June 1964, "LE/NR 7–1/K-O," EX LE, Box 144, WHCF, LBJL.

    White paid careful attention to the press coverage. In his memo to Manatos, he complained that "we continually catch hell from the newspapers."

61. Memorandum, Commissioner of Indian Affairs to Lee White, 15 July 1964, "NR 7–1/K," EX NR, Box 20, WHCF, LBJL

62. Memorandum, Jackson Graham to Lee C. White, 5 August 1964, "NR 7–1/K," EX NR, Box 20, WHCF, LBJL.

63. Congress, House, "Report No. 1821," to accompany H.R. 1794, 17 August 1964, 88th Cong., 2d sess.; Memo, White to Manatos, 15 June 1964; Congress, Senate, *Flowage Easement and Rights-of-Way Over Lands Within the Allegany Reservation—Conference Report,* 88th Cong., 2d sess., *Congressional Record* (17 August 1964), vol. 110, pt. 15, 19859–65; Congress, House, *Seneca Indian Nation,* 88th Cong., 2d sess., *Congressional Record* (18 August 1964), vol. 110, pt. 15, 20153–54; and *Allegheny [sic] Indian Reservation, N.Y., Statutes at Large,* 78, 738–43 (1964).

64. Memorandum, Commissioner of Indian Affairs to Lee C. White, 25 August 1964, "LE/NR 7–1/K-O," EX LE, Box 144, WHCF, LBJL; Memorandum, Jackson Graham to Lee C. White, 23 October 1964, "NR 7–1/K," EX NR, Box 20, WHCF, LBJL; and Memorandum, Acting Commissioner of Indian Affairs to Lee C. White, 29 October 1964, "NR 7–1/K," EX NR, Box 20, WHCF, LBJL.

    Disputes over the relocation of Gaiantwaka's remains continued after the bill signing. See Josephy, *Now That the Buffalo's Gone,* 143–49.

65. For the impact of the Kinzua Dam project on the Seneca Nation, see Bilharz, *Allegany Senecas,* 74–139; Senate, Committee on Interior and Insular Affairs, *Kinzua Dam,* 166; House, "Report No. 1128"; House, *Seneca Indian Nation, Congressional Record,* 20154; and "Seneca Tribe Honors Congressman Haley," *The Amerindian* 15 (September–October 1966): 3.

66. Senate, Committee on Interior and Insular Affairs, *Kinzua Dam,* 60, 108.

67. Goodell quotation from Committee on Education and Labor, *Economic Opportunity Act of 1964,* pt. 2, 1067.

68. Transcript, Carver Oral History, Interview no. 5, 18, JFKL; and Senate, *Flowage Easement, Congressional Record,* vol. 110, pt. 15, 19859–65.

69. Transcript, Carver Oral History, Interview no. 8, 85, JFKL.

70. Deward E. Walker, Jr., "Confederated Tribes of the Colville Reservation," in *Native America in the Twentieth Century,* ed. Davis, 132–33; Congress, House, Committee on Interior and Insular Affairs, *Colville Termination Legislation: Hearings before Subcommittee on Indian Affairs of the Committee on Interior and Insular Affairs,* 87th Cong., 2d sess., 15 May 1962, 11–12; and Kathleen A. Dahl, "The Battle Over Termination on the Colville Indian Reservation," *American Indian Culture and Research Journal* 18 (no. 1, 1994): 34.

71. Congress, Senate, Committee on Interior and Insular Affairs, Report 1068, to accompany H.R. 8236, 15 September 1961, 87th Cong., 1st sess.; and Transcript, 1977 Nash Oral History, 34–35, HSTL.

72. *Colville Indian Reservation, Wash., Statutes at Large,* 70, 626–27 (1956); House, Committee on Interior and Insular Affairs, *Colville Termination Legislation,* 15; and Congress, Senate, Committee on Interior and Insular Affairs, *Colville Indian Legislation: Hearings before the Subcommittee on Indian Affairs of the Committee on Interior and Insular Affairs,* 88th Cong., 1st sess., 24, 25, and 26 October, and 20 November 1963, 2–8, 277.

Jackson aide James H. Gamble had recommended that per capita payments be linked to a termination plan, arguing that "it is very unwise to make per capita payments in advance of a final agreed-upon terminal plan. This puts the cart before the horse." Memorandum, James H. Gamble to Henry M. Jackson, 12 March 1963, Folder 6, Box 203, Henry M. Jackson Papers, University of Washington Libraries, University of Washington, Seattle, Washington (hereinafter cited as HJP).

73. Senate, Committee on Interior and Insular Affairs, *Colville Indian Legislation,* 2–8, 277; for Colville tribal members' views, see 9–276. See also Dahl, "Colville Termination," 33–45; and Transcript, 1977 Nash Oral History, 34, HSTL.

74. Committee on Interior and Insular Affairs, *Colville Indian Legislation,* 277–84; *Indians, Confederated Tribes of the Colville Reservation, Statutes at Large,* 78, 755 (1964); and Transcript, 1977 Nash Oral History Interview, 34–35. Ironically, Holmes's argument echoed that of James Gamble, an avowed terminationist. See Memo, Gamble to Jackson, 12 March 1963.

75. Congress, Senate, Committee on Interior and Insular Affairs, *Colville Termination: Hearings before the Subcommittee on Indian Affairs of the Committee on Interior and Insular Affairs,* 89th Cong., 1st sess., 5 and 6 April 1965, 35–41. For Jackson's concern over Nash's alleged remarks, see Letter, Henry Jackson to John Carver, 3 March 1965, Folder 9, Box 33, JHP.

76. John Fahey, *The Kalispel Indians* (Norman: University of Oklahoma Press, 1986), 140–42, 152, 156–61; and Robert C. Carriker, "The Kalispel Tribe and the Indian Claims Commission," *Western Historical Quarterly* 9 (January 1978): 20–25.

77. Fahey, *The Kalispels,* 165–66 (quotation from p. 166); Carriker, "The Kalispel Tribe," 25; and Congress, Senate, Committee on Interior and Insular Affairs, *To Provide for the Disposition of Judgment Funds Now on Deposit to the Credit of the Lower Pend d'Oreille or Kalispel Tribe of Indians: Hearings before the Subcommittee on Indian Affairs of the Committee on Interior and Insular Affairs,* 88th Cong., 2d sess., 27 May 1964, microfiche edition.

  Both Fahey and Carriker claim that Kalispel committees, with some assistance from non-Indians, crafted the plan. In a 1964 memorandum, however, attorney Robert Dellwo charged that the BIA superintendent's office drafted the plan, which, because it had received tribal approval, he had no choice but to support. See "Memorandum to Senator Jackson from Bob Dellwo," n.d., Box 204, Folder 5, HJP.

78. Committee on Interior and Insular Affairs, *Kalispel Tribe,* 15, 22, 26.

79. Ibid., xxc; and "1961 Task Force Report," 13. For an example of the problems that per capita distributions created for Native Americans, see Robert L. Bennett, "Building Indian Economies with Land Settlement Funds," *Human Organization* 20, no. 4 (1961–62): 160.

80. Dellwo quotation from Fahey, *The Kalispels,* 166; Carriker, "The Kalispel Tribe," 26–27; Congress, House, Committee on Interior and Insular Affairs, Report 1492, to accompany H.R. 10973, 16 June 1964, 88th Cong., 2d sess.; and Congress, House, *Providing for the Disposition of Judgment Funds to the Credit of the Lower Pend d'Oreille or Kalispel Tribe of Indians,* 88th Cong., 2d sess., *Congressional Record* (21 July 1964), 16427.

81. *Kalispel Indians, Statutes at Large,* 78, 387 (1964); Congress, Senate, Committee on Interior and Insular Affairs, Report 1287, to accompany H.R. 10973, 31 July 1964, 88th Cong., 2d sess.

82. Ibid.

83. Carriker, "The Kalispel Tribe," 28–29.

84. Ibid., 29–30; and Fahey, *The Kalispels,* 170.

85. Fahey, *The Kalispels,* 170–71 (Nash quotation from p. 170); and Carriker, "The Kalispel Tribe," 29–30.

86. Quotation regarding Kalispel housing in Fahey, *The Kalispels,* 168.

87. Hough, *Development of Indian Resources,* 204; and MacDonald and Schwarz,

The Last Warrior, 305–7.

88. MacDonald and Schwarz, *The Last Warrior,* 305–7.

89. Homer Bigart, "For the Indian: Squalor in the Great Society," *New York Times,* 13 March 1966, 1, 67 (union quotation from p. 67). Bigart spoke with Nash while writing this story; see Transcript, 1977 Nash Oral History, 35; Transcript, Carver Oral History, Interview no. 5, 26–27; and Hough, *Development of Indian Resources,* 195.

90. Transcript, 1977 Nash Oral History, 28–29, HSTL (union quotation from p. 28, and other Nash quotations from p. 29); and Bigart, "For the Indian," 1, 67 (the Udall "blew up" quotation is from p. 1).

91. Memorandum, Lee White and John Macy to the President, 2 September 1965, "FG 145—Dept. of the Interior," Box 145, White House Central Files, Confidential Files, Lyndon B. Johnson Library, Austin, Texas (hereinafter cited as CF).

92. Ibid.

93. Schott and Hamilton, *People, Positions, and Power,* 169; Memorandum, Udall to the President, 15 November 1965, "FG 145—Dept. of the Interior," Box 145, CF; and Letter, Philleo Nash to Walter J. Burke, 10 December 1965, "Misc. 1965—Indians," Box 181, PNP.

94. Macy to the President, 14 December 1965, "FG 145—Dept. of the Interior," Box 145, CF; Letter, Hubert Humphrey to Philleo Nash, 26 December 1965, "Commissioner of Indian Affairs—Letters of Support about Resignation," Box 179, PNP; Letter, Joseph M. Montoya to Lyndon B. Johnson, 31 December 1965, "Commissioner of Indian Affairs—Letters of Support about Resignation," PNP, Box 179, HSTL; and Letter, Philleo Nash to Robert Treuer, 6 January 1966, "Correspondence File 1961–1965, 'T,'" Box 142, PNP.

95. Transcript, 1977 Nash Oral History, 42. Nash offers no date for his meeting with Udall. See Memorandum, John W. Macy, Jr., to the President, 9 March 1966, "Interior Affairs—Commissioner (Interior)," Office Files of John W. Macy, Jr., Lyndon B. Johnson Library, Austin, Texas (hereinafter cited as JMOF); Schott and Hamilton, *People, Positions, and Power,* 169, 206; Nash, "Human Values," 199; and Transcript, 1977 Nash Oral History, 43, HSTL.

96. Transcript, Carver Oral History, Interview no. 5, 36, JFKL.

97. Transcript, Carver Oral History, Interview no. 5, 32, 33, JFKL; Transcript, Nash Oral History, Interview no. 2, 41, JFKL; Transcript, Udall Oral History, Interview no. 2, 40, JFKL.

According to James Officer, Udall did not go to great lengths to accommodate Nash. Officer explained that when Nash attempted to meet with Udall, "he was often blocked by the secretary's administrative assistant and found himself spending literally hours in the outer office waiting his turn," an experience that Nash found "humiliating" and which led him to abandon efforts to see Udall. See Officer, "Anthropologist as Administrator," 15; and Transcript, 1977 Nash Oral History, 41, HSTL.

98. Transcript, Udall Oral History, Interview no. 3, 4, LBJL; Transcript, Udall Oral History, Interview no. 2, 40–41, JFKL.

99. Transcript, Carver Oral History, Interview no. 5, 34–35, JFKL.

100. Nash, "Human Values," 196; and Transcript, Nash Oral History, Interview no. 2, 42, JFKL.

101. Transcript, Nash Oral History, Interview no. 3, 60, JFKL; Nash, "Human Values," 197, 198; and Transcript, 1977 Nash Oral History, 35, HSTL.

102. Transcript, Nash Oral History, Interview no. 3, 60, JFKL; and Transcript, Nash Oral History, 31 October 1966, by Jerry Hess, Interview no. 9, 453–54, HSTL.

103. Nash, "Human Values," 198.

Margaret Connell Szasz quotes Nash as publicly stating, "There will be no more termination." However, his complete statement reads, "There will be no more termination unless a tribe is clearly ready for it and votes for it," a reiteration of Fred Seaton's 1958 pledge. See Szasz, "Philleo Nash," 317; and Donald Janson, "U.S. Moves to Spur Tribal Economies," *New York Times*, 5 September 1962, 80.

104. Vine Deloria, Jr., *Red Earth, White Lies: Native Americans and the Myth of Scientific Fact* (New York: Scribner, 1995), 29; Congress, Senate, *Commissioner of Indian Affairs*, 89th Cong., 2d sess., *Congressional Record* (13 April 1966), vol. 112, pt. 6, 8063; and "Nash as Commissioner—Five Years of Progress and Understanding," *NCAI Sentinel* 11 (winter 1966).

105. Szasz, "Philleo Nash," 320; and Transcript, 1977 Nash Oral History, 43, HSTL.

CHAPTER FIVE

1. Udall quotation from Memorandum, Udall to the President, 26 February 1966, "FG 145–6: 3/26/66—," EX FG, Box 208, WHCF, LBJL. Biographical information was assembled from Transcript, Robert Bennett Oral History, 13 November 1968, by Joe B. Frantz, 1–2, LBJL; Richard N. Ellis, "Robert

L. Bennett, 1966–69" in Kvasnicka and Viola, *The Commissioners*, 325; Congress, Senate, Committee on Interior and Insular Affairs, *The Nomination of Robert LaFollette Bennett, of Alaska, to be Commissioner of Indian Affairs*, 89th Cong., 2d sess., 1–2; and "Bennett, Robert LaFollette," in Charles Moritz, ed., *Current Biography Yearbook, 1967* (New York: H. W. Wilson), 29–31. Quotation from Robert L. Bennett, "New Era for the American Indian," *Natural History* 76 (February 1976): 7.

2. Moritz, "Bennett," 31; Burnette and Koster, *Road to Wounded Knee,* 161; Bennett, "Building Reservation Economies," 163; Remarks by Secretary Udall, 16 June 1964; and Letter, Corinne Locker to Rose Flanell, 30 June 1964, Folder 2, Box 11, CLP.

3. Press Release, "Bennett to be Deputy Commissioner of Indian Affairs, 19 October 1965, "DOI—News Releases—8–9/65," Federal Records, Department of the Interior, Box 13, LBJL; Transcript, 1977 Nash Oral History, 38, HSTL; and Transcript, Udall Oral History, Interview no. 3, 4, LBJL.

4. Transcript, Udall Oral History, Interview no. 3, 2, 3, LBJL; and Transcript, 1998 Udall Oral History.

5. Paul R. Wieck, "Bennett Already Baptized," *Albuquerque Journal,* 27 March 1966.

6. Ibid.; and Letter, Locker to William Byler, 15 March 1966, Folder 3, Box 11, CLP. For a slightly confused recounting of Nash's involvement, see Transcript, 1977 Nash Oral History, 37–39.

7. Senate Committee on Interior and Insular Affairs, *Nomination of Robert LaFollette Bennett,* 4–7.

   The AAIA sent no communication to the committee, perhaps because some members opposed the Bennett nomination. Corinne Locker hoped that the conflict with Anderson over the Albuquerque school might be the "coup de grace" for Bennett. See Letter, Locker to Byler, 15 March 1966.

8. Senate Committee on Interior and Insular Affairs, *Nomination of Robert LaFollette Bennett,* 37–43.

9. Ibid., 8–9; Fahey, *The Kalispels,* 182.

10. Senate Committee on Interior and Insular Affairs, *Nomination of Robert LaFollette Bennett,* 10, 12–13.

11. Ibid., 25–28.

12. Congress, Senate, Committee on Interior and Insular Affairs, "Executive Report No. 1, To accompany the nomination of Robert LaFollette Bennett, 8 April 1966," 89th Cong., 2d sess. Executive reports related to treaties or

nominations were not collected in the Serial Set. Some reports, including 89-2-R1 cited here, are available in the Congressional Information Service (CIS) microfilm collection.

13. Ibid. In 1964, Dellwo had complained to Jackson that "Bureau personnel proliferated on the reservation," immediately after the Kalispels received their judgment fund. See "Memorandum," n.d., Folder 5, Box 204, JHP.

14. Committee on Interior and Insular Affairs, Report 1.

15. Congress, Senate, *Commissioner of Indian Affairs,* 89th Cong., 2d sess., *Congressional Record* (13 April 1966), vol. 112, pt. 6, 8063; Lyndon B. Johnson, *Public Papers of the Presidents of the United States, Lyndon B. Johnson, 1966,* vol. 1 (Washington, D.C.: GPO, 1967), 457–59.

16. Letter and attached report, Robert L. Bennett to Henry M. Jackson, 11 July 1966. Copy available in Folder 10, Box 69, AAIAA.

17. Ibid.

18. Thomas O'Neill, "Politics and People: Senate Committee Finds Indians in Sorry Plight," *Newark Evening News,* 6 April 1966.

19. Congress, Senate, *American Indians—New Destiny,* 89th Cong., 2d sess., *Congressional Record* (21 April 1966), vol. 112, pt. 7, 8715–21.

20. Ibid. Mansfield made the laudatory remarks quoted. See Letter, Wendell Chino to Fred R. Harris, 10 June 1966, Folder 12, Box 41, Fred R. Harris Papers, Carl Albert Congressional Research and Studies Center, University of Oklahoma, Norman, Oklahoma (hereinafter cited as FHP).

21. Weekly Report to the President, April 12, 1966 From the Secretary of the Interior, 12 April 1966, "Interior, Dept. of," Box 127, CF; Letter, Lee Metcalf to Wallace Bear, 6 August 1966, "Indian Affairs (Various, 1961–1967)," Box 154, SUP; and "Senator Metcalf on Termination," *Indian Truth* 43 (October 1966): 14.

22. Congress, Senate, Committee on Interior and Insular Affairs, *Colville Termination: Hearing before the Subcommittee on Indian Affairs of the Committee on Interior and Insular Affairs,* 90th Cong., 1st sess., 8 June 1967, 2.

23. Thom quotation taken from D'Arcy McNickle, "The Indian Tests the Mainstream," *The Nation* 203 (26 September 1966): 276; and Letter, Washington State Project to Senator Jackson, 18 April 1966, Folder 20, Box 157, HJP.

24. William M. Blair, "Gains for Indians Vowed by Udall," *New York Times,* 23 March 1966, 27.

25. Castile, *To Show Heart,* 49; Vine Deloria, Jr., *Behind the Trail of Broken Treaties: An Indian Declaration of Independence* (Austin: University of Texas Press, 1974), 29; Donald Janson, "Indian Bureau Parley Rebuffs Tribes," *New York Times,* 14 April 1966, 27; Robert C. Day, "The Emergence of Indian Activism as a Social Movement," in *Native Americans Today: Sociological Perspectives,* ed. Howard M. Bahr, Bruce A. Chadwick, and Robert C. Day (New York: Harper & Row, 1972), 521; and Sam Steiner, *The New Indians* (New York: Harper & Row, 1968), 250–53. James Officer considered Steiner's discussion of the Santa Fe conference to be "somewhat fanciful." See Officer, "Assessment," 66 n13.

    Castile notes that there is no evidence Udall wanted to transfer OEO programs to the BIA. Donald Baker, general counsel for OEO, recalled in 1966 that Udall contacted Shriver, telling him that "you guys are doing such a great job with Indians; I want some help. I've obviously got to reorganize the BIA. Can I borrow a team?" This incident may have sparked concerns that the BIA wanted to control OEO programs. See Michael L. Gillette, *Launching the War on Poverty: An Oral History* (New York: Twayne Publishers, 1996), 124, 153.

26. "Indian Bureau Parley Rebuffs Tribes," *New York Times;* and Deloria, Jr., *Broken Treaties,* 29.

27. Deloria, Jr., *Broken Treaties,* 29–30; Steiner, *New Indians,* 253; and Donald Janson, "2 Indian Demands Granted by Udall," *New York Times,* 15 April 1966, 20.

    The sources cited above disagree on several minor points regarding the sequence of events at the Santa Fe conference. Thus, I have limited my account to those facts for which there is significant agreement. Deloria, who was present and who is usually a reliable reporter, writes that Udall asked the NCAI delegates to acquiesce in the termination of the Agua Caliente Tribe in California in return for "five years of peace for the tribes." If Udall did make such a statement, he made a notable error in judgment (see Deloria, *Broken Treaties,* 30).

28. Deloria, Jr., *Broken Treaties,* 31.

29. Clifford M. Lytle, Jr., "Vine Deloria, Jr. (1933–)," in *Leaders from the 1960s: A Biographical Sourcebook of American Activism,* ed. David DeLeon (Westport, Conn.: Greenwood Press, 1994), 72–74.

30. First quotation from Szasz, *Education and the American Indian,* 141; and Transcript, Informal Remarks by Secretary of the Interior Stewart L. Udall at the Bureau of Indian Affairs Conference, Santa Fe, New Mexico, April 15, 1966, at Morning Session on "The World of Work," 15 April 1966, "Vol. II

Documentary Supplement (2 of 2)," Box 2, Administrative History: Dept. of the Interior, LBJL.

31. Transcript, 1977 Nash Oral History, 26; and Transcript, Informal Remarks by Secretary, 15 April 1966.

32. Transcript, Informal Remarks by Secretary, 15 April 1966.

   At a press conference held later that day, Udall stated, "[W]e want to work very closely with the Indian people and the tribal leaders, and also with the business people and academic communities in ways they have never been involved before," indicating in his public remarks that Indians would be at least part of the policy process. See Transcript, Press Conference by Secretary of the Interior Stewart L. Udall at Santa Fe, N.M., 15 April 1966, Following a Conference on Indian Affairs, "Press Conferences—Jan.–April 1966," Box 128, SUP.

33. McNickle, "Indian Tests the Mainstream," 279; Cowger, *The Founding Years,* 31, 134–35; and Scott Bear Don't Walk, "McNickle, D'Arcy," in *Encyclopedia of North American Indians,* ed. Frederick E. Hoxie (Boston: Houghton Mifflin, 1996), 369–70.

34. Transcript, Informal Remarks by Secretary, 15 April 1966; and Ted Hulbert, "Congress to Get BIA Legislation to 'Free' Indians," *Albuquerque Journal,* 16 April 1966.

35. Transcript, Informal Remarks by Secretary, 15 April 1966.

36. Transcript, Press Conference, 15 April 1966; and Transcript, Press Conference, 22 April 1966, "Press Conferences—Jan.–April 1966," Box 128, SUP.

37. Memorandum, Udall to Commissioner Bennett, 29 April 1966, "Dept. of Interior (Bureau of Indian Affairs: Reorganization, etc.)," Box 127, SUP; and Memorandum, Frederick M. Haverland to Files, 2 May 1966, "Secretarial Meetings," Box 8, Robert L. Bennett Office Files, RG 75, National Archives, Washington, D.C. (hereinafter cited as RBP).

38. Memorandum, Commissioner of Indian Affairs to Under Secretary, 28 September 1966, Folder 19, Box 73, AAIAA; and Memorandum, Harry R. Anderson to Secretary Udall, 23 August 1966, "Secretarial Meetings," Box 8, RBP.

39. Donald Janson, "Indian Bureau Head Hails Udall Plan," *New York Times,* 17 April 1966, 81; Deloria, *Broken Treaties,* 30–31 (unattributed quotation from p. 31); Wise, *Red Man,* 393; and Chronology—Indian Resources Development Act, 12 August 1968, "Indian Resources Development Act (Omnibus Bill), 1966–67," Box 4, RBP. For the NCAI's procurement of the

draft, see Christopher Riggs, "American Indians, Economic Development and Self-Determination in the 1960s," *Pacific Historical Review* (forthcoming, August 2000).

40. Ellis, "Robert L. Bennett," 329; and Press Release, Regional Indian Meetings Set to Plan New Legislation, 17 September 1966, "Indian Affairs—News, 7/66–7/67," Box 34, Federal Records, Department of the Interior, LBJL.

41. Letter, Alvin M. Josephy, Jr., to Corinne Locker, 18 October 1966, Folder 3, Box 11, CLP; Letter, Corinne Locker to Alvin M. Josephy, Jr., 21 October 1966, Folder 3, Box 11, CLP; and Deloria, *Broken Treaties*, 31.

42. Letter, Josephy to Locker, 18 October 1966; and Letter, Locker to Josephy, 21 October 1966.

43. Steiner, *New Indians*, 271; and Memorandum, Commissioner of Indian Affairs to Under Secretary Luce, 20 January 1967, "Indian Resources Development Act (Omnibus Bill), 1966–67," Box 4, RBP.

44. "Administrative History," 27, "Vol. I, Part II (2 of 2)," Box 1, Administrative History, Department of the Interior, LBJL.

45. Letter, Vine Deloria, Jr., to Dr. Sol Tax, 20 January 1967, "10/5/64–2/29/68," EX IN, Box 1, WHCF, LBJL.
    Deloria was correct in his assessment that most Indian recommendations regarding the bill had been ignored. A study published in late 1967 concluded that the "very sketchy Bureau of Indian Affairs summary of recommendations [submitted by Indians] fails to state adequately the principal emphases apparent in the recommendations." See Deward E. Walker, "An Examination of American Indian Reaction to Proposals of the Commissioner of Indian Affairs for General Legislation 1967," *Northwest Anthropological Research Notes* 1 (fall 1967), 21.

46. Nancy Keegan Smith, "Presidential Task Force Operation During the Johnson Administration," *Presidential Studies Quarterly* 15 (spring 1985): 320–24 (Johnson quotation from p. 321); and Deloria, *Custer Died*, 27.

47. Notes, Meeting on Indians, 25 August 1966, "American Indians," Box 329, Office Files of James C. Gaither, Lyndon B. Johnson Library, Austin, Texas (hereinafter cited as JGOF); and Transcript, Udall Oral History, Interview no. 3, 12–13, LBJL.

48. "A Free Choice Program for American Indians: Report of the President's Task Force on American Indians," i, iii, December 1966, Box 3, Task Force Reports, Lyndon B. Johnson Library, Austin, Texas.

49. Ibid., i.

Task force member Herbert E. Striner restated many of the task force proposals in a paper submitted to Congress in 1968. See Herbert E. Striner, "Toward a Fundamental Program for the Training, Employment, and Economic Equality of the American Indian," in Congress, Subcommittee on Economic Progress of the Joint Economic Committee, *Federal Programs for the Development of Human Resources,* 90th Cong., 2d sess., 1968, 293–326.

50. Ibid., ii, 2, 10, 92, 102–4.

Douglas believed that "generally, a transfer has meant an increase in inefficiency and heavier financial burdens." For this and other objections, see Letter, L. W. Douglas to Walsh McDermott, 3 January 1967, "Pricing Files: Indians 1 of 2," Box 10, Office Files of John E. Ross and Stanford G. Robson, Lyndon B. Johnson Library, Austin, Texas (hereinafter cited as RROF).

51. Memorandum, Udall to the President, 2 September 1965, "HE 8–1 Air Pollution," EX HE, Box 22, WHCF, LBJL; and Transcript, Udall Oral History, Interview no. 7, 6 July 1970, by W. W. Moss, 137, JFKL.

52. Transcript, Udall Oral History, Interview no. 3, 18–20, LBJL.

53. Memorandum, Joe Califano to the President, 5 January 1967, "10/5/64–2/29/68," EX IN, Box 1, WHCF, LBJL.

54. Congress, House, Committee on Interior and Insular Affairs, *Policies, Programs and Activities of the Department of the Interior, Part II,* 90th Cong., 1st sess., 27 January 1967, 2; and William M. Blair, "Panel Asks Shift of Indian Bureau," *New York Times,* 28 January 1967, 14.

55. Memorandum, Charles F. Luce to Joseph Califano, 27 January 1967, "Pricing Files: Indians 1 of 2," Box 10, RROF.

56. "Panel Asks Shift," *New York Times;* Memorandum, John W. Gardner to the President, 11 February 1967, "10/5/64–2/29/68," EX IN, Box 1, WHCF, LBJL; and Memorandum, Joe Califano to the President, 13 February 1967, "10/5/64–2/29/68," EX IN, Box 1, WHCF, LBJL.

57. Deloria, *Custer Died,* 159–60; and Douglas E. Kneeland, "Gardner Urges Indian Unit Shift," *New York Times,* 18 February 1967, 10.

Deloria allegedly stated on a 5 February television broadcast that he favored the transfer but did not think the NCAI would support it. See Memorandum for the Record, 10 February 1967, "Indian Affairs—Commissioner (Interior)," JMOF.

Wayne Aspinall acquired a transcript of Gardner's speech, which apparently left him unmoved. In a memorandum to the Indian affairs subcommittee regarding the speech, Aspinall stated that "Subcommittee

Chairman Haley and I have made our position abundantly clear on this proposal." See Memorandum, Wayne N. Aspinall to All Members of the Subcommittee on Indian Affairs, 21 March 1967, "Wounded Knee," JHP.

58. Letter, Earl Boyd Pierce to Jim Jones, 1 March 1967, "Ex FG 145–6, 3/26/66," FG, Box 208, WHCF, LBJL; Resolution, Intertribal Council of the Five Civilized Tribes, 2 March 1967, attached to Letter, Carl Albert to Henry Hall Wilson, Jr., 20 March 1967, "FG 145–6, 3/26/66," EX FG, Box 208, WHCF, LBJL; and Letter, Carl Albert to Governor Overton James, 20 March 1967, Folder 39, Box 63, Departmental Files, Carl Albert Papers, Carl Albert Congressional Research and Studies Center, University of Oklahoma, Norman, Oklahoma (hereinafter cited as CAP).

59. Statement of the Oglala Sioux Tribe on the Proposal to Transfer the Bureau of Indian Affairs From the Department of the Interior to the Department of Health, Education and Welfare, 10 March 1967, attached to Letter, Paul M. Popple to Mildred Young, 21 March 1967, "In/O Gen," GEN IN, Box 4, WHCF, LBJL.

60. Memorandum, John W. Gardner to the President, 22 March 1967, "Transfer of Bureau of Indian Affairs to HEW (Proposed), 1966–1967," Box 150, SUP; Transcript, Udall Oral History, Interview no. 3, 18, LBJL; Castile, *To Show Heart,* 46–47; and Letter, Stewart L. Udall to Mike Mansfield, 28 July 1967, "Transfer of Bureau of Indian Affairs to HEW (Proposed), 1966–1967," Box 150, SUP.

61. "A Free Choice Program for American Indians," 84.

62. Ibid., 98–99.

63. Steiner, *New Indians,* 283–85; Letter, Indian Conference on Policy and Legislation to President Johnson, 2 February 1967, attached to letter, T. W. Taylor to Joseph Califano, Jr., 15 February 1967, "12/21/66—," GEN IN, Box 2, WHCF, LBJL.

64. Letter, Indian Conference on Policy and Legislation to President Johnson.

65. Ibid.

66. Letter, Pueblo of Acoma to Joseph M. Montoya, 19 February 1967, Folder 11, Box 118, Joseph M. Montoya Papers, Center for Southwest Research, University of New Mexico, Albuquerque, New Mexico; and Chronology—Indian Resources Development Act, 12 August 1968. Unattributed quotation from Letter, Commissioner of Indian Affairs to James Officer, 6 December 1967, "Indian Resources Development Act (Omnibus Bill), 1966–67," Box 4, RBP. See also Letter, Luce to Califano, 11 May 1967, "LE/IN Ex," EX LE, Box 74, WHCF, LBJL.

67. Letter, Luce to Califano, 11 May 1967; Memorandum, Udall to Califano, 12 May 1967, "LE/IN Ex," EX LE, Box 74, WHCF, LBJL; Memorandum, Califano to the President, 13 May 1967, "LE/IN," EX LE, Box 74, WHCF, LBJL; and Congress, House, Committee on Interior and Insular Affairs, *Indian Resources Development Act of 1967: Hearings before the Subcommittee on Indian Affairs of the Committee on Interior and Insular Affairs,* 90th Cong., 1st sess., 13 and 14 July 1967, 1, 11.

68. "Administrative History," 27; House, Committee on Interior and Insular Affairs, *Indian Resources Development Act,* 1–32.

69. House, Committee on Interior and Insular Affairs, *Indian Resources Development Act,* 1–32, 37–43.
     Section 17 of the Indian Reorganization Act of 1934 had allowed for the chartering of corporations, but few tribes had done so, in part because the relationship between the tribal government and the corporation was vague. Title II of the Indian Resources Development Act was intended to clarify the authority of the corporations.

70. Ibid., 19, 33.

71. Committee Check List: Omnibus Bill, attached to Memo, Udall to Califano, 12 May 1967; Congress, Senate, *Economic Development and Management of Resources of Individual Indians and Tribes,* 90th Cong., 1st sess., *Congressional Record* (18 May 1967), vol. 113, pt. 10, 13201; Congress, House, *Public Bills and Resolutions,* 90th Cong., 1st sess., *Congressional Record* (6 June 1967), vol. 113, pt. 11, 14926; Deloria, *Broken Treaties,* 32; and William C. Selover, "Congress Charts Self-Help to Lift Status of the Indian," *Christian Science Monitor,* 10 June 1967, 6.

72. "Congress Charts Self-Help," *Christian Science Monitor.*

73. "Administrative History," 27; and House, Committee on Interior and Insular Affairs, *Indian Resources Development Act of 1967,* 1, 35.

74. House, Committee on Interior and Insular Affairs, *Indian Resources Development Act of 1967,* 45, 55.

75. Ibid., 58–62.

76. Ibid., 92; Transcript, Deloria Oral History, 3; Letter, Lewis L. Zadoka to Stewart Udall, n.d., "Interior," Box 44, Legislative Series, TSP; Letter, Mad Bear to President Johnson, 14 July 1967, "Le/In," EX LE, WHCF, Box 74, LBJL; and Letter, Richard Roessel, Jr., to Joseph Califano, 3 June 1967, "Le/In," GEN LE, Box 74, WHCF, LBJL.

77. Letter, Paul Pitts to Senator A. S. Mike Monroney, 11 August 1967, Folder

8, Box 83, A. S. Mike Monroney Papers, Carl Albert Congressional Research and Studies Center, University of Oklahoma, Norman Oklahoma (hereinafter cited as AMP); and Attachment to Letter, Carl Albert to Overton James, 13 July 1967, Folder 65, Box 101, Legislative Series, CAP.

78. Memorandum, Congressional Relations Officer to Commissioner of Indian Affairs, 31 August 1967, "Indian Resources Development Act (Omnibus Bill), 1966–67," Box 4, RBP; and Memorandum, Commissioner of Indian Affairs to James E. Officer, 6 December 1967, "Indian Resources Development Act (Omnibus Bill), 1966–67," Box 4, RBP.

79. Letter, Commissioner to James Officer, 6 December 1967; Resolution #1, As Amended, attached to Letter, Forest Gerard to Commissioner of Indian Affairs, 12 October 1967, "National Congress of American Indians," Box 6, RBP.

80. Letter, Forest Gerard to Commissioner of Indian Affairs, 12 October 1967.

81. Udall, "State of the Indian Nation," 555–56.

82. Report, Udall to the President, 12 December 1967, "Interior, Dept. of, 1967—," Box 127, CF.

83. Letter, Vine Deloria, Jr., to Leslie Dunbar, 31 October 1967, "NCAI Fund, Inc. (General Support)," Box 2S454, Ford Foundation Archives, Center for American History, University of Texas, Austin, Texas (hereinafter cited as FFA).

CHAPTER SIX

1. Transcript, Udall Oral History, Interview no. 3, 6–7, LBJL.

2. Burnette, *Road to Wounded Knee,* 161.

3. Newsletter, League of Nations Pan.-Am. Indians, n.d., Folder 8, Box 74, FHP; Letter, Lee Motah to Robert L. Bennett, Folder 20, Box 74, FHP; and Deloria, *Broken Treaties,* 31.

4. House, Committee on Interior and Insular Affairs, *Activities of the Department of the Interior,* 1967, Part II, 3–4.

5. Congress, Senate, Committee on Appropriations, *Department of the Interior and Related Agencies Appropriations for Fiscal Year 1970: Hearings before a Subcommittee of the Committee on Appropriations,* 91st Cong., 1st sess., 192–94.

6. House, Committee on Interior and Insular Affairs, *Activities of the*

Department of the Interior, Part II, 1967, 4; and Senate, Committee on Appropriations, *Appropriations for Fiscal Year 1970,* 193–94.

7. House, Committee on Interior and Insular Affairs, *Activities of the Department of the Interior,* Part II, 1967, 4–5; Congress, House, Committee on Appropriations, *Department of the Interior and Related Agencies Appropriations for 1968: Hearings before a Subcommittee of the Committee on Appropriations,* Part I, 90th Cong., 1st sess., 21 February 1967, 758, 764; and Congress, House, Committee on Appropriations, *Appropriations for 1970: Hearings before a Subcommittee of the Committee on Appropriations,* Part II, 91st Cong., 1st sess., 6 March 1969, 128.

8. Szasz, *Education and the American Indian,* 121–22, 142; and House, Committee on Appropriations, *Appropriations for 1968,* Part I, 748.

9. Officer, "Indian Service," 85–86; and 1977 Nash Oral History, 39.

10. Transcript, Udall Oral History, Interview no. 3, 7, LBJL; Szasz, *Education and the American Indian,* 142; Memorandum, Udall to the President, 1 June 1966, "Ex FG 145–6, 3/26/66—," FG, Box 208, WHCF, LBJL; and House, Committee on Interior and Insular Affairs, *Activities of the Department of the Interior,* Part II, 1967, 3.

    Bennett's role in the personnel selection is unclear. Szasz calls Marburger "Udall's personal choice."

11. Memorandum, Commissioner of Indian Affairs to Secretary of the Interior, 5 January 1968, "Legislation," Box 5, RBP.

12. Congress, Senate, *Indian Policy—1966,* 89th Cong., 2d sess., *Congressional Record* (13 October 1967), vol. 112, pt. 20, 26571–75; excerpts reprinted in Josephy, *Red Power,* 60–65.

13. Letter, George McGovern to Robert F. Kennedy, 29 January 1968, "Indian Affairs Subcommittee," Box 26, George S. McGovern Papers, Seeley G. Mudd Manuscript Library, Princeton University, Princeton, New Jersey; author interview with Fred R. Harris, 3 April 1998, Albuquerque, New Mexico; and Transcript, McGovern Oral History, Interview by Paige Mulholland, 30 April 1969, 23, LBJL.

    The McGovern papers contain very little material on Indian affairs, another indication that he had little success during his tenure as subcommittee chairman.

14. Bilharz, *Allegany Senecas,* 99; and Memorandum, "Meeting with a delegation of Seneca Indians," 21 August 1967, "Seneca," Box 8, RBP.

15. Ellis, "Robert L. Bennett," 327–28.

16. Memo, Commissioner to Secretary, 5 January 1968.

17. Letter, Robert L. Bennett to A. S. Mike Monroney, 22 January 1968, Folder 8, Box 93, AMP; and Letter, Chief Julian B. BlueJacket to Hon. Mike Monroney, 5 January 1968, Folder 8, Box 93, AMP.

18. Szasz, *Education and the American Indian,* 143.

19. Interior Department Bureau of Indian Affairs, *Indian Affairs 1967: A Progress Report from the Commissioner of Indian Affairs,* 5–6; and Interior Department Bureau of Indian Affairs, *Indian Affairs 1968: A Progress Report from the Commissioner of Indian Affairs,* 6.

20. Szasz, *Education and the American Indian,* 171–73. For a critical assessment of the community aspect of Rough Rock, see Castile, *To Show Heart,* 37–40.

21. Fred R. Harris, *Potomac Fever* (New York: W. W. Norton & Co., 1977), 126; and Szasz, *Education and the American Indian,* 149.

22. Congress, Senate, Committee on Labor and Public Welfare, *Indian Education: Hearings before the Special Subcommittee on Indian Education of the Committee on Labor and Public Welfare,* pt. 1, 90th Cong., 1st and 2d sessions, 14 December 1967, 4 January 1968, 4, 5, 56; Homer Bigart, "Tribal Leaders Assail School," *New York Times,* 15 December 1967, 11; and "Kennedy Deplores Nation's 'Betrayal' of Indian Education," *New York Times,* 3 January 1968, 41.

23. For a discussion of the LBJ-RFK rivalry, see Jeff Shesol, *Mutual Contempt: Lyndon Johnson, Robert Kennedy, and the Feud that Defined a Decade* (New York: W. W. Norton, 1997).

24. Brugge, *Navajo-Hopi Land Dispute,* 139–44; and Catherine Feher-Elston, *Children of the Sacred Ground: America's Last Indian War* (Flagstaff, Ariz.: Northland Publishing, 1988), 118.

25. Ibid., 145; Letter, Bennett to Graham E. Holmes, 8 July 1966, reproduced in Congress, Senate, Committee on Appropriations, *Development Needs of the Former Bennett Freeze Area: Hearings before a Subcommittee of the Committee on Appropriations,* 103d Cong., 2d sess., 9 July 1993, 13–15; Feher-Elston, *Children of the Sacred Ground,* 118; and MacDonald and Schwarz, *Last Warrior,* 308.

26. Brugge, *Navajo-Hopi Land Dispute,* 157; Letter, Bennett to Holmes, 8 July 1966; and MacDonald and Schwarz, *Last Warrior,* 308.

Emily Benedek contends that "All the residents of the Bennett Freeze Area are Navajos." This statement was accurate at the time she published but not at the time Bennett issued the order. See Benedek, *The Wind Won't Know Me,* 296.

27. Letter, Bennett to Holmes, 8 July 1966; and Brugge, *Navajo-Hopi Land Dispute,* 146.

28. Brugge, *Navajo-Hopi Land Dispute,* 156, 186; Feher-Elston, *Children of the Sacred Ground,* 118; and MacDonald and Schwarz, *Last Warrior,* 308–10.

29. Brugge, *Navajo-Hopi Land Dispute,* 161–65, 181–86, 189–95.

30. Senate, Committee on Appropriations, *Former Bennett Freeze Area,* 7–9; Feher-Elston, *Children of the Sacred Ground,* 118; and MacDonald and Schwarz, *Last Warrior,* 308–9.

    The 1994 court decision granted the Hopis some land and retained the freeze in a small area. See Senate, Committee on Appropriations, *Former Bennett Freeze Area,* 26, 32.

31. Senate, Committee on Appropriations, *Former Bennett Freeze Area,* 7–9.

32. Ibid., 30, 55.

33. Brugge, *Navajo-Hopi Land Dispute,* 145–46.

34. Suzanne Gordon, *Black Mesa: The Angel of Death* (New York: The John Day Company, 1973), 9, 12.

35. Udall quotation from Alvin Josephy, Jr., "The Murder of the Southwest," *Audubon* 73 (July 1971): 62–63; Richard O. Clemmer, "Black Mesa and the Hopi," in *Native Americans and Energy Development,* ed. Joseph G. Jorgensen, et al. (Cambridge: Anthropology Resource Center, 1978), 17.

36. "Navajo Group Renews Feud with Udall," *Albuquerque Journal,* 13 June 1965; Brugge, *Navajo-Hopi Land Dispute,* 136; and Telegram, Severe Vaughn and others, to Stewart Udall, 11 June 1965, attached to Letter, Norman Littell to Lee C. White, 15 June 1965, "IN/Navajo" EX IN, Box 3, WHCF, LBJL.

37. Brugge, *Navajo-Hopi Land Dispute,* 138–41; Holmes quotation from Iverson, *Navajo Nation,* 105.

    The lease was with the Sentry Royalty Company, a subsidiary of Peabody, but was commonly known as the Peabody lease because Peabody would eventually take over the mining operations. See Charles F. Wilkinson, "Home Dance, the Hopi, and Black Mesa Coal: Conquest and Endurance in the American Southwest," *Brigham Young University Law Review* No. 2 (1996): 465–66.

38. Lynn A. Robbins, "Energy Developments and the Navajo Nation," in *Native Americans and Energy Development,* 42–43; Iverson, *Navajo Nation,* 105–7 (quotation from p. 105); and Brugge, *Navajo-Hopi Land Dispute,* 140–41.

39. Smith quotations from Iverson, *Navajo Nation,* 106, and Josephy, "Murder of the Southwest," 64. See also Robbins, "Energy Developments," 42–43.

40. Wilkinson, "Home Dance," 465–66; and Josephy, "Murder of the Southwest," 66.

   Although he denied the allegations, Boyden was in the employ of Peabody Coal at the time he advised the Tribal Council to sign the lease. See Wilkinson, "Home Dance," 469–70.

41. Clemmer, "Black Mesa and the Hopi," 17, 26, 29; Wilkinson, "Home Dance," 465; and Josephy, "Murder of the Southwest," 66.

42. Clemmer, "Black Mesa and the Hopi," 24–27; and Josephy, "Murder of the Southwest," 66.

43. Wilkinson, "Home Dance," 473; Josephy, "Murder of the Southwest," 66; and Clemmer, "Black Mesa and the Hopi," 28 n45.

44. Josephy, "Murder of the Southwest," 65; and Clemmer, "Black Mesa and the Hopi," 17, 28.

45. See Gordon's *Black Mesa* for a spirited (and polemical) protest of the mining operations. See also Marjane Ambler, *Breaking the Iron Bonds: Indian Control of Energy Development* (Lawrence: University Press of Kansas, 1990), 60; and Wilkinson, "Home Dance," 480.

46. *United States Statutes at Large,* 23, sec. 53, 26 (1883–1885); Robert D. Arnold, *Alaska Native Land Claims* (Anchorage: Alaska Native Foundation, 1976), 68–79; and Donald Craig Mitchell, *Sold American: The Story of Alaska Natives and Their Land, 1867–1959* (Hanover: University Press of New England, 1997), 376–79. For a brief synopsis of the Alaskan land claims dispute based largely on Arnold's work, see Claus-M. Naske and Herman E. Slotnick, *Alaska: A History of the 49th State,* 2d ed.(Norman: University of Oklahoma Press, 1987), 186–208.

47. *To provide for the admission of the State of Alaska into the Union, Statutes at Large,* 72, 339–40 (1958).

48. "1961 Task Force Report," 72–74.

49. "Report to the Secretary of the Interior by the Task Force on Alaska Native Claims," 28 December 1962, foreword, 67–71 (copy available in "1967–68 Task Force on American Indians," Box 194, JGOF); and Arnold, *Alaska Native Land Claims,* 80–81.

50. *Task Force on Alaska Native Claims,* 67–71.

51. Arnold, *Alaska Native Land Claims,* 105.

52. Ibid., 102, 103–4, 105; and Memorandum, Commissioner of Indian Affairs to Secretary of the Interior, 20 November 1964.

53. Senate Committee on Interior and Insular Affairs, *Nomination of Robert L. Bennett,* 33–34.

54. Senate Executive Report No. 1, 6–7.

55. Mitchell, *Sold American,* 379; and Arnold, *Alaska Native Land Claims,* 112–14.

   Gruening and his colleagues discovered that the Interior Department was ignoring the protests sometime in mid-1966. See Ernest Gruening, *Many Battles: The Autobiography of Ernest Gruening* (New York: Liveright, 1973), 505.

56. Memorandum, Udall to Commissioner Bennett, 29 April 1966; and Arnold, *Alaska Native Land Claims,* 112–14.

57. Mitchell, *Sold American,* 380; *Federal Register* 31, 8 December 1966, 15494; and Arnold, *Alaska Native Land Claims,* 117–19.

   Because many of the claims overlapped, the total acreage claimed exceeded the size of the state of Alaska.

58. "Alaskans Dispute Freeze on Land," *New York Times,* 11 June 1967, 11; Mitchell, *Sold American,* 380; Walter J. Hickel, *Who Owns America?* (Englewood Cliffs, N.J.: Prentice-Hall, Inc., 1971), 20 n6. Udall quotation from Arnold, *Alaska Native Land Claims,* 118.

59. Memorandum, Charles F. Luce to Joseph A. Califano, 25 January 1967, "Pricing Files: Indians 1 of 2," Box 10, RROF; Senate Executive Report No. 1, 7; and Letter, Stewart L. Udall to Hubert H. Humphrey, 15 June 1967, reprinted in Congress, Senate, Committee on Interior and Insular Affairs, *Alaska Native Land Claims: Hearings before the Committee on Interior and Insular Affairs,* 90th Cong., 2d sess., 8, 9, and 10 February 1968, 20–21.

60. Report to the President, June 13, 1967 From the Secretary of the Interior, "Interior, Dept. of, 1967—," Box 127, CF; Arnold, *Alaska Native Land Claims,* 119; Senate, Committee on Interior and Insular Affairs, *Alaska Native Land Claims,* 1, 21–22; and Report to the President, November 28, 1967 From the Secretary of the Interior, "Interior, Dept. of, 1967—," Box 127, CF.

61. Report to the President, 28 November 1967; and Mary Clay Berry, *The Alaska Pipeline: The Politics of Oil and Native Land Claims* (Bloomington: Indiana University Press, 1975), 51.

62. Report to the President, 28 November 1967.

63. Senate, Committee on Interior and Insular Affairs, *Alaska Native Land Claims,* 31, 224, 228.

64. Congress, Senate, Committee on Interior and Insular Affairs, *Alaska Native Land Claims: Hearings before the Committee on Interior and Insular Affairs,* Part 2, 90th Cong., 2d sess., 12 July 1968, 543, 549.

65. Ibid., 517–22, 543.

66. Ibid., 548, 555; Hickel, *Who Owns America?,* 5, 20 n6; and *Federal Register* 34 (23 January 1969), 1025.

67. Arnold, *Alaska Native Land Claims,* 125–26; and E. W. Kenworthy, "'Udall's Freeze' on Claims for U.S. Land Keeps Governor Hickel and Many Other Alaskans Heated Up," *New York Times,* 3 January 1969, 11.

    The final settlement, which extinguished aboriginal land claims, awarded Native Alaskans title to 44 million acres of land and $962.5 million dollars in compensation.

68. For a discussion of Bartlett and Native Alaskans, see Mitchell, *Sold American,* 332, 375.

69. Transcript, Udall Oral History, Interview no. 3, 7–8, LBJL.

70. Memorandum, Joseph Califano to Lee C. White, 19 August 1967, reprinted in "Interagency 1967 Task Force on Indians," Box 20, TF.

71. Ibid.; and Memorandum, Joseph Califano to Lee C. White, 14 September 1967, reprinted in "Report of the Interagency Task Force on American Indians."

72. Memorandum, Lee C. White to Joseph Califano, 23 October 1967, reprinted in "Interagency 1967 Task Force on Indians"; and Memorandum, Lee C. White to Mr. Califano, 23 October 1967, "EX SP 2–3/1968/ In Indian Message Backup Material IV," EX SP, Box 122, WHCF, LBJL.

73. Memo, White to Mr. Califano, 23 October 1967; and "Report of the Interagency Task Force on American Indians," 23 October 1967, 2, "Interagency 1967 Task Force on Indians."

74. "Report of the Interagency Task Force on American Indians," 2–3, 33–35.

75. Memo, White to Mr. Califano, 23 October 1967; and Memorandum, Joe Manes to Earl Darrah, 27 October 1967, reprinted in "Interagency 1967 Task Force on Indians;" Transcript, Udall Oral History, Interview no. 3, 13, LBJL.

    In early 1967 the Interior Department and HEW worked on a joint program to draft a special message to be combined with a Labor Department message on migrant labor. This Indian message was never delivered. See Memorandum, Charles F. Luce to Joseph Califano, 26

January 1967, "Indians/Mig. Workers," Box 67, Office Files of Joseph A. Califano, Jr., Lyndon B. Johnson Library, Austin, Texas.

76. Memorandum, Ervin Duggan to Matthew Nimetz, 24 February 1968, "EX Sp 2–3/1968/In Indian Message Backup Material V," EX SP, Box 122, WHCF, LBJL; Memorandum, Lee White to Joseph A. Califano, 26 February 1968, "EX Sp 2–3/1968/In Indian Message Backup Material V," EX SP, Box 122, WHCF, LBJL; and Memorandum, "Ervin" to "Matthew," n.d., "EX Sp 2–3/1968/In Indian Message Backup Material I," EX SP, Box 122, WHCF, LBJL.

77. Memorandum, Stewart Udall to Joseph Califano, 2 March 1968, "EX Sp 2–3/1968/In Indian Message," EX SP, Box 122, WHCF, LBJL.

78. Memorandum, Joe Califano to the President, 2 March 1968, "EX Sp 2–3/1968/In Indian Message Backup Material II," EX SP, Box 122, WHCF, LBJL; Memorandum, Joe Califano to Mr. President, "EX Sp 2–3/1968/In Indian Message 3/6/68," EX SP, Box 122, WHCF, LBJL; Lyndon B. Johnson, *Public Papers of the Presidents of the United States, Lyndon B. Johnson, 1968–69,* vol. 1 (Washington, D.C.: GPO, 1970), 335–44.

    The conflict with Kennedy's actions prompted Ervin Duggan to note that "Joe [Califano] should stress that this Message is not an attempt to rebut Bobby Kennedy." Johnson surely put it to that purpose. See Memorandum, "To Matthew," n.d., "EX Sp 2–3/1968/In Indian Message Backup Material I," EX SP, Box 122, WHCF, LBJL.

    The "Special Message to Congress on the Problems of the American Indian, 'The Forgotten American'" was only one of several such messages released by the White House in early 1968. During the first three months of that year, Johnson sent a total of eighteen special messages to Congress. See President, *Public Papers,* 1968–69, Book I, xiii–xxvi.

79. Johnson, *Public Papers,* 1968–69, Book I, 335–44.

80. Transcript, Udall Oral History, Interview no. 3, 13, LBJL; Johnson, *Public Papers,* 1968–69, Book I, 335–44; and Officer, "Indian Service," 79.

81. Letter, Richard A. Halfmoon to Stewart Udahl [*sic*], 22 March 1968, "EX Sp 2–3/1968/In Indian Message 3/6/68," EX SP, Box 122, WHCF, LBJL; and Letter, W. W. Keeler to President Johnson, 18 March 1968, "GEN Sp 2–3/IN Indian Message," GEN IN, Box 123, WHCF, LBJL.

82. Congress, Senate, *The American Indian—Message from the President,* (H. Doc. 272), 90th Cong., 2d sess., *Congressional Record* (6 March 1968), vol. 114, pt. 5, 5521; Transcript, Bennett Oral History, 4, LBJL; and Johnson, *Public Papers,* 1968–69, Book I, 336. For a critical rhetorical analysis of Johnson's message, see Robbins, "The Forgotten American," 31–33.

Donald Fixico writes that "President Johnson expressed opposition to unilateral termination in a message before a national meeting in Kansas City in February 1967." However, the speaker was HEW Secretary John Gardner, who assured his audience that the "President is opposed to termination," a statement that may have been true but would have been far more impressive had Johnson made it. See Fixico, *Termination*, 195; and "Remarks by John W. Gardner," attached to memo, Aspinall to Subcommittee, 21 March 1967, JHP.

83. "A Free Choice Program for American Indians," 10; Draft memorandum, to Mr. Califano, n.d., "Pricing Files: Indians 1 of 2," Box 10, RROF; and Memorandum, White to Califano, 23 October 1967.

84. Memorandum, Udall to Califano, 2 March 1968; Ralph Nader, "Lo, the Poor Indian," *New Republic* 158 (30 March 1968): 14.

85. Congress, Senate, Committee on the Judiciary, *Constitutional Rights of the American Indian: Hearings before the Subcommittee on Constitutional Rights of the Committee on the Judiciary,* Part I, 87th Cong., 1st sess., 29, 30, and 31 August, 1 September 1961, 1; Robert Hill Winfrey, Jr., "Civil Rights and the American Indian: Through the 1960s" (Ph.D. diss., University of Oklahoma, 1986), 168; Philp, *Indian Self-Rule,* 216; and Deloria and Lytle, *The Nations Within,* 207.

   Ervin's papers contain little material regarding Indian civil rights beyond subcommittee reports. See files under Senate Records, Series I, Correspondence Files, Legislative 1963, JC, Constitutional Rights Subcommittee, Samuel J. Ervin, Jr. Papers, Southern Historical Collection, Wilson Library, University of North Carolina, Chapel Hill, North Carolina.

86. For Ervin's attitudes toward civil rights, see Sam J. Ervin, Jr., *Preserving the Constitution: The Autobiography of Senator Sam Ervin* (Charlottesville, Virginia: The Michie Co., 1984), 163–85.

87. U.S. Commission on Civil Rights, *Justice: 1961 Commission on Civil Rights Report,* Book 5 (Washington, D.C.: GPO, 1961), 131, 133, 158.

88. Senate, Committee on the Judiciary, *Constitutional Rights of the American Indian,* Part I, 3. For a full treatment of this issue, see Wunder, *"Retained by the People."*

89. Congress, Senate, *Bills and Joint Resolutions Introduced,* 89th Cong., 1st sess., *Congressional Record* (2 February 1965), vol. 111, pt. 2, 1784; and Winfrey, "Civil Rights," 188. Winfrey provides a thorough account of the hearings. See Congress, Senate, Committee on the Judiciary, *Constitutional Rights of the American Indian: Hearings before the Subcommittee on*

Constitutional Rights of the Committee on the Judiciary, Part 5, 89th Cong., 1st sess., 22–24, 29 June 1965, 2–14.

90. Ibid., 3–4, 9–12.

91. Ibid., 148, 190–91, 194–95.

92. Congress, Senate, *Proposed Legislation to Protect Rights of Indians,* 89th Cong., 1st sess., *Congressional Record* (2 February 1965), vol. 111, pt. 2, 1799; and Congress, Senate, Committee on the Judiciary Committee on the Judiciary, Committee Print, Subcommittee on Constitutional Rights of the Committee on the Judiciary, *Summary Report of Hearings and Investigations,* 89th Cong., 2d sess., 1–27.

93. Congress, Senate, *Bills and Joint Resolutions Introduced,* 90th Cong., 1st sess., *Congressional Record* (23 May 1967), vol. 113, pt. 10, 13461; and Ervin, *Preserving the Constitution,* 203. For a history of the open housing legislation, see Thomas Clarkin, "The Fair Housing Act of 1968," (master's report, University of Texas, 1993); Winfrey, "Civil Rights," 199–201; and Supplemental memorandum, 2 November 1967, "Constitutional Rights" (no box number available), AAIAA.

94. Deloria and Lytle, *Nations Within,* 210; *Indian Record,* 28, copy available in "Indian Message Responses," Office Files of Frederick Panzer, Lyndon B. Johnson Library, Austin, Texas; and Kimmis Hendrick, "American Indians Juggle Rights and Indianhood," *Christian Science Monitor,* 7 March 1968, 3.

95. Johnson, *Public Papers,* 1968–69, Book I, 342; and Press Release, "Ervin Praises Call for Indian Rights Bill, 6 March 1968," "EX Sp 2–3/1968/In Indian Message 3/6/68," EX SP, Box 122, WHCF, LBJL.

96. Ervin, *Preserving the Constitution,* 203–4; and Congress, Senate, *Interference with Civil Rights,* 90th Cong., 2d sess., *Congressional Record* (8 March 1968), vol. 114, pt. 5, 5835–38.

97. Memorandum, JEO to SLU, 27 March 1968, "S.L.U. and Staff (James Officer)," Box 138, SUP.

98. Clarkin, "Fair Housing"; and President, *Public Papers,* 1968–69, Book I, 509–10.

99. Congress, Senate, Committee on the Judiciary, *Constitutional Rights of the American Indian: Hearings before the Subcommittee on Constitutional Rights of the Committee on the Judiciary,* Part 4, 88th Cong., 1st sess., 7 March 1963, 900. See also Winfrey, "Civil Rights," 189; and Philp, *Indian Self-Rule,* 216.

100. Deloria and Lytle, *American Indians, American Justice,* 131–36; and Wunder, *"Retained by the People,"* 141–44, 153–56.

101. 1968 NCAI Resolutions, Resolution No. 7, copy available in "Gaither: Indians-General (1)," Box 15, JGOF, LBJL; Brugge, *Navajo-Hopi Land Dispute,* 198; and Ellis, "Robert L. Bennett," 330.

102. For a brief discussion of Bruce's tenure as commissioner, see Joseph H. Cash, "Louis Rook Bruce (1969–73)," in Kvasnicka and Viola, *Commissioners,* 333–40.

CONCLUSION

1. Richard M. Nixon, *Public Papers of the Presidents of the United States, Richard M. Nixon, 1970* (Washington, D.C.: GPO, 1971), 564–76.

2. Ibid., 567.

3. Congress did not formally abandon termination until it passed the Tribally Controlled Schools Act of 1988, which declared that Congress "hereby repudiates and rejects House Concurrent Resolution 108 of the 83d Congress and any policy of unilateral termination of Federal relations with any Indian Nation." See *Augustus F. Hawkins-Robert T. Stafford Elementary and Secondary School Improvement Amendments of 1988. Statutes at Large,* 102, pt. 1, 386 (1988).

4. Garment, *Crazy Rhythm,* 225.

5. Old Person quoted in Deloria, *Of Utmost Good Faith,* 219; and Memorandum, Bennett to Udall, 5 January 1968.

6. Congress, Senate, *Introduction of Bills and Resolutions,* 92d Cong., 2d sess., *Congressional Record* (9 February 1972), vol. 118, pt. 5, 3316; and Transcript, Verkler Oral History, Interview no. 3, 138–39, SHO. See also Emma R. Gross, *Contemporary Federal Policy Toward American Indians* (New York: Greenwood Press, 1989), 79, 91 n2.

   Jackson's conversion was apparently less than complete. James Abourezk (D.-S.D.), who became chairman of the Indian Affairs subcommittee in 1973, later complained that "It appeared to me that Scoop was there to make certain, among other things, that Indians did not interfere with whites anywhere in the United States, particularly in Washington, his home state." James Abourezk, *Advise & Dissent: Memoirs of South Dakota and the U.S. Senate* (Chicago: Lawrence Hill Books, 1989), 215.

7. Lee Metcalf remains an interesting exception to this pattern whose career demands greater study.

8. Transcript, Udall Oral History, Interview no. 3, 11, LBJL. Jackson quotation

from Ognibene, *Scoop,* 134. See also Memorandum, Bennett to Udall, 5 January 1968.

9. House, Committee on Interior and Insular Affairs, *Indian Resources Development Act,* 48–49; and Transcript, Press Conference, 304–5, 15 April 1966, "Press Conferences, Jan.–April 1966," Box 128, SUP.

10. Officer quotation from Castile, *To Show Heart,* 17; and Transcript, Udall Oral History, Interview no. 3, 12–13, LBJL.

11. Udall, "State of the Indian Nation," 554.

12. Deloria, *Custer,* 259.

13. Kathryn L. MacKay, "Warrior Into Welder: A History of Federal Employment Programs for American Indians 1878–1972" (Ph.D. diss., University of Utah, 1987), 256–60. For a discussion of critical evaluations, see Riggs, "Indians, Liberalism," 6–12.

14. Transcript, Udall Oral History, Interview no. 3, 16, LBJL.

15. Senese, *Self-determination,* 68–82. For quotation, see Task Force on Indian Affairs, "Implementing Change Through Government," *Human Organization* 20:12 (1962): 136.

16. AICC, *Declaration,* 6; and Resolution of the Indian Conference on Policy and Legislation, attached to Letter, Indian Conference and Policy and Legislation to President Johnson, 2 February 1977.

17. Burt, "Western Tribes and Balance Sheets," 495.

18. U.S. Bureau of the Census, *Census of Population: 1970. Subject Reports. Final Report PC(2)–1F. American Indians* (Washington, D.C.: GPO, 1973), 18, 27, 120; and U.S. Bureau of the Census, *Vol. 1, Characteristics of the Population. Part 1, United States Summary—Section 2* (Washington, D.C.: GPO, 1973), 860, 861.

   Because the figures concerning Indian income were derived from areas with populations exceeding 10,000, they ignore the lower income and educational levels of remote and isolated Native Americans, and thus do not accurately represent the Indian population as a whole.

19. Burnette, *Road to Wounded Knee,* 162.

20. Transcript, Udall Oral History, Interview no. 3, 21, LBJL; Vine Deloria, Jr., "Memo on Present State of Indians Affairs," n.d., NCAI Fund, Inc. (General Support), Box 2S454, FFA; Transcript, Deloria Oral History, 6; Cowger, *Founding Years,* 138–44, 147–49; and Deloria, *Custer Died,* 217–24.

BIBLIOGRAPHY

ARCHIVAL AND MANUSCRIPT COLLECTIONS

Arizona Historical Association, Arizona State University, Phoenix, Arizona
        Paul J. Fannin Papers
Carl Albert Congressional Research and Studies Center, University of
Oklahoma, Norman, Oklahoma
        Carl Albert Papers (CAP)
        Fred R. Harris Papers (FHP)
        A. S. Mike Monroney Papers (AMP)
        Thomas J. Steed Papers (TSP)
Center for American History, University of Texas, Austin, Texas. Ford
Foundation Archives (FFA)
Center for Southwest Research, University of New Mexico, Albuquerque, New
Mexico
        Joseph M. Montoya Papers
        Navajo-Hopi Land Dispute Manuscript Collection
        William Zimmerman Papers
Florida Southern College Library, Lakeland, Florida
        James A. Haley Papers (JHP)

Harry S. Truman Library, Independence, Missouri (HSTL)
    William A. Brophy Papers (WBP)
    Philleo Nash Papers (PNP)
Humanities Research Center, University of Texas, Austin, Texas
    Oliver La Farge Papers
Indiana University of Pennsylvania, Indiana, Pennsylvania
    John P. Saylor Papers (JSP)
John F. Kennedy Library, Boston, Massachusetts (JFKL)
    White House Central Files (WHCF)
    Lee C. White Papers (LWP)
Lyndon B. Johnson Library, Austin, Texas (LBJL)
    Administrative Histories
    Diary and Appointment Logs
    Federal Records
    Legislative Background and Domestic Crises File
    Office Files of Joseph A. Califano, Jr.
    Office Files of James C. Gaither (JGOF)
    Office Files of Frederick Panzer
    Office Files of John W. Macy, Jr. (JMOF)
    Office Files of John E. Ross and Stanford G. Robson (RROF)
    Task Force Reports
    White House Central Files, Confidential Files (CF)
    White House Central Files, Subject Files (WHCF)
Manuscripts Division, Library of Congress, Washington, D.C. (LOC)
    Clinton P. Anderson Papers (CAP)
National Archives, Washington, D.C.
    Robert L. Bennett Office Files, RG 75 (RBP)
Seeley G. Mudd Manuscript Library, Princeton University, Princeton, New Jersey
    Association of American Indian Affairs Archives (AAIAA)
    Corinne Locker Papers (CLP)
    George S. McGovern Papers (GMP)
Senate Historical Office, Washington, D.C. (SHO)
Southern Historical Collection, Wilson Library, University of North Carolina, Chapel Hill, North Carolina
    Samuel J. Ervin, Jr. Papers
Special Collections, University of Arizona, Tucson, Arizona
    Morris K. Udall Papers (MUP)
    Stewart L. Udall Papers (SUP)

University of Washington Libraries, University of Washington, Seattle, Washington
>   Henry M. Jackson Papers (HJP)
>   Lloyd Meeds Papers
Western History Collections, University of Oklahoma, Norman, Oklahoma
>   American Indian File

Published Sources, Dissertations, and Theses

Abourezk, James G. *Advise & Dissent: Memoirs of South Dakota and the U.S. Senate.* Chicago: Lawrence Hill Books, 1989.

Ambler, Marjane. *Breaking the Iron Bonds: Indian Control of Energy Development.* Lawrence: University Press of Kansas, 1990.

"American Indian Capital Conference on Poverty." *Indian Truth* 41 (June 1964): 13–15.

American Indian Chicago Conference. *Declaration of Indian Purpose.* Chicago: American Indian Chicago Conference, 1961.

Anderson, Clinton P. *Outsider in the Senate: Senator Clinton P. Anderson's Memoirs.* New York: World Publishing Co., 1970.

Arnold, Robert D. *Alaska Native Land Claims.* Anchorage: Alaska Native Foundation, 1976.

Ashby, LeRoy and Rod Gramer. *Fighting the Odds: The Life of Senator Frank Church.* Pullman, Wash.: Washington State University Press, 1994.

Bear Don't Walk, Scott. "McNickle, Darcy." In *Encyclopedia of North American Indians,* edited by Frederick E. Hoxie, 369–70. Boston: Houghton Mifflin, 1996.

Benedek, Emily. *The Wind Won't Know Me: A History of the Navajo-Hopi Land Dispute.* New York: Alfred A. Knopf, 1992.

Bennett, Robert L. "Building Indian Economies with Land Settlement Funds." *Human Organization* 20:4 (1961–62): 159–63.

———. "New Era for the American Indian." *Natural History* 75 (February 1967): 6–11.

Bernstein, Alison R. *American Indians and World War II: Toward A New Era in Indian Affairs.* Norman: University of Oklahoma Press, 1991.

Bernstein, Irving. *Guns or Butter: The Presidency of Lyndon Johnson.* New York: Oxford University Press, 1996.

Berry, Mary Clay. *The Alaska Pipeline: The Politics of Oil and Native Land Claims.* Bloomington: University of Indiana Press, 1975.

Bilharz, Joy A. *The Allegany Senecas and Kinzua Dam: Forced Relocation Through Two Generations*. Lincoln: University of Nebraska Press, 1998.

Boise Cascade Center for Community Development. *Indian Economic Development: An Evaluation of EDA's Selected Indian Reservation Program*. Vol. II, *Individual Reservation Reports*. N.p., 1972.

Bordewich, Fergus M. *Killing the White Man's Indian: Reinventing Native Americans at the End of the Twentieth Century*. New York: Anchor Books, 1996.

Brophy, William A. and Sophie D. Aberle, comps. *The Indian: America's Unfinished Business*. Norman: University of Oklahoma Press, 1966.

Brugge, David M. *The Navajo-Hopi Land Dispute: An American Tragedy*. Albuquerque: University of New Mexico Press, 1994.

Burnette, Robert. *The Tortured Americans*. Englewood Cliffs, N.J.: Prentice-Hall, Inc., 1971.

Burnette, Robert and John Koster. *The Road to Wounded Knee*. New York: Bantam Books, 1974.

Burt, Larry W. *Tribalism in Crisis: Federal Indian Policy, 1953–1961*. Albuquerque: University of New Mexico Press, 1982.

———. "Western Tribes and Balance Sheets: Business Development Programs in the 1960s and 1970s." *Western Historical Quarterly* 23 (November 1992): 475–95.

Butler, Raymond A. "The Bureau of Indian Affairs: Activities Since 1945." *Annals of the American Academy of Political and Social Science* 436 (March 1978): 50–60.

Cahn, Edward S., ed. *Our Brother's Keeper: The Indian in White America*. New York: World Publishing Co., 1969.

Califano, Joseph A., Jr. *The Triumph and Tragedy of Lyndon Johnson: The White House Years*. New York: Simon & Schuster, 1991.

"Capitol [sic] Conference on Indian Poverty Sets Forth Needs and Aims." *The Amerindian* 12 (May–June 1964): 1–2.

Carriker, Robert C. "The Kalispel Tribe and the Indian Claims Commission Experience." *Western Historical Quarterly* 9 (January 1978): 19–32.

Cash, Joseph H. "Louis Rook Bruce, 1969–73." In *The Commissioners of Indian Affairs, 1824–1977*, edited by Kvasnicka and Viola, 333–40.

Castile, George Pierre. *To Show Heart: Native American Self-Determination and Federal Indian Policy, 1960–1975*. Tucson: University of Arizona Press, 1998.

Clarkin, Thomas Francis. "The Open Housing Act of 1968." Master's report, University of Texas, 1993.

Clemmer, Richard O. "Black Mesa and the Hopi." In *Native Americans and Energy Development*, edited by Jorgensen, et al., 17–34.

Clifford, Clark. *Counsel to the President: A Memoir.* New York: Random House, 1991.

Cobb, Daniel M. "Philosophy of an Indian War: Indian Community Action in the Johnson Administration's War on Poverty, 1964–1968." *American Indian Culture and Research Journal* 22, no. 2 (1998): 71–102.

Collier, John. "The United States Indian." In *Understanding Minority Groups*, edited by John Gittler, 33–57. New York: John Wiley & Sons, 1956.

Commission on the Rights, Liberties, and Responsibilities of the American Indian. *A Program For Indian Citizens: A Summary Report, January 1961.* N.p., 1961.

Congressional Quarterly's Guide to Congress. 4th ed. Washington, D.C.: Congressional Quarterly, Inc., 1991.

Congressional Quarterly's Guide to U.S. Elections. 3d ed. Washington, D.C.: Congressional Quarterly, Inc., 1994.

Cowger, Thomas W. *The National Congress of American Indians: The Founding Years.* Lincoln: University of Nebraska Press, 1999.

Crow Dog, Mary and Richard Erdoes. *Lakota Woman.* New York: Grove Weidenfeld, 1990.

Dahl, Kathleen A. "The Battle Over Termination on the Colville Indian Reservation." *American Indian Culture and Research Journal* 18, no. 1 (1994): 29–53.

Dallek, Robert. *Lone Star Rising: Lyndon Johnson and His Times, 1908–1960.* New York: Oxford University Press, 1991.

Davis, Mary B., ed. *Native America in the Twentieth Century: An Encyclopedia.* New York: Garland Publishing, 1994.

Day, Robert C. "The Emergence of Indian Activism as a Social Movement." In *Native Americans Today: Sociological Perspectives*, edited by Howard M. Bahr, Bruce A. Chadwick, and Robert C. Day, 506–32. New York: Harper & Row, 1972.

Deloria, Philip S. "The Era of Indian Self-Determination: An Overview." In *Indian Self-Rule*, edited by Philp, 191–207.

Deloria, Vine, Jr. *Behind the Trail of Broken Treaties: An Indian Declaration of Independence.* Austin: University of Texas Press, 1974.

———. *Custer Died For Your Sins: An Indian Manifesto.* New York: Macmillan Company, 1969.

———. "The Lummi Indian Community: The Fisherman of the Pacific

Northwest." In *American Indian Economic Development,* edited by Stanley, 87–158.

———. *Red Earth, White Lies: Native Americans and the Myth of Scientific Fact.* New York: Scribner, 1995.

———. *We Talk, You Listen: New Tribes, New Turf.* New York: Macmillan Company, 1970.

Deloria, Vine, Jr., ed. *Of Utmost Good Faith.* San Francisco: Straight Arrow Books, 1971.

Deloria, Vine, Jr. and Clifford M. Lytle. *American Indians, American Justice.* Austin: University of Texas Press, 1983.

———. *The Nations Within: The Past and the Future of American Indian Sovereignty.* New York: Pantheon Books, 1984.

Drinnon, Richard. *Keeper of Concentration Camps: Dillon S. Meyer and American Racism.* Berkeley: University of California Press, 1987.

Eggan, Fred. "Philleo Nash: The Education of an Applied Anthropologist." In *Applied Anthropologist and Public Servant,* ed. Landman and Halpern, 7–10.

Ellis, Richard N. "Robert L. Bennett, 1966–69." In *The Commissioners of Indian Affairs,* edited by Kvasnicka and Viola, 311–23.

Ervin, Sam J., Jr. *Preserving the Constitution: The Autobiography of Senator Sam Ervin.* Charlottesville, Va.: The Michie Co., 1984.

Fahey, John. *The Kalispel Indians.* Norman: University of Oklahoma Press, 1986.

Feher-Elston, Catherine. *Children of the Sacred Ground: America's Last Indian War.* Flagstaff, Ariz.: Northland Publishing, 1988.

———. "Navajo-Hopi Land Controversy." *Native America in the Twentieth Century,* edited by Davis, 386–89.

Fenno, Richard F., Jr. *Congressmen in Committees.* Boston: Little, Brown and Company, 1973.

Feraca, Stephen E. *Why Don't They Give Them Guns: The Great American Indian Myth.* Lanham, Md.: University Press of America, 1990.

Finger, John R. *Cherokee Americans: The Eastern Band of Cherokees in the Twentieth Century.* Lincoln: University of Nebraska, 1991.

Fisher, Louis. *Presidential Spending Power.* Princeton: Princeton University Press, 1975.

Fixico, Donald L. *Termination and Relocation: Federal Indian Policy, 1945–1960.* Albuquerque: University of New Mexico Press, 1986.

Garment, Leonard. *Crazy Rhythm: My Journey from Brooklyn, Jazz, and Wall Street to Nixon's White House, Watergate, and Beyond . . .* New York:

Times Books, 1997.

Gillette, Michael L. *Launching the War on Poverty: An Oral History.* New York: Twayne Publishers, 1996.

Gordon, Suzanne. *Black Mesa: The Angel of Death.* New York: The John Day Company, 1973.

Graham, Hugh Davis. *The Uncertain Triumph: Federal Education Policy in the Kennedy and Johnson Years.* Chapel Hill: University of North Carolina, 1984.

Gross, Emma R. *Contemporary Federal Policy Toward American Indians.* New York: Greenwood Press, 1989.

Gruening, Ernest. *Many Battles: The Autobiography of Ernest Gruening.* New York: Liveright, 1973.

Harris, Fred R. *Potomac Fever.* New York: W. W. Norton & Co., 1977.

Hasse, Larry J. "Termination and Assimilation: Federal Indian Policy, 1943 to 1961." Ph.D. diss., Washington State University, 1974.

Hauptman, Laurence M. *The Iroquois Struggle for Survival: World War II to Red Power.* Syracuse, N.Y.: Syracuse University Press, 1986.

———. *Tribes and Tribulations: Misconceptions About American Indians and Their Histories.* Albuquerque: University of New Mexico Press, 1995.

Hauptman, Laurence and Jack Campisi. "The Voice of Eastern Indians: The American Indian Chicago Conference and the Movement for Federal Recognition." *Proceedings of the American Philosophical Society* 132 (December 1988): 316–29.

Heller, Francis H., ed. *The Truman White House: The Administration of the Presidency, 1945–1953.* Lawrence: Regents Press of Kansas, 1980.

Hickel, Walter J. *Who Owns America?* Englewood Cliffs, N.J.: Prentice-Hall, Inc., 1971.

Hoikkala, Paivi H. "Mothers and Community Builders: Salt River Pima and Maricopa Women in Community Action." In *Negotiators of Change: Historical Perspectives on Native American Women,* edited by Nancy Shoemaker, 213–34. New York: Routledge, 1995.

Hough, Henry W. *Development of Indian Resources.* Denver: World Press, Inc., 1967.

Iverson, Peter. "Legal Counsel and the Navajo Nation Since 1945." *American Indian Quarterly* 3 (spring 1977): 1–15.

———. *The Navajo Nation.* Westport, Conn.: Greenwood Press, 1981.

Jaimes, M. Annette. "The Hollow Icon: An American Indian Analysis of the Kennedy Myth and Federal Indian Policy." *Wicazo Sa Review* 4 (spring

1990): 34–44.

Johnson, Claudia T. *Lady Bird: A White House Diary*. New York: Holt, Rinehart and Winston, 1970.

Johnson, Donald Bruce and Kirk H. Porter. *National Party Platforms, 1840–1972*. Urbana: University of Illinois Press, 1973.

Johnson, Lyndon B. *The Vantage Point: Perspectives of the Presidency, 1963–1969*. New York: Holt, Rinehart and Winston, 1971.

Jorgensen, Joseph G., Richard O. Clemmer, Ronald A. Little, Nancy J. Owens, and Lynn A. Robbins, eds. *Native Americans and Energy Development*. Cambridge: Anthropology Resources Center, 1978.

Josephy, Alvin, Jr. "The Murder of the Southwest." *Audubon* 73 (July 1971): 52–67.

Josephy, Alvin M., Jr. *The American Indian and the Bureau of Indian Affairs, 1969: A Study, with Recommendations*. Toronto: Indian-Eskimo Association of Canada, 1969.

———. *Now That the Buffalo's Gone: A Study of Today's American Indians*. New York: Alfred A. Knopf, 1982.

———. *Red Power: The American Indians' Fight for Freedom*. Lincoln: University of Nebraska Press, 1971.

Kammer, Jerry. *The Second Long Walk: The Navajo-Hopi Land Dispute*. Albuquerque: University of New Mexico Press, 1980.

Kappler, Charles J. *Indian Treaties, 1778–1883*. New York: Interland Publishing, 1972.

Kelly, William H. "Indian Adjustment and the History of Indian Affairs." *Arizona Law Review* 10 (winter 1968): 559–77.

Kersey, Harry A., Jr. *An Assumption of Sovereignty: Social and Political Transformation among the Florida Seminoles, 1953–1979*. Lincoln: University of Nebraska Press, 1996.

Kickingbird, Kirke. "Trust Responsibilities and Trust Funds." In *Native America in the Twentieth Century*, edited by Davis, 658–59.

Knoche, Beth Ritter. "Termination, Self-Determination and Restoration: The Northern Ponca Case." Master's thesis, University of Nebraska, 1990.

Kravitz, Sanford. "The Community Action Program—Past, Present, and Its Future?" In *On Fighting Poverty: Perspectives From Experience*, edited by James L. Sundquist, 52–69. New York: Basic Books, 1969.

Kutler, Stanley I. *The Wars of Watergate: The Last Crisis of Richard Nixon*. New York: Alfred A. Knopf, 1990.

Kvasnicka, Robert M. and Herman J. Viola, eds. *The Commissioners of Indian Affairs, 1824–1977*. Lincoln: University of Nebraska Press, 1979.

La Farge, Oliver. "Termination of Federal Supervision: Disintegration and the American Indians." *Annals of the American Academy of Political and Social Science* 311 (May 1957): 41–46.

Landman, Ruth H. and Katherine Spencer Halpern. *Applied Anthropologist and Public Servant: The Life and Work of Philleo Nash,* ed. Ruth H. Landman and Katherine Spencer Halpern. Washington, D.C.: American Anthropological Association, 1989.

Lawson, Michael L. *Dammed Indians: The Pick-Sloan Plan and the Missouri River Sioux, 1944–1980.* Norman: University of Oklahoma Press, 1982.

Lazarus, Edward. *Black Hills, White Justice: The Sioux Nation Versus the United States, 1775 to the Present.* New York: HarperCollins, 1991.

LeUnes, Barbara Laverne Blythe. "The Conservation Philosophy of Stewart L. Udall, 1961–1968." Ph.D. diss., Texas A&M University, 1977.

Levitan, Sar A. *Federal Aid to Depressed Areas: An Evaluation of the Area Redevelopment Administration.* Baltimore: Johns Hopkins Press, 1964.

———. *The Great Society's Poor Law: A New Approach to Poverty.* Baltimore: Johns Hopkins Press, 1969.

Levitan, Sar A. and Barbara Hetrick. *Big Brother's Indian Programs—With Reservations.* New York: McGraw-Hill, 1971.

Littell, Norman C. *My Roosevelt Years.* Edited by Jonathan Dembo. Seattle: University of Washington Press, 1987.

Lowe, Marjorie L. "'Let's Make It Happen': W. W. Keeler and Cherokee Renewal." *The Chronicles of Oklahoma* 74 (summer 1996): 116–29.

Lurie, Nancy Oestreich. "The Voice of the American Indian: Report on the American Indian Chicago Conference." *Current Anthropology* 2 (December 1961): 478–500.

Lytle, Clifford M. "Vine Deloria, Jr." In *Leaders from the 1960s: A Biographical Sourcebook of American Activism,* edited by David DeLeon, 72–79. Westport, Conn.: Greenwood Press, 1994.

MacDonald, Peter and Ted Schwarz. *The Last Warrior: Peter MacDonald and the Navajo Nation.* New York: Orion Books, 1993.

MacKay, Kathryn L. "Warrior into Welder: A History of Federal Programs for American Indians, 1878–1972." Ph.D. diss., University of Utah, 1987.

Manuel, Henry F., Juliann Ramon, and Bernard L. Fontana. "Dressing for the Window: Papago Indians and Economic Development." In *American Indian Economic Development,* edited by Stanley, 511–77.

Martin, Jill E. "A Year and a Spring of My Existence: Felix Cohen and the Handbook of Federal Indian Law." *Western Legal History* 8 (winter/spring 1995): 35–60.

McNickle, D'Arcy. "The Indian Tests the Mainstream." *The Nation* 203 (26 September 1966): 275–79.

———. *Native American Tribalism: Indian Survivals and Renewals.* New York: Oxford University Press, 1973.

Means, Russell and Marvin J. Wolf. *Where White Men Fear to Tread: The Autobiography of Russell Means.* New York: St. Martin's Press, 1995.

Metcalf, Lee. "The Need for Revision of Federal Policy in Indian Affairs." *Indian Truth* 35 (January–March 1958): 1–8.

Milkman, Raymond H., Christopher Bladen, Beverly Lyford, and Howard L. Walton, eds. *Alleviating Economic Distress: Evaluating a Federal Effort.* Lexington, Mass.: Lexington Books, 1972.

Mitchell, Donald Craig. *Sold American: A Story of Alaska Natives and Their Land, 1867–1959: the Army to Statehood.* Hanover: University Press of New England, 1997.

Morgan, Arthur E. *Dams and Other Disasters: A Century of the Army Corps of Engineers in Civil Works.* Boston: Porter Sargent Publishing, 1971.

Moritz, Charles, ed. *Current Biography Yearbook, 1961.* New York: H. W. Wilson Co., 1961.

———. *Current Biography Yearbook, 1962.* New York: H. W. Wilson Co., 1962.

———. *Current Biography Yearbook, 1967.* New York: H. W. Wilson Co., 1967.

Nader, Ralph. "Lo, the Poor Indian." *New Republic* 158 (30 March 1968): 14–15.

"Nash as Commissioner—Five Years of Progress and Understanding." *NCAI Sentinel* 11 (winter 1966).

Nash, Philleo. "Anthropologist in the White House." In *Applied Anthropologist and Public Servant,* ed. Landman and Halpern, 3–6.

———. "Science, Politics, and Human Values: A Memoir." *Human Organization* 45 (fall 1986): 189–201.

Naske, Claus-M. and Herman E. Slotnick. *Alaska: A History of the 49th State.* 2d ed. Norman: University of Oklahoma Press, 1987.

"Navajo Proposed For Indian Commissioner." *The Amerindian* 9 (January–February 1961): 1.

Officer, James E. "The Bureau of Indian Affairs Since 1945: An Assessment." *Annals of the American Academy of Political and Social Science* 436 (March 1978): 61–72.

———. "Philleo Nash: Anthropologist as Administrator." In *Applied Anthropologist and Public Servant,* ed. Landman and Halpern, 11–15.

———. "Termination as Federal Policy: An Overview." In *Indian Self-Rule,* edited by Philp, 114–28.

————. "The Indian Service and Its Evolution." In *The Aggressions of Civilization: Federal Indian Policy Since the 1880s*, edited by Sandra L. Cadwalader and Vine Deloria, Jr., 59–103. Philadelphia: Temple University Press, 1984.

Ognibene, Peter J. *Scoop: The Life and Politics of Henry M. Jackson*. New York: Stein and Day, 1975.

Opotowsky, Stan. *The Kennedy Government*. London: George G. Harrap & Co., 1961.

Ourada, Patricia K. *The Menominee Indians: A History*. Norman: University of Oklahoma Press, 1979.

Parker, Dorothy R. *Singing An Indian Song: A Biography of D'Arcy McNickle*. Lincoln: University of Nebraska Press, 1992.

Parman, Donald L. *Indians and the American West in the Twentieth Century*. Bloomington: Indiana University Press, 1994.

Peroff, Nicholas C. *Menominee Drums: Tribal Termination and Restoration, 1954–1974*. Norman: University of Oklahoma Press, 1982.

Philp, Kenneth R. "Termination: A Legacy of the Indian New Deal." *Western Historical Quarterly* 24 (April 1983): 165–80.

————. *Termination Revisited: American Indians on the Trail to Self-Determination, 1933–1953*. Lincoln: University of Nebraska Press, 1999.

Philp, Kenneth R., ed. *Indian Self-Rule: First-Hand Accounts of Indian-White Relations from Roosevelt to Reagan*. Current Issues in the American West series, vol. IV. Salt Lake City: Howe Brothers, 1986.

Prucha, Francis Paul. *The Great Father: The United States Government and the American Indians*. 2 vols. Lincoln: University of Nebraska Press, 1984.

————. *The Indian in American Society: From the Revolutionary War to the Present*. Berkeley: University of California Press, 1985.

Prucha, Francis Paul, ed. *Documents of United States Indian Policy*. 2d ed. Lincoln: University of Nebraska Press, 1990.

Rawls, James J. *Chief Red Fox Is Dead: A History of Native Americans Since 1945*. Fort Worth: Harcourt Brace College Publishers, 1996.

Riggs, Christopher. "Americans Indians, Economic Development and Self-Determination in the 1960s." *Pacific Historical Review*. In press.

————. "Indians, Liberalism, and Lyndon Johnson's Great Society, 1963–1969." Ph.D. diss., University of Colorado, 1997.

Robbins, Lynn A. "Energy Developments and the Navajo Nation." In *Native Americans and Energy Development*, edited by Jorgensen, et al., 35–48.

Robbins, Rebecca L. "The Forgotten American: A Foundation for Contemporary Indian Self-Determination." *Wicazo Sa Review* 4 (spring 1990): 27–33.

Rosenberg, Ruth. "Zah, Peterson." In *Notable Native Americans,* edited by
Sharon Malinowski, 474–76. New York: Gale Research, Inc., 1995.

Scheirbeck, Helen Maynor. "Education, Public Policy and the American
Indian." Ph.D. diss., Virginia Polytechnic and State University, 1980.

Schifter, Richard. "The Legislative Record." *Indian Affairs* 62 (February–April
1966): 2.

———. "Trends in Federal Indian Administration." *South Dakota Law Review*
15 (winter 1970): 1–21.

Schott, Richard L. and Dagmar S. Hamilton. *People, Positions, and Power: The
Political Appointments of Lyndon Johnson.* Chicago: University of
Chicago Press, 1983.

"Senator Metcalf on Termination." *Indian Truth* 43 (October 1966): 14.

"Seneca Tribe Honors Congressman Haley." *The Amerindian* 15
(September–October 1966): 6.

Senese, Guy B. *Self-Determination and the Social Education of Native Americans.*
New York: Praeger, 1991.

Shesol, Jeff. *Mutual Contempt: Lyndon Johnson, Robert Kennedy, and the Feud
That Defined a Decade.* New York: W. W. Norton, 1997.

Smith, Nancy Keegan. "Presidential Task Force Operations During the
Johnson Administration." *Presidential Studies Quarterly* 15 (spring
1985): 320–29.

Smith, Paul Chaat and Robert Allen Warrior. *Like a Hurricane: The Indian
Movement from Alcatraz to Wounded Knee.* New York: The New Press,
1996.

Sorkin, Alan L. *American Indians and Federal Aid.* Washington, D.C.:
Brookings Institution, 1971.

Stanley, Sam, ed. *American Indian Economic Development.* The Hague: Mouton
Publishers, 1978.

Steiner, Stan. *The New Indians.* New York: Harper & Row, 1968.

Stevens, Susan McCulloch. "Passamaquoddy Economic Development in
Cultural and Historical Perspective." In *American Indian Economic
Development,* edited by Stanley, 511–77.

Szasz, Margaret. *Education and the American Indian: The Road to Self-
Determination, 1928–1973.* Albuquerque: University of New Mexico
Press, 1974.

Szasz, Margaret Connell. "Philleo Nash." In *The Commissioners of Indian
Affairs,* edited by Kvasnicka and Viola, 311–23.

Task Force on Indian Affairs. "Implementing Change Through Government."
Human Organization 21 no. 2 (1962): 125–36.

Taylor, Theodore W. *The Bureau of Indian Affairs*. Boulder: Westview Press, 1984.

Taylor, Walter. "The Treaty We Broke." *Nation* 193 (2 September 1961): 120–21.

Thomas, Lately. *When Even Angels Wept: The Senator Joseph McCarthy Affair— A Story Without a Hero*. New York: William Morrow and Co., 1973.

Tjerandsen, Carl. *Education for Citizenship: A Foundation's Experience*. Santa Cruz, Calif.: Emil Schwarzhaupt Foundation, Inc., 1980.

"To Hold Capitol [sic] Conference on Indian Poverty." *The Amerindian* 12 (March–April 1964): 3.

Udall, Stewart L. *The Quiet Crisis*. New York: Holt, Rinehart and Winston, 1963.

————. "The State of the Indian Nation—An Introduction." *Arizona Law Review* 10 (winter 1968): 553–57.

Unger, Irwin. *The Best of Intentions: The Triumphs and Failures of the Great Society Under Kennedy, Johnson, and Nixon*. New York: Doubleday, 1996.

Walker, Deward E., Jr. "An Examination of American Indian Reaction to Proposals of the Commissioner of Indian Affairs for General Legislation 1967." *Northwest Anthropological Research Notes* 1 (fall 1967): 1–178.

————. "Confederated Tribes of the Colville Reservation." In *Native America in the Twentieth Century*, edited by Davis, 132–33.

Warden, Richard D. *Metcalf of Montana: How a Senator Makes Government Work*. Washington, D.C.: Acropolis Books, 1965.

Watkins, Arthur V. "Termination of Federal Supervision The Removal of Restrictions over Indian Property and Person." *Annals of the American Academy of Political and Social Science* 311 (May 1957): 47–55.

Weber, Michael P. *Don't Call Me Boss: David L. Lawrence, Pittsburgh's Renaissance Mayor*. Pittsburgh: University of Pittsburgh Press, 1988.

"What Indians Want." *New Republic* 143 (19 December 1960): 7–8.

Wilkinson, Charles F. "Home Dance, the Hopi, and Black Mesa Coal: Conquest and Endurance in the American Southwest." *Brigham Young University Law Review*, no. 2 (1996): 449–82.

Wilson, James J. "OEO Indian Programs: New Hope For Old Emma." *Communities in Action* 1 (Aug.–Sept. 1965): 24–26.

Winfrey, Robert Hill Jr. "Civil Rights and the American Indian: Through the 1960s." Ph.D. diss., University of Oklahoma, 1986.

Wise, Jennings C. *The Red Man in the New World Drama: A Politico-Legal Study with a Pageantry of American Indian History*. Edited and revised by Vine Deloria, Jr. New York: Macmillan Company, 1971.

Wunder, John R. *"Retained by the People": A History of American Indians and the Bill of Rights*. New York: Oxford University Press, 1994.

Young, Robert W. *A Political History of the Navajo Tribe*. Tsaile, Navajo Nation, Ariz.: Navajo Community College Press, 1978.

U.S. Government Documents

An Act to provide for a per capita distribution of Menominee tribal funds and authorize the withdrawal of the Menominee Tribe from Federal Jurisdiction. Statutes at Large. 68 (1954).

"Anderson, Clinton Presba." In *Biographical Directory of the United States Congress, 1774–1989*, 534.

Area Redevelopment Act. Statutes at Large. 75 (1961).

Allegheny [sic] Reservation, N.Y., Seneca Nation. Statutes at Large. 78 (1964).

"Aspinall, Wayne Norviel." In *Biographical Directory of the United States Congress, 1774–1989*, 552.

Augustus F. Hawkins-Robert T. Stafford Elementary and Secondary School Improvement Amendments of 1988. Statutes at Large. 102 (1988).

Biographical Directory of the United States Congress, 1774–1989. Bicentennial Edition. Washington, D.C.: GPO, 1989.

Colville Indian Reservation, Wash. Statutes at Large. 70 (1956).

Economic Opportunity Act. Statutes at Large. 78 (1964).

Eisenhower, Dwight D. *Public Papers of the Presidents of the United States, Dwight D. Eisenhower, 1953*. Washington, D.C.: GPO, 1960.

Elementary and Secondary Education Act of 1965. Statutes at Large. 79 (1965).

Federal Register. 31 (8 December 1966): 15,494.

———. 34 (23 January 1969), 1025.

Freedom of Communications: The Joint Appearances of Senator John F. Kennedy and Vice-President Richard M. Nixon, Presidential Campaign of 1960. Washington, D.C.: GPO, 1961.

Freedom of Communications: The Speeches of Senator John F. Kennedy, Presidential Campaign of 1960. Washington, D.C.: GPO, 1961.

"House Concurrent Resolution 108." *Statutes at Large*. 67 (1953).

Indians. Statutes at Large. 76 (1962).

Indians, Confederated Tribes of the Colville Reservation. Statutes at Large. 78 (1964).

Indians, leasing of restricted land. Statutes at Large. 69 (1955).

"Indian, State jurisdiction over criminal and civil offenses." *Statutes at Large*. 67 (1953).

Johnson, Lyndon B. *Public Papers of the Presidents of the United States, Lyndon B. Johnson, 1963–1964.* Vol. 1. Washington, D.C.: GPO, 1965.

———. *Public Papers of the Presidents of the United States, Lyndon B. Johnson, 1966.* Vol. 1. Washington, D.C.: GPO, 1967.

———. *Public Papers of the Presidents of the United States, Lyndon B. Johnson, 1968–1969.* Vol. 1. Washington, D.C.: GPO, 1970.

Kalispel Indians. Statutes at Large. 78 (1964).

Kennedy, John F. *Public Papers of the Presidents of the United States, John F. Kennedy, 1961.* Washington, D.C.: GPO, 1962.

———. *Public Papers of the Presidents of the United States, John F. Kennedy, 1962.* Washington, D.C.: GPO, 1963.

Menominee County, Wis., assistance. Statutes at Large. 76 (1962).

Nixon, Richard M. *Public Papers of the Presidents of the United States, Richard M. Nixon, 1970.* Washington, D.C.: GPO, 1971.

To provide for the admission of the State of Alaska into the Union. Statutes at Large. 72 (1958).

"Udall, Stewart Lee." *Biographical Directory of the United States Congress, 1774–1989,* 1966.

U.S. Bureau of the Census. *U.S. Census of Population: 1960. General Social and Economic Characteristics, United States Summary. Final Report PC(11)–1C.* Washington, D.C.: GPO, 1962.

———. *U.S. Census of Population: 1960. Subject Reports. Nonwhite Population by Race. Final Report PC(2)–1C.* Washington, D.C.: GPO, 1963.

———. *U.S. Census of Population: 1970. Subject Reports. Final Report PC92)–1F. American Indians.* Washington, D.C.: GPO, 1973.

———. *U.S. Census of Population: 1970. Vol. 1, Characteristics of the Population. Part 1, United States Summary—Section 2.* Washington, D.C.: GPO, 1973.

U.S. Commission on Civil Rights. *Justice: 1961 Commission on Civil Rights Report, Book 5.* Washington, D.C.: GPO, 1961.

U.S. Comptroller General of the United States. "Review of Certain Aspects of the Program for the Termination of Federal Supervision Over Indian Affairs." 1961.

U.S. Congress. House. *Allegany Indian Reservation—Seneca Nation.* 88th Cong., 2d sess. *Congressional Record* (14 April 1964), vol. 110, pt. 6.

———. *Authorizing Acquisition of and Payment for Flowage Easement and Rights-of-Way Within the Allegany Indian Reservation in New York.* 88th Cong., 2d sess. *Congressional Record* (7 February 1964), vol. 110, pt. 2.

———. *Loans to Indian Tribes for Public Works or Facilities.* 87th Cong., 2d sess. *Congressional Record* (5 October 1962), vol. 108, pt. 17.

———. *Menominee Tribe of Wisconsin.* 83d Cong., 1st sess. *Congressional Record* (1 August 1953), vol. 99, pt. 8.

———. *Providing Assistance to Menominee County, Wis.* 87th Cong., 2d sess. *Congressional Record* (20 March 1962), vol. 108, pt. 4.

———. *Providing for the Disposition of Judgment Funds to the Lower Pend d'Oreille or Kalispel Tribe of Indians.* 88th Cong., 2d sess. *Congressional Record* (21 July 1964), vol. 110, pt. 12.

———. *Public Appropriations Bill, 1961.* 86th Cong., 2d sess. *Congressional Record* (25 May 1960), vol. 106, pt. 8.

———. *Public Bills and Resolutions.* 90th Cong., 1st sess. *Congressional Record* (6 June 1967), vol. 113, pt. 11.

———. *Public Works and Economic Development Act of 1965.* 89th Cong., 1st sess. *Congressional Record* (12 August 1965), vol. 111, pt. 15.

———. *Remarks on Indian Affairs.* 84th Cong., 2d sess. *Congressional Record* (28 March 1956), vol. 102, pt. 5.

———. *Seneca Indian Nation.* 88th Cong., 2d sess. *Congressional Record* (18 August 1964), vol. 110, pt. 15.

U.S. Congress. House. Committee on Appropriations. *Appropriations for 1970: Hearings before a Subcommittee of the Committee on Appropriations.* Part II. 91st Cong., 1st sess., 6 March 1969.

———. *Department of the Interior and Related Agencies Appropriations for 1964: Hearings before a Subcommittee of the Committee on Appropriations.* 88th Cong., 1st sess., 28 January–21 February 1963.

———. *Department of the Interior and Related Agencies Appropriations for 1965: Hearings before a Subcommittee of the Committee on Appropriations.* 88th Cong., 2d sess., 28 January–21 February 1964.

———. *Department of the Interior and Related Agencies Appropriations for 1966: Hearings before a Subcommittee of the Committee on Appropriations.* Part 1. 89th Cong., 1st sess., 2 February–3 March 1965.

———. *Department of the Interior and Related Agencies Appropriations for 1968: Hearing before a Subcommittee of the Committee on Appropriations.* Part 1. 90th Cong., 1st sess., 21 February 1967.

U.S. Congress. House. Committee on Education and Labor. *Economic Opportunity Act Amendments of 1967: Hearings before the Committee on Education and Labor.* Appendix. 90th Cong., 1st sess., 1967.

———. *Economic Opportunity Act Amendments of 1967: Hearings before the Committee on Education and Labor.* Part 2. 90th Cong., 1st sess., 19–23, 26 and 28 June, 10 July 1967.

————. *Economic Opportunity Act Amendments of 1967: Hearings before the Committee on Education and Labor.* Part 3. 90th Cong., 1st sess., 12–14, 17–19 July 1967.

————. *Economic Opportunity Act of 1964: Hearings before the Subcommittee on the War on Poverty of the Committee on Education and Labor.* Part 1. 88th Cong., 2d sess., 17–20 March; 7–10, 13 and 14 April, 1964.

————. *Economic Opportunity Act of 1964: Hearings before the Subcommittee on the War on Poverty of the Committee on Education and Labor.* Part 2. 88th Cong., 2d sess., 15–17, 20 and 21 June, 1964.

————. *Elementary and Secondary Education Amendments of 1966: Hearings before the General Subcommittee on Education and Labor.* Part 2. 89th Cong., 1st sess., 15–18, 22 and 23 March 1966.

U.S. Congress. House. Committee on Interior and Insular Affairs. *Colville Termination Legislation: Hearing before the Subcommittee on Indian Affairs of the Committee on Interior and Insular Affairs.* 87th Cong., 2d sess., 15 May 1962.

————. *Indian Resources Development Act of 1967: Hearings before the Subcommittee on Indian Affairs of the Committee on Interior and Insular Affairs.* 90th Cong., 1st sess., 13 and 14 July 1967.

————. *Kinzua Dam (Seneca Indian Relocation): Hearings before the Subcommittee on Indian Affairs of the Committee on Interior and Insular Affairs.* 88th Cong., 1st sess., 18 May; 15–16 July; 8, 9, 12, 19, and 20 August; 31 October; 1 November; 9–10 December 1963.

————. *Policies, Programs, and Activities of the Department of the Interior: Hearings before the Committee on Interior and Insular Affairs.* 88th Cong., 1st sess., 31 January–11 February 1963.

————. *Policies, Programs, and Activities of the Department of the Interior, Part II: Hearing before the Committee on Interior and Insular Affairs.* 90th Cong., 1st sess., 27 January 1967.

U.S. Congress. House. Committee on Public Works. *Public Works and Economic Development Act of 1965: Hearings before the Committee on Public Works.* 89th Cong., 1st sess., 10–14, 18, 19, and 26 May 1965.

U.S. Congress. Joint Economic Committee. *Federal Programs for the Development of Human Resources: Hearing before the Subcommittee on Economic Progress of the Joint Economic Committee.* 90th Cong., 2d sess. Joint Committee Print. Washington, D.C.: GPO, 1968.

U.S. Congress. Joint Economic Committee. Subcommittee on Economy in Government of the Joint Economic Committee. *Toward Economic Development for Native Communities: A Compendium of Papers.* 91st

Cong., 1st sess. Joint Committee Print. Washington, D.C.: GPO, 1969.

U.S. Congress. Senate. *Additional Co-sponsors of Bills.* 89th Cong., 1st sess. *Congressional Record* (7 April 1965), vol. 111, pt. 6.

————. *Amendment of the Indian Long-Term Leasing Act.* 88th Cong., 1st sess. *Congressional Record* (28 August 1963), vol. 109, pt. 12.

————. *The American Indian—Message from the President* (H. Doc. 272). 90th Cong., 2d sess. *Congressional Record* (6 March 1968), vol. 114, pt. 5.

————. *American Indians—New Destiny.* 89th Cong., 2d sess. *Congressional Record* (21 April 1966), vol. 112, pt. 7.

————. *Announcement of hearings on Nomination of Philleo Nash to be Commissioner of Indian Affairs.* 87th Cong., 1st sess. *Congressional Record* (9 August 1961), vol. 107, pt. 11.

————. *Announcement of hearings on S. 1392, Relating to the Indian Heirship Land Problem.* 87th Cong., 1st sess. *Congressional Record* (18 July 1961), vol. 107, pt. 10.

————. *Bills and Joint Resolution Introduced.* 90th Cong., 1st sess. *Congressional Record* (23 May 1967), vol. 113, pt. 10.

————. *Bills and Joint Resolutions Introduced.* 89th Cong., 1st sess. *Congressional Record* (2 February 1965), vol. 111, pt. 2.

————. *Commissioner of Indian Affairs.* 87th Cong., 1st sess. *Congressional Record* (20 September 1961), vol. 107, pt. 15.

————. *Commissioner of Indian Affairs.* 89th Cong., 2d sess. *Congressional Record* (13 April 1966), vol. 112, pt. 6.

————. *Economic Development and Management of Individual Indians and Indian Tribes.* 90th Cong., 1st sess. *Congressional Record* (18 May 1967), vol. 113, pt. 10.

————. *Federal Responsibility Toward Indians.* 86th Cong., 1st sess. *Congressional Record* (2 March 1959), vol. 105, pt. 3.

————. *Flowage Easement and Rights-of-Way Over Lands Within the Allegany Reservation—Conference Report.* 88th Cong., 2d sess. *Congressional Record* (17 August 1964), vol. 110, pt. 15.

————. *Indian Heirship Land Problem.* 88th Cong., 1st sess. *Congressional Record* (11 October 1963), vol. 109, pt. 14.

————. *Indian Policy—1966.* 89th Cong., 2d sess. *Congressional Record* (13 October 1966), vol. 112, pt. 20.

————. *Interference with Civil Rights.* 90th Cong., 2d sess. *Congressional Record* (8 March 1968), vol. 114, pt. 5.

————. *Introduction of Bills and Joint Resolutions.* 92d Cong., 2d sess. *Congressional Record* (9 February 1972), vol. 118, pt. 5.

———. *Nomination of Stewart Udall to be Secretary of the Interior.* 87th Cong., 1st sess. *Congressional Record* (21 January 1961), vol. 107, pt. 1.

———. *Payment for Flowage Easement and Rights-of-Way Over Lands Within the Allegany Indian Reservation, N.Y.* 88th Cong., 2d sess. *Congressional Record* (14 April 1964), vol. 110, pt. 6.

———. *Philleo Nash.* 82d Cong., 2d sess. *Congressional Record* (29 January 1952), vol. 98, pt. 1.

———. *Proposed Legislation to Protect Rights of Indians.* 89th Cong., 1st sess. *Congressional Record* (2 February 1965), vol. 111, pt. 2.

———. *Public Works and Economic Development Act of 1965.* 89th Cong., 1st sess. *Congressional Record* (1 April 1965), vol. 111, pt. 5.

———. *Public Works and Economic Development Act of 1965.* 89th Cong., 1st sess. *Congressional Record* (1 June 1965), vol. 111, pt. 9.

———. *Relocation of the Seneca Nation.* 88th Cong., 2d sess. *Congressional Record* (30 March 1964), vol. 110, pt. 5.

———. *Unemployment in Certain Economically Depressed Areas.* 84th Cong., 2d sess. *Congressional Record* (26 July 1956), vol. 102, pt. 11.

U.S. Congress. Senate. Committee on Appropriations. *Department of the Interior and Related Agencies Appropriations for Fiscal Year 1970: Hearing before a Subcommittee of the Committee on Appropriations.* 91st Cong., 1st sess., 12 March 1969.

———. *Development Needs of the Former Bennett Freeze Area: Hearing before a Subcommittee of the Committee on Appropriations.* 103d Cong., 2d sess., 9 July 1993.

U.S. Congress. Senate. Committee on Banking and Currency. *Area Redevelopment—1961: Hearings before the Subcommittee of the Committee on Banking and Currency.* 87th Cong., 1st sess., 18, 19, and 26 January and 20 February 1961.

———. *Public Works and Economic Development: Hearings before the Subcommittee of the Committee on Banking and Currency.* 89th Cong., 1st sess., 4–7 May 1965.

U.S. Congress. Senate. Committee on Interior and Insular Affairs. *Alaska Native Land Claims: Hearings before the Committee on Interior and Insular Affairs.* 90th Cong., 2d sess., 8, 9, and 10 February 1968.

———. *Alaska Native Land Claims: Hearing before the Committee on Interior and Insular Affairs. Part 2.* 90th Cong., 2d sess., 12 July 1968.

———. *Amendments to the Menominee Termination Act: Hearings before the Subcommittee on Indian Affairs of the Committee on Interior and Insular Affairs.* 87th Cong., 1st sess., 18, 19, and 24 April 1961.

———. *Colville Indian Legislation: Hearings before the Subcommittee on Indian Affairs of the Committee on Interior and Insular Affairs.* 88th Cong., 1st sess., 24, 25 and 26 October, and 20 November 1963.

———. *Colville Termination: Hearings before the Subcommittee on Indian Affairs of the Committee on Interior and Insular Affairs.* 89th Cong., 1st sess., 5 and 6 April 1965.

———. *Colville Termination: Hearing before the Subcommittee on Indian Affairs of the Committee on Interior and Insular Affairs.* 90th Cong., 1st sess., 8 June 1967.

———. *Indian Heirship Land Problem: Hearings before the Subcommittee on Indian Affairs of the Committee on Interior and Insular Affairs.* 87th Cong., 1st sess., 9 and 10 August 1961.

———. *Indian Heirship Land Problem: Hearings before the Subcommittee on Indian Affairs of the Committee on Interior and Insular Affairs.* 87th Cong., 2d sess., 2 and 3 April 1962.

———. *Indian Heirship Land Problem: Hearings before the Subcommittee on Indian Affairs of the Committee on Interior and Insular Affairs.* 88th Cong., 1st sess., 29 and 30 April 1963.

———. *Kinzua Dam (Seneca Indian Relocation): Hearing before the Subcommittee on Indian Affairs of the Committee on Interior and Insular Affairs.* 88th Cong., 2d sess., 2 March 1964.

———. *The Nomination of Philleo Nash to be Commissioner of Indian Affairs: Hearings before the Committee on Interior and Insular Affairs.* 87th Cong., 1st sess., 14 and 17 August 1961.

———. *The Nomination of Philleo Nash to be Commissioner of Indian Affairs, Executive Session: Hearing before the Committee on Interior and Insular Affairs.* 87th Cong., 1st sess., 8 September 1961. Microfiche.

———. *The Nomination of Robert LaFollette Bennett, of Alaska, to be Commissioner of Indian Affairs: Hearing before the Committee on Interior and Insular Affairs.* 89th Cong., 2d sess., 1 April 1966.

———. *The Nomination of Stewart L. Udall to be Secretary of the Interior: Hearing Before the Committee on Interior and Insular Affairs.* 87th Cong., 1st sess., 13 January 1961.

———. *Providing for the Division of the Tribal Assets of the Ponca Tribe of Native Americans of Nebraska among the Members of the Tribe, and for other purposes.* Senate Report 1623. 87th Cong., 2d sess., 25 June 1962.

———. *To Provide for the Disposition of Judgment Funds Now on Deposit to the Credit of the Lower Pend d'Oreille or Kalispel Tribe of Indians: Hearings before the Subcommittee on Indian Affairs of the Committee on Interior and Insular Affairs.* 88th Cong., 2d sess., 27 May 1964. Microfiche.

U.S. Congress. Senate. Committee on the Judiciary. *Constitutional Rights of the American Indian: Hearings before the Subcommittee on Constitutional Rights of the Committee on the Judiciary.* Part I. 87th Cong., 1st sess., 29–31 August, 1 September 1961.

———. *Constitutional Rights of the American Indian: Hearing before the Subcommittee on Constitutional Rights of the Committee on the Judiciary.* Part 4. 88th Cong., 1st sess., 7 March 1963.

———. *Constitutional Rights of the American Indian: Hearings before the Subcommittee on Constitutional Rights of the Committee on the Judiciary.* Part 5. 89th Cong., 1st sess., 22–24, 29 June 1965.

———. *Summary Report of Hearings and Investigations of the Subcommittee on Constitutional Rights of the Committee on the Judiciary.* 89th Cong., 2d sess.

U.S. Congress. Senate. Committee on Labor and Public Welfare. *Area Redevelopment: Hearings before the Subcommittee on Labor of the Committee on Labor and Public Welfare.* 84th Cong., 2d sess., 24, 25 and 27 February; 20, 22, 23, 26, 28 and 29 March; 26 April 1956.

———. *Economic Opportunity Act of 1964: Hearings before the Select Committee on Poverty of the Committee on Labor and Public Welfare.* 88th Cong., 2d sess., 17, 18, 23 and 25 June 1964.

———. *Examination of the War on Poverty: Hearing before the Subcommittee on Employment, Manpower, and Poverty of the Committee on Labor and Public Welfare.* Part 3. 90th Cong., 1st sess., 24 April 1967.

———. *Examination of the War on Poverty: Hearing before the Subcommittee on Employment, Manpower, and Poverty of the Committee on Labor and Public Welfare.* Part 14. 90th Cong., 1st sess. Miscellaneous Appendix.

———. *Indian Education: Hearings before the Special Subcommittee on Indian Education of the Committee on Labor and Public Welfare.* 90th Cong., 1st and 2d sessions, 14 and 15 December 1967, 4 January 1968.

U.S. Department of Commerce. Area Redevelopment Administration. *Annual Report on the Area Redevelopment Administration of the U.S. Department of Commerce, 1962.*

———. *Economic Growth in American Communities: Annual Report on the Area Redevelopment Administration of the U.S. Department of Commerce, 1963.*

———. *More Jobs Where Needed: Annual Report on the Area Redevelopment Administration of the U.S. Department of Commerce, 1964.*

U.S. Department of Commerce. Economic Development Administration. *Annual Report 1967.*

———. *Jobs For America: Economic Development Administration Annual Report, Fiscal 1969.*

———. *1968 Progress Report of the Economic Development Administration.*

U.S. Department of the Interior. *Annual Report of the Secretary of the Interior, 1961.*

———. *Annual Report of the Secretary of the Interior, 1962.*

———. "Report to the Secretary of the Interior by the Task Force on Alaska Native Affairs." 1962.

———. "Report to the Secretary of the Interior by the Task Force on Indian Affairs." 1961.

U.S. Department of the Interior. Bureau of Indian Affairs. *Developing Indian Employment Opportunities,* by Keith L. Fay. Bureau of Indian Affairs, n.d.

———. *A History of Indian Policy,* by S. Lyman Tyler. Bureau of Indian Affairs, 1973.

———. *Indian Affairs 1964: A Progress Report from the Commissioner of Indian Affairs.*

———. *Indian Affairs 1965: A Progress Report from the Commissioner of Indian Affairs.*

———. *Indian Affairs 1967: A Progress Report from the Commissioner of Indian Affairs.*

———. *Indian Affairs 1968: A Progress Report from the Commissioner of Indian Affairs.*

U.S. Office of Economic Opportunity. *As the Seed is Sown.* 4th Annual Report. Office of Economic Opportunity, 1968.

———. *The Quiet Revolution.* 2d Annual Report. Office of Economic Opportunity, 1966.

———. *The Tide of Progress.* 3d Annual Report. Office of Economic Opportunity, 1967.

COURT CASES

Littell v. *Udall,* 242 F. Supp. 635 (1965); 366 F. 2d 668 (1966); 87 SCt. 713.

Seneca Nation of Indians v. *Wilber M. Brucker, Secretary of the Army, et al.,* 162 F. Supp. 580 (1958); 79 S. Ct. 1294 (1959).

United States v. *21,250 Acres of Land, More or Less, Situate in Cattaraugus County,* 161 F. Supp. 376 (1957).

NEWSPAPERS

New York Times, 8 December 1960; 17 February 1961; 22 February 1961; 3
    August 1961; 10–11 May 1964; 13 March 1966; 23 March 1966;
    14–15 April 1966; 17 April 1966; 28 January 1967; 18 February
    1967; 11 June 1967; 15 December 1967; 3 January 1968; 3 January
    1969.
Washington Post, 24 June 1960; 8 April 1961; 7 August 1961; 10–11 May
    1964.

ORAL HISTORIES

Anderson, Clinton Presba. Member of Congress from New Mexico, 1941–45,
    1949–73. Interview by John F. Stewart. Washington, D.C., 14 April
    1967. Oral History Collection, JFKL.
Aspinall, Wayne Norviel. Member of Congress from Colorado, 1949–73.
    Interview by Nancy Whistler. Palisades, Colorado, 15 February 1979.
    Former Members of Congress Collection, Manuscripts Division, LOC.
Batt, William L. Administrator, Area Redevelopment Administration,
    1961–65. Interview by Larry J. Hackman. Washington, D.C., 26
    October, 1966. Oral History Collection, JFKL.
Bennett, Robert L. Commissioner of Indian Affairs, 1966–69. Interview by Joe
    B. Frantz. Washington, D.C., 13 November 1969. Oral History
    Collection, LBJL.
Boatner, Charles K. Assistant to the Secretary of the Interior; Director of Press
    Information, Department of the Interior, 1964–70. Interview by
    Michael L. Gillette. Fort Worth, Texas, 2 June 1976. Interview no. 4.
    Oral History Collection, LBJL.
Carver, John A. Assistant Secretary of the Interior, 1961–64. Interview by
    John Stewart. Washington, D.C., 20 September 1968. Interview no. 2.
    Oral History Collection, JFKL.
———. Interviews by William W. Moss. Washington, D.C., 7 October 1969,
    Interview no. 5; 18 November 1969, no. 7; 25 November 1969, no. 8.
    Oral History Collection, JFKL.
Hughes, Phillip S. Deputy Director, Bureau of the Budget, 1966–69. Interview
    by David McComb. Washington, D.C., 7 March 1969. Oral History
    Collection, LBJL.

McGovern, George S. Member of Congress from South Dakota, 1963–81. Interview by Paige Mulholland. Location not identified. 30 April 1969. Oral History Collection, LBJL.

McGuire, Marie C. Commissioner of Public Housing. Interview by William McHugh. Washington, D.C., 3 April 1967. Oral History Collection, JFKL.

Nash, Philleo. Commissioner of Indian Affairs, 1961–66. Interview by Charles T. Morrisey. Washington, D.C., 8 March 1966. Interview no. 2. Oral History Collection, JFKL.

———. Interviews by Jerry N. Hess. Washington, D.C., 24 June 1966, Interview no. 1; 17 October 1966, no. 6; 31 October 1966, no. 9; 5 June 1967, no. 13. Oral History Collection, HSTL.

———. Interview by William W. Moss. Washington, D.C., 26 February 1971. Interview no. 3. Oral History Collection, JFKL.

———. Interviewer and location not identified. April 1977. Box 208, PNP.

Udall, Stewart. Secretary of the Interior, 1961–69. Interviews by Joe B. Frantz. Washington, D.C., 18 April 1969, Interview no. 1; 19 May 1969, no. 2; 29 July 1969, no. 3. Oral History Collection, LBJL.

———. Interviews by W. W. Moss. Washington, D.C., 16 February 1970, no. 2; 2 June 1970, no. 6; 6 June 1970, no. 7. Oral History Collection, JFKL.

Verkler, Jerry T. Staff Director, Senate Interior and Insular Affairs Committee, 1963–74. Interviews by Donald A. Ritchie. Washington, D.C., 30 January 1992, Interview no. 1; 30 January 1992, no. 2; 3 February 1992, no. 3. Oral History Collection, SHO.

Unpublished Interviews and Correspondence

Deloria, Vine, Jr. Executive Director, National Congress of American Indians, 1964–68. Interview by Christopher Riggs, 17 July 1999, Golden, Colorado. Transcript. Author's collection.

Harris, Fred. U.S. Senate, 1964–73. Interview by author, 3 April 1998, Albuquerque, New Mexico. Tape recording. Author's collection.

Schifter, Richard, Bethesda, Maryland, to author, Austin, Texas, 19 August 1998. Author's collection.

Udall, Stewart L. Secretary of the Interior, 1961–69. Interview by author, 3 April 1998, Santa Fe, New Mexico. Tape recording. Author's collection.

INDEX

DATE DUE

GAYLORD			PRINTED IN U.S.A.